BEING RECONCILED

Being Reconciled offers an entirely fresh treatment of the ethical and theological dimensions of reconciliation in the context of the complex questions of the Gift. It reconsiders notions of freedom and exchange in relation to Christian doctrine which understands Creation, Grace and Incarnation as heavenly gifts, but the Fall, evil and violence as refusal of those gifts. In a sustained and rigorous response to the works of Derrida, Levinas, Marion, Žižek, Hauerwas and the 'Radical Evil' school, John Milbank posits the daring view that only transmission of the forgiveness offered by the Divine Humanity makes reconciliation possible on earth. Any philosophical understanding of forgiveness and redemption therefore requires theological completion.

A genuinely Christian understanding of reconciliation, says Milbank, involves a drastic reconception of philosophical notions of reality and of Christ's relationship to human society – one not confined to material items and exchanges, but engaging with processes of evil, atonement, forgiveness and grace. Working on the premise that theology, unlike philosophy, regards all things as gifts, but contending that the true gift is always involved in gift-exchange, *Being Reconciled* argues for forgiveness as the public renewing of a positive exchange of gifts that overcomes the privation of evil, rather than as a negative and private gesture that refuses a positivity of evil. It is only meaningful in the perpetual synergy of human offering and divine gift, eternally transferred and renewed through infinite and multiple reciprocities.

Both a critique of post-Kantian modernity, and a further development of a distinctive new theology that engages with questions of metaphysics, historicity, culture and politics, *Being Reconciled* is the first in a series of writings centred on the Gift. It is an original and vivid new account of reconciliation and forgiveness by a leading international theologian.

John Milbank is the Frances Myers Ball Professor of Philosophical Theology at the University of Virginia. He is a co-editor of the Radical Orthodoxy series, including its original first volume *Radical Orthodoxy: A New Theology* (Routledge, 1999), and is co-author with Catherine Pickstock of *Truth in Aquinas* (Routledge, 2000) and author of *The Word Made Strange* (1997).

RADICAL ORTHODOXY SERIES
Edited by John Milbank, Catherine Pickstock
and Graham Ward

Radical orthodoxy combines a sophisticated understanding of contemporary thought, modern and postmodern, with a theological perspective that looks back to the origins of the Church. It is the most talked-about development in contemporary theology.

RADICAL ORTHODOXY
edited by John Milbank, Catherine Pickstock and Graham Ward

DIVINE ECONOMY
D. Stephen Long

TRUTH IN AQUINAS
John Milbank and Catherine Pickstock

CITIES OF GOD
Graham Ward

LIBERATION THEOLOGY AFTER THE END OF HISTORY
Daniel M. Bell, Jr

GENEALOGY OF NIHILISM
Conor Cunningham

SPEECH AND THEOLOGY
James K.A. Smith

CULTURE AND THE THOMIST TRADITION
Tracey Rowland

BEING RECONCILED
John Milbank

BEING RECONCILED

Ontology and pardon

John Milbank

Routledge
Taylor & Francis Group

LONDON AND NEW YORK

First published 2003
by Routledge
11 New Fetter Lane, London EC4P 4EE

Simultaneously published in the USA and Canada
by Routledge
29 West 35th Street, New York, NY 10001

Reprinted 2004 (twice)

Routledge is an imprint of the Taylor & Francis Group

© 2003 John Milbank

Typeset in New Baskerville by
Keystroke, Jacaranda Lodge, Wolverhampton
Printed and bound in Great Britain by
TJ International Ltd, Padstow, Cornwall

British Library Cataloguing in Publication Data
A catalogue record for this book is available from the British Library

Library of Congress Cataloging in Publication Data
Milbank, John
Being reconciled: ontology and pardon/John Milbank.
p. cm. – (Radical orthodoxy series)
Includes bibliographical references and index.
1. Reconciliation–Religious aspects–Christianity.
3. Philosophical theology. I. Title. II. Series.

BT265.3 M55 2003
234′.5–dc21   2002032638

ISBN 0–415–30524–1 (hbk)
ISBN 0–415–30525–X (pbk)

In memory of my father
John Douglas Milbank (1920–2002)

But this is Cotswold, Severn: when these go stale
Then the all-universal and wide decree shall fail
Of world's binding, and earth's dust apart be loosed,
And man's worship of all grey comforts be abused,
To mere wonder at lightning and torrentous strong flying hail.

Ivor Gurney, from
'Friendly are Meadows'

. . . it's as if
We had left our house for five minutes to mail a letter
And during that time the living room had changed places
With the room behind the mirror over the fireplace
        W.H. Auden, from *For the Time Being: A Christmas Oratorio*

Parfois prend le miroir
Entre ciel et chambre
Dans ces mains le minime
Soleil terrestre.

Et des choses, des noms
C'est comme si
Les voies, les espérances se rejoignaient
A même rive.

On se prend à rêver
Que les mots ne sont pas
A l'aval de ce fleuve, fleuve de paix,
Trop pour le monde,

Et que parler n'est pas
Trancher l'artère
De l'agneau qui, confiant,
Suit la parole.
        Yves Bonnefoy, from
    'A Même Rive' in *Les Planches Courbes*

CONTENTS

PREFACE

The following book is the first in a projected series of writings concerning 'gift'.

Why 'gift' exactly? The primary reason is that gift is a kind of trancendental category in relation to all the topoi of theology, in a similar fashion to 'word'. Creation and grace are gifts; Incarnation is the supreme gift; the Fall, evil and violence are the refusal of gift; atonement is the renewed and hyperbolic gift that is for-giveness; the supreme name of the Holy Spirit is *donum* (according to Augustine); the Church is the community that is given to humanity and is constituted through the harmonious blending of diverse gifts (according to the apostle Paul).

In a sense, therefore, these writings will form a sequel to *The Word Made Strange* which offered a fragmentary treatment of the field of Christian doctrine from the transcendental (not transcendentalist!) perspective of *verbum*, which is associated with God the Son. This linguistic perspective is now not left behind, but complemented by the angle of *donum* which is associated with God the Spirit. To theology will be added an equally intermittent theopneumatics.

Why is this addition required? So far, my theological project has been primarily focused upon 'participation', but in a new way.[1] Traditionally, *methexis* concerned a sharing of being and knowledge in the Divine. Those who still espouse this perspective tend to play down the importance of language, culture, time and historicity as encouraging a relativism incompatible with any vision of a metaphysical order. Those on the other hand who stress these factors tend to do so at the expense of such a vision.

Against this dismal alternative, I have always tried to suggest that participation can be extended also to language, history and culture: the whole realm of human *making*. Not only do being and knowledge participate in a God who is and who comprehends; also human making participates in a God who is infinite poetic utterance: the second person of the Trinity. Thus when we contingently but authentically make things and reshape ourselves through time, we are not estranged from the eternal, but enter further into its recesses by what for us is the only possible route.

Such a perspective is anticipated by theurgic neoplatonism, but only completed by a Christian theurgy as partially envisaged by Dionysius and Augustine. For in the end, this perspective is *liturgical*, since liturgy already assumes the descent of the Divine in and through our praise of the Divine. A metaphysics of the participation of the poetic at once envisages all true *poesis* as liturgy, and at the same time must itself be a contingent temporal liturgical perfomance as well as an expression of *theoria*.[2] Of course I am still trying to think through the massive *aporias* that result from such a perspective.

However, culture is not just about production (*poesis*). It is also constituted through exchange. The arguments of *Theology and Social Theory: Beyond Secular Reason* against the notion of a 'social science' were all intended to show that this false concept rests always upon an arbitrary privileging of either production over exchange (Marx), or else exchange over production (Durkheim), when in reality any such privileging is incoherent in terms of social ontology. We only exchange in producing; but equally only those in relation produce, and all productions involve exchanges.

For Augustine, the *donum* that is the Holy Spirit is not only a free one-way gift (though it is also that), but in addition the realization of a perpetual exchange between the Father and the Son. This exchange results from the production of the Son; but equally, the Son is only brought to birth through the procession of the desire that is the Holy Spirit: a desire for communion, and a desire that even exceeds the closed communion of a dyad, looking for infinite and multiple reciprocities (though the closed perfection of the dyad is the ground for the latter; one has no figure of amorous promiscuity here).

Thus the notion of a participation of the poetic in an infinite *poesis* is to be complemented by the notion of a participation of reciprocal exchanges in an infinite reciprocity which is the divine *donum*. I am not however speaking here simply of a 'dramatic' dimension. In fact, to the contrary, as will emerge clearly in the second book, my interest in 'gift-exchange' rejects any one-sided 'personalism'. It will be noticed that I have adopted as organizing principles, not the philosophical transcendentals – truth, goodness, beauty, etc., but rather irreducibly theological ones: *verbum, donum. Verbum* adds to truth the liturgical performance of truth; likewise, *donum* adds to goodness a sacramental dealing with the world of objects (seen as both *anathemata* and sacrificial *donata*) as alone allowing the emergence of a subject who is not a mere *libido dominandi*. In *my* dramatic therefore, 'things' are equally, or perhaps more the primary players than are 'persons' – although both these categories are fundamentally disturbed in their usual meanings. (Clearly I am offering a contrast with von Balthasar here; however, these structural differences may scarcely extend at all to a substantive contrast – nor, of course, do I pretend to anything like his plenitude of continuous treatment.)

The *methexis* of donation, which complements the *methexis* of language, has two aspects. First of all, for theology there are no 'givens', only 'gifts'. Normally, in our secular society, one can say 'Oh, there's a box', an inert 'given', and then maybe in addition one can say, 'yes, it was a gift'. But in Creation there are only givens in so far as they are also gifts: if one sees only objects, then one mis-apprehends and fails to recognize true natures. Here something can only be at all as a gift, and furthermore never ceases to be constantly given; in this case the act of giving is never something that reverts to the past tense.

It is just *because* things as created can only be as gifts, just because their being is freely derived, that one has to speak of Creation in terms of participation and of analogical likeness of the gift to the giver – since if his mark is not upon the gift, how else shall we know that it is a gift? Those who imagine that participation is for Christian theology some sort of alien Hellenistic theme (besides the fact that they can never have read the Bible with any attention) fail to see just this, as they equally fail to see that for Greek philosophy there was an uncreated material residue that was not created, and so not a gift, and which therefore *limited* the sway of *methexis*.

The second aspect of the *methexis* of donation is linked to the argument (which will only be fully made in the second book) that gift is an exchange as well as an offering without return, since it is asymmetrical reciprocity and non-identical repetition. Because gift is gift-exchange, participation of the created gifts in the divine giver is also participation in a Trinitarian God.

This defence of gift-exchange involves a strong engagement with social theory. In this sense, my sequence on gift constitutes also a sequel to *Theology and Social Theory: Beyond Secular Reason*. Compared with the latter volume, the engagement is much more positive in character: however, nothing here is being retracted – rather I am concerned to learn from social theory in its more historical, ethnographic and less ideological aspects.

This volume in the series is concerned with for-giveness, or par-don (in Anglo-French). Projected future writings will concern the relation of gift to being and to God, and its ethnographic and historical instances.

The present volume occupies a less directly ontological terrain inasmuch as it is concerned with the restoration of a refused and ruptured gift. Why begin 'the wrong way round' with this secondariness?

Well, first of all, since we inhabit a broken world, this is to follow the *ordo intelligendi* rather than the *ordo essendi*, which run in opposite directions, as Aristotle declared. Since knowledge consists in *seeing* this reversal, however, it is equally valid to start with either – a mere matter of convenience of presentation.

So were it simply a matter of tracing the lineaments of gift in being, one could start either way around. But the circumstance of *fallenness*, diagnosed by theology, prevents, without the instance of the gift of grace, knowledge from being knowledge in glimpsing the reversal that dethrones its own primacy. This has given rise to many complex disputes between Thomists and Scotists, which I will touch upon in this book, concerning what belongs to finite being and knowledge, and what belongs only to *fallen* finitude (with Scotists tending to see the *conversio ad phantasmata* as only a consequence of our *status lapsus*).

So to start with the restoration of the gift is to stress our fallen condition, and the lack of ease of escape from this: thus the following pages are riddled with *angst* and *aporias*. This approach also, in the third place, has a pedagogic advantage: it begins with the dilemmas of experience, before proceeding to a more abstract, collective and historical approach.

Nevertheless, the fact of fallenness does not really disturb the equilibrium between the order of knowledge and the order of being. Fallenness is only known under grace, and hence theology may equally well begin ontologically with Creation, as gnoseologically with the Fall.

However, there is a fourth, Christological factor which tilts the balance, and which bears upon the thing that is centrally at issue in this book – namely the relation between ontology and pardon. If, according to the Thomist view to which I subscribe, the occasion for incarnation was our deliverance, then nevertheless for Aquinas, in accordance with Chalcedonian logic, the upshot of the Incarnation exceeds its occasion. The result of the contingency of deliverance is paradoxically the eternal inclusion of a human nature under a divine enhypostasization. Since God is impassable, although this circumstance only begins to be in time, this beginning-to-be must somehow belong eternally to God. All this comes to a head in Chapter 4.

The task here is to think through this paradox, without lapsing into idealist *gnosis* which ontologizes a necessary passage through evil. In some fashion, although God's goodness is prior to evil, God is eternally for-giving as well as eternally giving; just as he is eternally humanity as well as God. This is an aspect of what some Russian theologians have deemed the 'sophiological' mystery of God being eternally more than God, even though there is nothing more than God, and Creation is not necessitated.

The choice then to begin with forgiveness is a choice for a radically Christocentric theology and equally for a theology centred upon the hypostatic descent of the Spirit in the Church. It is a choice for a theology of God-Manhood and deification, as the more radically Christian option.

But since reconciliation is an historical event, if there has eternally been an event of restoration of Being surplus to Being, then this perspective disturbs the sway of pure ontology and demands that Being comprise the gift of a contingent event – *not*, however, I would contend, a gift before being, since a pre-ontological *unum* is yet more static than being, and events have to be *actual*. But certainly Being as also giving, Being as also energy (*dynamis*), Being as also *Sophia*.

* * * *

I am greatly indebted to the faculty and students of the Divinity Faculty at the University of Cambridge, and of the Department of Religious Studies at the University of Virginia, as well as to many others too numerous to mention, stretching over a period of thirty years. Without the help of all these people, I could never have engendered the following theses.

Earlier versions of some chapters of the book have appeared as follows: 'Darkness and Silence: Evil and the Western Legacy' (Chapter 1) in John Caputo, ed., *The Religious* (Oxford: Blackwell, 2002); 'Forgiveness and Incarnation' (Chapters 3 and 4) in John Caputo et al., eds, *Questioning God* (Bloomington Indiana: Indiana University Press, 2001); 'Christ the Exception' (Chapters 5 and 6) in *Reflections*, vol. 5, Spring 2002 (Center of Theological Inquiry, Princeton); 'The Last of the Last: Theology, Authority and Democracy' (Chapter 7) in *Revista Portuguesa da Filosofia*, Tomo LVIII, Fasc. 2, 2002; 'The Midwinter Sacrifice' (Chapter 8) in *Studies in Christian Ethics*, vol. 10, no. 2 (Edinburgh: T. and T. Clark, 1997); 'Socialism of the Gift, Socialism by Grace' (Chapter 9) in *New Blackfriars*, December 1996; 'The Gospel of Affinity' (Chapter 10) in *Ethical Perspectives*, vol. 7, no. 4, December 2000 (Catholic University of Leuven: European Centre for Ethics). I should like to thank all the publishers and journals involved for their permission to reproduce this material. Thanks are also due to Faber and Faber, London, for permission to reproduce an extract from W.H. Auden's poem 'For the Time Being', in W.H. Auden *For the Time Being* (1935), to Mercure de France for permission to reproduce an extract from Yves Bonnefoy's poem 'A Même Rive' in *Les Planches Courbes* (2001), and likewise to Oxford University Press for permission to reproduce an extract from Ivor Gurney's poem 'Friendly are Meadows' in *Selected Poems* (1997).

Finally, my enormous thanks are due to Donna Packard, who word-processed the final manuscript, and to its editors: Roger Thorpe, Julene Knox, Clare Johnson, Ruth Whittington, Richard Willis and Colin Morgan.

1

EVIL

Darkness and silence

I

Traditionally, in Greek, Christian and Jewish thought evil has been denied any positive foothold in being. It has not been seen as a real force or quality, but as the absence of force and quality, and as the privation of being itself. It has not been regarded as glamorous, but as sterile; never as more, always as less. For many recent philosophers, however (e.g. Jacob Rogozinski, Slavoj Zizek, J.-L. Nancy), this view appears inadequate in the face of what they consider to be the unprecedented evil of the twentieth century: the mass organization of totalitarian control and terror, systematic genocide, and the enslavement of people who are deliberately worked to the point of enfeeblement and then slaughtered.[1] Such evil, they argue, cannot be regarded as privative, because this view claims that evil arises only from the deliberate pursuit of a lesser good. Power directed towards extermination suggests rather destruction and annihilation pursued perversely for its own sake, as an alternative end in itself. Such an impulse towards the pure negation of being, as towards the cold infliction of suffering – that may not even be enjoyed by its perpetrators – suggests that the will to destroy is a positive and surd attribute of being itself and no mere inhibition of being in its plenitude. This supposed positive evil for its own sake is often dubbed 'radical evil', following a term used by Immauel Kant in his book *Religion Within the Bounds of Mere Reason*.[2] With some plausibility, Kant's account of evil is seen as encouraging a break with the traditional privation view focused upon being in general, in favour of a view focused purely upon the finite human will. This new view comprehends evil as a positively willed denial of the good and so as a pure act of perversity without ground. The development of such a position is traced from Kant, through Schelling, to Heidegger.

In this way, a specifically modern *theory* of evil is held to be adequate to account for a specifically modern extremism of evil *practice*, which the theory, nonetheless, predates. Despite this predating, which might suggest some causal link, the modern practical extremity of evil is held to be, at least in part, the outcome of a far older Western tradition of metaphysical

1

reflection on evil which trivializes it and underrates it. So not only is evil as privation refuted by Auschwitz, it is also indicted by it as responsible for such an outcome. Evil denied as mere denial leaves us unvigilant against its real positivity.

This position, then, traces no lineage to the Holocaust from the specifically German and modern accounts of radical evil, yet asserts, perhaps all too vaguely, a lineage from the age-old western metaphysical understanding of evil as privation. Here, however, the advocates of 'radical evil' (or 'postmodern Kantians', as I will henceforth describe them), have to face the diametrically opposite alignment of theoretical and practical evil proposed by Heidegger's pupil, Hannah Arendt, and arguably against her former teacher.[3] For Arendt, famously, the mass murderer Adolf Eichmann, on trial in Jerusalem, discloses not a pre-Satanic will to evil, nor a lust for horror, but instead 'the banality of evil', an incremental and pathetic inadequacy of motive which escalated imperceptibly into complicity with unimaginable wickedness. It has now been shown, against those prone (for various reasons) to doubt this, that Arendt's account of evil as 'banal' is most certainly linked with her Augustinian predilections, and support for Augustine's account of evil as negative.[4] Thus the horror of Auschwitz, for Arendt, is not the revelation of evil perpetrated for its own sake, but rather a demonstration that even the most seemingly absolute evil tends to be carried out by people who imagine, albeit reluctantly, that they are fulfilling the goods of order, obedience, political stability and social peace.

In this fashion, Arendt implicitly saw the Western metaphysical account of evil in terms of privation as confirmed, not denied, by the Holocaust. *A fortiori*, therefore, this traditional theory of evil was not for her complicit with the modern practical excess of evil. In addition, Arendt established very astutely certain links between a debased Kantianism, and the co-operation of many of the German people with the implementing of the final solution.[5] To this degree she also raised the question of a link between the modern theory of evil and the modern excessive practice of evil. And where she did, in her political theory, deploy Kant favourably, she adverted to social convergence in judgement, which is linked, by Kant, with the beautiful, and not to the common experience of the natural sublime that for Kant has profoundly to do both with respect for the formal law, *and* with radical evil.[6]

Despite this opening of the issue concerning the relation between modern theory of evil and modern evil as practised, Arendt veered well away from any indictment of Kant as such. *Debased* Kantianism is culpable, not the real Kantian philosophical legacy. Thus while, in relation to the Holocaust, the ancient view of evil is confirmed and therefore exonerated, the modern, positive view of evil is not accused of a certain responsibility. And yet this intellectual lineage would seem to be, at least *prima facie*, more plausible in terms of time, locality and proximity than the supposed genealogy which traces back to Western onto-theology. It would allow some significance to the predating of the modern practice of evil by the modern theory of evil. After all, the opponents of the privation theory have already contended for the profound alignment of radical evil with the Holocaust, since this theory alone is held adequately to interpret it. Supposing, instead, that privation theory can interpret the Holocaust, then this alignment would appear very differently: not as the retrospective match of event to detached theory, but as the prior perverse attempt to enact a false theory. Instead of the view that the negation of evil as merely negative permits its positivity to erupt, one would have the view that the false assertion of evil as positive leads to an impossible quest to enact such positivity, which can in reality only unleash a bad infinite of further and further privation, since being will not *permit* any final solution, any finished or perfected evil.

Nevertheless one can see immediately, from this formulation, why Arendt could not have traced the genealogy it expresses, quite apart from her residual respect for Kant. To ascribe causality to the pursuit of the Satanic illusion, the illusion of the pursuit of evil for its own sake, appears clean contrary to the invocation of the banality of evil behaviour. And Arendt, as many have pointed out, had all too little to say about the psychology of the *instigators* of the final solution, rather than that of people who must be judged its mere executives, albeit paramount ones, like Eichmann. All the same, this is not to say that a privation theory, nor even aspects of a banality theory, cannot apply also to the instigators. Hitler and his henchmen were not exactly Satanists, and their articulations of their motives were not like that of the Californian Charles Manson or the English 'Moors murderer' Ian Brady – a close student of de Sade and decadent literature. In these extreme cases one has something like the illusion of the belief that evil is being performed for its own sake, although privation theory is able to discern amidst this vaunted Satanic glory the pathetic desire for control in those whose high self-esteem has been in no way socially confirmed.[7] Something of that may, indeed, have been operative amongst the Nazi cohorts, but they still articulated their defective desires more positively, in terms of the promotion of the racial health and excellence of humanity: indeed in their paganism or atheism they remained all too humanist, and Hitler sought avowedly to produce a human being worthy of worship.[8] Likewise, the suppression and, finally, liquidation of the Jews was not articulated in nihilistic terms, but could be viewed as 'rational', given that one's objective was to secure a German power absolutely untainted by socialism and the influence of international commerce, and a German identity based on cultural uniformity and demotion of the Christian and Biblical legacy in favour of a Nordic one.

The Nazis did not, therefore, like Charles Manson, avowedly elect radical evil, saying 'Be Thou my Good'. Such Satanism discovers itself to be an illusion at the point where it finds it can establish no stable positive kingdom of evil, nor encompass absolute destruction of being, but instead can only unleash an ever-escalating slide of deprivation which will usually cease with self-destruction. Clearly, the theory of radical evil is not implicated in the Holocaust in this extreme Satanic fashion. However, in a much more subtle fashion, it may after all, be implicated. Here one can claim first of all (as I will later demonstrate), that Nazi concepts of universal power and legality were much more compatible with, and even derived from, the Kantian categorical imperative, than Arendt allowed. In the second place, one can claim that if the Nazis still affirmed a Kantian free will as their good, then they also inherited the *aporias* of this free will, as half-admitted by Kant in *Religion Within the Bounds of Mere Reason*. For these *aporias*, there is no clear way of distinguishing between the will which genuinely wills freedom, and the will which wills against itself, restraining freedom: this self-opposition for Kant characterizes the evil will.[9] As we shall see, these *aporias* arise because of the lack, in Kant, at this highest level, of any teleology which can discriminate the good substance of what is willed from a deficient instance of such substance. Here, instead, the only thing willed is the law of free-willing itself, which defines legality as untrammelled autonomy, and it might seem that the free will to bind oneself equally instantiates such autonomy. At the very least one can ask, exactly how is one to discriminate between the will binding itself to be free, and the will binding itself in unfreedom, if there is no desirable content here to prove the goodness of the genuine good will to freedom?

But if this is really the case with Kant, then one must face up to something which seems at first sight highly unlikely: namely that political totalitarianism and terror really could, with a certain plausibility, pose as the fulfilling of the categorical imperative, just as much as the most stringent code of personal self-denial. Later we shall see more clearly how these opposites can converge and mutually reinforce each other. In effect, the promotion of formal freedom can become akin to the systematic promotion of the inhibition of freedom by an imperceptible slide. And such self-deceiving espousal of evil would in practice be very like the setting up of a Satanic organisation. Here also, no stable realm of evil would result, but instead the pace of privation of being would be horrendously quickened.

In what follows I shall offer, in the first place, a further defence and exposition of the view of evil as privation and banality. I shall therefore argue that it can apply also to modern extreme evil, and is in no sense responsible for this evil. However, in the second place, beyond Arendt, I shall argue that the modern, positive theory of evil *is* in a measure responsible for the modern actuality of evil.

II

To begin with, however, I must offer a much fuller exposition of the modern theory of evil as positive and 'radical'.

Contemporary proponents of this view start with the proposition that totalitarian phenomena of the twentieth century, and in particular the Holocaust, exhibit something uniquely terrible. These phenomena include, of course, state terror enacted in the name of socialism. However, while I do not doubt that the Soviet State, like the Nazi one, was intrinsically criminal, I would claim that this criminality flowed from Lenin's nihilism, from the exacerbation of modern state sovereignty, and certainly also from Marxist productivism and anti-agrarianism, but not from socialism as such. Indeed, the presence of genuine socialist ideals allowed the Soviet State later somewhat to reform itself, whereas the more unadulterated nihilism of the Nazis led shortly to self-destruction. On the other hand, European and American liberal democracy has also engendered a continuous horror almost as grave as the Holocaust, and a more troublingly sustainable mode of nihilism, appropriately disguised by an unparalleled reign of *kitsch* (including the American Holocaust industry): this is the sequence of deliberate terror and extermination deployed against civilian populations as a primary instrument of war and neo-colonial power from the Congo and the Philippines through Hiroshima, Palestine, Kenya, Algeria and Vietnam to the Gulf War and Afghanistan. This sequential instance – unparalleled in pre-modernity – shows that the source of terror is *not* simply 'totalitarianism', but rather the emptiness of secular power as such. It also shows that 'liberal democracy' is a mere virtual circus designed to entertain the middle-classes of the privileged world. For in its global instance, liberal capitalist power is also totalizing and utterly inhuman. The rapid dismantlement, since September 11, 2001, in both Britain and the USA, of age-old Anglo-Saxon liberties (including *Habeas Corpus*), reveals that once the empty heart of liberal sovereignty, which pursues only naked power (whether of the totality or the individual) for its own sake, is threatened, global terror is quickly injected into the domestic scene also.

If we allow that 'totalitarianism' be replaced by the wider concept of 'secular immanence', which is totalizing and terroristic because it acknowledges no supra-human power beyond itself by which it might be measured and limited, then we can still agree that twentieth-century politics has displayed something unprecedently sinister. For in the instances of the Holocaust, the Gulag and US foreign policy, law has itself consented to criminal principles and dedicated the resources of the State to mass murder on a legal, organized and bureaucratic basis. In particular, in the case of the Holocaust (although there are certainly some earlier imperial near-analogues), sections of the population deemed difficult or surplus to requirement were not simply oppressed or incarcerated, but were literally worked to death and discarded. So whereas previous slave economies still preserved some sense of the human status of the slaves, here this was denied in the context of a new hierarchical humanism which restricted full humanity to certain racial, physical and mental ideals.[10]

For the postmodern Kantians, this new degree of malevolence suggests in effect a will towards evil for its own sake, not merely evil as a lack of reality, or a lack of power, but evil as an alternative and viable exercise of power, whereby some human beings can devote themselves primarily to the destruction of others. This is now revealed as a possibility: it worked – scarcely any Jews now inhabit Germany. And if evil is now revealed as having equal potency with the good, an equal potency which proceeds to an equal actuality, then it is also shown as proceeding entirely from the rational will. It would surely be unthinkable to proffer any excuses for the Holocaust, or to lay out a set of mitigating circumstances. Yet the postmodern Kantians suggest that privation theory unfolds precisely by offering mitigating circumstances for all evil, so allowing radical evil to slip through its theor-etical net. What it amounts to, they argue, is a kind of justification of being, an ontodicy (by analogy with theodicy), which also exonerates all creatures who exist, including human beings. For privation theory, all being as being is good, and since all power in order to be effective manifests the actuality of being, all power, as power, is good, and evil not only is impotent but can even be defined, at least in one valid way, as weakness and impotence (this is underscored most heavily by Dionysius the Areopagite).[11] It follows that, since the will is a potency, it is only actual and effective when it wills the good; hence for both Dionysius and Augustine, it is not exactly the case that evil can be willed: rather there is evil precisely to the degree that there is an absence of willing. No one, as willing, wills anything but the good, and evil only affects the will to the extent that a deficient good is being willed.[12]

This exoneration of the will as such suggests, to the postmodern Kantians, that thereby the will is excused, and evil displaced from human origin. Instead of a primary referral of evil to potency and will, privation theory seems to imply a root of evil prior to power and will, in impersonal ontological circumstances, or rather in meontological circumstances.[13] For according to Jewish and Christian tradition, at least up to Maimonides and Aquinas, Being in its pure self-origination is infinite, and if Being as such is good, then, also, the infinite as such is good, indefeasibly good, beyond the possibility of swerving. Hence it would seem that goodness is a property of non-limitation, and not a derivative of personal election. Conversely, if evil is only possible for finite creatures, then finitude can always be proffered as something of an excuse: the will falls into evil by choosing the lesser good (since to will at all it must will *some* good), but here it is a victim of its finite partiality of perspective, and its finite lack of power to affirm. Indeed, even St Paul appears entirely to exonerate the will, lamenting that he does what he hates, the opposite of what he wants to do (Romans 7: 15, 18; Galatians 5: 17). Thereby he blames the incapacity of his flesh, but not exactly the purity of his intentions. For where the will has failed to will what it should, then, for this traditional metaphysical perspective, it has failed to will in some measure, and the will is held captive by something prior to will: either, for the ancient Greeks, materiality as such; or else for Jews and Christians, certain perverse habits that hold our materiality and psychic passions in their grip.[14] Thus while it might seem that privation theory, by defining evil as lack of being, prevents any rooting of evil in the ontological, in fact it does affirm such rooting. For since evil is rooted in finitude, and the finite is caused by the infinite, the infinite is the real ultimate source of lack, the ontological of the meontological. And because the infinite is essentially impersonal, freedom as the origin of evil is here subordinated to ontological *cause* as the origin of evil. In this way, it is argued by the postmodern Kantians, human evil is mystified, and blame shifted to a metaphysical scenario.

Yet at the same time, their apparently more humanist account involves also an *alternative* metaphysical scenario. They wish to regard the alternative good/evil in pre-ontological terms as entirely prior to the distinction between infinite and finite. This means, for them, that the finite will as such, in willing the good of the other, can manifest the extreme of goodness, an infinite good, if you like.[15] But conversely, as they concede, following Schelling, this must also mean that the infinite can manifest the extreme of evil.[16] Thus for Schelling, the good will of God is the result of a radical decision within the dark indifferent ground of the infinite, and this alone ensures that God *really* is good, according to any fashion of goodness that we can understand. God's goodness also is a loving decision; it is an offer, a free gift, not an inevitability. Were it the latter, how could we be grateful, how could we feel infinitely loved? (Schelling has a certain point here, even though I shall later dissent.)

III

In articulating their post-Holocaust alternative to privation theory, the postmodern Kantians draw primarily upon Kant's account of radical evil, which they see as explicitly or implicitly developed by Schelling and Heidegger.

In Kant's account, evil is not really referred to finitude and so not primarily to any sort of lack or deficiency. He produces instead a theory of the pure 'self-binding' of the will, which is sometimes seen as his qualification of the Enlightenment, and retrieval, or even purer expression, of a Biblical, Pauline and Augustinian thematic.[17] But this is a mistake; radical evil is *not* original sin (even though Kant sees it as the rational rethinking of the latter), and it *is* an enlightenment substitute for original sin, in a fashion that I shall demonstrate.

First of all, however, I shall try to explicate the traditional view of evil, free will and original sin, particularly in its Augustinian version. Let us return, initially, to my invocation of St Paul. In his understanding of will, he still assumes a Biblical and Hellenic teleology: human beings are created to will the love of God as their final end and beatitude. As created they have a certain foretaste of the vision of God, and sufficient power to pursue this vision as they ought. When the will does pursue this vision, it is free from perverse, unnatural restrictions of its appointed nature, which thereby inhibits its freedom as such, for the inner reality of creaturely freedom is just this passing beyond given finite nature in diverse ways towards the infinite. Will is nothing other, as Augustine makes clear in *De Libero Arbitrio*, than the site of the *dynamism* of the participation of the finite in the infinite, in the case of rational creatures (angels and humans).[18] Thus 'will' arises where a rational vision, not as yet full accessible, lures forward through our desire our finite potency. It follows that will as such cannot fail of the choice of its final end without in some measure slipping away from its freedom. And this slipping away *cannot*, either for St Paul or Augustine, be accomplished by a surd choice of will alone, since will is nothing but the impact of omnipotent infinite reason upon finite rational power. Instead, the slipping must involve either or both an unnatural restriction of intellectual reason and of forceful capacity. St Paul dwells upon the latter, Augustine on both: for Augustine we cannot will what we will to will, because the inherited sin of Adam has impaired both our vision and our potency. If there was any pure 'sin of the will' (unknown to the Greeks), then this was the original sin of Adam himself, who, enjoying perfect vision and perfect capacity and so perfect freedom, nonetheless freely and without ground willed these things away.[19] This act, for Augustine, is strictly baffling and incomprehensible. It is not at all *explained* by free will, because free will in its natural created state knows only the willing of the good, under the compulsion of the vision of the good, and no choice between good and evil at all. To the contrary, the very, as it were, 'fictional' notion that there is such a choice, was invented by Adam at the Fall (or by Satan in the angelic Fall). The problem of the Fall is the sheer apparent impossibility of this invention, the imagining of a false simulacrum within the repleteness of reality. This imagining alone erects an illusory autonomy, or self-governance of the will, since it is precisely the will of a creature to hold sway over himself, in disregard of his appointed substantive end. That is to say, it is the will to prefer the identical repetition of emptiness of rule for no purpose, but rather for its own sake, over submission to the natural superiority of the infinite which must be perceived in ever-renewed, non-identical repetition. Indeed finitude alone renders this delusion possible, yet finitude here is not really, as critics of privation theory imagine, invoked as an excuse, since the entire life of the finite, as created out of nothing, resides in its orientation to the infinite. Thus to assert the pure self-governing of the finite entity over against the infinite, which, as boundless, *cannot* be self-governing in this fashion, is also to deny that which sustains its bounds and specific substance, in favour of an emptiness, an *infinite* emptiness, which alone belongs to it solely.

Since Adam's choice was for the illusion of a finite autonomy of the will (that is to say, for the idea of a groundless free choice between good and evil as expressing the very essence of freedom), it is not at all true to say that, for Christian theology, the descendants of Adam inherit a tendency to evil which is primarily a tendency of *the will*. To the contrary, this would be to perpetuate Adam's fantasy. Instead, the reality of Adam's election is revealed first and foremost as loss of the vision of God and as physical death and incapacity of the body. As a result of this twin impairment, will as desire lacks both vision and capacity, and degenerates into concupiscence: the original sin of Adam which through ignorance and weakness we tend to repeat.

But then how, it might be asked, if the will is so inhibited, does St Paul think he can even will the good, although not carry it out? The answer is provided by Augustine in *De Libero Arbitrio*. Matching the aberrant leading role taken by the will at the Fall is the aberrant leading role taken by the will under grace. The miracle of grace consists in our capacity to desire truth beyond our intellectual and forceful inhibitions.[20] To be sure, for Augustine following Plato, all human knowing is an interplay between always already knowing something and not yet knowing it, which amounts to the thesis that for us (ontologically and so even for Adam), fully knowing something is *always* in some measure the desire to know it. In this way, it has to be understood that, in Augustine, the vision which 'governs' the will is nonetheless a vision only secured also *through* right will. Moreover, since effective will must be enacted, a true and unimpaired potency is also essential for the enjoyment of vision (in the much later *De Trinitate*, such 'trinitarian' equality of power, understanding and will is much more emphatically expressed). The loss primarily of vision and impulsion (rather than will/desire) after the Fall, implies the cessation or at least inhibition of the interplay between the already and the not yet of cognition – leaving the will to circle vainly in its own orbit. Just as, before the Fall, the lure of true vision pulled desire towards itself, so, now, after the Fall, the loss of vision weakens drastically the impulse of desire (while the loss of power equally impairs its capacity to express itself). Yet God does not restore our plight by proffering us primarily true vision and power once more; rather his new accommodation remains appropriately true to our finitely necessary interplay of already and not yet, by now *accentuating* the role of desire upon which such interplay depends. Hence what God, by grace, restores to us, in the face of the loss of the magnetic poles of the already of power and the not yet of fully attained knowledge (it should be realised that power and knowledge are finally, in God, transcendentally co-extensive), is precisely the 'middle' of interplay between them, the middle of desire which reintegrates their magnetism. This is the gift to us of the hyperbolic presence of the Spirit.

It will be seen from the above that it is not at all the case for Augustine, as in post-Reformation misreadings of his work, that after the Fall, human beings are left with a will to the good which is illusory and 'unrighteous' and only to be cured by grace through the Incarnation.[21] To the contrary, Augustine affirms that the original justification assured to humans by divine grace before the Fall is seamlessly continued as the offer of redeeming grace through Christ which becomes immediately available by typological anticipation after the Fall.[22] In consequence, for Augustine (and he never retracted this) *no one*, after the Fall, is guilty as an individual on account of original sin which is the guilt of Adam (even if Augustine in later works – a position repeated by Aquinas – says that we are guilty simply *as* members – like the hands of a murderer – of the human race). People are only guilty if they refuse the offer of grace and remain content with their deficient inheritance.[23] (Augustine never later denies the proleptic availability of the grace of Christ, even if he lamentably comes to speak of the non-election of some in relation to this grace.) And this grace arrives precisely *as* our immediately renewed capacity for a free-willing of submission to God. Thus if we experience original sin as the frustration of our will and consequent concupiscence (as is more stressed from *Ad Simplicianum* onwards), then this is only because this will to fulfil the law is itself grace, and therefore, as James Alison has argued, original sin is only disclosed in the light of our salvation in Christ.[24] It is clear that in no way are grace and free will here set over against each other in a Lutheran fashion. Instead, the gift of grace consists in a miraculously restored desire for God, despite the loss of original vision and capacity.

But if will operating properly as will is guided, for Augustine, by a true vision, how is it able to take the lead in our restoration? How can purification of vision and capacity first of all be induced by a true desiring? To understand this, we have to understand the complex double hierarchy of will and virtue, which Augustine explains in the *De Libero Arbitrio*. He declares there that possessed intellectual and moral virtues lie hierarchically above the will, since virtue *as* virtue can only be good, while the will can be good or bad (meaning that the will can perversely inhibit itself). Nevertheless, he also asserts that the will wills a good *beyond* the good of virtue (beyond, therefore, one can note, the pagan conception of the good).[25] What is this good beyond virtue? Augustine describes 'a virtue' as the possession of an individual, which *as* virtue he cannot lose, since virtue lost is vice. By contrast, the will desires, beyond virtue, an inaccessible divine good, which can never belong to an individual, and can only be enjoyed in common. This superabundant good is shared between us, and never possessed: just like sunlight, says Augustine, which is more truly precious than gold, even though gold can be held through private ownership. This good, since it is infinite and above us, and held securely by God, *can* be lost by us, unlike virtue as virtue. Nevertheless, insecure will, which should be guided by secure virtue, still takes the lead over virtue, because true virtue is less fundamentally a possession than it is a sharing in the common good. Such sharing in what surpasses us is only ever to be attained by desire, even if a true desire, for Augustine, involves a kind of true, but inchoate, envisaging. (This analysis shows that the accentuated role of will in Augustine is specifically allied to Platonism rather than Aristotelianism.)

However, if desire exceeds virtue in the direction of the more common and universal, then it *also*, according to *De Libero Arbitrio*, exceeds virtue in the direction of the more individual and particular. For the will is linked not just to discrimination of right from wrong, and the following of truth rather than falsehood, but also with idiosyncratic, but equally valid, moral and aesthetic preferences. There is a real 'proto-romantic' dimension here. Thus, Augustine says, some in a landscape will admire more the 'height of a mountain', others the 'verdure of a forest', others 'the pulsing tranquillity of the sea'; and in like fashion the cleaving of desire to the good refracts it according to our specific local affinities.[26] In this way, the will for Augustine at once directs us beyond private virtue to the common good, and yet at the same time does so through a desire necessarily more individuated than virtues like patience, taken in the abstract, which though privately possessed, like gold, show, also like gold, the same identical quality in all instances. This is why 'will' in Augustine names the drastic participatory tension between the infinitely general and the finitely particular. And it is clear that this tension has for him also a political dimension, since it implies the equipoise of the mediating 'aristocracy' of virtue with the 'democracy' of will, commonality and varied affinity. Thus towards the end of Book 1 of *De Libero Arbitrio*, Augustine affirms clearly that theology requires a politics economically adapted to times and places: monarchy or aristocracy should be the norm where few are virtuous, and therefore the Good is not much refracted; but democracy should be the norm where the Good is widely (and we can infer, variously) distributed. This same tension indicates also an 'economic' dimension in every sense: enjoyment in common does not inhibit individual expression, rather each is the precondition of the other.

In this light one can see that Adam's error was to deny this ontological tension which at once validates individual expressiveness and collective sharing, in favour of a confinement to the middle of 'virtue', or to merely *private* possession of the nonetheless *abstractly general* (whose abstraction travesties the real superabundant infinite varied specificity of the true divine universal – described in other terms by Maximus the Confessor as the identity of the infinitely various *Logoi* with the one *Logos*: see *Ambiguum* 7). His error was, by an act of will, to deny the aspect in which will is hierarchically superior to virtue, and instead to affirm only the one-sided hierarchy of virtue over the will, or desire. This is tantamount to denying the participatory aspect of virtue, and imagining that one can entirely possess, with absolute security, one's own virtue. However, where the security of virtue depends upon oneself, this is simply because one wills virtue, entirely through a volition claiming (illusorily) to be autonomous and spontaneous. This will is poised, supposedly like the post-Kantian will, equally between good and evil. Illusory self-possession of virtue 'above' the will, nonetheless entirely depends upon an imagined self-possession of the will (as the Stoics saw). Adam's error was to imagine that he could possess his own will. And

11

the legacy of this error is that human beings think of the highest good, in Stoic fashion, as that which can be self-possessed, and is not subject to external erosion. The Good is now thought of as the exercise of the most autonomous, which is free will.

By contrast, for Augustine, free will is inherently our own only as alien to us. In consequence it is returned to us as the arrival from outside of grace, and as the restoration of a good that we can only enjoy in common, and yet must receive according to our own unique affinities. To will here means to be moved beyond oneself towards a sharing and ontological distribution (according to real requirement, not formal equality), of the inexhaustible common good. It is through this moving that desire attracts once more to itself true vision, and draws along with it new resources of power for self-realization.

IV

Turning back now, to Kant, one finds instead an entirely different picture. He is not concerned with a lack of power to do good, since for him this would be contradictory: 'ought implies can'. Nor is he concerned with a lack of guiding vision, since he has defined the Good *as* a good will, or more precisely as the law which freedom gives itself, and which secures freedom. Since the Good is primarily in this fashion law, it first of all concerns the form or manner in which things are done, and is indifferent as to content. To introduce some substantive good or aim towards such good into one's *primary* understanding of what is 'right' is, for Kant, actually to subvert morality.[27] 'Ends' are only admissible for Kant as a secondary consideration, and they concern first our willing of our perfect submission to the *formality* of duty, and second, our willing of the happiness of others, where 'happiness' means a mere empirical state, and *not* something inherently consequent upon virtue.[28] It is true that, owing to the conditions of our understanding, we cannot fully grasp the noumenally formal in itself as unmediated by the phenomenally substantive; but this ensures that freedom and its law remain for us an ineffable idea. Thus, both as formal and as ineffable, the Kantian 'right' which orientates the Good entirely exceeds all envisaging. In no sense could radical evil for him connote loss of vision of the infinite, since the bounds between the finite and the infinite are permanently fixed and permit of no participatory mediation. For Kant, we will, adequately, as finite creatures, with reference only to our finitude; at the same time, we do invoke a noumenal infinitude in which our spirits are truly at home – yet this infinitude only impinges on the finite as the empty and incomprehensible formality of freedom which is inexplicably able to interrupt the fatedness of phenomenal causality.

Therefore Kant does not regard the will as bound by incapacity or blindness in the intellectualist and historicist fashion of St Paul and Augustine

– which is as Biblical as it is Greek. To the contrary, he regards the will as self-bound, as mysteriously unable to will will, or as willing against itself, pathologically. He is not concerned with a Pauline acting contrary to what one wills, but with an innate failure of the will itself to will freedom. This failure has, for Kant, two aspects. First of all, we tend to adopt non-moral maxims instead of moral ones: this means that where one's actions should embody in their most immediate meaning and palpability a maxim that we could will to turn into a universal law – for example the imperative to tell the truth – they tend, instead, to be contaminated by a pragmatic and egoistic concern for individual or collective material survival and well-being – hence we usually succumb to the temptation to lie.[29] Now it might seem that here Kant does, indeed, see freedom as trammelled by the flesh in the manner of St Paul. However, this is not the case, because, in the Pauline instance, as developed by Augustine, there is a certain continuity between the lower passions and the higher desire for God. (Were it not so, for St Paul, then sexual union with a prostitute would not be able to contaminate our collective bodily union with Christ.) Correctly orientated and disciplined, the lower passions should encourage and give way to the higher desire, and indeed this mediation is essential, so that, given corrupt passions, given corrupt *flesh*, no person can truly love God – and St Paul spilt much ink denying such a self-deluding illusion. However, for Kant, there is no such sphere of participatory mediation between the physical and the psychic. For him it is rather a given that the sensory is neither moral nor immoral, but instead amoral, and so naturally orientated towards self-preservation and self-enjoyment. In consequence morality is not for him primarily a matter of the reorientation of the feelings, or the passions. Rather, a necessary 'moral feeling' is the paradoxical feeling of 'the sublime' which is the feeling of a break with feeling, or the counter-attractive attraction of self-sacrifice.[30] This sublimity also mediates, by rupture and not by participation, between the sensory with its natural egotism and the noumenal or spiritual with its equally natural and inevitable upholding of the freedom of self along with the freedom of others. Given that we are free as noumenal, and that this freedom is both intellectually and competently sufficient unto itself (as not for St Paul and Augustine), there is, in principle, absolutely no reason for it to be externally contaminated. Thus in no way for Kant, as for the Greeks, the Church fathers and high scholastics, might perverse sensory passions inevitably pull downwards the good will, unless entirely of its own perverse volition this will elects to substitute contingent for categorical ends.

In this way, Kantian 'Radical Evil' is a far more unsoundable mystery than Augustinian 'original sin'. And a second aspect to our failure to will freedom redoubles the mystery. Here we do not adopt non-moral maxims, but rather dilute our adoption of moral ones.[31] Kant avers that the dilution is always present, and even that the degree of such dilution is radically undecidable.

This situation arises from the necessary role of 'moral feeling' in his account of morality. Given that morality is the law of the noumenal outside the bounds of our understanding, which is confined to the phenomenal, practical reason requires to be sensorily 'schematized' (or 'pictured' with an intrinsic appropriateness). However, unlike the categories of theoretical understanding, which are *orientated* to the phenomenal, practical reason cannot, as reason, which is concerned with what lies beyond the phenomenal, be schematized in any truly legitimate sense.[32] Normally, Kant declares, it is improperly 'symbolized' according to a merely formal analogy, and schematized only at the curious point where we register, negatively, a break with the phenomenal when it becomes sublimely infinitized. Such a break Kant associates with heroism and self-sacrifice. Now in so far as these human phenomena belong with the natural sublime, they are not in any way for Kant necessarily moral: to the contrary, they concern our pride in, and awe at, a natural resistance to, and transcending of, nature. By contrast, Kant declares that the moral law in itself has nothing to do with sacrifice and admiration for sacrifice, which we tend to associate with the superogatory. Instead, the moral law commands only duty, and no one deserves admiration for fulfilling the minimum of duty; only disdain if they fail to do so.[33] And yet, according to Kant, we have *no* immediate access to this stringency and purity of duty, because for us the law of freedom is an essentially unknown idea, which, indeed, we can only affirm through 'rational faith'; we are assured of freedom exclusively at the point where we feel the attraction of giving up phenomenal well-being, or are led to admire such renunciation. Hence the moral law is registered improperly as moral feeling, or the strange attraction of sacrifice. (Even in the case where a sensory inclination *happens* to coincide with duty we only exercise virtue, according to Kant, when we are motivated purely by duty, so here also the sensory inclination must be sacrificed.)

However, this state of affairs drives the entire Kantian theory of ethics into irresolvable *aporias*, as he half-concedes. We are supposed to know the moral law *a priori*, without recourse (as with theoretical reason) to the application of categories to sensible intuition. And yet, if the moral law is only registered through the schematization of the natural sublime, then Kant is forced to supplement his case for the *a priori* status of the moral law, as he does in the *Critique of Judgement*, through illegitimate appeal to the admiration of all men in all ages for the heroism of sacrifice, as an inchoate registering of the categorical imperative (the problem here being, why has something the most humanly vital and so democratically knowable by all, even the most theoretically stupid, namely the categorical imperative, only just been discovered – by Kant?).[34]

But then of course, the problem ensues, how is one ever to know that sacrificial motives are pure? How is one sure that even a Thomas More died for the moral law, and not out of self-pride or the love of admiration?[35] And how is one to discriminate within oneself, if only a feeling of love of self-sacrifice registers the law, and yet *even this feeling* contaminates the purity of duty and is only valid in so far as this feeling constantly negates itself, sacrificing even the love of sacrifice? If this sacrifice even of sacrifice is, still, nevertheless sacrifice, how to distinguish a diminution of love of sacrifice and denial of self, from a subtle increase of love of sacrifice and affirmation of self?

This is the aporetic situation more or less admitted by Kant in *Religion Within the Bounds of Mere Reason*. Here it is notable that some of the empirical instances he gives of 'radical evil', particularly horrific slaughter in wars conducted for their own sakes, lie all too close to the instances of heroism practised for its own sake which he had earlier seen as evidence for the universal but inchoate registering of the categorical imperative.[36] However, the case, in Kantian terms, for regarding 'radical evil' as *a priori*, appears stronger than the case for the categorical imperative, since the *a priori* character of radical evil resides in the very undecidable uncertainty regarding human motivation as just described. If radical evil is more clearly *a priori* than the categorical imperative, then this implies, beyond Kant, that the reality of freedom itself, and its law, must remain uncertain (within the terms of a Kantian perspective).

As the self-binding of will, radical evil is a given fact precisely in the sense of an *a priori*. It is not, for Kant, like original sin, a biologically or socially inherited reality, because for him nothing in the causal order can affect the order of freedom. Nor, like original sin, is it a contingent event which distorts the created order, and one can note here that original sin, by remaining with narrative and an endless regress, is really *less* hypostatized and ahistorical than radical evil. Instead, radical evil is co-given along with freedom as an inherent possibility of freedom. This makes sense, because if what defines freedom is not its willing of an infinite goal which allows the flourishing of the free creature, but rather the willing of freedom as such, then freedom can only be free if it might will against itself. For this reason, radical evil is *implied by* enlightenment autonomy and does not qualify it – though only Kant was clever enough to see this. Pure freedom is as free in self-denial as in self-affirmation. And we have further seen that actually, under these conditions, self-denial becomes indistinguishable from self-affirmation.

In point of fact, though, Kant does not entirely admit the pure positivity of the evil will. He retains a minimal attachment to privation theory, by distinguishing *Wille* from *Willkür*: however much the latter acting will may elect the unfree, it can never entirely pervert the former pure faculty of will which is orientated to its own freedom and not its own destruction.[37] Nevertheless, this Kantian distinction appears unstable, precisely because Kant regards evil as a positive possibility constitutive of freedom as such. For Christian tradition, this was not the case: to the contrary, it regarded evil as the very *invention* of counter-possibility – of possibility in the drastic sense of an alternative to the actual. Therefore, by making such counter-possibility a surd dimension of the will, Kant lodges possibility within being as co-equal with actuality. In order for freedom to be actual, the capacity for self-destruction must lurk; in consequence, freedom appears more original than either actuality or possibility, indeed prior to being and non-being. It was this implication of radical evil which was developed by Schelling, and we can now see that the problem with his de-ontologization and de-infinitization of the Good is that thereby it inherits the Kantian problem of an undedicability between good and evil.[38] If God decides to share a neutral infinite with us, what renders this a gift, rather than a kind of establishing of empire via a grant of being? How might the gift of being not be perhaps disguised domination, unless the infinite we are granted to share in is in itself unshakable, as infinite peace and harmony according to a substantive aesthetic measure? Since peace and harmony and affinity only make sense as subjectively experienced and judged, there is after all really no danger that the ineluctable infinite Good might be merely impersonal.

After Schelling, the God-beyond-God of a ground of freedom prior to good and evil is transmuted by Heidegger into the ontological that is identical with nothing and indifferent to the resolute ontic decision for actuality.[39] Indeed, the ground for the authentic autonomy of this decision which fully admits its contingency remains a preserving of the sense of the equal validity of cancelling such a decision: this preserving constitutes our necessary 'guilt' in the face of Being. Jean-Luc Nancy rightly worries that both this ontic humanist affirmation and its reverse face of resignation to the indifference of fate – whereby the ontological can only manifest itself in occluding itself (as apologetically resorted to by the later Heidegger, at the end of the Nazi era) – are both complicit with the Holocaust.[40] And yet Heidegger is logical within the terms of the legacy of radical evil: to desire, like Nancy, that the will to affirmation have ontological priority, is, in effect, to reassert the vision of good as ontological and evil as privative. If Nancy were able to admit this, then he would also be able to admit that it is perverse to suggest that the extremity of modern evil reveals the co-primacy of evil in power and in being. For this renders all being and all power superior either to good or to evil, and therefore ensures that any act of power is legitimate and 'good' is undecidably good or evil.

Or to put it in another fashion: where good is not identical with being as such, willed good has only an 'ironic' fictional status – and in the end no one acts in the name of a fiction. This is one crucial reason why there cannot really be a *secular* privation theory: secularity will not see being as such as good and so will have to identify the Good in terms other than the full presence of the actual. The nearest one gets to such a secular theory is Spinoza, and later Nietzsche, but Spinoza still has an immanent God, and being and power remain convertible with the Good. Nonetheless, his immanentism means that evil in the cosmos, which is deficient weakness, is fated and inevitable, and in this way it would seem that evil does get lodged in being and privation is compromised, unless the perspectives of becoming have no true reality. One can conclude, therefore, that privation theory does require transcendence and creation *ex nihilo*.

Where, by contrast, being is rendered in secular fashion as indifferent to good and evil, Auschwitz is falsely accorded the status of a revelation; in this way taking evil seriously by granting it positive status passes over into resignation to the sway of evil itself. In this way Hitler enjoys a ghostly theoretical victory.

V

It will be recalled that the main objection of the postmodern Kantians to privation theory was that it provides an ontological excuse for evil which diminishes the responsibility of freedom. Now, however, it can be seen that this charge should be thrown back at them. For on their view, the decision for evil is referred to a prior possibility for such freedom – to a freedom prior to freedom and indifferent to good and evil, which alone establishes freedom as freedom. The demonic breaking in of such a radical pre-personal freedom which is *prior* to decision (Schelling's 'dark ground') surely cannot be blamed on the person so possessed? So this is really an ontological (or para-ontological) excuse. Moreover, worse still, where one starts by asserting that the Good has its ground in freedom *rather than* Being, one inevitably winds up by saying that Being (or a possibility before Being), as neither good nor evil, itself trumps freedom. Even if at first it allows it, it must in the end obliterate it, since without participatory mediation between a partially good finite, and an absolutely good infinite, the finite good will only arises through a concealment of Being with which it is essentially in conflict.

By contrast, the privation theory avoids all excuses, by denying that evil is lodged in any reality, power or being whatsoever. Somehow, it is impossibly instigated by will alone. If it is true, as we have seen, that it is not really *caused* by freedom, since freedom, as free, causes only the Good, then this shows that the bad will cannot *even* blame a possibility lodged within the order of causality (within which freedom, for the tradition, as not for Kant, itself lies). And as for the idea that privation theory offers finitude as an excuse, this may apply to the ancient Greeks, but not to Augustine and Dionysius. For them there is nothing defective in finitude as such; rather what is defective is the disallowing of finite things from reaching their own proper finite share of perfection. (For Dionysius, it should be noted, privation is more the removal of the Good than the removal of Being, since the Good for him lies beyond Being; however this detail does not really affect the present argument.)[41]

Thus evil for the Christian tradition was radically without cause – indeed it was not even self-caused, but was rather the (impossible) refusal of cause.

17

In this way privation theory offers not an 'explanation' of evil, but instead rigorously remains with its inexplicability, for 'explanation' can pertain only to existence, and here evil is not seen as something in existence. Indeed it is regarded for this reason as not even explicable *in principle*, not even explicable for God. Since evil is in this way *so* problematic that it falls outside the range of *problema*, there has never been for theologians any 'problem of evil'. The idea that there is such a problem has only arisen since, roughly, the time of Leibniz. As inherited evil was held to have already impaired our finitude, there was, indeed, for the authentic tradition, *in us* a causal bias to evil; yet since grace renews our will, our evil decision to refuse grace is as groundless and causeless as Adam's original sin. For this reason, according to Augustine, the origin of evil must be passed over as 'darkness and silence', as if there were a dreadful *apophasis* of evil that parodied the *apophasis* of the Divine.[42] Because evil is uncaused, there is indeed a sense in which it possesses us like an anti-cause proceeding from a Satanic black hole: as J.-L. Marion argues – the non-existence of the Devil *is* the existence of the Devil.[43] But when evil possesses us, not only are we responsible for this possession, it is also the case that this possession delivers the very phenomenon of autonomous responsibility. Evil is just that for which alone we are solely responsible. Evil is self-governing autonomy – evil *is* the Kantian good, the modern good.

Since evil is for privation theory so radically uncaused, it does not require to be justified by an ontodicy. Indeed, the rise of theodicy, and so of ontodicy, is much more correlated with a post-Scotist univocity of Being, and a sense that, if the finite equally *is*, as much as the infinite, then even the lacking that is evil equally *is* along with the good – in consequence the presence of evil must be 'justified' in terms of providential design.[44] (It is true that that this has some germs within the Church Fathers, but they confined it to a correct insistence that certain local pains and sufferings are not reallly evil but can indeed, like thirst that will be quenched, contribute to the overall good.)[45]

VI

From such theodicy and ontodicy, the theory of radical evil is in truth by no means immune. If, for Kant, human good will is only evidenced in resistance to suffering, then certainly non-moral evil in nature plays for him a providential role. But in addition, the most 'signal' virtue is for Kant displayed in our resistance to other human beings. Here moral evil, also, is a providential training ground for virtue, because Kant explicitly states that only the exercise of heroism in warfare (which, it will be recalled, is a sublime schema of the moral law), could have gradually trained up the strength of the will, such that it is finally able to resist its own self-denial, and to arrive at the moral preconditions for the establishing of 'perpetual peace' amongst the nations. The passage to moral virtue via the sublime also traverses the exercise of radical evil, just as the path to civilized peace lies dialetically through warfare. Like the neo-fascist master-psychologist of J.G. Ballard's visionary novel *Super-Cannes*, wherein high-powered executives are permitted recreational violence amongst the marginalized, Kant already holds that the moral impulse can only arise where our psychopathic impulses are also allowed a certain exercise.

However, we have already seen how this theodicy and ontodicy comes unstuck: the purportedly moral self-overcoming will might still be the natural heroic will – at once sublime and radically evil, or one might well say, Miltonically Satanic. How is one to decide? As Jacques Lacan pointed out, the Sadean sadistic will also wills only its own freedom, and is also prepared to sacrifice comfort, security and survival for the sake of its own exercise.[46]

But Kant was near to conceding this problem. How did he try to cope with it? The answer is that he sought to supplement morality with grace. Supposedly, Kant brings religion within the bounds of reason by reducing it to morality, but we have already seen how practical reason problematically transgresses the bounds established by theoretical reason, since it claims knowledge of noumenal freedom. And we have also seen how, when moral knowledge is brought back within the schematic bounds of the phenomenal, our claim to know the noumenal as moral is rendered uncertain. Thus practical reason, if it is to be saved, must, on the grounds of its own rational demand, be *supplemented* by religious faith. *Religion within the Bounds of Mere Reason* should really be entitled 'reason outside its own bounds in the sphere of religion'. For it turns out that ethics, the essence of religion, cannot after all dispense with the mere *parerga* or 'inessentials' of religion which exceed, for Kant, the ethical. Thus it cannot dispense with unmerited grace, with the Sacraments, with the organized Church.[47] Grace must be invoked, because we can only distinguish the will to freedom from radical evil if we have faith that our aspiration to a good will is graciously taken by God as equivalent to his infinite and ineluctably holy will (here Kant clearly has not gone as far as Schelling). To have this faith is also to have faith in an eschatological discrimination, when the good wills are finally divided from the bad wills, and the mere empirical pursuit of egoistic happiness is finally subordinated to freedom, since the virtuous are rewarded with happiness and the vicious with unhappiness. Moreover, this faith cannot merely be entertained by individuals, because radical evil arises for Kant (here influenced by Rousseau), only from cultural association which gives rise to envy and greed and so forth, and contaminates a supposed 'private' exercise of moral autonomy.[48] (One can contrast Augustine here, for whom, as we have seen, the good will is enjoyment, according to a specific refraction that is not in rivalry with other specific refractions, of an essentially common good.) The only way, according to Kant, to combat this corruption of the inward by the social, is to set up, not merely a State founded on a social contract and directed by a general will, but also a Church which seeks really to overcome, and not merely to inhibit, the inner desires of egotism. A Church is supposed, for Kant, to engender a kind of 'general moral will'. And its Sacraments, although arbitrary signs, are necessary reminders of the hope of the *eschaton*, without which morality remains uncertain.[49]

In this fashion, the theory of radical evil, which is supposed to locate evil within human limits, must after all, as Kant admits (though not his con- temporary heirs), in order to avoid antinomianism, invoke divine grace. However, Kantian free will is not, like Augustinian free will, identified with grace as the gift *par excellence* of grace. Instead, for Kant, freedom is no gift, but an inert *given*, and equally given along with it, is radical evil: so if it is a gift, it is a poisoned one. And as for Luther, free will as such cannot aspire to God; this Lutheran legacy is part of what leads Kant to conclude that finite will simply in itself is 'bound'.[50] Thus, bizarrely enough, Kantian grace is *far more* positivistically and pietistically irruptive than Augustinian or Thomist grace. For it does not give free will, but juristically supplements its (ontologically) *given* deficiency, since here the will to the good has reduced to the mere will to have a good will in the hope that God, by grace, will *impute* to us a good will.

If the Kantian account of grace and free will as it were parodies the Augustinian one, then so also does his account of the Church. For the Augustinian, as for the Pauline vision, the *ecclesia* aspires to, and partially realizes, a real harmony of differentiated persons by blending together a diversity of characters and roles according to a beautiful and analogical affinity that is rooted in the Church's manifestation of the incarnate *Logos*. Kant seems almost to come near to this, and yet the diverse persons in his Church are only united under the abstract formal resemblance of their wills, and only aspire to be 'one body' according to a just matching of happiness to freedom. It is not that here the specific happiness which is also the specific freedom of one person (according to a teleological flourishing) is concretely blended with the specific free happiness of another, according to the advent of affinity under grace, as for the Pauline view which Augustine elaborated. (Not seeing this distinction, Arendt, like many others, overrates the anti-liberal potential of 'beautiful' reflexive judgement in the third critique.)[51]

And in this way it becomes apparent that radical evil does *not* offer a secular view of evil, but only an alternative theology, which is an alternative account both of theological reason and of divine revelation to the tradi- tional account provided by Christian privation theory. Now then, we can attempt a theological discrimination between the two. And what is apparent is that, paradoxically, only privation theory (plus original sin and Satanic possession), allow for a *human* discrimination of good and evil in the here and now, and so the possibility of a substantively just social order. By con- trast, the theology of radical evil is also a theology of radical eschatological postponement of a guaranteed good and a guaranteed justice. And this theology cannot really allow any *anticipation* of the *eschaton*.

VII

It is finally the political implications of the Kantian legacy which I wish to explore. I have already defended at length the view of evil as privation which undergirds the view of evil as banal. The two views are not, however, identical: it is possible for negativity to take a sublime quasi-heroic form. Nevertheless, one can extend Arendt's theory of banality by arguing that this quasi-Satanism of the perpetrators of State horror is usually prepared by an incremental piling up of small deficient preferences which gradually and 'accidentally' (as Aquinas argued) produce the monstrous. (Aquinas after Dionysius speaks of 'accidental' causing of evil [S.T. I. Q. 49 a 1; *De malo* Q. 1. a 3; Dionysius D.N. V. 32] where Augustine seems to speak of no causing at all. However, by this they mean that pursuit of a too limited good 'accidentally' causes the lack of good that should ensue. This is an odd sort of accidentality, since it really brings nothing about, and involves not merely a non-intended consequence, but also an overlooked one.)

To give an example of this 'accidental' process: in the seventeenth-century English colony of Virginia, female servants proved at once unruly and over-dependent on their masters in circumstances of instability and great reliance upon women's labour. It proved harder and harder to grant them relative independence after their apprenticeships, and also harder and harder to ensure the legitimacy of their offspring. Gradually, their servitude drifted into slavery, and inheritance for slaves was directed for obvious reasons of convenience through the female line (though the *irrelevance* of paternity also gave savage licence to rape and seduction by masters). Soon, with the expansion of the African slave trade, there were more black female servants and slaves than white (there were initially many freed Africans, and conversely some *de facto* white slaves). Soon after that, there was a preponderance of black female slaves (male Africans being more able legally to establish an agrarian independence), and then their children, female and male, were all members of a black slave class. In 1662, all this was finally codified in law. Although it is true that a slave trade and embryonic racist ideologies – including the idea that black women were more suited to outdoor labour – preceded these developments, the legal confirmation of *de facto* slavery and the exclusive linking of a slave-class to race (intially defined though, more in terms of religion than of colour), nevertheless came about through the incremental effect of a series of petty puritanical and disciplinary approaches to a very real chaos, rather than from any fully-fledged ideological pro-gramme. The latter only emerged in the wake of sedimented events.[52]

Such a stress upon the 'accidental' factor in this case alerts us to the truth that an almost fully-fledged slave economy was less a diabolical aberration in the recent history of the West, than something that many typical features of Western modernity (disciplinary puritanism, enhanced patriarchalism, neo-republican dreams) could gradually engender in certain extreme circumstances.

Likewise, in the case of the Holocaust, the Satanism of the final solution was the outcome, as Alain Badiou (n. 13) rightly insists, of a long drift of deficient science, deficient philosophy, deficient politics, deficient religion and deficient sociality. To take the converse view, and to imagine that Hitler was a deliberate Satanist, or even that a Manson can attain a fully Satanic perspective, is to lend credence to that saddest of all the errors of evil (and of Satan) whereby it always imagines that it is yet more evil than it really is. For evil to be at all, it must still deploy and invoke some good, yet it would like to forget this: evil as positive is evil's own fondest illusion. Insisting in this way upon the pathos of evil and upon its creeping and incremental character by no means, as many fear, involves a taking away from the responsibility of individual wills. On the contrary, this insistence points to the gravity of even the smallest responsibilities and the dangers of apparently good intentions (which it does *not* quite deem as tragically unavoidable); also it does not excuse or regard as inevitable the long-encouraged emergence of 'monstrous' wills. Nor does this insistence tend to deny the unprecedented character of the Holocaust: all that it denies is the notion of a metaphysical revelation of an unexpected ontological status for evil. By contrast, it points to the Holocaust's real disclosure of the terrible capacities of an ancient depravity whose character, nonetheless, retains all too tediously its perennial nature. (Even if it be pointed out that many minor implementers of the 'logic' of the final solution indulged their own sadism, one should see that even sadism has its pathos and pathetic pursuit of displaced goods. Bernhard Schlik's – in many ways problematic – novel *The Reader* illustrates this point: the sadism of a female camp official is inseparable from the fact of her illiteracy, which has led her to select this job as one of the few where this fact can be disguised.)

In addition, a stress upon the pathos of evil which insists more than the thesis of 'radical evil' upon the political, incremental dimension of Nazism tends to indicate how the Holocaust is imbricated with modernity, and very likely foreshadows further unspeakable horrors to come.

But if the final solution was the outcome of a long incremental drift, then we must finally ask, was the Kantian legacy itself part of this process?

Hannah Arendt in part considered this to be the case. Adolf Eichmann did, as she noted, have a self-admitted Kantian habit of mind in so far as he thought sovereign law must be obeyed, must be obeyed without exception, and must be obeyed beyond the call of duty in the spirit of the letter.[53] For Arendt, it is this popularized Kantianism which explains how the utterly inefficient Nazis were nonetheless able to co-opt the internalized efficiency of the German people.

However, Arendt took Eichmann's Kantian habit to be a parody of Kantian nobility – and indeed it appears that Eichmann himself had thought so. Thus she says that, for the ineffability of the sovereign law of free will as such, Eichmann had substituted the sovereign will of the Führer. This is not to be confused with the command of the categorical imperative. But are they really so distinct? And was Eichmann merely parodying?

Politics, for Kant, though rooted in the moral law, has to deal mainly with the contingent, empirical imperatives of material well-being. However, we have seen how the categorical imperative has to be schematized and symbolized in terms of these lesser imperatives. And the Kantian account of the just polity suggests indeed that the self-governing State symbolizes the self-governing moral individual according to a formal analogy ('symbol' for Kant, always denotes a mere common ratio, which is also how he understands 'analogy'). This analogy involves nothing more nor less than *the division of powers*. At the centre of the State should stand an unchanging sovereign power, whose issuing of laws without enacting them renders it akin to the transcendent law of freedom in the individual. Kant himself makes this analogy when, in *Religion Within the Bounds of Mere Reason* he compares God the Father who is the ultimate source of the moral law, to a political sovereign.[54] God the Son is then compared to a political executive, and also to the individual will which is incited by moral feeling to obey the ineffable law. Thus we see that, for Kant, the political executive is akin to individual moral activity, inspired by moral feeling. Finally, God the Holy Spirit is at once like the political judiciary and the individual judgement. These two are akin, because they both seek to apply the law to particular circumstances, and to match freedom to happiness, according to extrinsic desert, not intrinsic co-belonging. In this way Kant, in keeping with his logic of essential inessentials (*parerga*), reveals that his hierarchy of cold duty over warm feeling is grounded in a heterodox and Arian Trinity. At the same time he reveals how the same Trinity secures a political sovereignty which can be taken as absolute and persisting over and above what is enacted and judged in its name.

To be absolutely fair to Kant here, he is clear that tyranny results when the powers are confused with each other and especially when the executive usurps the sovereignty.[55] By this measure Hitler would surely have been deemed a tyrant. Kant allows for the popular overthrow of a corrupt executive and judiciary, and this was the basis for his qualified support for the French Revolution. Nevertheless, in his famous footnote on regicide in the *Metaphysics of Morals*, Kant ferociously disallows overthrow of the sovereign power as utterly contradictory.[56] So where sovereign and executive have utterly coalesced, albeit through usurpation (as in the Nazi case), what Kantian basis remains to support resistance and non-obedience, even if the original usurpation was denounced, since the *de jure* basis of sovereignty in Kant seems to reduce to the *de facto*? For Kant, sovereign political authority is the point where moral and political rule, categorical and contingent imperative, actually come together. Since the sovereign power embodies the collective general will, and is the absolute source of all legality, to will against the sovereign power in person is to will against political legality. This cannot be universally willed, under the maxim 'I will to destroy a corrupt sovereign power', because it removes the very basis of legality, just as lying, for Kant, destroys the possibility of trust and thus of all free association. Hence regicide *does* fall foul of the categorical imperative, and to oppose the political sovereign *is* to oppose the moral sovereign.

This conclusion really results because the ground of legitimacy in Kant is entirely one of immanent consent and procedural emission from a consensually established centre: thus he cannot allow that a substantive natural law would remain, even in the absence of sovereign power. To the contrary, the only political law of nature for Kant is that there must be an earthly sovereign centre if there is to be collective justice. Here the closed bounds of human reason which disallow a mediation of the infinite also absolutize established human authority. This absolutization is very extreme in Kant, since he describes regicide as the *supreme* instance of radical evil and of sublime horror, almost displacing the crucifixion of the Son of God in this respect. Here the only thing that prevents regicide as an act of freedom from being seen as an act of moral liberation is the identification of the sovereign idea of freedom we must respect, with a *given*, established, specific exercise of freedom by a political ruler. But then how else, short of the *eschaton, are* we now, in Kantian terms, to discriminate a good will from a bad one? Even though Kant never drew this conclusion, it seems to follow, if one thinks through his *aporias* to their ends. Kantian morality, deconstructed, says, you know your will is good when you obey the law of the State without exception and beyond the call of duty. Eichmann had it more right than he appears to have known.

If this analysis is correct, then the Nazi episode casts suspicion not just upon Fichte or Müller or Nietzsche or Heidegger, but on the main lines of the Germanic philosophical legacy to which the second half of the twentieth century has remained in some ways too dangerously subservient. This is not, however, to indict an entire culture, because Kant's most decisive and insightful opponents – Jacobi, Hamann, Herder – were also German and also strongly informed a later Germanic tradition. Moreover, in relation to the Nazis, many other currents are equally culpable, including an originally British evolutionism in some of its manifestations.[57] But the ambiguity of the Kantian legacy does raise specifically the question which must still haunt us, that of the collusion between liberalism and totalitarianism. Moral liberalism tends to engender an uneasy oscillation between absolute promotion of one's own freedom for any goal whatsoever, and absolute sacrifice to the freedom of the other, again without any conditions as to the goals that others should pursue. Writ large at the level of the State, this produces a giant-scale oscillation between a present collective identity as an end in itself, and the endless self-sacrifice of individuals for the sake of a better future. Thus political liberalism itself engenders today an increasingly joyless and puritanical world in which we work harder and harder towards obscure ends, while 'surplus' populations of the young, the old, the cultural misfits and the poor are increasingly marginalized, disciplined, put to degrading work or indeed simply destroyed – all, perhaps, as Ballard implies, for the psychopathological amusement of the successful. The liberal state already exhibits a certain totalitarian drift and may always become really totalitarian at the point where its empty heart is besieged by an irrational cult of race, class, science, style or belief. Indeed, since September 11, 2001, this narrow gulf may already have been crossed.

The slide of liberalism toward totality confirms that where free will as such as identified with the Good, the promotion of self-respect and autonomy will be simultaneously and indistinguishably the promotion of self-inhibition and radical evil; the most noble will be also the psychopathological. But for privation theory it is this very promotion of abstract free autonomy that itself enshrines what is evil, and radically deficient.

2

VIOLENCE

Double passivity

I

Is the question of evil the same as the question of violence? It might seem so, since all violence is evil – even justified violence is the justification of a lesser evil. But is all evil violence? For the theory of radical evil, the answer might be no: evil does not remove or destroy; instead it sets up its own dark kingdom. But we have seen the incoherence of this view. For the theory of evil as privative, by contrast, evil always removes and destroys. The depriving of good is perforce also a disturbing of the peace. Inversely, if peace is a harmonious plenitude, when it is disturbed there is always an instance of noisy distortion, which impairs just distribution.

So evil is violence, violence is evil. But why then are there two words for the same thing? Pure synonymity? Not exactly. Were evil simply violence, then one might take it that peace was simply an absence of conflict. But for privation theory peace is also positive justice, harmony and affinity. Peace is also the Good and the True and the Beautiful. It is rather the theory of radical evil which tends to view peace as mere absence of disturbance, as the non-violation of 'the other' by a will which respects freedom. So even if this perspective interprets the will to evil as a positive volition, it still defines its action as a formal invasion of freedom rather than a destruction of substance or a turning from a *telos*. If evil is radical, then it only disturbs the peace, and does not also conceal the Good. Evil here is a like a club: as a weapon it is positive and neutral; but in its effect it is simply negative, illegitimate invasion. Here there are two supposedly indisputable visibilities: one of the positive willing agent, the other of manifest violence.

Privation theory, however, denies all this obviousness. It questions the evidence of both visibilities. First of all, violence is never merely witnessed; it must also be judged. Is the outstretched arm a push, assault or a stay? Is the crack of the whip a spur, a dishonouring, a rebuke or a caress? It is clear that apparent violence may not after all be violence. Secondly, and inversely, the asserting will may in reality be negative, as was argued in Chapter 1. In this case apparently non-violent and neutral assertion is, after all, privation and therefore violence.

So in terms of the effect of evil, the theory of radical evil focuses *too much* upon violence. Life, after all, is one invasion after another: if invasion as such is violence, goodness is the Rousseauian secluded glade. But if, rather, we must discriminate amongst invasions, then violence is only violence when it ruins an essence (how something should be) or diverts from a goal (how something should develop). In this case, violence is violence when it is also evil.

On the other hand, the theory of radical evil also disguises an invisible violence. For privation theory, evil is not simply the psychopathic will to violence. As we have seen, the theory of radical evil, when deconstructed, logically asserts that the moral will is also the psychopathic will, and even that the psychopathic impulse must be allowed play in order *both* to stimulate and train, *and* to provoke in reaction, the moral impulse (this is Ballard's Nietzscheanism without French polish). Privation theory is only able to overcome this diagnosis of human nature by insisting upon the ontological contingency of pathology as original sin – *even if* this be rooted also in our biology. It asserts that originally, and more properly, human nature has a self-transcending character which orientates it towards the supernatural. Hence our reality is not measured by our apparent capacity, but by our aspiration.[1] Against the given, one appeals to the lost and renewed gift of grace, and the fact that our given perversity is *unsoundable*: the most searching psychoanalysis is forced to speak of death-drives, fundamental sadisms and so forth. Privation theory rightly reflects that the minimum of sense that can be made here concerns a deluded pursuit of more substantive and abiding pleasures.

But most crucially of all, privation theory *levels* the moral will with the psychopathic will. The theory of radical evil thinks through an ethics of immanence rooted in the human will and not the event of grace (to which even the atheist Badiou must appeal, in opposing this theory).[2] It logically concludes to a pre-moral undecidability between the sublime and the psychopathic. Privation theory only releases us from this abyss of horror by fully owning up to the levelling of 'the moral' and 'the immoral' indicated by the theory of radical evil. It points out that the 'good' will to freedom in its unteleological neutrality is bound to be as evil as it is good. Hence the positive assertion of private autonomy is judged to be *just as* evil as its evidently evil and perverse enjoyment of heteronomous interferences (the Sadeian reality of the Kantian subject). Such autonomy is exposed by privation theory as deprivation of our participation in being as gift: in this way privation theory attacks as evil not just exterior and visible destruction, but also interior and invisible self-assertion. The latter is here diagnosed *as also* evil; but this means as also secretly violent: a violence against Being, an attempted and illusory violence against God.

In the end, for privation theory there is a perfect convertibility of evil with violence. The evil acting will is as violent as the evil external act, because both are equally *deficient* in character. For the theory of radical evil, by contrast, only the external act and not the acting will is violent – this matches the fact that the will and not the act is 'evil'. For this theory also construes the act, as we have seen, too much merely as violent and not also as the evil distortion of the Good. Privation theory sees disturbing of the peace also as inhibition of the Good, and is only able to diagnose the evil will as *occult violence* because it interprets it also as an inhibition of a participation in infinite plenitudinous goodness.

II

What follows in this chapter is an attempt to read violence in terms of the above theory that evil and violence are convertible but not identical: exactly like a couple of malign transcendentals. The same relation pertains, of course, between evil and falsity, evil and disunity, evil and nullity, evil and ugliness – all of which anti-transcendentals play some sort of latent role in my account. That 'violence' is also an anti-transcendental, naturally implies that peace is a transcendental: a position implicitly affirmed by Dionysius, Augustine, Aquinas and Cusanus.[3]

I have already tried to show the main consequences of this theory: first of all, if evil converts with violence, then evil is never positive. Secondly, if violence converts with evil, then violence is never simply *evident*, because we have to *judge* whether a substantive good has been impaired. Thus a kind of 'phenomenological pacifism' which shies away rigidly from 'apparent' violence is here ruled out. Instead, violence has always to be diagnosed, and in a double fashion. Much apparent violence may be exonerated, while much occulted violence must be disinterred. What we are mainly concerned with, therefore, is the question of violence and spectatorship.

In three different ways, it seems to me, those in the wealthy middle-class West today have become characteristically *onlookers* of violence, rather than (at least for now) participants in enactments of violence. We no longer carry daggers in our belts and whip them out at the slightest provocation – like, for example, the young J.S. Bach when faced with a recalcitrant viola de gamba player. Instead, we watch endless scenes of violence in filmed recordings – scenes of violence in wild nature, human violence in remote places, or else of simulated, fictional violence.

This is the first and most obvious way in which we have become primarily onlookers of violence. Later in this chapter I will address the debate about the relative dangers or else innocuousness of watching violence, especially fictional violence. These reflections will lead to the paradoxical conclusion that looking at violence is actually *more violent* than participating in violence – that to be violent *is* actually to survey in a detached, uninvolved fashion a scene of suffering; the *most* violence lies in an occulted violence. Clearly this conclusion will tend to undercut any assumption that because we are primarily the watchers of violence, we are removed from it and live in an essentially post-violent society.

This conclusion also has implications for the other two ways in which we have become onlookers of violence. The second way concerns our gaze upon the past: history has been increasingly regarded ever since the eighteenth century as the place where savage acts took place on the basis of superstition and confessional prejudice; and where such acts persist, as for example in the Balkans or the Near East, this is seen today as a kind of historical hangover, affecting only the margins of our modern world. But the question here is, if we experience a sense of moral superiority when we gaze, passively, at a violent past wherein active intervention is now, by definition, forever impossible (because of the irreversibility of time) are we, in fact, analogically or even literally *doing violence* to the past?

The third way concerns the increasing recommendation in modern times, but especially in the United States, of refraining from actual physical violence as the exercise of a supreme good; for example, in the sphere of punishment.[4] Frequently this pacifism has been associated with the setting-up of quasi-utopian communities in a removed wilderness, or else with groups, like the Quakers, committed primarily to international and commercial rather than national and political activities, and often the promoters of penal reform. The pacifist outlook seems to assume that where one is presented with acts of violence in real life – either towards others or to oneself – then to retain the stance of *onlooker* is morally superior to undertaking a defensive counter-violence. The pacifist elects to *gaze at violence*, and he maintains this stance even if he turns his face away from a violent spectacle, since it persists in his memory. But in fact, this question of averting one's gaze also points towards the issue which I will return to later concerning the counter-intuitive character of the pacifist outlook; and one can note here that the very notion of the counter-intuitive has metaphorical links with 'averting one's gaze'. For if the pacifist is confronted with an act of violence against the innocent which he is not going to meet with counter-violence – shall we say, a posse of marauding Apaches about to assault pioneering women and children, or else a bunch of gung-ho American pilots about to bomb into submission 'subversives' in the Third World – then does he stay and watch, or does he shrink quietly away to his prayers? If he does the latter, if he averts his gaze, then how will not the innocent, catching this act out of the corner of their terrified eyes, not perceive here the signifiers of indifference or embarrassment? On the other hand, if he stays to watch, how will they not discern in his gaze of pious sorrow a trace of the non-intervening *voyeur*? Pacifism, then, is counter-intuitive down two possible forks; it is aporetic, and therefore impossible for humanity as ordinarily understood.

Moreover, the implication of these reflections is that the refusal of physical counter-violence itself cannot avoid the taint of malice, or the communication of a violent intention. Failure to see this itself derives from a failure sufficiently to look, to the second power, at the scene of violence plus onlookers: failure, then, of a sufficiently explored, sufficiently involved and sympathetic, rather than detached intention. Failure in other words, of an adequate phenomenology of the scene of violence which nevertheless judges as much as it discerns.

But if this is the case, then it is not simply that pacifism as non-violence is less moral than the defensive use of physical violence. It is also that pacifism, as looking at violence, is at least as violent, and probably more absolutely violent, than actual physically violent interventions. This then will confirm my more general conclusion which I have yet to argue – that gazing at violence is the greatest violence, indeed the very essence of violence.

It is this conclusion which I now wish to establish, in relation to the first site of spectatorship – namely the watching of recorded violence, real or feigned.

III

The question of taking pleasure in violent spectacle has been with us at least since eighteenth-century discussions of the aesthetics of the sublime.

Edmund Burke was by no means alone in this period in raising the spectre of a perverse pleasure in the horrific and repellent. John Dennis already linked the experience of the sublime to 'enthusiastic terror' and James Beattie noted, somewhat uneasily, the 'gloomy satisfaction' that we take in shipwrecks and other catastrophes held within a secure, distancing frame.[5] The distinguishing of the experience of the sublime from both the experience of beauty and of the commitment to virtue raised for the first time in modernity a theme that helps to define it, namely the claimed recognition of an aesthetic realm indifferent to the ethical – that garden of delights which nurtures the *fleurs du mal.* (Although in the end the tortured and Kabbalistic Baudelaire was seeking to release a beauty trapped by modern urban evil – like the affection of a prostitute, or the glance of a lost stranger – that is also an alienated goodness which the plenitude of the *Kalon* – Beauty and Goodness – requires in order to be itself.)

One may conjecture that in ages when horror pressed in upon people from all sides, it was less easily rendered a spectacle, and that with the rise of the possibility of safe tourism to threatening places, and equally the increased likelihood of urban encounter with horrors that merely 'pass one by', the possibility of gazing with impunity at the fascinatingly catastrophic was vastly increased. However, this social circumstance is surely not what was decisive, for antiquity and the Middle Ages were dimly aware of such psychological possibilities. In the *Republic*, Plato tells of Leontion, who, noticing some executed corpses lying outside the north wall of Athens, experienced an almost irresistible desire, warring with his disgust, to go up and look at them. And in the *Confessions*, Augustine notes that we may often

30

attend the theatre because we enjoy being made sad by 'tragical passages' we could not ourselves 'endure to suffer'; this theatrical drug is for him no true medicine, since it achieves no catharsis, but rather induces addiction.[6] Yet neither Plato nor Augustine saw in these phenomena a dreadful possibility, reality's dark blooms. Instead, for both they are to do with a fascination with nothingness, which is a false fascination, always predatory on the reality it gradually erodes.

To modernity this interpretation, which reduces the perverse urges to banality, seems implausible: is not the lure to enjoy destruction *as lure* something intensely positive? But the clue to the truth of the diminished intensity of this lure, compared with the urges to create and enjoy life, lies in the circumstance of spectatorship. As Augustine notes, my enjoyable commiseration with the sufferings on stage is linked with the impossibility of my intervening to alleviate them (for they are feigned); hence the whole experience depends upon an absolute bar against reciprocal participation sealed by a double passivity: the scene exhibited is only there at all to be watched, but since watching is all the watchers can do, they are themselves confined to a *telos* of mere reception. Neither the players nor the audience may actively intervene in the other sphere, and each sphere – stage and audience – is only there for the other one. Naturally, life as a whole could not be like this, because then nothing would ever happen: we would all remain stuck in the final tableau of a masque, or confined to our seats as a perpetual audience. Therefore, the whole point of every spectacle is that it must end, and indeed what the audience has come to see is how it will end, or in other words the manner of its death.

So it ceases to be the case that the problem is one of certain spectacles of death which arouse intense enjoyment. Instead, the point is that every staged 'scene' is a scene of horror, a spectacle of termination, and that it is so because the artificial creation of the situation of pure spectacle is a recreational relaxation precisely as a diminution of life, or its real interactive excitements, its real consummations and overwhelmings by power (which is not violence, if the power be really power – that is a manifestation of the actual). It follows that the circumstance of spectacle is a de-intensification of being, and that in itself it *is* the spectacle of destruction – a drama which to be justified must be re-integrated as ritual through its staged gestures of return and resurrection. It further follows that just as only the Eucharist renders the gaze at the crucified God non-perverse, the purest spectacles of pure destruction represent the lowest degree of intensity, the most drugged and frozen tableaux. Here one is either a pure sadist, or a pure masochist, but in either case utterly passive, and indeed relieved of the degree of activity which informs every reception in order for it to be *a response* or mode of interpretation or intervention. Without the middle between active and passive – which is more properly an entirely 'active reception' or non-identical repetition of activity[7] – passivity itself vanishes down the gulf of its last gaze upon the *nihil* of achieved destruction, or the last presentation of that destruction.

But then why, (post)modernity will ask, are artistic scenes of violence able to re-awake us from our complacent bourgeois slumbers and remind us of our framing by natural death and violence? The answer is that this slumbering is itself a nihilistic embrace of death in disguise: it has already relaxed life by restricting the dangers of unexpected death precisely through the increase of death-like petrified spectacle everywhere: of routine securities guaranteed by the acting out of the same scripts, and the witnessing of these actings out by the various policing agents, such that neither performance nor judgements of the performance (following the rule book) can interfere with each other's prescribed operations.[8] Contemporary bourgeois life which is now in the main a sterile, uncreative and proletarianized reproduction of 'information' (as the insurgents of May 1968 already diagnosed) is therefore already theatre, and therefore (given the conclusions above) already the theatre of cruelty, and all that is lacking in the bourgeois is not knowing this to be the case.

Art and the theatre only wake it up to this fact, and offer in addition that increased intensity which comes 'at the last gasp', when the secret seeker of death, faced with death's arrival, at last recoils from it, as well as recognizing and explicitly embracing the object of his desire. But by the same token, the theatre of cruelty, like all merely sublime art, only realizes to the full the bourgeois urge to diminution of the real. The fact that at last it reveals and exposes that tiny degree-almost-zero of remaining intensity which persists even in the least intense of all lives, disguises from view that its spectacle of horror is the least intense thing imaginable. A breezy day in Peckham, a bus-ride to Upminster, would be less suburban.

But there again, modernity asks, and has asked ever since the eighteenth century, were not primitive times, the times of invention, danger, uncertainty, adventure and closeness to nature, also the times of exhibitions of ritual violence? Rituals in which all participated, which were therefore not mere theatre. And is it not precisely such ritual, such active, engaged, participatory art, with no active and passive, no artists versus spectators of art, which the modern *avant-garde* seeks to reclaim?

But to this one must answer, resolutely, that while indeed, 'ritual' was no mere domain for 'primitive' societies over against the everyday (as Talal Asad had rightly insisted),[9] yet even so, just to the degree that this ritual incorporated experiences of ritual violence, which means framed violence you can *safely* watch, boundaries had to be established and zones of non-interference set up between performers and spectators. That is to say, ritual violence, violent sacrifice and violent initiation must *already* constitute to a degree a realm of theatre, and the continuous re-invocation of primitive ritual by theatrical modernity should therefore cease to surprise us.

By contrast, the purest urge to non-theatrical ritual, to a ritual coincident with life, and without performers and spectators, is surely not to be located in 'the primitive'. Rather, one might look for it, first of all, in Plato's vision in the *Laws* of a city with a festival for every day of the year, which offered itself to the gods through its conversion of every procedure into dance and music;[10] secondly, in the monotheistic faiths which tend to view the highest sacrifice as praise offered harmoniously by all, in such a fashion that all sing and all hear, while all transpire upwards with their song into the secret heavenly sanctuary and all expect to return, for a while, to the flow of temporary life. Here, therefore, violent (later non-violent) sacrifice establishes no partitions between the killed who departs and the living who remain, or between the licensed killers and an audience watching from a safe distance (even monotheistic sacrificial procedures are approximated to the purely liturgical, non-theatrical pattern).[11]

The above considerations suggest, therefore, that a modern 'society of the spectacle' retreats from the pure liturgy of monotheism to a pagan theatricality. And like paganism, it invests its hopes in a controllable economy of violence: where this much and no more blood was once shed to appease the gods, now this much and no more simulated violence, or rather as much simulated violence as you like, will appease our 'aggressive urges'; and in the absence of real wars to watch (from a safe distance) ensure that, indeed, no more real wars or mass oppressions ever again occur. From the horrors of the Second World War and of Auschwitz has been reborn, again, such a would-be atoning art, which seeks to face up to, present, repeat symbolically and so prophylactically, the unimaginable, the sublimely inconceivable atrocity. We cannot run away from this, it is implied (by Hermann Nitsch, Damien Hirst, J.G. Ballard and so forth), for now it has occurred, we have to admit the unlimited degree of our thrilling at such spectacle, and art alone, art with a boldness of rupture to match that of Auschwitz, can now purge away our complicity, and take upon itself the future salvific prevention of equivalent or worse real calamities in the future.

In this way modern art, which is increasingly only an art of the sublime – of shock and rupture without attraction – recycles the disturbance of a Baudelairean aesthetic diabolism (and removes its saving ambiguity) as the ultimate Aristotelian catharsis; the true pagan, priestly virtue. But two things are overlooked here: the one theoretical, the other historical. The first, theoretical point, is that all violence is, in a sense, simulated: to be successfully violent we must shield ourselves from the effects of violence; to enjoy violence we must switch off our capacities for sympathy. In short we must, in this instance uniquely, be spectators of the deeds we perform. And here intervention in the plot, as in an interactive computer game, does *not at all* cancel the boundary between performer and spectator, but only perfects it: the player on stage I can apparently kill from my seat in the audience is all the more a player watched by me or whom I simply watch;

even the players manipulated by me, in a virtual reality without upshot for my love, are all the more under the control of my gaze, all the more reduced to the realization of my pre-existent fantasies. By comparison, a play I did not write *may* alter my life, and to that degree does not so purely happen only on stage as the fantasy I can 'interactively' control.

But the best spectacle of all is the most apparently real and yet controlled. In fact it is the real terrified individual who can truly relay to me a pure passivity, and which I therefore can most enjoy according to the perverse canons of enjoyment of the same pure passivity (meaning the degree zero of activity just before death). That is to say, the only purgation which will satisfy is the real killing, the real sacrifice: artists have begun to re-arrange dead animals and the organic world in order to intensify (as they think) sublime rupture, just as their increasingly indistinguishable allies in iniquity, many 'scientists', are also re-arranging reality in the name of 'the beautiful,' or our endless increasing needs for more food, more variety, more prolonged 'life', more 'normal' life and increasingly more choice, more strangeness (at this point they join hands with the artists, the technicians of sublimity). But if the degree of shock is never quite enough, if the stakes of catharsis forever rise, and if, also, the most perfectly simulated violence is actual violence (as has just been demonstrated) then the demand to purge horror by horror is the demand for . . . horror.

This is the point aptly described by J.G. Ballard in *Super-Cannes* as 'stepping through Alice's looking glass' – the point at which we live actually in the world of simulation and, for example, kill real people with real bombs, yet without real risk or loss of life to 'our own' side, as in the Gulf and Afghanistan wars. Or else again, the point at which we propose to put on trial, torture and execute real people, but in secret, in a virtual legality outside normal legitimacy, but nonetheless permit 'the victim' to watch – as proposed in the United States for dealing with 'terrorists'. Here occurs no reversion to public execution which displayed the objectivity of the law, since not all can now be spectators. Instead it is the purest and most unprecedently barbaric indulgence by the State of psychopathic impulses to private vengeance. Perhaps soon, indeed, as Ballard envisages, 'therapeutic' suspensions of legitimacy permitting the enactment of perverse crimes in secret by the privileged few will be covertly allowed.[12] Since September 11, 2001, we have clearly stepped through the looking-glass.

Therefore it turns out that the stringent crudities of Plato and Augustine are more perceptive than the subtleties of Aristotle: the drug of violence is no dialectical *pharmakon*, but merely addictive. Tragedy offers no catharsis as the purely tragic, and if hope remains, it must rather reside in the possibility that there are no innate 'aggressive urges', or rather that they are a naturally and culturally contingent historical legacy.

Here one can ask, just how would one locate them, given that almost every known instance of aggression can be linked with some occasion of aggression, or actual aggression which precedes it? If this fact of a chain of aggressive acts brings us up against 'pointless aggression', and if such radical aggression can again erupt *de novo* in any given instance, then its pointlessness is an absolute mystery and we *do not know* how to understand it *or* express it or perform it in terms of recognizable reasons or pleasures or delights. (Even in animal nature aggressivity far exceeds function.) To point to 'exercise of power' will not do here, since power over something still involves 'a point' which resides in a measure of pleasure in, and appreciation of, the thing or person controlled by power; *absolute* power for its own sake without these interactive dimensions would kill the thing or person controlled, and in thereby losing its power become once more pointless, without assignable reason or pleasure. At this juncture the celebration of the purely sublime has to take refuge in sheer *mystique*. One can note here the double thrust of privation theory: evil is 'explicable' as the pursuit of the lesser good, yet a diminished pursuit is ultimately nihilistic, and so not explicable at all. This is not, however, positive radical evil, but a radical negativity.

It follows that neither in terms of the privated pursuit of peace, nor as a surd mode of mysterious anti-action which 'is' not, since it denies actuality, is one justified in envisaging aggressivity as innate. Rather it is fiction, theatre and contaminated mythology which itself trades upon this invented tragic scenario.

Plato was therefore right: acceptable poetry is liturgical praise of the divine and heroic, but mimesis within a fictional frame is to be eschewed – or received only, we may qualify, if integrated back into a liturgical frame by its own self-negating gestures within that frame: as Milton achieves in *Paradise Lost*. If drama involves *only* negative capability, and no subtly insinuated act of real subjective commitment by the author to his words, then it becomes nihilistic. This was Wittgenstein's suspicion concerning Shakespeare: that he was no true hymnic *Dichter*. Yet it was surely a misreading. Shakespeare's villains and anti-heroes are precisely captured by the abyss of pure drama, and this *tragic delusion* is clearly condemned by framing liturgical gestures of resurrection, which increasingly punctuated and closed his plays. In this way, as Keats discerned, negative capability encourages a sublime gesture of faith rather than one of gnosis or auto-biographical self-absorption.[13]

But without such liturgical recouping of negative capability, the theatrical and fictional inherently tends to the spectacle of violence which is real violence. Is it not after all clear that if violence is culpable as denying (ending) some reality, then it is culpable for *pretending* something; while conversely, what fictionalizes is violent unless it doubles this irony by another irony intended to reinforce a real already threatened by pretence (in this way Socratic irony was a counter-fiction).[14] Thus Plato's refusal of epic and theatrical fictions about the gods which are intended – unlike hymns and instructive myths of origins – merely to divert us or to reflect our given humanity, is *exactly the same gesture* as his refusal of violence within the divine realm.[15]

The second, historical point, is that in our recent past, science and art have always first mimed the horrors to come. Unteleological evolutionism (the Darwinian variety; now scientifically somewhat in eclipse) more or less demanded eugenicizing, since if we are outcomes of chance, we require redesigning. It sought to shore up liberalism with a greater 'beauty' of convenience, but engendered only a greater means of totalitarian, expert control over an ignorant, submissive populace. Likewise, *avant-garde* art of the kind which sought either to relieve the monotony of modern life (Salvador Dali, for example) or else to augment and make palpable its speed for the sake of ensuring our deepest passionate satisfaction (Italian futurism) in fact encouraged the yet more sublime vision of the imposition of unimaginable force and horror by a few political artists upon their many willing admirers. (Other instances of the modernist *avant-garde*, however, constituted a genuine protest.) So what may the far more shocking interventions of 1990s art and science (engendered precisely by the liberal response to a horror it seeks to prevent from happening again) betoken for the present century?

We are all too soon beginning to see . . .

IV

At this point it is time to revert to the two other issues concerning violence and spectacle. First of all, our gaze upon the past.

If we merely look upon the violent past in judgement, do we not reproduce the scene of double passivity? Do we not assume that the conflict and illusions of the past are over, and no longer inflect the course of events today? Inversely, do we not assume that the past, since it is finished with, cannot in any sense be resumed and redeemed?

We get in this position of double passivity *vis-à-vis* the past, where we imagine that violence is essentially over, and so frameable by our gaze. We then do violence to the past, because we render it *too* different from our present, and fail to sympathize with its dilemmas.

Violence is far from over, and if anything has been increased by being abstracted and generalized. Today, violence is like the regularity of breathing, which goes on all the time and is a fire so slow (fire, since it is oxidization) that we do not notice that it is fire. Likewise, we do not today see brutality – especially the exclusion and elimination of those who fail in the competition of the marketplace. Now that knowledge is also subject to the market, and the quest for truth has consequently been abandoned in favour of the sloshing about of 'information', we do not notice that since information is a valuable product – inhibiting random chaos and threatened by the entropy of out-of-dateness – it assumes that many will lack information and will be socially defined as the uninformed or else the deficient in personal data (according to entirely standardized criteria).

Truth, by contrast, is not like this, since it does not stand in contrast to chaos as an island of arbitrary systems, and cannot become out of date. Because of its consequent non-vanity, truth is marked by plenitude and democratic availability: it is Augustine's sunlight.

Computers though, in so far as they impose the reign of information, are the enemies of truth and democracy. Our gaze at their screens is the constitution through watching and receiving of inherently violent trans-actions which in the end, when we step through their looking-glass, always involve real physical violence.

On line, therefore, we are clubbing each other to death, but invisibly, very very gradually and at a huge remove. When this process does appear, then we finally see what we collectively do, but assume that it has nothing to do with us, individually. But just as breathing is the most massive combustion, so also this slowed-down and distributed violence is actually increased violence, like a torture that is all the more torture through being long drawn-out.

Likewise, it is increased as a trade in violence, or in abstract, purposeless power: power for *its own sake*, which is another definition of what constitutes violence. Modern economics and politics have discovered how to instil a kind of order from the systematization of the random, the pursuit of dis-order, the battle of all with all. There is nonetheless a dialectic at work here, because the increasing pursuit of power through simulations of the real – the competitions for signs, images, logos, genes and *patents* for all these things – potentially places in the hands of random individuals extraordinary capacities for violent interactions (which in the end are brutally physical) – through computer network subversions and chemical and biological mutations. Soon we might all be Gollums, scrabbling for a binding ring of power which every individual may in theory wield. The only antidote to this logical extension of capitalist freedom is a terroristic policing of 'terrorism', such as is now being put into place.

By contrast, the violence of the past, though more physical, was more measured. In the era of the great world faiths it resulted, accidentally, in a sense, from the pursuit of peace – from their visions of peace, or of a reality that enabled peaceableness to be attained, and therefore from an envisioned ontological peaceableness (this is especially the case, I would argue, for the monotheistic faiths). By contrast, modernity has tended to despair of this vision and to espouse instead theses of ontological conflict, which suggest – often with increasing despair – that violence can only be tempered, not eradicated.

Hence we have no reason to patronize or despise the past. Of course the major religions were violent in practice and in certain ways they were justified in being so – even if they also resorted, in their human fallibility, often to excessive and unjustifiable violence. Since they believed that they possessed keys to the harmonization of human life in accord with reality, they inevitably at times deployed coercion when faced with those who opposed this reality in various ways. And sometimes they *should* have done just this; it was a matter of proper self-belief. The liberal enlightenment also pursued a vision of universal peace and also defended it coercively. The only difference is that the liberal vision is less generous (less 'liberal' in fact), and is in a sense also a vision of universalized violence. Hence its coercive defence of its peace often seems indistinguishable from a defence of the arbitrary – law from criminality. By contrast, violence enacted in the name of a substantive *telos* can more plausibly pose as essentially educational, as a self-denying coercive ordinance.

The real point here is, that although Christianity, for example, certainly requires in the end *free consent* to the truth, it does not fetishize this freedom merely as a correct mode of approach: truth is what most matters, and moreover a *collective* commitment to the truth, since truth itself is the shareable and the harmonious. Thus in certain circumstances, the young, the deluded, those relatively lacking in vision require to be coerced as gently as possible. Anyone professing to be shocked by this is, I submit, naively unreflective about what in reality he already accepts (for example in the secular schooling of the young) and is thinking in over-individualistic and over-voluntaristic terms that are ontologically impossible.

There is also one specific consideration that applies to Christianity alone which should be taken into account: Christianity is the religion which risks subordinating the law, since the formal generality of the law, while it may inhibit violence, is itself a mode of counter-violence. Instead, Christianity looks, for salvation and an entire realized peace, to the infinite and unpredictable variety in occurrence of the Good: a radically unleashed *phronesis*, which is also the attentive but unroutinized self-giving of charity. But to subordinate the barriers and taboos of the law is also to take a terrible risk – the risk of the advent of a totally unleashed violence, instead of the *eschaton* of peace. Here, perhaps, lies the most acute Jewish critique of Christianity – namely that, like the Norse Loki it has unchained the hound of *danger* – allowed it, in Franz Steiner's phase, to march into the heart of civilization in a fashion that I have already described.[16] The Christian, though, can only abide by her commitment to all or nothing.

In a sense then, yes, Christianity has led to violence: first, because it is a universalizing religion; second, because it aims so high. The best is always likely to turn out to be also the worst. But why, then, should we patronize our ancestors and the unimaginably complex and perilous situations in which they found themselves, by apologizing on their behalf? In a word, we cannot as human beings suppose that violence is entirely unavoidable, in so far as it runs the educative risks of redemption.

And this leads me back to the third issue of violence and spectacle, namely pacifism. Here the main point has already been made: pacifism is aporetic because both gazing at and averting one's gaze from violence are intuitively complicit with its instance. Christian pacifism then, has to erect itself as a counter-intuitive doctrine. But then why (as Stanley Hauerwas asks) should not theology challenge intuitions which may be embedded in our fallen nature? Well, it seems to me that the intuitions violated here are not fallen ones but created ones, for the impulse to protect the innocent is rooted in our animality, embodiment and finitude.

There is an analogy here to Bernard Williams's insistence that ethics should not be so counter-intuitive or counter-naturalistic as to challenge our natural impulse always to save our own nearest and dearest first in the event of a common catastrophe.[17] To take any other position is again to deny our finitiude, and our limited range of intense capacity for affection and attention. One can see this by asking the question, suppose the neglected nearest and dearest survive, despite our neglect? With the best intentions or respect for our altruism, how will they, as warm-blooded animals, really *read* our pious neutrality? Will not the whole future of our relations with them be coloured by our choice? Not surprisingly, perhaps, most Christians have so confused Kant and Comte with the gospels, that they do not realize that Aquinas would have been in essential agreement with Williams here, and that the entire Christian tradition at least up to the time of the Angelic doctor interpreted *agape* as 'neighbour love' to mean precisely a preferential love for those nearest to us, those with the most inherited, realized and developed affinity with us, as well as those strangers with whom suddenly we are bonded whether we like it or not, by instances of distress, shared experience or preferred comfort.[18] The Samaritan is also the neighbour, and Jesus is clearly *not* here teaching us to respect or help strangers only as strangers. Nevertheless, one should interpret the parable to mean, in addition and inversely, that the daily neighbour is also the arriving stranger through time (see Chapter 9 below) and this reading duly qualifies, without cancelling, the main point that has just been made.

This specificity of given proximity, which is yet also the endlessly surprising gift of renewed contingent arrival, is *our only* creaturely way to participate in God's equal love for all. The latter, then, can only be implemented on earth, collectively and socially as a vast web of interlocking affinities within a common but sufficiently accommodating and varied culture. Without this theological view, one collapses into over-precious *aporias* about the treatment of some being also the neglect of others.

Somewhat similar considerations apply to our relation to the innocent, or relatively innocent. We are not, and should not aspire to be, angels, equally close to all. On the contrary, we are naturally closer to the endangered, or to those we interpret as such, or to those whose cause we sympathize with. We *should* defend – even sometimes with violence – what we believe in, though with the knowledge that we may well be mistaken. Otherwise we are not risking some sort of conjecture as to the nature of the Good – and if we fail to do this, then the Good itself will fade into unreality, since we are both finite and fallen, and do not yet enjoy a beatified immediate intuition of goodness in all its plenitudinous immediacy.

This, I think, is the key to what Charles Péguy called 'the mysterious charity' of Jeanne d'Arc: even in a situation of very complex and often sordid human passions she had to seek to elect the relative good, and even physically to fight for it, given that otherwise it would be destroyed.[19]

Of course, as Augustine implied, any good you have to fight for is not the absolute Good. The very reason for fighting for something is that it is threatened, and obviously the real absolute Good is never threatened in this kind of way. But since we only have weak intimations of the absolute Good and only enjoy these in theory when conjoined with some practical attempt to enact it in fragile finite structures, pacifism is like a kind of over-apophatic iconoclasm, which despises the necessary fragility of these realized intimations. It seeks to have a kind of cheap and easy participation in the eternal; it tries to leap out of our finitude, embodiment and fragility. In this way, pacifism strangely colludes with its seeming opposite, the Machiavellian and pagan republican error of seeking to immortalize and maintain forever what is fragile, and bound, in the end, to pass away. (This may be one reason why pacifism tends to dominate United States radicalism.) Either to underrate or to overrate the fragile is a terrible mistake, and interrupts the economy of the participation of time in eternity.

A reading of Péguy's verse play, *Le Mystère de la Charité de Jeanne d'Arc* gives rise to several reflections which are relevant to the issues that I am trying to resolve here. For one thing, Jeanne's lay status is crucial. There is something about the absolute demonization of all war and conflict which smacks of a clerical despising of the laity from within the walls of a monastery or a presbytery, wherein the need to oppose, to deceive, etc. may at least *appear* not to arise with the same exigency.[20] Even if Dostoyevsky's monasticization of all society is, in a sense, a correct aim (if this means trying to bring about a liturgical society), one can nevertheless see that the monasticization of the whole of society is much more difficult than the monasticization of a celibate few. For this general attempt to produce a liturgical society has to reckon with both sex and conflict. And the placing of sex outside the purview of the sacred is in a way highly parallel to the absolute condemnation of warfare. In both cases, one has to do with a kind of despising of the lay Christian, and an inability really to think of a way in which a lay Christian can be a Christian at all.

In the Middle Ages, the elaboration of the notion of chivalry was, to a small degree, an attempt to elaborate a lay theology in a way that I think very few people now understand. This lay theology resisted an unintelligent clerical squeamishness about sex: as the *Roman de la Rose* asks, if clerical chastity is the 'highest' path and the likeliest to attain beatitude, then should not God will it for all humans? Yet that would be inconsistent with God's approval of nature and generation. Only the Olympian gods, the authors of this work argue, were jealous of the human physical bliss of the golden age; such an attitude is alien to the God of creation and grace, and therefore sexual puritanism is pagan and not Christian.

Chivalric theology also resisted an unintelligent clerical preciosity concerning conflict, using just the same argument. Wolfram von Eschenbach in his *Parzival* points out through the mouth of his protagonist that if clerical non-violence is 'the highest' then fighting a just war would imperil one's salvation, at least to some degree.[21] If some wars are just, they lie therefore within the scope of providence, and such impairment therefore seems inconsistent with divine justice and grace. (One should nonetheless accept that this point is in tension with another equally valid point: namely that *some* people – clerical and lay – should exhibit already the eschatological life of peace. Sexual abstinence however – if sexuality is a good – cannot really parallel this. The celibate path is rather a matter of remaining in childish innocence in a certain respect, as a reminder of the danger of fallen sexuality, with its reduction of human to animal passions which for humans, unlike animals, is evil and violent.)

Now Péguy in many ways revived these lay concerns, and not surprisingly, and not of course without terrible ambiguities, he adhered to a renewed cultus of the female warrior Jeanne d'Arc. But his strange drama exhibits other features which allow us to make further and surprising connections. Throughout its course he meditates in a more or less Jewish fashion on the fact that it seems that the atonement has not worked and that in the end Christ and the Church have been refused. It also raises the issue of the *contingency* of the Incarnation and Crucifixion. Jeanne d'Arc says repeatedly: yes, Jesus was refused and executed in his time, but the peasants and knights of France would not have refused him. Equally, though, and with seeming contradiction, she suggests that Christ's message could *only* have been preserved because it arrived to the exceptional people of Israel at an exceptional moment.

Her extreme double naivety has a sophisticated point – how can we entirely know that elsewhere Jesus's appeal would not have worked or else would have utterly failed? This then links up to the further point that if the atonement is to be effective, if it is really to be an atonement at all, then it must be verbal in order to be nominal; received in order to be precedent. That is to say, received (first of all by Mary) only through the hypostatic presence amongst us of the Holy Spirit which is the Church. In this way a more Pneumatological approach to atonement recovers also a Jewish perspective, while inversely the Christological dimension provides the language and presence of a finality of atonement lacking within Judaism.

For atonement to be ontologically actual, Christ's appeal must still after all work within history: there must really in some sense exist the *ecclesia*. His example must somewhere and somehow be followed and this mimesis must

41

clearly involve further acts of mutual atoning which realizes the hypostatic presence of the Holy Spirit.

So one can say that a certain Jewish dimension seems for Péguy, the *Dreyfusard*, to supervene upon the Christian: first of all, in terms of the need for continued atonement, and for a collective redemption that requires the 'right positioning' of all in relation to all in space and time through mutual exchange. (As in the Jewish mystical gathering up and re-weaving together of the lost 'divine sparks'; this should not of course be interpreted as betokening any sort of catastrophe in the eternal, only the aporetic loss of divine glory in the world through the Fall, which God immediately corrects, although our own realisation of this correcting must be gradual.)

Secondly, in terms of a renewed apocalyptic. Yes, Péguy seems to say, the road to redemption lies through suffering evil, rather than betraying truth, and yet even in order to suffer evil and thereby defeat it, evil must not *only* be undergone but also *opposed*. Otherwise, there is a sense in which atonement has failed. This insight comprehends why the New Testament ends in a renewed Jewish fashion: with apocalypse. For even metaphoric war, or opposing, is still nevertheless war, and in suffering evil we do not only in a sense accept it, but only suffer it precisely because we also oppose it, and therefore are at war with the demonic.

To be sure, evil as ultimately nothing need not be opposed, yet evil as predatory upon the positive – as confining the positive to an 'enclave' where its nature as relative good is threatened, because it no longer communicates with the supreme Good (like Baudelaire's *fleurs du mal*) – must be opposed, must be *refused*, else it is simply accepted. Even if one says 'I oppose all violence', the word 'oppose' gives the game away: violence has tragically sucked even you, the pacifist, into its *agon*. Standing aloof, not intervening when you might – this mere gaze – is *also* an act: it *opposes* the violent person by violently leaving him to his violence and not trying to stop him in his tracks. Contrariwise, it *is* important actively and chivalrously to oppose violence: for example to stop someone from going as far as murder, even if one thereby kills him, for soon (now or hereafter) he may come to repent of his intentions, whereas it is far more difficult to repent of the actual deed. Not to see this is to underrate the importance of act and to fall prey to a Kantian privileging of motivation.

It is because we can only be good collectively that we cannot exercise pure peaceableness alone. Once there is violence, we are all inevitably violent. And violence can only be eradicated collectively, by a strange apocalyptic counter-violence, which is in the end a divine prerogative, yet is also obscurely anticipated within time. This is why, for St Paul, although every Christian is a farmer, he is also a soldier 'who should never get entangled in civilian pursuits' (II Timothy 2). Christians do, indeed, believe perfect peace to be the ultimate ontological reality and so to be attainable. But in that case, peace names the *eschaton*, the final goal; if there is peaceableness on the way to his goal, then this is a peculiarly intersubjective virtue. I rather doubt whether individual exercise of 'peaceableness' has very much meaning. For now, we must rather try together to be peaceable. In the penultimate, which both peace and conflict now sometimes anticipate, there will be fought the unthinkable and for us aporetic 'conflict against conflict'. However, in the ultimate beyond the last battle, even the refusal of evil will be redundant: then there will be only peace.

Because 'peaceableness' was never exactly seen as an individual virtue, I suspect that these were no real 'pacifisms' in pre-modernity, and that pacifism is profoundly linked with individualism. Likewise, it is linked with an over-valuation of freedom, since it assumes that forcing a person's will is the worst thing possible; even though in subtle ways, we of course do this all the time.

We therefore should not and even cannot be pacifists. Instead, prior to the ultimate, we are always partially already in the apocalyptic situation of 'opposing force', if by force one means the attempt to disturb, for egoistic reasons, the harmony of reality. In opposing force, we are always tragically deploying the enemy's means. We are like Frodo Baggins's servant Samwise, putting on the ring of evil force in order to remain invisible and escape the orcs, so that his master may ultimately destroy this symbol of abstracted power for its own sake – which, like the ring of Gyges in Plato's *Republic*, notably confers invisibility on the wearer. In the *Lord of the Rings*, there is a complex blend of double risk: renunciation of absolute power – the *copied* and *stolen* master ring which is not, like the lesser, originally wrought rings, a *gift* – combined with occasional trickery of that power, leads to a victory that nonetheless appears to be a lucky accident, or else the work of providence.[22] Likewise, we can only try to force force with reserve and with hopeful risk that distorted realities will come to repent. This is the best we can do; our scenario is apocalyptic, not utopian.

If the above considerations are sound, then we can see that the spectator of sublime artistic violence, the Christian apologist for the Christian past, and the Christian pacifist idealist, all actually enact different versions of the same scenario of double passivity which constitutes any 'fictional' spectacle. In this way the past is distorted into fiction, and present situations which demand our risky response are likewise distorted. But we have also seen that watching fictional violence does not just lead to violence, nor is it just a variant of violence. Rather, it is violence itself: the 'safe' gaze into the looking-glass of narcissistic perversity. This gaze always invites an actual step behind the looking-glass into the world where now, as always (and yet now more than ever before), violence is real because it is always only virtual, just as non-liturgical virtuality is always violence.

And the virtuality of violence converts diabolically with the negativity of evil, revealing pure virtuality to be violence, just as lack of being is evil, or virtuality to be evil, just as negativity is violence. This is the Cross, the anti-chiasmus.

3

FORGIVENESS

The double waters

I

How are evil and violence to be overcome? If we are to be saved from their grip, then we must partake of the waters of forgiveness which flow down the slopes of Mount Purgatory. However, right from the top, these waters divide: down the near slope pour the waters of Lethe, or of forgetting; down the farther side rush the waters of Eunoë, or of positive remembrance. According to Dante, this stream 'non adopra se quinci a quindi pria non ē gustato [it works not if first it be not tasted on this side and on that]'.[1]

Forgiveness, therefore – the forgiveness that we in the West have been given to remember – is poised vertiginously between obliteration and a recollection that amounts to a restoration. It is either, or both, a negative gesture and a positive deed. The most ancient, pre-Christian cognates for something at least akin to 'forgiveness' suggest mostly the former: Greek *aphesis* is a letting go, or dismissal; Latin *ignoscere* is an overlooking or not-knowing, and in the Old Testament the God of Mercy is said to hide human faults behind his back. If there was any question, for the Romans, of a deed here, or of an active donation, then the gesture of forgiving was not itself seen as a gift, but what was offered (*dare*) was either impunity (*venia*) or, once again, oblivion as to the past.[2]

Only in a later era at once Christian and feudal do the vernacular tongues suggest that forgiveness is a positive offering. Both the Latinate and Germanic languages now deploy words designating a hyperbolic giving: *pardonner, perdonare, perdonar, vergeben, forgive*.[3] In both cases, the main force of the prefix seems to be one of emphasis – here giving is extreme because one-sided and unprompted, a gift to the undeserving. At the same time, it is not clear that negativity is not also connoted. In English the prefix 'for' may be an intensifier (as in forread, forfrighted), but it may also be a negator (as in foredeem, forhale).[4] Perhaps forgiveness, since it gives up, or forswears a legitimate ground of complaint, suggests a kind of negative giving which benignly removes – the giving of a gift which fortunately destroys. This is exactly how, in *Works of Love*, Søren Kierkegaard understood forgiveness: namely, as the counterpart of Creation, which miraculously brings being out of nothing; and of hope, which turns an absence into a presence.[5] By contrast, for Kierkegaard, forgiveness with equal miraculousness decreases, and causes what is, not merely to be as if it were not, but literally not to be. It is precisely this absurdity of forgiveness which leads the Danish philosopher to insist that it is a reality only of divine grace and only to be known as real by human faith. Indeed since, for Kierkegaard, the gift of Creation appears to bring about existence, while the negating anti-gift of forgiving grace removes it, he seems to invoke here a metaontological register of 'donology'.

However, one may already pose the question as to whether, in this respect, and with regard to his exclusive understanding of forgiveness as negation, Kierkegaard is not the heir to specifically late mediaeval, early modern and Reformation developments. For whatever the linguistic evidence, there is no doubt that, for the earlier Christian era, negativity was doubly qualified by something positive. In fact,the positivity of forgiveness was the counterpart to the negativity of evil.

By our human efforts alone, we could, indeed, for this period, like the pagan Virgil, arrive at the waters of Lethe, but to arrive at the waters of positive remembrance we required already prevenient grace, personified for Dante by the figure of Matilda who presides as a new Proserpine (that earlier female *figura* of a necessary half-and-half) over the earthly paradise.[6] Thus, for the high Middle Ages, the forgiveness and repentance which is specifically the grant of grace was mediated only through the sacrament of penance, which is the first instance of a new, positive dimension to forgiveness. In penitence, repentance is more than an attitude, it is also a public sign, a gesture, an offering which somehow 'makes up' for a past error. But this positivity might indeed appear to be a mere prelude to the negating anti-gift of pardon as mediated by the priest, an overture required by the legalism of mediaeval Christian thought. Such legalism may seem to be exemplified in Thomas Aquinas's stipulation that whereas *human* forgiveness may be offered in the absence of repentance, divine forgiveness cannot be so offered.[7] However, it turns out that legalism is not what is in evidence here, but something almost like the reverse: whereas human forgiving may or may not induce repentance, says Aquinas, divine forgiveness necessarily does so. Therefore, in Aquinas, archetypal, exemplary divine forgiveness is not a mere blotting-out, as it frequently becomes in later theologies, for which a putatively pure, utterly unelicited divine forgiveness only forgets and ignores the past. By contrast, the forgiveness realized through repentance looks initially at damaged past events which it then seeks to transform. Following this latter model, divine forgiveness for Aquinas is the provision to the one forgiven of the positive means not merely to make restitution for an injustice, but to make a restitution so complete that one is utterly reconciled with the one wronged (here God himself) and one's relationship with him can flow in future so smoothly that it is exactly, as Kierkegaard later put it, as if it had never suffered any 'jolt' whatsoever.[8] And since divine forgiveness was, for Aquinas and the Middle Ages in general, mediated by the Church through the sacrament of penance, it was to some extent the case that, at an interhuman level also, to forgive someone was actively to bring about reconciliation through the provision to the other of a positive means of recompense.[9]

However, at times this action might go beyond merely providing opportunity for recompense and become a matter of oneself offering recompense in an act of substitution. Thus the second positive dimension to mediaeval pardon concerns the proximity of this notion to ideas of atonement. Supremely, of course, God was held to have offered us forgiveness, even for original sin, through his Incarnation, suffering and death as a man. Whether God could, nonetheless, have forgiven our sins without such recourse was a crucial matter of debate within mediaeval theology. Yet whatever was concluded on this issue, it was unavoidable that, as a matter of record, divine forgiveness had taken the initial form of suffering in our stead. Here, one is tempted to say, forgiveness has become literally for-giving, giving the gift on behalf of the other; in this Christological instance it is the divine Son through his assumed human nature making the return offering of true worship to the Father – a return which humanity should make, but since the Fall can make no longer. Such an assimilation of the prefix 'for' to its prepositional use may well be without etymological warrant; nevertheless it appropriately conveys the Christian assimilation of forgiveness to substitutionary atonement. Here it is the case that guilt so incapacitates the *habitus* that first of all an innocent other must show one the way of penitence, which only thenceforward becomes imitable, even by the guilty. Of course such a logic was not confined to the supreme Christological instance; rather, the intersubjective contagion of works of piety and intercession was central for mediaeval faith and practice.

One could say that the double addition of positivity to forgiveness belonged within a cultural matrix which did not firmly distinguish mercy from justice and thought of all giving, including forgiving, not as ideally pure, free and disinterested, but rather as situated within an economy of exchange and obligation.[10] This was not, however, a capitalist exchange, even in disguised or latent form (as Marxists such as Pierre Bourdieu have claimed). The gift was not a commodity refusing to declare itself, because it returned non-identically, at no absolutely required time, and thereby always preserved a reciprocity that was asymmetrical and in consequence not abstractly equivalent to other reciprocities.[11] In a somewhat parallel fashion, the circulating economy of forgiveness could not be reduced to a workable calculus of self-interest, trading sin for sin, like debt for debt, in the ultimate interest of one's eternal self-preservation. No such simple reduction was possible, because the high mediaeval theology of forgiveness was a paradoxical attempt to economize the aneconomic. For this theology, sin was the refusal not simply of a measurable divine justice, but rather an immeasurable divine grace. As such a refusal of an infinite free gift, it was without human, calculable remedy and was only to be remedied by the incalculable mystery of God himself enduring, innocently, this lack of his own grace, and so giving us, once again, this grace in the mode of a suffering that heals.[12] Therefore, for this outlook, what we are offered once again through Christ's atonement is without measure and without price, and the only penance demanded of us in return for this forgiveness is the non-price of acceptance, even if such acceptance must be shown, manifested and realized in this or that appropriate action according to time and place.

Likewise, the contagion of merit and intercession, though it was still, and crucially, a trade of sorts, was an impossible and miraculous trade in the infinite, a seeking to restore, by all and for all, the repayment of a debt due which is nothing but an infinite free accepting. Just for this reason, Aquinas insisted that human forgiveness could not wait on a human penance which it could not, like divine forgiveness, guarantee; instead, forgiveness, as negative cancellation only attained through positive enabling and substitutionary undergoing, had to be freely and infinitely offered without price to the neighbour, as the gospels had demanded. Therefore forgiveness obeyed no ordinary, calculable economy, since it was without finite price. Nonetheless, the aim of forgiveness was not a lone, self-righteous certainty of the will to exonerate (without regard to circumstances or the repentance of the other), but rather charity, which the Middle Ages regarded less as a performance than as a *state* of fraternal, friendly and harmonious co-existence. The aim, in other words, was reconciliation, where the bond of love is an exchange of infinite love.

Yet since this exchange, though without limits, was also according to finite measure, concrete issues of fair distribution and the rectification of past unfairness and violent seizures were not to be ignored. (Hence there was no sense of an infinite obligation to give which we entirely fail to realize.) Infinite giving, in order to be participated in, must be manifest for now in an aesthetic sense of who is to give, what, where and when, and what might be an appropriately shaped response or recompense in the case of something judged to be lacking. Just because the goal sought was not the private subjective sustaining (with indifference to objects) of a pure and absolute negative commitment to ignore all faults one suffers from others, but rather concrete reconciliation based on mutual agreement as to the right distribution of objects (and an agreement whose justice must be validated by a third party), forgiveness in this era was not as yet interruptively counterposed to justice and issues of positive recompense. Instead, one could say, for the Christian understanding up to the high mediaeval period, forgiveness was the name of the order which carried justice into the eternal, a justice beyond justice which assumed that if all was to be fairly set right, then all must be reconciled in the truth, whose pattern is such that the reconciliation is infinite and beyond all possible finite undoing. It is for this reason, that before going to meet Beatrice in the celestial paradise, Dante must become reconciled with her under the auspices of Matilda in the earthly paradise.[13] Indeed, this sequence makes clear that there will be no individual preceding to heaven *until* the Fallen order of the earth is restored through a measured reconciliation.

From the high mediaeval period, therefore, we have been bequeathed a certain legacy of forgiveness as unlimited positive circulation, which contrasts with the antique understanding of forgiveness as a mere negative gesture. Nevertheless, since this epoch, the increasing sundering of gift from contract, and of mercy (including divine mercy) from justice, encouraged first by new theological assumptions and new ecclesial practices, has apparently ensured an overwhelming cultural re-insertion of forgiveness as negativity – a counterpart to the reconceiving of evil as positive.

This notion of a simple re-insertion is, however, misleading: for in classical times there was mostly no real recommendation of forgiveness in a post-Christian sense. In this period, the 'overlooking' of fault referred either to a pragmatic ignoring of it for self-interested reasons, or else to the taking into account of mitigating circumstances and involuntary motions.[14] And, in fact, acts of arbitrary 'mercy' were viewed with suspicion as exonerating malefactors and raising benefactors above the normal sway of legality. Within, for example, the ancient Greek *strictly finite* regime of justice and gift-exchange, *aphesis* was indeed often regarded as an arbitrary intrusion, breaking maliciously into a balanced and regular interchange between equals.[15] For the sake of this interchange, the Greeks were prepared mostly to sacrifice the difficult exception and the unreconciled and aggrieved individual (though one must read Plato's *Laws* and to a degree Aristotle's *Ethics* as protesting against this). Preparedness to violate the law in the name of charity or mercy was more associated with oriental despotic empires, from which Israel herself learned much.[16] Here, however, forgiveness was very much an act of sovereign whim, a gesture of pure negative cancellation, and an act quite prepared to violate justice. In so far as many modern Christian versions of forgiveness, as exemplified by Kierkegaard, recommend a unilateral act of ontological cancellation, then they would seem to be long-term legatees of this oriental despotism, protracted to infinity in the late mediaeval reconception of God as a reserve of absolute, infinite untram-melled power and will. (One should note here that there was already a *theological* invention of pure unasked-for forgiveness, and that postmodern versions of this merely repeat in secular guise this later theology.)

It might be claimed, notwithstanding, that this modern Christian position is a legitimate extrapolation from the Bible. For up until the time of the Babylonian exile, there is little evidence for a strong Hebraic notion of forgiveness, other than ideas of mitigation according to circumstance and for future mutual interest.[17] Strong notions of forgiveness seem rather to have arisen from that epochal Hebraic projection of empire into the transcendent as a power able to overrule and belittle all human despotism.[18] Hence in Deutero-Isaiah, Ezekiel and Jeremiah, God is endowed with an unlimited will to forgive. However, the Hebrew projection is scarcely to be understood as itself an exaltation of the despotic, and in consequence the will to forgive of the Hebrew God is not a will to pure forgetfulness of fault. To the contrary, a new sense of the need for, and the possibility of, a far-reaching divine forgiveness for extreme sins is accompanied, in texts of a mainly priestly origin, by a renewed sense of the need for ritual purifications and acts of atonement. So far from these two considerations running in counterpoise, it is rather the case that there is an increasing expectation of an eschatological day when God will offer – perhaps in the shape of some shadowy human figure – a new possibility of final expiation. Here, one might say, forgiveness has entered into a mixed constitution: the monarchic component of interruption of legal process by fiat has become blended with an aristocratic sense of appropriate equity in time and place and a democratic sense of restitution from within, according to immanently absorbed norms. Such a mixed constitution of forgiveness is supremely realized in the Incarnation, where the estranged and alien sovereign is restored to rule through the consensual self-legislation of humanity (in Christ and his body the Church) under norms of taught and received objective measure. After the Incarnation, contrary to Jewish expectation, there is held to begin not a reign of realized forgiveness, but a time when divine forgiveness can be somewhat mediated by human beings: a time for which justice is infinitized as forgiveness.

So already I wish provisionally to suggest that the most compelling Western legacy of forgiveness presents it as a positive mixed constitution – exemplified ideally not in an oriental empire, but in something like the Logres of King Arthur – who, in the romance of *Tristram*, is shown to offer forgiveness and reconciliation to the adulterous lovers, in opposition to the unmerciful justice of King Mark of Cornwall.[19] By contrast, the negative and unilateral post-late-mediaeval and Reformation sense of forgiveness perverts this constitution into a despotism now to be exercised as anarchy. If there is something legitimate in forgiveness as negation, then this surely is but a negation of negation, an absorption into the positive through suffering of evil, which is of its nature privative in the first place. In consequence, forgiveness is not, as for Kierkegaard, a decreation, but rather the uninterrupted flow of the one initial Creation through and despite, as he puts it, the 'jolt' of fault. Here the donological remains ontological.

II

Up till now, I have traced the tension between forgiveness as negative gesture and forgiveness as positive gift. Already, though, we have glimpsed the lineaments of a second tension, between forgiveness as human and forgiveness as divine. Let us suppose, first of all, that we are asking whether or not forgiveness can be enacted between human beings today in terms of the resources for thinking about forgiveness in both negative and positive terms as so far described.

It seems to me that a purely interhuman forgiveness will then appear to be impossible in terms of five major *aporias*.

(a) Who is to forgive?

First of all, there is the question of who is to forgive. Here, one signpost at the divided way reads 'the victim', while the other reads 'sovereign authority'. Of course, as now reiterated piously *ad nauseam*, only the victim can forgive, since only she has suffered the wrong and only she can be reconciled. But even this chosen fork of victimage proves a path that cannot really be taken. Quite simply, the victims will never appear to exonerate us. In the first place, they are far too numerous: since an evil deed is contagious, it is impossible to know how far the consequences of even the simplest and most minor misdemeanour extends. That is its terror; that is why all wrong is so absolutely wrong. Therefore, the infinite jury of victims can never be summoned to the consistorial court of penitence. And second, as is often pointed out, the true victims do not survive at all to be able to proffer pardon. Forgiveness is, always for us in time, only a reality that is proven to be possible for the weaker, the easier cases: those dead and pulverized in their fury and despair will never rise in time to prove that they can surmount these attitudes.

However, even if we could locate and summon the victims, which we cannot do exhaustively, and so not into adequate exoneration, do they really enjoy an exclusive or primary right to exonerate? Part of the problem here is already latent in what has just been said: since there is never only *one* victim, the claim of this victim exclusively to forgive a fault is like an anarchic appropriation of sovereignty; all the other, often untraceable victims are thereby betrayed. Moreover, private forgiveness always implies an inter-ruption of public justice which is associated with the perspective of a third party. If it is thought of in negative terms, then a fault is simply overlooked: the raped girl, victim of a man who was once her lover, forgives him and never brings him to court. If it is rather thought of in positive terms, then the upshot is still the same: the raped girl exacts from her ex-lover her own conditions for recompense and reconciliation, but if these are *just* conditions, then do not they require public, third-party assessment?

(Although, according to the New Testament, all Christians are expected to settle things among themselves out of the secular court, a certain ecclesial trial is still involved.) Thereby, however, the forgiving victim might legitimately incur public outrage; her loyalty to a friend may betray other women, past or future possible victims of the same man, or else still other women rendered more vulnerable to similar acts in parallel situations by the girl's refusal to expose, and make an example of, this particular criminal. What makes her, after all, the right one to do the forgiving, rather than all those other women? Moreover, since any rape renders all women less secure and all men less trusted and more liable themselves to false accusations of rape and therefore *also* less secure, this crime is an attack on the whole community. It follows, therefore, that only the sovereign representative of this community should be properly empowered to forgive. But if he, she or it were to do so, this would be offering the chance for making reparation and achieving rehabilitation to a dangerous rapist, while his actual, damaged victims persisted in hatred and bitterness toward him; then we should not feel that he had been forgiven. And where are we to locate the sovereign power to represent all those injured who may lie unknown beyond any traceable boundary of space and time? Therefore, neither the victim nor the sovereign power may forgive, and there is no human forgiveness.

(b) Forgiveness in time

Secondly, there is the question of how, in any sense at all, a past fault can be removed. The problem is one of *time*. For there is no problem with a spatial mistake. The person blocking the entrance can simply be removed. But *that* he blocked the entrance for a time, and prevented such and such another person from getting through, so crucially delaying her, and so forth, can never be altered, or changed, ever. Writers such as Vladimir Jankélévitch have asked, in the wake of the Holocaust, whether an absolute imperative to forgive is not nihilistic, since it amounts to the will to abolish misdeeds from our memory, thereby ensuring a complicity with the perpetrators.[20] For Jankélévitch, more specifically, the order of time runs counter to forgiveness, because, first of all, if past events can be wiped out from our reckoning, we are ignoring the ineluctable discreteness of past moments, through which alone time occurs and finite being arises at all. Secondly, it runs counter to forgiveness, because certain events perpetrated in time, and supremely the Holocaust, manifest a radical evil (of just the kind discussed in Chapter 1) to which wickedness is unmotivated by even the illusion of good. Whereas, in the case of an inadequate will to the good resulting in a deficient deed, one may appeal to the fundamentally good will of the perpetrator and redeem his deed through a remembering of it in its aspects of a positive desire for the Good, thereby shedding only what was lacking and perverted about it (and therefore never fully there in the first place), in the case of an absolutely perverse will there is no seed of conscience to be cultivated, and its resulting deed is pure positive horror. Such horror cannot, like a privation, be legitimately forgotten, and yet, if remembered, it cannot possibly be redeemed. This wound must forever fester.

Besides Jankélévitch's issue of the reversibility of time and of radical evil, one may mention a third problematic of time and forgiveness, which involves, once again, the vanishing of the victim. As we have already seen, the primary problem here is that the most victimized are always already dead, so that apologizing to them in one's own name or in the name of one's ancestors seems smug and futile and even, in a certain way, as I argued in Chapter 2, patronizing to the villains of the past, who did not enjoy our interests or perspectives – which themselves, indeed, may be less absolute than we imagine. Hence we may well deplore the millennial futility of apologizing to Galileo, the victims of the crusades, exterminated Amerindians, and so forth. Either apologizing for, or else offering forgiveness on behalf of, one's ancestors, seems a dubious procedure. But does not the same dubiety invade also one's relationship even to one's own past self? How can I apologize now, after the heat of the moment, for my anger then, within it? More crucially, how can I forgive now, when the effects of injury have somewhat abated, the wrong I suffered then, enduring its full and unmitigated impact? One may say, indeed, that this problem is only serious if one entertains a Humean scepticism as to the continuity of identity; however, even if one does not go that far, there remains a rupture between the person first injured and the same person later offering forgiveness, were it to occur merely one minute later. For one *cannot* receive injury at the psychic level, which is alone relevant here, without experiencing a weakening, and resentment and anger about that weakening. And where the cause of the injury is received as personal, one receives a malicious intent, concerning which one cannot fail to feel fury. There can be no distinguishing the sin from the sinner in this case, because sin is a manifestation of personality and is always specifically characterized as proceeding from *this* individual or set of individuals. Refusing to hate the sinner despite his sin can only mean endeavouring to attend to what remains positively loveable in him despite his sin, not pretending to love what is not loveable and does not deserve love. (The reverse view is actually yet more post-late-mediaeval distortion of the Gospel.) Thus, inevitably and unavoidably, victims pass through a moment of hatred for those who have offended them. This is why victims are dangerous, this is why victims – which means all of us – are corrupted, weakened and poisoned by that which they at first innocently suffer. But if victims must at first hate, then what worth their eventual offering of forgiveness? Is it that they later repent their first hatred, thereby betraying from their newfound relative comfort their earlier violated selves? And is not such a gesture futile, since it cannot wipe out the fact of their earlier hatred, nor even perhaps entirely expunge it from memory?

Having stated these three dimensions to the *aporia* of forgiveness and time, it must however immediately be asked whether they can be mitigated if one invokes the Augustinian account of the inseparability of time and memory. For does not what has so far been said assume that time is a series of punctual, discrete moments? Yet this is clearly not the case, since every past moment has always already become present, and then, in turn, future. Therefore, as Augustine perhaps most fully realized (although this insight is already present in Aristotle), the past only occurs initially through the supplement of the trace it leaves in the future – a trace which, in *De Musica*, Augustine clearly (like Aristotle) regards as ontological, although in the *Confessions* he explicates the psyche as the most intense, complex and reflexive site of such traces.[21] The past, on this understanding, only *is* through memory, and while this does not abolish the ontological inviolability and irreversibility of pastness, it does mean that the event in its very originality is open to alteration and mutation. As Augustine correctly saw, one cannot imagine, and there could not be, any entirely discrete past event unaffected by what came later, just as, to use his example, a note in music is only situated and defined by its place in a sequence, such that the end of a musical composition still to be heard can change the nature of what we have already heard.[22] Certainly there are limits to alteration, even though they cannot be specified: the note remains this note, however far the new relations it enters into may re-disclose it. Nevertheless, these reflections reveal that the past is not strictly unalterable and that the remembered past, although provisional and revisable, is not a sort of hypothesis that can never be confirmed, but is rather itself the ontologically real past.

Now of course it is no accident that Augustine began to develop a temporal rather than spatial ontology of finitude in the course of writing a work of *confession*, in which he seeks to obtain forgiveness for his past life and reconciliation with God. Augustine realized, in effect, that the Christian promotion of forgiveness in time demanded drastic ontological revision, if certain *aporias* were to be overcome. Thus with respect to the first of our temporal problematics of forgiveness, as stated by Jankélévitch: it is not that forgiveness nihilistically pretends to obliterate past evidence, but rather than this past existence is itself preserved, developed and altered through re-narration. In this re-narration one comes to understand why oneself or others made errors, in terms of the delusions that arose through mistaking lesser goods for the greater. As to the third of our problematics of time and forgiveness (all aspects of the one *aporia*), the inevitable past hatred undergone by the victim, this also is not to be regarded as something punctual and static, as if the 'first' past were still somehow really there. While Jankélévitch is right to insist on a certain stubborn resistance of 'pastness', he is wrong to ignore the fact that the 'passing away' of time reveals a complicity of time with the nothingness of finitude in itself – a complicity which nonetheless furnishes the ground for the possibility of redemption. For since evil is only manifest in the finite, not the infinite, which as infinite and enduring is without rupture or impairment of power, it can indeed absolutely fall away, because finitude in its own right is nothing whatsoever and only receives being as participation in the infinite. Hence time, which was first the time of gift, becomes, after the intrusion of evil, the time of mercy. The victim comes to remember and revise his past hatred more objectively as a correct refusal of the negative, and of the impairment of his own power; but at the same time, through re-narration he is able to situate and qualify this hatred in relation to a renewed understanding of the deluded motives of his violator. Most crucially, his offering of forgiveness involves not simply a cancellation of his earlier hatred, but a kind of dispossession of his own hatred, as he comes to understand (in a fashion well described by Spinoza) how his negative reaction belonged to a whole sequence of (nonetheless not Spinozistically fated) events mostly outside his control.

Eventually, at the heart of his hatred, he rediscovers the love for his own and others' real good, which essentially motivated it, and sees indeed that this love is the entire, real, actual content of hatred, since what was really hated was the negative impairment of charity and goodness. What was hated was nothing, and in consequence, hatred actually falls away from the positively remembered reconstituted past which is the real past. One has passed through Lethe to the waters of Eunoë, where all flows through the earthly paradise without one jolt, as if horror has never been, as, indeed, in a sense it has not. It is here exactly as Borges put it in his late story *The Rose of Paracelsus* – the Fall means, precisely, not to realize that one is still in the earthly paradise; redemption, conversely, is the restoration of paradise to our perception.[23]

From the above we can see that there is a clear connection between the Augustinian theory of time as memory which permits forgiveness, on the one hand, and his account of evil as privation on the other. For evil can only pass away, be forgiven and forgotten, if not only the past can be revised, but also what is deficient in the past can be revised out of existence. This means that what really and fully occurs and has the capacity to recur in memory is the good and positive. In a much more drastic and radical sense than Nietzsche, Augustine really did think that 'only the active returns' (and not the reactive).

But of course what arises here is a question with respect to Jankélévitch's second problematic: can one sustain this Christian ontology of forgiveness in the wake of the Holocaust of Jewry? In my view, one must say yes, not out of a kind of sustaining of nerve, but because precisely the Holocaust requires all the more such a visionary response. By contrast, as I argued in Chapter 1, talk of radical evil, an absolutely corrupted will, a motive-less crime that can never be atoned, and so forth, falsely *glamourizes* this (perhaps) most terrible of events, by rendering it outside all comprehension whatsoever, and thereby absolutizes it, granting it a demonic status equivalent to divinity, and finally perpetuates its terror, since what is unredeemed remains in force. The argument which runs '*This* evil was so terrible that we belittle its horror if we describe it as negative' effectively means that this evil was really so impressive that we had better accord it a status in being equivalent to the Good.[24] Thus whereas the soldiers simply and rightly, if belatedly, sent in the tanks and arrested the perpetrators, the philosophers choose rather to resurrect this horror as ontological victory. Bowing down to the remains of the camps as though before an idol, they solemnly proclaim a surd and ineliminable evil so serious that art from henceforward must confine itself to fashioning little figurines of atrocity.

One prefers, surely, the crude common sense of the soldiers. The greatest atrocity requires all the more an access of hope, the greatest evil calls out all the more for an impossible forgiveness and reconciliation, else, quite simply, such evil *remains in force.* As uncomprehended, unresumed, we must still live in the echoes of its illusions (as the return of neo-Darwinism,[25] eugenicism, and an art of pure sublime rapture, would all seem to indicate). In contrast to myths of 'radical evil', as I argued, one should rather recognize that the most terrible thing about the Holocaust was that *even this* event was brought about through a chain of seemingly 'good reasons' – economic, cultural, scientific, peace-seeking – whose delusory appeal is unfortunately *not* alien to our common humanity. Mere lack of good, we can now all the more see, is a sufficiently terrible thing in itself. Moreover, this status of mere lack allows us still to ascribe the Holocaust to the contingency of perversity, and therefore to realize that its malice need never be repeated either in deed or in unhealed memory.

It has been seen therefore that the *aporia* of forgiveness and time may be overcome through the double Augustinian vision – first, of ecstatic time which is already memory and second, of evil as privation. However, it must now be made explicit that this is necessarily a theological vision. Time as remembered in its ontological positivity is only real because it participates in the divine, infinite eternal memory. Otherwise it would be destined to pass away, like the original merely past past, into pure oblivion, thereby rendering the Good and actual ontologically as nugatory as the privative and deficient. For indeed where there is no envisaged creation *ex nihilo,* but only the pure irruption of Being through time out of a nothingness with which it is contradictorily identical (as for Heidegger), then it may well be arguable that what negates or deprives is in every way as positive as the seemingly good and actual, since all being must for this vision only arise as the secret concealment of a simultaneous deprivation: the ontic regarded as the mask of an ontological ultimacy which manifests itself only as irreducible removal.[26] Likewise, since here ontological recollection by resolute *Dasein* dissipates the appearance of discrete ontic moments into the contentless pure flux of immanent ontological passage (without any analogical mediation of the ontological through the ontic), such recollection, if we are to continue to think at all, must return us to the necessary illusion of discrete present instances, as proffering indeed the only serious basis for human ethical life. Thus, unlike the Augustinian *ecstasis* of time, the Heideggerean version cannot be ethically lived, and delivers us, after all, to the calculus of momentary instances. In consequence, it does indeed leave us with past facts unalterable in their record of horror and ontologically positive in their very negativity. Likewise, it underwrites a dualism between infinite forgiveness and finite justice. A supposedly pure and negative forgiveness equated with the ontological can only be actualized via its manifestation in the calculus of just exchange between finite ontic instances, whereby it is cancelled as pure forgiveness. This disallows the possibility that the finite exchange of reconciliation, achieved through a positive ontological remembering and transformation of past time, might itself mediate an infinite forgiveness. For the latter perspective, this infinite forgiveness is seen as a divine plenitude of exchange and not as a transcendental abyss of one-way passage from nothing to nothing.

It follows, therefore, that if we seek forgiveness in purely human terms according to the canons of pure immanence, the *aporias* of forgiveness and time will indeed stand, offering us no possibility of forgiveness whatsoever.

(c) *Forgiveness and forgetting*

A third *aporia* of human forgiveness concerns the question of forgiving and forgetting. If, as we have just seen, for a purely immanentist perspective past events must remain marooned in their pastness (for all that this is an ontic illusion), then it would seem that the only possibility of forgiveness resides in a negative forgetting. The truth of such forgetting would, however, be on a level with the truth of all forgetting of purely ontic experience, which is bound up with an inevitable 'anxiety' as to ultimate meaning and purpose. Hence we would here only forgive and forget to the same non-ethical measure that we were able to surmount finitude itself.

However, even allowing this problem as to whether one is here speaking of ethical forgiveness at all, there is a further difficulty. Where, as for the immanentist perspective, past hatred is immutable and subject to no alchemy of transformation, then so long as one hates one does not forgive, and so long as there remains a fault present for one, one does not forgive. By contrast, in a case where this fault no longer impinges, then this must be because it has been entirely forgotten. Once forgotten, the fault can be forgiven. But of course, once the fault has been forgotten it no longer needs to be forgiven, and therefore as soon as forgiveness becomes possible, it is already redundant.

An immanentist account of time confines one, therefore, to a view of forgiveness as negation. But this turns out, for the reason just given, to be a gesture impossible to perform.

(d) *The trade in forgiveness*

The fourth *aporia* of forgiveness concerns the question of purity of motive. We have seen that where forgiveness is thought of as having positive dimensions of penance and substitution, it is inherently a matter of exchange and reconciliation. In this case the question of purity of motive does not really arise, because what the forgiver seeks to achieve is not a state of personal disinterested benevolence, but rather an instance of ontological harmony between himself and another, such that his own self-realization and happiness is ineluctably bound up with the other's, and vice versa.

For this Christianized eudaimonism, my interest in my own happiness cannot compromise the disinterest of my will to forgive, since my happiness is from the outset less a possession than a relational *ecstasis*: my fulfilling myself by orientating myself beyond myself to the other; my realizing myself by expressing myself and letting myself go, and receiving back from the other a new interpretation of myself.[27] Here to forgive is to restore that order of free unlimited exchange of charity which was interrupted by sin. For this reason, to forgive is, as the gospels insist, immediately to receive forgiveness; Kierkegaard says that my forgiving and being forgiven belong together as the sky reflected in the sea and the sky itself.[28] It might seem, of course, that if one forgives in order, or partly in order, to be forgiven, there is a trade in forgiveness such that, after all, Christian forgiveness does not escape the calculative prudence of Greek *aphesia* and Latin *ignoscere*. However, this would be again to overlook the aneconomic economy of pardon. For this economy, to offer charity, whether as original gift or restorative forgiveness, is only possible if one is *already* receiving the infinite divine charity, since charity is not an empty disposition (as it later became), but the ontological bond between God and creatures, whereby creatures only are as the receiving of the divine gift and the unqualified return of this gift in the very act of receiving. Because this bond is also the ground of a correct harmonious relation between creatures, such a return is impossible if the gift is not also passed on from creature to creature in accord with the divine spirit of generosity. Hence giving, since it is not enacted in order to achieve purity of motive but to establish a reciprocity, is already a receiving according to a reception transcendentally prior to any purely possessive calculation of what one might, perhaps, receive by giving. And, likewise, to forgive is to re-establish a reciprocity only possible as the attainment of a mysterious harmony through its participation in the divine infinite harmony. As the human forgiver is himself a sinner, he must re-receive this harmony in order to be able to forgive. His forgiving of the other, therefore, shows that he is divinely forgiven, or rather his forgiving of the other is the very instance of himself being divinely forgiven.

There is, therefore, no question of a secret trade in forgiveness, nor of an inevitably contaminating motive of hope for forgiveness for oneself, within the terms of a construal of forgiveness as both divine and positive. These issues arise only for an immanent and negative perspective. Here, as we have seen, to forgive must mean a gesture of negating the past, and must be regarded as genuine, not in terms of a positive upshot of reconciliation – since this cannot here come about with the perpetrator *as* perpetrator – but rather in terms of the forgiveness being done entirely for its own sake of refusing resentment and ignoring wrong. But the trouble then, of course, is that forgiveness never can be offered for its own sake. Rather, every pardoner is indeed Chaucer's pardoner, who tells narratives showing that greed leads to death but himself hopes that pardon can break this chain of fatality.[29] Thus he deploys pardon calculatively as a warding-off, or absolute escape from, death. To this end he receives payment for his telling of narratives about greed leading to death and for his offering of papal pardons that will suspend this logic. But finally his own offering of pardons to temper the upshot of greed is itself motivated by the basest of all greed: an easy, wandering life of cheap prestige, petty power and worldly goods at the cost of little effort. This trade in pardon does indeed condone and increase human injustice, according to the worst fears of the ancient democratic and egalitarian Greeks. The pardoner is the anarchic agent of the remote Roman tyrant.

Chaucer depicts, perhaps, the growing corruption of the mediaeval economy of forgiveness, whereby it was turning into a cheap forgiveness of mere negative gesture, which nonetheless had to be bought dearly. It may seem as if the Reformation removed this price and ended the trade, but at a profound level that is not so. For every habitual and humble pardoner, in the very awareness of his free pardoning, congratulates himself and awards himself a high status, if his goal be purity of motive rather than actual concrete reconciliation, *which no possessed virtue can guarantee*, and which arrives always, miraculously, by grace.

Such a sense of high status carries with it also a consciousness of anarchic power and of the binding of those remitted in an infinite indebtedness. Furthermore, it guarantees an easy, picaresque lifestyle, again like that of Chaucer's pardoner, since the habitual and easy forgiver travels light through time by instantly ridding himself of the terrible burdens of injuries done to him and the terrible difficulties involved in seeking reconciliation (within infinite justice) with others. Since to forgive negatively and easily does not necessarily improve the character of the one forgiven, and may have the opposite effect, it seems that the real motivation of pure disinterested forgiveness is rather the avoiding of suffering, by pretending one has not been injured after all. Therefore, the merely negative pardoner is an adept of cheap forgiveness, as far from the genuine struggles of Christian existence as Bonhoeffer's adept of cheap grace. By contrast, although Aquinas indeed, as we saw, insists that human beings must offer forgiveness even in the absence of penitence, he only regards this offer as an initial and incomplete stage in the bringing about of reconciliation: the initiating gesture creates a negative space for an eventual positive upshot.

(e) Forgiveness and finality

The fifth *aporia* of forgiveness concerns forgiveness and finality. Where, again, forgiveness is regarded as negative, then the total forgetting of a fault implies that forgiveness has the last word over against both fault and just indignation. As Vladimir Jankélévitch points out, however, that 'last word' might be regarded as both dangerous and deluding. For if, indeed, one should not harbour resentment, then equally one should not forget injustice, not only in order to honour the memories of its victims, but also in order to remind oneself of possible future danger. By merely forgiving, by contrast, one forgets this danger or the possibility that a past malefactor may act viciously once again, perhaps precisely by abusing one's very forgiveness. As Jankélévitch puts it, 'where grace abounds, sin may abound all the more,' as well as vice versa.[30] Therefore, it seems that to forgive one must utterly forget, as if this alone guarantees an ultimate and irreversible reconciliation, and yet in forgetting one is blinding oneself to an actual or possible absence of reconciliation.

In this way every secular performance of forgiveness poses as an illusory *eschaton*. And because its finality is a chimaera, it offers not more security within human relationships, but rather an undesirable hesitation between increased security and increased insecurity. This arises in the following fashion. The implication of secular forgiving is that its obliterative finality has established an unshakable security hitherto absent. For, up till now, within a given specific human relationship, where all has gone smoothly without fault or grievance, there remains a sense of something untested. Will love survive the breaking of faith by one party? It seems that only forgiveness demonstrates that it can, and therefore discloses, irreplaceably, the depth of the relationship. However, if the offence is merely forgotten, then nothing after all has been gained. But if, to the contrary, it is remembered, then there is no forgiveness, precisely because the retained fact that a bond *could* be ruptured seems to place an unsurpassable barrier before the gate of Eden and to suggest that the bond was weaker than supposed. Therefore, since human forgiveness is not really final, it no more strengthens a relationship than a fault necessarily weakens it.

The above reflections upon this last *aporia* illuminate by contrast the significance of positive and divine forgiveness. Where the offender has positively offered penance, then indeed forgiveness may tilt the balance toward stability, since repentance can indicate an improvement of character beyond the latent tendency which led to the commission of a fault. Because the fault has exposed this tendency and permits its extirpation, it becomes indeed a kind of *felix culpa*, and forgiveness can be regarded as a gain on an erstwhile semi-illusory innocence of interaction. At the same time, the revelation of the possibility of fault still does, indeed, insinuate a germ of insecurity. And here forgiveness can only offer finality – without which security, indeed, *there could be no reconciliation* – through a participation in real, divine, eschatological finality. In consequence there is an inescapable logic to the original Biblical notion of positive forgiveness as only arriving with the *eschaton,* or else partially as its anticipation.

III

The foregoing consideration of the five *aporias* of forgiveness has confirmed that positive notions of forgiveness tend to regard it as first of all divine, since the prime paradigm for positive forgiveness is the Incarnation and Atonement. By contrast, negative notions are associated first of all with a theology focused more upon the divine fiat than upon the Incarnation, and, secondly, with a secular outlook unable to countenance the recuperation of time by eternity. As we have seen, the *aporias* of time, forgetting, motive and finality apply only to these negative accounts, especially in their secular form. However, the first *aporia* of the appropriate pardonee crosses the threshold between negative and positive, human and divine.

For this *aporia* seems to suggest that no human forgiveness, negative or positive, is possible, since the victims cannot be found, and neither victim nor sovereign may adequately forgive. Perhaps, then, this suggests that only God can forgive, since he alone is an adequate sovereign authority who can represent us all. This conclusion is partially correct, but it of course runs up against the problem of how we can be forgiven by God if human victims do not in fact forgive us. Such a forgiveness would surely be no more than nominal. Furthermore, a human sovereign power in some measure suffers what those it represents suffer, but not so God, who is perfectly in act, beyond all suffering. Thus God is so disconnected from all victimage, so impervious to offence, that it seems that he has nothing to forgive. Indeed, one mystical theologian of the late mediaeval period, Julian of Norwich, roundly declared that God does not forgive, since he cannot be offended, but only continues to give, despite our rejection of his gift. For Julian, sin as negative remains so entirely outside the divine comprehension (as negative it is not really something to be known) that from the divine point of view it is simply as if humanity has suffered an incomprehensible and even involuntary disaster, since no will enjoying beatitude could genuinely choose evil.[31]

It would appear then that neither human beings nor God can offer forgiveness. God may go on giving despite sin, but how is his gift, which is always of peace, mediated to us, if no human reconciliation can be effected?

4

INCARNATION

The sovereign victim

I

If, as the last chapter concluded, forgiveness can be neither human nor divine, then it would seem appropriate to ask whether this is why, for us in the West, forgiveness began as the work of divine humanity. It may not, indeed, be the case that the notion of incarnation resolves in a fully satisfactory manner the *aporia* of the pardonee, or of who is to forgive; but perhaps, by pointing to the mystery of the God-Man, it points to the only imaginable site of such resolution.

For here we have the unique instance of the sovereign victim. As Thomas Aquinas put it: 'the most efficacious argument for His Divinity has been this: without the support of the secular power he has changed the whole world for the better.'[1] As unique sovereign victim, perhaps, the God-Man was alone able to inaugurate forgiveness; for here was not a single instantiation of human nature, victimized like all humans by other humans, but rather a human victim suffering the maximum possible victimage, by virtue of its person-ification by the divine *Logos*, all-wise and all-innocent and therefore able to let the human nature plumb the full depths and implications of suffering. In this way a single suffering became also a sovereign suffering, capable of representing all suffering and of forgiving on behalf of all victims. One can note here that it is also a uniquely personal sovereignty, whereas human sovereignty – which only exists in *modern* political theory – is necessarily an impersonal cipher to which all our freedoms are initially sacrificed.

This sovereign victim is also able to forgive, unlike other human beings, at the very original instance of hurt, without a single jolt of rancour, since in the divinely enhypostasized human nature, suffering is paradoxically undergone in a wholly accepting, actively receptive fashion, in such a way that this undergoing is itself offered as a gift. Indeed, the suffering Christ is without qualification forgiveness from the outset, and not merely after repenting of his initial anger as a victim (which we cannot avoid) precisely because his human nature and will is imbued with the shape, character, idiom or *tropos* of the pure divine gift, which, as Julian of Norwich argued, never needs to forgive since it is never offended. As Maximus the Confessor established, Christ's human will, being imbued by the divine *tropos*, is a separate will by nature, but not by *gnome* or intention – see *Opusculum* 3.

Such an eternal divine gift only becomes forgiveness when in Christ it is *not* God forgiving us (since he has no need to) but humanity forgiving humanity. Therefore divine redemption is not God's forgiving us, but rather his giving us the gift of the capacity for forgiveness. And this can only be given in the first instance by the Trinity to Christ's humanity, because, first of all, only his victimage will be sovereign, and second, only he will be able absolutely and entirely to break with that rancour which normally must precede forgiveness and continue to contaminate it. Usually, forgiveness is occasioned by resentment and so remains somewhat grudging; with Christ's humanity alone there arises a pure forgiveness, since this really *surpasses* forgiveness, and is rather the unbroken continued giving of the divine gift as also the offering of a suffering actively undergone.

Yet nevertheless, despite this suggestion of how forgiveness might be possible, a disquiet must remain, a disquiet felt by those who asked Christ, 'By what right do you forgive sins?' One can answer, by right of conjoined divinity and humanity, by right of sovereign victimhood. And yet, if Christ, by reason of his enhypostasization by the infinite and innocent *Logos*, is as it were 'virtually' all victims, able to speak in their name, still he may not usurp their freedom, and if we are forgiven by Christ, but not, say, by Beatrice, we may still feel that we hover between the waters of Lethe and the waters of Eunoë. It is for this reason that the gift of intrahuman forgiveness offered by the whole Trinity to Christ's humanity is passed on by Christ to us as the hypostatic presence amongst us in time of the Holy Spirit, the bond of exchange and mutual giving within the Trinity. As participators through the Sacraments and membership of the body of Christ in the divine humanity, we now also begin to be capable of a forgiveness on sufficient authority and without taint of rancour. However, it remains our task to forgive and to go on receiving the forgiveness of other human beings, since what God offers us is not his negative forgiveness, but the positive possibility of intrahuman reconciliation. God is already reconciled to us, but only when Queen Matilda shows us once again the earthly paradise will we be reconciled to God.

II

If the above gives the lineaments of a theology of incarnational forgiveness, one may still nonetheless ask about its ontological foundation. Just how is the sovereign also a victim? Is this mysterious impossibility entirely impenetrable? Can we hope further to lift the veil of the *aporia*?

One may note here, first of all, that perhaps it should be untroubling to us that forgiveness appears to our understanding to be impossible. For theology considers what are, to us, three absolute impossibilities. First of all, there is the impossibility that anything else should exist outside of God, who is replete Being. For this to be possible, God must have gone outside of himself, and yet there is no exterior to God, no sum which might add to his amount. But then on top of this impossibility of Creation, theology overlays the second impossibility of sin, namely that creatures enjoying to their appropriate degree the absolute, and enjoying this only by grace of the absolute, might discover an illusory 'of themselves' wherewith to reject the absolute in the name of something lesser. Although, indeed, sin in itself is only loss and the desire of something less, the first sin that imagined sin does appear to be a surd, ungrounded will to the nullity of self-grounding autonomy, as we saw in Chapter 1. Finally, on top of this impossibility, theology overlays the third impossibility of redemption for a fault which, since it cuts finite being off from (infinite) reality, would appear to be without redress, even by that reality. It should surely result in absolute extinction, and one may note here that theology up to the High Middle Ages generally maintained that Creation only remained in being after the Fall through the proleptic working of the Incarnation.

In consequence of this theological vision, the Christian legacy has worked in terms of not one, but three ontologies of the impossible, all seamlessly laid on top of each other without break, and yet without necessary connection, like a double palimpsest. We now only glimpse the impossibility of Creation through the impossibility of the Fall, and both through the impossibility of the Redemption, even though Creation does not entail Fall, nor Fall, Redemption. For us, now, the impossible reality of a retrieval of absolute loss preserves and discloses again the impossibility of this loss, which in turn preserves and discloses again the impossibility that anything could first have been received from absolute plenitude.

It is difficult, nonetheless, for theology to remain with the thought of the impossibility of redemption, which is precisely the impossibility of forgiveness. The temptation is to claim too strong an insight into the ground of its possibility, thereby rendering it a kind of ineluctable necessity or a mere rebound effect of interrupted contractual exchange. Thus Anselm, for all the brilliant subtlety and correctness of much of his Christology, which certainly describes an aneconomic sacrifice of God to us and not a measurable debt paid by us to God,[2] nevertheless perhaps too much suggests that one can grasp how an infinite loss may be rectified. In some sense, certainly, as he suggests, this must be through the re-offering of the finite to the infinite by the infinite in person, but to imply that this logic is more than aesthetically compelling (if he does so, and he may not) is to advance too far. First of all, the suggestion that God cannot of necessity suffer loss and dishonour to his glory tends to overlook the point that any such loss is strictly 'impossible' for God. God cannot become a victim, and therefore is in no way drawn by absolute necessity into forgiveness. In the second place, since sin is the absolute refusal of the absolute, or a totally 'impossible' negation of what cannot be negated, it is not clear that even the absolute can now retrieve the finite from its captivity within itself.

Indeed, for reasons not totally unlike these two considerations, these aspects of Anselm's position were frequently rejected in later High Scholastic theology. Thus divine redemption and forgiveness came to be grounded not in an automatic reaction to the loss of glory, but rather in the free divine willing of the Good, even though such willing was taken absolutely to characterize the divine nature and not to be a matter of caprice.[3] At the same time, the possibility of divine redemption and forgiveness started to be based not upon an Anselmian equation of infinite with finite, but rather upon the mysterious depths of divine creative capacity, deemed somehow able to restore that which has refused its own created status. These positions were common to Thomas Aquinas and to Duns Scotus, even though their respective explications of these positions dramatically diverged. (It is terribly tempting in this instance to compare Anselm with Hegel, and Aquinas and Scotus with the later Schelling.)

In the remainder of this chapter, I want to show how Aquinas's Christology thought through as far as possible the problematic of a divine-human commencement of forgiveness conceived as positive, while Scotus's Christ-ology undid the vital link between forgiveness and incarnation, thereby inaugurating the reign of aspiration to purely negative forgiveness which, as we have seen, cannot be achieved and effects no reconciliation. I will also show that whereas Aquinas's subordination of ontology to theology permits him to ground forgiveness in ultimate reality, Scotus's first beginning of onto-theology involves also an onto-Christology which renders forgiveness a secondary, restricted and arbitrary instance within the divine goodness. Hence, it turns out that a unilateral and negative conception of the Good belongs from the outset within the logic of onto-theology, whereas it is frequently presented as its opposite. Inversely, an account of forgiveness as a positive exchange and reconciliation belongs to the logic of a theology that is in excess of metaphysics.

III

For Aquinas, it is possible that God, according to his *potentia absoluta*, might have forgiven us without the incarnation of the *Logos*.[4] A divine decree of negative obliteration allied to an act of positive recreation would in theory have been sufficient. By this assertion, Thomas assures us that God had no need to be appeased in order to become reconciled to us and that instead, in himself, he always and eternally was reconciled to us. One can express this in the terms already favoured, which declare that God does not need to forgive since he goes on giving. For Aquinas, therefore, the Incarnation does not bring about this reconciliation for God, but rather mediates this reconciliation to us, making it effective for us and in us, so ensuring that we, too, are reconciled.

He argues that the actual means of incarnation and atonement adopted for our salvation, while not absolutely necessitated, were nonetheless 'convenient', fitting, suitable for this purpose.[5] They possess the necessity, in Aquinas's own illustration, not of going in a certain direction to reach a certain goal, but of travelling most conveniently, or appropriately – for example, on horseback.[6] This sense of *convenientia* hovers, therefore, between the necessitated and the arbitrary and as such (as Gilbert Narcisse has argued at length) it is clearly an *aesthetic* notion closely allied to terms such as *proportio, harmonia, ordinatio* and *analogia*.[7] A certain pleasing *logos* is exhibited here beyond merely capricious arrangement, and yet God is not bound to this order in the same way that he is bound to conclude that $a = a$ and is not *not a*. Nevertheless, for Aquinas the counterfactual invocation of *potentia absoluta* is an essentially abstract, logical moment, designed to indicate where God is not impersonally, ineluctably constrained. It is not, as for later Scholastics, following more a model derived from later canon law, a kind of reserve power which may, at a whim, intervene to interrupt the conventional norms of *potentia ordinata*.[8] Rather, for Aquinas, *all* that God actually does belongs to his *potentia ordinata*, which is not an order of caprice, but itself reflects the eternal divine sense of justice and appropriateness. Therefore Aquinas's God is 'compelled' not only by the absolute exigencies of logical possibility, but also by something one may dub 'actual necessity', or the agreeable that appears in the harmonious proportions of an infinite actual order. This is then reflected in the divine economy.

Aquinas lists several different ways in which the order of incarnation was 'convenient', and declares that he only cites a few, since their number is infinite.[9] But two modes are especially relevant here. First of all, the notion that it is aesthetically fitting that since we fell as a consequence of Adam's pride and the rebellion of his sensory faculties, we should be restored through divine humility and re-education of the understanding by the senses. Christ follows and shows us the path through suffering and despair to a despising of our morality and the regaining of eternal life.[10] This shows that while, for Aquinas, God *could* have restored us just through his continued gift, he nonetheless so respects human freedom and the legacy of human history that he seeks also positively to forgive us by tracing himself, as only an innocent man can, the perfect ways of penitence which we are to follow.

A second instance of *convenientia* is also important. It is appropriate that God should draw near to humanity in this most radical and unexpected fashion, because God as infinite and replete cannot be rivalled, and therefore can give himself entirely – even his own divine nature.[11] Here Aquinas is exploiting to the full the mystery of the first theological impossibility, that of Creation. Just because there is no outside to God, God can most freely and ecstatically exceed himself; just because God cannot share *anything*, he can share *everything*. It is partially because of his intense sense of this paradox that Aquinas espouses ontologically strong notions of deification. Adam was created to enjoy the beatific vision and to share without reserve, to the (for us unknown) measure of human personhood, in the divine nature.[12] And significantly, Aquinas cites this predestination of Adam as a further ground for the *convenientia* of the Incarnation; humanity has a *natural* kinship with the supernatural; humanity bears the image of God, rather as the Son bears the image of the Father; finally, humanity as a rational animal synthesizes the whole work of Creation in a way the angels do not – it is 'appropriate' that this finite totality be conjoined with infinite plenitude.[13]

All this is also relevant to the thematic of forgiveness. Aquinas's account of divine non-rivalry means that God, being all, is uniquely only able to give of himself. Since all that is, is of God, things only suspire by a return to God, which is realized through humanity the microcosm, the crown of Creation. Hence while, for Aquinas, Creation is in one sense an entirely one-way gift, in another it is an absolute exchange, since the gift is only received in its return to God, just as deified humanity comes more and more to participate in the Son's return to the Father within the Trinity. And since, for Aquinas, the Creation is not really outside of God, it is, through humanity, able to make an adequate return of love and honour to God. *Without the Incarnation* for Aquinas (we shall shortly see the contrast with Scotus here), God is able in the Creation to realize a *telos* commensurate with his own infinite nature. One might ask: how can this be, since anything other than God is less than God? But the point here is that this very other to God is so problematic that Aquinas realizes that it can only be possible as a *self-exceeding* – that is to say as the lesser and other to God which only exists (through humanity) as always cancelling this lesserness and otherness. Here the final upshot – deification – is extraordinarily in excess of the original goal – Creation – since it would be pointless for God to aim for deification, which is already himself. This strange structure – outcome in excess of goal – only applies to the relation between God and Creation, and is a result of its 'impossibility'.

Given this context of exchange between infinite and finite, whereby it belongs intrinsically to human nature 'to exact' deification (albeit through the divine grace by which alone it is human), God does not, for Aquinas, gain an adequate return for his infinite love only through the Incarnation. The ground of incarnation is not then for him, the completion of the infinite–finite gift-exchange. Rather, the occasion for incarnation is God's free will to redeem according to his goodness, and hence the occasion for incarnation is the offer of *forgiveness* – although in the sense already described of an offering of the possibility of reconciliation with God and other human beings. The difficulty though, of imagining how God can offer us this reconciliation, is, as we have seen, the sheer apparent impossibility of retrieving a deficient act which is itself an impossible will to destruction. Here, as we have also already seen, Aquinas seems to claim less insight than Anselm: he does not exactly 'grasp' the conjoining of finite to infinite as necessitated, but nonetheless he can envisage something of its 'appropriateness' in the beauty of the narratives which relate this conjoining. It is not so much that God *had* to become incarnate in order to retrieve us, and that we can comprehend the 'possibility' of this, as, rather, that it seems 'fitting' that a God whose absolute giving has been thwarted (inconceivably) should somehow miraculously redouble this giving. Hence the intimate link established by Aquinas between deification and hominization: where deification is refused by us, God still wills nonetheless to bring it about through the making of a human nature actually to subsist in a divine hypostasis. And here, once again, Aquinas insists that *of necessity* this did not have to be the person of the *Logos*, rather than any other person of the Trinity; rather, this was merely aesthetically 'right' because of the affinity between the Son as image and humanity as image.[14]

But the problem here it would seem is how, if God in Creation gave absolutely, such that deification adequately completes the infinite–finite gift exchange, he can possibly give anything more. The answer may be that in Creation God gave himself unreservedly to creatures, including the grace of beatification, and never gives *to creatures* anything more than this. However, in the Incarnation he causes a human creature not just to receive as finite the infinite in due measure, but actually to be, in its entire, unrepeatable, specifically characterized and incommunicable *suppositum* or self-subsistence, God himself, as 'appropriated' to that persona which is the *Logos*. This is not so much a new gift of God to humanity, as a making of a human nature also to be the means of absolute uninterrupted giving – by which means, as I have suggested, God is alone able to inaugurate forgiveness on earth.

Nevertheless, if the Incarnation is not a further gift, it still brings about something in excess even of absolute divine gift, namely the conjoining of humanity to divinity. This is indeed a sharing in excess of gift, in excess of Creation, even though there was nothing originally withheld. Thus while the occasion and goal of incarnation for Aquinas was *not* (as later for Scotus, as we shall describe) ontological completion of the Creation, but rather the offering of forgiveness (in the sense of the possibility of positive reconciliation), nonetheless there appears to arise as an outcome of this purpose something ontologically in excess of it, something therefore ontologically in excess even of forgiveness and reconciliation. For the Incarnation was no temporary instrument to be left behind: now, for always in time, and so from eternity, human nature through Christ is directly impersonated by the *Logos*, in such a way that we may worship Christ's human appearance without idolatry. If Christ's humanity eternally subsists in the *Logos*, meaning that the *Logos* is both *suppositum* of divinity and *also suppositum* of this particular humanity, then in some sense the world was created by and through the baby in Bethlehem. In some sense also, the human offence which required the Incarnation was always, also, an offence against the incarnate one. We are to rejoice in and adore the resurrected humanity not because it has redeemed us (as if we were paying a due price) but simply because it is glorious and causes us to exult.

In consequence Aquinas explicitly calls attention to the *felix culpa* pronounced at the lighting of the Easter candle, and is apprised also of the fact that, via redemption, Mary has also received a status beyond that of Adam, since her assent to the Incarnation was essential to human re-creation (whereas Adam did not assent to his creation) and the enhypostasis of the human nature.[15] Aquinas (unlike Scotus) was in tune with the thrust of the famous lines of the folkloric carol: 'O ne had the apple taken been. . . . Ne had our Lady a'been Heavene's Queen.' It is significant that Scotus had to resort to an alternative mode of exalting Mary – namely the doctrine of her immaculate conception – which focuses not on her own will but on divine predetermination.

However, does it *really seem 'fitting'* (and it did not, later to Scotus) that through fault a higher status should eventually be realized? Does not this downgrading of innocence to secondary status conversely elevate the merely *reactive* virtue of forgiveness over the purity of original giving? And does this notion not seem to underwrite the debatable view, as described in the previous chapter, that forgiveness is more final than fault? Lastly, as Scotus argued, if the conjoining of humanity in person to the divinity is a higher good (as it is) than even the saving of humanity, then must not this have been God's primary intent in the Incarnation?[16]

None of these problems should be lightly dismissed, and indeed the *felix culpa* is too easily celebrated in sermons of tipsy casualness. However, let us attempt to deal with them in order. First of all, there is no sense in Aquinas that pre-fallen innocence was lacking in any perfection, any more than this was the case for the original created order without incarnation. And one must remember that real innocence is unknown to us; it is a state where malice is unimaginable for the good will and so is not, after all, equivalent to a seemingly secure untested good relationship prior to any serious fault, such as we might encounter in our fallen state. We distrust the untested character of such a relationship precisely because we know that its participants are already creatures susceptible to temptation, since unlike our unfallen first parents, they already know what temptation is.

In the second place, real, positive Christological forgiveness is, as has been shown, not reactive, since it is only the sustained giving of the original gift, despite its refusal. For this reason, forgiveness in response to fault is not a reaction superior to an original action, since it is *only* this continued action, neither more nor less.

In the third place, it may indeed be the case that, in human experience, to know reconciliation after rupture is yet more joyous than an original state of tranquility. Yet we should hesitate over this too facile analogy. Once again, we have never known real innocence, and therefore cannot compare the joys of reconciliation with the joys of innocence. If, nonetheless, it be insisted here that we have known innocence to some degree and yet do experience a more intense joy in the arrival of reconciliation after the rupture of this innocence, then one should still note that this is partly because one has a sense of something final – of a relationship tested and shown to be absolutely binding; were we to imagine in reconciliation that there might be further ruptures, our joy would no longer be unconfined. In a sense, therefore, there is something in the outcome of forgiveness which exceeds its occasion and goal, which is the instrumental healing of a relationship. Yet as we have seen, such finality in human forgiveness is only more than illusion where it participates (after the Incarnation and before the *parousia*) in eschatological finality itself. Therefore only the advance arrival of the *eschaton* in the middle of history guarantees the finality of forgiveness, and, in consequence, forgiveness as such.

But precisely what is it that renders Christ's forgiveness final, and ensures that, whereas the deified Adam could fall, those deified through participation in Christ's humanity enhypostasized by the *Logos* can never fall again? (A point which Christian theology found at first difficult to establish, as Origen's writing indicate.) Presumably one must say, just this new absolute degree of conjoining between infinite and finite, whereby the reality of victimage, which may seek to forgive, does so absolutely and before rancour, since it is infused with the idiom of uninterrupted sovereign gift. In this fashion, following Maximus, there is in Christ no hesitant, wavering human *gnome*, independent of the divine *gnome* which expresses the divine *tropos*.

In the fourth place, one must still deal with the Scotist point that God must will, primarily, the higher goal first. However this objection first of all too easily assumes that there can be something for creatures higher than deification. The Incarnation stands higher than deification for Aquinas's understanding, not because it realizes a higher finite goal for the Creation, but because here God's own infinite *telos* in himself has become also the realization (though incomprehensibly with no real addition to God, and no 'real relation' of God to it, as Thomas puts it)[17] of this particular human nature *in atomo*. This is the case for Aquinas in the *Tertia Pars*, because he recognizes only one *esse* in Christ, which is the divine *esse* itself.[18] For this reason, God gains nothing in glory through the Incarnation, since he gains only himself, which is no gain.

Secondly, the Scotist objection fails to realize that, as we have seen, the paradoxical structure of outcome exceeding occasion and cause is not peculiar to the Thomist account of incarnation as motivated by the will to forgive, but is already the structure of all divine activity, since it explicates the impossibility of creation. God's goal is the existence of creatures outside himself, yet since there is nothing outside God, all creatures suspire (through humanity – and I am conscious of supplementing Aquinas with Maximus here) only in returning to God and attaining an outcome in excess of their first occasioning. The structure of divine redemption simply repeats this structure of divine creation, and therefore the ontological excess of the hypostatic union over its instrumental occasion in turn explicates the impossibility of this redemption. God can only restore what has gone wrong by rendering it also at one point (but to which all other points are connected – and there are many thorny problems here) united with him, identical in subsistent character to him, even though this 'adds' nothing to his own character.

But there is also a further, crucial consideration. Just a little earlier it was suggested that the structure 'outcome exceeding occasion' is *also* the structure of all forgiveness in so far as it requires finality, even though this finality can only be provided Christologically. Hence indeed it seems that while the Incarnation is ontologically in excess of our being forgiven, this circumstance alone is precisely what ensures that we *are* forgiven. To receive forgiveness is not only to continue to receive the gift through and despite Kierkegaard's 'jolt'; it is also to receive the intensified gift of identity with the giver, an identity of shared *character*, idiom, ethos or *tropos* which still respects independence of will – although the wills unite in a shared intention. In this way, we need to add Maximus's Christological insights to Augustine's insights on time in order fully to grasp forgiveness. Where people differ, struggle and quarrel, then finally the only solution is to become one flesh, to forge one shared identity, one harmony, one tone, one flavour, which does not mean that asymmetrical contributions to this are denied (though in the case of the divine-human union, there is, of course, really no intrinsic human contribution to the shared *persona*). It may be unpopular to say this, but reconciliation is the absoluteness of shared taste, the freedom of the dance in joint measure which is the gift of lovers to an audience – their transmitted bond which binds a community to them, just as the bond of the Holy Spirit forges the hypostatic union.

Forgiveness, therefore, perfects gift-exchange as *fusion*. If gift-exchange retains free gift as non-identical repetition and asymmetrical reciprocity, then forgiveness exceeds this to the measure that in perfected exchange every surprise is anticipated by the other, since the surprise she offers is also the surprise he arrives at in that very instance, as requiring a perfectly *improvised* and yet absolutely consensual dance. But since, as we have seen, forgiveness is only inaugurated by the sovereign victim, this perfection of exchange as fusion is first granted to us in the idiomatic characterizing of victim as sovereign, sovereign as victim. It is their relation, their dance, that first and alone reconciles.

All this seems to point to a further inescapable mystery. To receive forgiveness, we have discovered, can only mean to receive the God-Man, and to receive him as an outcome which infinitely exceeds the forgiveness he proffers, although this exceeding *is* after all forgiveness, since forgiveness is unshakable finality. Such a process implies that while there is indeed no

Hegelian necessity for fault if we are to reach the highest human goal, and no reason too blithely to celebrate fault, that all the same a narrative course of alienation and restoration *does* appear to occasion an ontological revision (it is this cautiously 'Hegelian' Thomism which the subtle exegesis of Michel Corbin points toward).[19] This is not indeed, as for Hegel, an ontological revision for God, but it is still an ontological revision for the Creation in relation to God, since for forgiveness to become possible it is necessary that *now the Logos comes to be* not merely the *suppositum* of the divine nature, but also of human nature as manifest in this individual, Jesus Christ. Certainly this hypostatic union is for Aquinas created and in no real relation to God from the divine perspective: in such a way that it is not, for God, a new thing that he is now the subsistent base of a creature, but rather there is this new mode of being only for the creature and for us. All the same, not just the Creation in itself but its relation to God is thereby revised. *Now* it begins to be true, although it must also be retrospectively true (just as Adam, according to Aquinas, even though he did not know he was to fall, still proleptically anticipated Christ in his enjoyment of the beatific vision),[20] that the Creation is sustained not only through participation in, but – in a mediated sense – through union with, God. Equally, now it begins to be true, though it must have been true always, that *analogia* or *convenientia* is not just approximation of humanity to God, but even the appropriate blending together in one idiom or *tropos* of the one with the other.

So if forgiveness is a reality, then it seems that it is somehow not subordinate to ontology, or rather that being is now shown in time as forgiveness and finality and as revisable via narrative. Here, therefore, finite ontology does not yield to, but nonetheless coincides with, eschatology.

One must deliberately refrain, however, from any actual ascription of 'event' as involving change to God: this would be incompatible with his aseity. Nevertheless, the implication of Chalcedonian doctrine appears to be that God is not only infinite *esse*, outside time, but also the subject of this particular series of events in time resumed as a resurrected human nature through all eternity. Moreover, Aquinas's peculiar metaphysics deliberately negotiate this circumstance in a way that perhaps has never been fully noted. For Aquinas, the notion of God as *esse* exceeds metaphysics and belongs to *sacra doctrina*, since metaphysics (as Aristotle failed to realize), in thinking only general, transcendental categories, *cannot*, after all, think the transgeneric character of being (as recognized by Aristotle), since *esse* is as much present in the individual and accidental as in the general and the substantive.[21] Hence the knowledge enjoyed by the divine *esse*, unlike the knowledge of the metaphysician, stretches down to every last particular.[22] And so from the divine perspective of *esse*, there is indeed a comprehension of event in excess of the mere falling of events under general ontological categories, since the yet more 'general' perspective of *esse* fractures the sway of generality itself. *Esse* as infinite *actus* is itself an infinite though unchanging occurrence or event which is if anything more hyper-specific than super-general. From the point of view of *esse*, an instance can break out of a preceding framework, just as the perfection of the divine eminent knowledge of a fallen thrush is identical in the divine essence to his knowledge of the category 'birds'.

It is this understanding of the divine transgeneric *esse* which then forms the ground for Aquinas's insistence that there is only the one divine *esse* in the divine humanity. There cannot, for Aquinas, be another finite, human *esse* (although there is, of course, a human *essentia*), because this would either be an accident added to the divine *suppositum* – which cannot receive accidents any more than it can be accidentally conjoined to the humanity (since God cannot be the accident of a creature) – or else another substance so added, which would be equally impossible, since the divine substance is infinite and replete.

For many commentators, and perhaps most mediaeval Scholastic theologians, this refusal of either substantive or accidental additions to the *Logos* has seemed to exhaust all possibilities of union with humanity.[23] However, this is to fail to grasp the subtleties of Thomas's metaphysical innovations. Since *esse* is non-generically common to substance and accident, it is indifferent to either, and yet God is supremely *esse*. Therefore he lies beyond the substance/accident contrast in his *essentia*, and since the persons of the Trinity are identical with this *essentia*, this self-subsistence also exceeds the contrast of essential versus additional. Inversely, the divine *esse* is identical with, and manifest as, the three 'incommunicabilities' of personhood. It *is* their peculiar, though subsistently interrelated, 'ways' of being.

Hence when Aquinas speaks of the one *esse* of the divine humanity, he means, somewhat like Maximus the Confessor (though he is less explicit), that all that there *is* in Christ is the one way of being that characterizes the eternal *Logos*.[24] Because *esse* is as much event and instance as general structure, and because as manifest in a 'way' of being it is somewhat like an eternal 'narrative' constitution that forms character (in the *perichoresis* of the Trinity), it is able to be entirely communicated to a finite instance. A 'way' of being slips out of the infinite into a perfect reflection in the finite. Both finite and infinite, it seems, can exhibit one and the same specific character of love in the perfect fusion that is forgiveness. Therefore while, for Aquinas, Jesus's humanity has a fully human mind, will and even individuality, it still does not possess a human personhood or *suppositum*, because this involves absolute self-subsistence, incommunicability and uniqueness, and all of Jesus's individual human nature subsists in and is held together in consistency of character by (again this is more explicit in Maximus) the eternal hypostasis of the Son.[25] This hypostasis, as a 'way' of being, is beyond substance and accident, and just for this reason is able to receive an 'addition' to itself which is not really an addition (altering its essence) and yet is not accidental either. Aquinas gives many instances at the finite level of 'proper accident', or of additions beyond minimal essence which still belong properly to a thing's being or 'character'. In the Christological instance also, he cites finite analogues, specifically the relation of a body to a hand.[26] Here he explains that one can have a body without a hand, and yet a hand is not an entirely accidental instrument of the body as, for example, is an axe. A hand is rather an 'organic' instrument of the human body, and here it is important to bear in mind that Aquinas, in his commentary on the *De Anima*, supports and augments the remarkable Aristotelian view that only men of extreme sensitivity of touch are intelligent.[27]

Thus while, of course, Aquinas considers that handless men are men, he can scarcely think that hands are purely 'accidental' to a rational animal. An organic instrument is neither substantial nor accidental, but is still an integral part of the *esse* and specific personal *suppositum* of the individual. And with charming brilliance, Aquinas notes that a sixth finger on a hand may be an accidental deformity, yet since it is *useful* to his owner, it has become an integral part of him.[28] He compares the hypostatic union precisely to the growth of a sixth finger.

For Aquinas therefore, since God is both *esse* and tri-personal, he is open to the arrival of an event which causes something else to belong to him, not accidentally and not essentially, but rather as exhibiting precisely the same way of being – the same dance, in the same measure. But in Aquinas's metaphysics, this existential character *is* the real, is the true concrete reality which upholds everything. Hence to be conjoined this way is not to be weakly or metaphorically conjoined, nor merely conjoined by like *habitus* (a position he specifically rejects),[29] but to be joined in substantive actuality.

Nevertheless, for Aquinas this event, this arrival, involves nothing new for God; it is not a real relation for him. Thus the human nature of Christ belongs integrally to the *Logos* and its being is only the being of the *Logos*, and yet, to its human attribute, the *Logos* is not really related. This seems highly strange, yet it is really an outcome of the same old impossibility of something being outside God when there is no outside of God. God for Aquinas is not really related to the Creation, and yet the Creation is real, and really participates in him. Likewise, God is not really related to the divine humanity, and yet the latter also is real and is really so fused with God that now God is, also, human (since the *Logos* is the subject, also, of human attributes). However, just as Aquinas says that God perfectly knows the Creation through knowledge of how his essence may be participated, so it would seem that one must also say (as Aquinas, however, explicitly does not), that God knows perfectly the hypostatic union through knowledge of how a finite event may be absolutely conjoined to his *esse*. And also that just as for Aquinas God foreknows that he will create and so utters the *Logos* in this foreknowledge, so also one should add to Aquinas (to be consistent with his thought) that God utters the *Logos* in foreknowledge of sin and his appropriate, fitting response to it through the hypostatic union.

But in that case, always and from eternity, God as giver is also the God who proffers divine-human forgiveness. Always and from eternity, temporal event is conjoined to *esse*. Always and from eternity, God is also humanity. Always and from eternity, ontologic is also eschatologic, and what is must also be told. Here is the ontology beyond ontology of pardon.

This need to tell even of God, since he is also in himself a telling, arises from the mysterious and incomprehensible paradox that God is as originally forgiving (or rather the giver of forgiving) as he is giving.

So our reflections on Aquinas have shown that if forgiveness can only be commenced by the divine sovereign victim, this also reveals forgiveness to be an outcome exceeding its own occasion and the perfection of gift-exchange with fusion. Finally, we have seen that the recognition of God as the provider of forgiveness (so correctly characterized) entails that the infinite always was, if certainly not (as for Hegel) really related to the finite, nonetheless eminently fused with it at a certain incomprehensible point of identity.

IV

As a melancholy postscript to these reflections, it can now be explained how Duns Scotus removed, for a time, the possibility of an authentic under-standing of forgiveness along the lines I have indicated.

For Duns Scotus, as is well known, the ultimate motivation for incarnation was not the forgiveness of humanity. We have already seen the weakness of much of the reasoning to this conclusion. However, his position is only fully comprehensible when one realizes that he did not grant to Adam in the earthly paradise an orientation by nature to the beatific vision.[30] Since, for Scotus, being is transcendentally indifferent to infinite and finite, as also to active and potential, albeit that the former terms are allowed to be more exemplary as to intensity or degree or *gradus*, the finite Creation fully *is*, in its own right as Creation, and holds ground ontologically, simply as what God has determined it shall be.[31] Lost from this perspective is a full sense of the impossibility of creation: for where this is grasped, as by Aquinas, then it is also seen that finitude as constituted only by the infinite must, in order to suspire, be self-cancelling. Here the finite creature fully conscious of its finitude must aspire to return to God and to comprehend his finitude in the vision of his maker. In consequence, for Aquinas, human beings simply as human were ordained to the beatific vision and to deification.

For Scotus, by contrast, such ordination is merely a divinely willed supplement. But in consequence, creatures as creatures do not appear to Scotus as capable of making a return of love to the Creator commensurate with the gift of creation. For this reason God, who for Scotus is bound of his own necessity to will the highest good, is inevitably inclined to will (albeit freely) the Incarnation, in order that here a creature via his conjunction with the infinite *Logos* may offer back to God an infinite return of love.[32] The problem with this conception is that it appears to downgrade humanity and not to allow that humans of their very nature (if this be followed) offer the highest return possible by creatures. As we have already seen, Christ in a sense offers nothing higher than a creature considered only *as* creature. Thus for Aquinas there is no question of the Incarnation increasing God's reception of finite glory, as there appears to be for Duns Scotus.

But the most curious thing about Scotus's scheme is that while, in a sense, it offers incarnation instead of deification, where Aquinas sees deification as the ground of possibility of incarnation (shocking as this may seem), the inhibition regarding deification, founded on univocity of being, actually restricts also any strong account of the hypostatic union. Hence in Scotus's view, while indeed Christ's humanity somehow makes an infinite return of love to God through the *Logos*, as purely human it enjoys only finite merit; whereas for Aquinas, who developed a strong Alexandrian view of the *communicatio idiomatum*, this merit was infinite.[33] Likewise for Scotus, again in contrast to Aquinas, Christ's human nature is not fully engraced, is not indefectible, and does not enjoy the beatific vision through fusion with the divine nature in the one divine hypostasis, but instead is elevated in these three ways purely by divine decree which need not have been enacted.[34] In kindred fashion for Scotus, the indefeasibility of the final persistence of the blessed in enjoying the beatific vision does not derive from the vision itself as secured by our participation in the hypostatic union, but rather is, once again, a merely extrinsic grant of the divine will.[35]

So while the ground of incarnation is for Scotus onto-Christological rather than redemptive, it is difficult to see how in fact this union, which is supposed to perfect the Creation, is any reality of itself, as opposed to a kind of imposed structure. Accordingly Scotus, knowing no medium between substance and accident, regarded Christ's humanity as an accidental addition to the *Logos*, though of course the *Logos* was still for him in no real relation to it.[36] Supposedly Scotus thought that an accident in dependence on a substance need not realize any potential in that substance (which would be inappropriate for God); but one cannot come to possess any accident which comes in some, albeit temporary way to characterize oneself, without it realizing some potential in one – otherwise an accident is just an external possession. (The Avicennian idea of distinct formalities in a single substance, taken over by Scotus, encourages just this conception – which really undoes, rather than transcends, the logic of substance and accident.) If that indeed is what Scotus is really talking about (or even if one allowed that there can be an accident not realizing a potential), then it still is the case that God cannot receive anything into his *esse* or *persona* that is not essential and not assimilated to his own essence. Scotus only thinks in these terms because his elevation of finite being to ontological equality with infinite being in terms of sharing in a transgeneric attribute – if not in terms of mode and degree – ensures that a real sense of its participatory character is lost, and in consequence it must be thought as standing 'spatially' alongside the infinite. Thus in the Christological instance, Christ's humanity, if it is to remain real for Scotus, must enjoy an *esse* of its own. And indeed, its individuality seems in effect to amount for him to human personhood, since he understands human personhood only negatively, as a not-being-dependent on something higher.[37] Therefore all the essential ingredients of human personality – individuality, animality, rationality – are there in Christ for Scotus; it is simply that all this is included in a purer self-subsistence. While Aquinas indeed thinks in somewhat similar terms, he also allows personality as a positive, specifically characterized incommunicability, which as something human *really is not there* in Christ, whereas a positive divine personality *is* present.

It appears then, that while one might be attracted by the Scotist view of the Incarnation as pure active gift, and not reactive forgiveness, that the divine-human union accompanying this account is in fact extremely tenuous. This has implications for how Scotus conceives the secondary purpose of the Incarnation, contingent upon sin, which is indeed the forgiveness of human sins. Here once again a weak sense of participation (reduced to a matter of degrees of perfection that stops short of the infinite, thought of as a positively different *modus*, whereas for Aquinas 'infinite' is a negative term related primarily to our *modus significandi*)[38] means that Scotus thinks that even original sin is only finite and only requires finite merit, which a mere human being could render in compensation.[39] Thus God could, by his *potentia absoluta*, have appointed a merely human saviour, and indeed, since Christ's human merits are finite, it would seem that through the Incarnation we are only humanly redeemed for Scotus. And as a result of all this, forgiveness as conceived by Aquinas has been in every way lost to view.

First of all, Christ's offering of finite merit and satisfaction fulfils the demands of divine justice, not of divine mercy. The latter operates much more by fiat, and since the *pattern* of satisfaction realized by Christ is no longer its means of operation, it is difficult to see how this fiat any longer expresses itself in what is 'convenient' – even if Scotus still deploys the term. God simply decrees the adequacy of what Christ does and conjoins with it his forgiveness. For Scotus, the divine justice and grace-imbued mercy are now 'formally distinct', just as happiness (as self-realization) and justice are formally distinct (the devil being held to have fallen through a neglect only of the latter).[40]

In either case, Scotus assumes that where, from our point of view, concepts can be conceptually distinguished, this is because they directly indicate distinct essences external to our perception; by contrast Aquinas locates essence much more in the mind and describes much more of a gulf between mental understanding and ontological states of affairs.[41] Such

Scotist essences are simple and inviolate, so that if we project them to the infinite, this may increase their intensity but not alter their inner core of identity. Accordingly, divine justice and mercy and happiness are essentially the same in nature as ours, and remain 'formally distinct' in God. Even though they are 'really identical' in him, this is only in so far as they reside 'virtually' in his single essence which is infinite. God's understanding of this infinite essence is his 'first instance', but in his consequent 'instances' he produces from his understandings the essences of things as *finite* and as formally distinguished from himself and each other.[42] Hence through the formal distinction, Scotus over-elevates the absoluteness of finite simplicities and simultaneously compromises the absoluteness of the divine simplicity. Indeed, he says explicitly that since simplicity is univocally shared between God and creatures, infinity and not simplicity must primarily characterize God.[43] In this way he interprets Anselm's *Monologion* to mean that we know God in terms of infinite degrees of perfections that we grasp in their simple essence quite apart from God, arguing that to refer a perfection analogously to God adds nothing to our knowledge of this perfection.[44] This totally obliterates the 'phenemonological' dimension implicit in Aquinas (and in Anselm, following Augustine), which assumes that to grasp a perfection *is* to see the infinite shining though the finite and calling the finite above itself.[45]

For Scotus therefore, we can grasp 'mercy' and 'justice' non-theologically as distinct in their essences – else why would there be two concepts, he reasons, disallowing the notion that perhaps they are *really* distinct only for our deficient ontological experience. In this way he already thinks of mercy in 'secular' terms, and so as outside of justice. As such it becomes a matter of mere negative decree or withholding – this notion of mercy he then projects upon God.

Thus we can see that, in the first instance, Scotus loses Aquinas's sense of forgiveness as positive and inherently divine. In the second instance, he also loses Aquinas's sense of it being only possible through the Incarnation as the work of the God-Man, or the sovereign victim. This is because he is scarcely able to think of the hypostatic union at all, and has to patch it up with divine decrees, in any case deemed adequate for our forgiveness without the mediating work of penance and substitution. Scotus never, like Aquinas, allows that merit automatically elicits grace, since it is (for Aquinas) itself the result and manifestation of grace.[46] Once more, Scotus's ontic conception of God makes him think of divine initiative and human response as external to each other, in such a way that our merit becomes too much ours, or at any rate something that does not of itself return to God, but rather something which God may or may not graciously receive. One consequence of this loss of a sense of participation is therefore a loss also of a sense of exchange between infinite and finite. God becomes more of a one-way giver and, significantly, this unilateralism of the gift seems here to be a *consequence* of a reduction of God to one ontic pole within a common univocalized being. So whereas a finite being that *was not* of itself had itself to return, and indeed God, as loyal to his own *esse* and its transcendental norms of beauty and justice, 'had to' guarantee this return, now a finite being need not of itself return, and God is not of himself bound to receive it. Already therefore, the Scotist God has become more like a bestowing tyrant and the 'mixed constitution' of gift-exchange and positive forgiveness has begun to be dissolved.

In the third instance, Scotus loses also Aquinas's sense of forgiveness as 'outcome exceeding occasion'. As we have seen, he rejects this essentially because his doctrine of univocity obscures a sense of the impossibility of creation and the way in which, as a consequence, the entire divine economy involves an outcome exceeding occasion. But with this loss, Scotus can no longer think a finality intrinsic to forgiveness, but must resort to a God who simply 'decides' that the blessed need not fall again, although he withheld this benefit from Adam.

In the fourth instance, Scotus loses forgiveness as fusion, because he disallows deification as a ground for incarnation and in consequence cannot think the divine-human union through character or *tropos*.

In the fifth and final instance, Scotus loses divine *esse* as conjoined to temporal event, and the divine gift as also eternally divine forgiveness. His onto-theology necessitates also an onto-Christology, because it disallows deification and requires something else to provide the divine requirement of glory from the creation. But an onto-Christology, when conjoined to the view that a merely finite human fault could have been corrected by minor, finite means, ensures that none of the narrative, typological and aesthetic seriousness of Christ's suffering and passion is carried up into his pre-ordained eternal destiny in an organic rather than a merely accidental fashion. So while the Scotist God is eternally also man, this man also remains accidentally outside God, and in consequence it does not seem that this God is eternally also forgiveness. By contrast, in the Thomist scheme, where Christological outcome is ontologically in excess of Christological purpose, and this excess over forgiveness nonetheless *is* forgiveness, God is seen as from eternity in his own foreordination also human, and therefore, through this fusion, as eternally forgiving.

5

CRUCIFIXION

Obscure deliverance

I

Evil is to be overcome by forgiveness. As likewise is violence . . . Yet just as violence is convertible with evil, but distinguished from it according to our *modus cognoscendi* (but not by any formal distinction), so also there is a distinction to be made by us between escape from violence and escape from evil, even though they are two entirely coinciding aspects of the same process, like the front and the back of a depthless strip.

Forgiveness restores the Good. But in another aspect X, it restores peace. What is this other aspect? If forgiveness endures and compensates for evil, X suffers violence without violent opposition, and yet at the same time positively opposes violence with a counter-violence to violence as such, which positively reasserts peace (see the discussions in Chapter 2). X has no obvious name, but lies somewhere between passion and rule, exercising at once both victimhood and sovereignty, as we saw in Chapters 3 and 4.

It follows that the name of X might be cruciformity, or *imitatio Christi.* As incarnate, as we saw in Chapter 4, Christ forgave, in the sense of offering again to humans, as a gift, the possibility of their mutual reconciliation. But also, as persecuted and crucified, Christ overcame violence and restored peace. He first instituted and fulfilled X as indeed the *via crucis*, which involves in its anti-chiasmus both violence and suffering, as well as evil and negation.

But we have already spoken of sovereign victimhood. Then what is really the missing aspect?

One must recall the issue of violence and visibility. Privation theory exposes the hidden violence of autonomous self-assertion because it reads violence as negation of the infinite positive plenitude of the Good. The process of forgiveness carries out just this reading, and performs its implications.

But as we saw in Chapter 2, privation theory also calls for a discrimination amongst apparent violence: some of this truly is deprivation of the Good, and therefore also violent. Some of it is not, and therefore is not, after all, violent. The theory of radical evil, by contrast, which tends to be sheerly phenomenological, accepts the idea of a naive intuition of visible violence, and therefore defines violence merely as intrusion, as an obvious impinging upon the terrain of 'the other'. But since life consists of nothing but heteronomy, this opens the way to the terrorism of political correctness, which of course serves the purposes of liberal capitalism and the liberal state and encourages their new turn towards terroristic Fichtean policing of supposed 'natural right'. These theorists, as Alain Badiou argues in his *Ethics*, propound an ethics without politics which in fact subserves the worst politics. If violence is visible interference with the other, then it can be 'ethically' judged, without advertance to collective political purposes, questions of just distribution and so forth.

But where violence must be discriminated, there one has always a political dimension to the ethical. The aspect of violence, more obviously than the aspect of evil, concerns the realm of *visible* disturbance, and therefore the public, political realm. Evil is found in an occulted violence and so lies more within an 'interior', even if this private aspect is also, in the end, also political. But violence displays an apparent evil which seems to have the positivity of destruction, even though discrimination declares some of this 'destruction' not to be so, and furthermore decrypts real destruction as pathetically negative after all.

The 'evil' aspect, and its remedy, forgiveness, therefore are relatively ethical. But the 'violent' aspect and the *via crucis*, are relatively political, even though there is no true *ethics* without the *polis*, and no true *polis* without the idea of the Good. Not only is violence more visible, and in consequence more political than evil, it is also more political because here apparent violence must be collectively judged in terms of evil, whereas in the case of evil, an occulted 'private' evil (as negation) must be covertly exposed by the heroic individual operating in the back alleys of the night, as also violence.

As is well known, many apparently innocent visible processes – of the economy, of the bureaucracy, of information – are in fact violent. Inversely, many appearances of violence, such as the loud jangle of church bells, or the thrusting of a political demonstration upon people's attention, or the forceful closing down of a factory or an information network, are in fact peaceful. Both these statements are of course judgements: there is violence in one case and peace in another in relation to the justice of the ends pursued – *not* as extrinsic means, but as embryonic ends (this has nothing to do with ends justifying means). But this is the point: claims to see violence are always diagnostic, in relation to accounts of the political, collective Good; the apparently purely 'ethical' option of the Levinasians and advocates of radical evil (excepting Zizek here) only disguises the judgement they make in terms of their espousal of political and economic liberalism.

Therefore we need to supplement an account of forgiveness with an account of the *via crucis*. It has already been argued that forgiveness cannot be handled merely ontologically as an eternally immanent 'given' possibility, but is rather a possibility that has only arrived in history as the actuality of *an event*, which transforms the way things 'are'. This is the event of the Incarnation which revises finite ontology and more radically discloses that eternal *esse* was, from eternity, also a happening.

This event, as we also saw in the last chapter, concerns the advent of the sovereign victim. But so far we have explored this notion more according to its esoteric, ethical, 'private' and ontological aspect (concerning the relations of time to eternity). This must now be supplemented by an exploration of its exoteric, political, public and historical eventual aspect – remembering always that the ethical and the political are distinct only for our *modus cognoscendi*.

What should this exploration involve? Above all a double discrimination. First of all a discrimination of the violence undergone by Christ – in what *sense* was he subject to violence, if at all? Who was the violent agent here? What brought about his death?

Secondly, an echoing of the discrimination Christ himself performed. If he did suffer violence, then what political project was he positively negating, and what other political project was he positively recommending? ('Political' here extends beyond the notion of legitimated violence to that of the peaceful order of the *Civitas Dei*.) What did he see and thereby suffer as violence? What did he envisage instead as perpetual peace?

II

So why did Jesus die? The gospels present us with a very confusing and complex account. Jesus deliberately returned to Jerusalem, although he seems to have known that this was to court danger. He was 'betrayed' by one of his disciples, although it is unclear why this betrayal was necessary, nor in what it consisted. After his betrayal and seizure, he was, according to the synoptic accounts, arraigned before the Sanhedrin, who accused him of denouncing the temple, of disregarding the law and of claiming to be the Son of God. Then however, the high priest and elders handed Jesus over to Pilate, the Roman governor, asserting that he was a rebel who had set himself up as a king of the Jews against Caesar. Pilate subjected Jesus to enigmatic and ironic questioning, and, according to St Luke's gospel, in turn handed him over to Herod, the Greek king of Judea and Roman puppet. Herod could find him guilty of nothing and returned him to Pilate (Luke 23).

In an obscure decision, Pilate is then presented as having at once condemned Jesus to death in deference to the crowd's wish to release Barabbas rather than Jesus, and at the same time as having 'handed Jesus over' to the Jerusalem mob to do what they liked with: '. . . but Jesus he delivered up to their will. And as they led him away they seized on Simon of Cyrene . . .' (Luke 23: 25–6). Yet this 'doing what they like' took the form of appropriating the Roman judicial punishment of crucifixion: 'Pilate said to them, "Take him yourselves and crucify him, for I find no crime in him"' (John 19: 6). In Matthew's gospel, Pilate elaborately washes his hands before the crowd and declares 'I am innocent of this man's blood: see to it yourselves' before 'delivering' Jesus to be crucified (Matthew 27: 24–6). Even Mark's gospel says, ambiguously, that 'Pilate, wishing to satisfy the mob . . . delivered him to be crucified' (Mark 15: 15). Comparison with Matthew's version plausibly suggests that this means indeed that Pilate 'handed over' Jesus to the mob. Given this near unanimity, there is really no clear reason, as we shall further see below, to assume that the gospel writers merely invented the role of the crowd in order to exonerate the Romans. It is true that in Mark (15: 16) it is the soldiers not the crowd who lead Jesus away, but this does not render impossible a joint mob-military action, as Mark's 'deliver' may indicate. By now we should know that Mark's brevity is no necessary sign of greater historicity, and is as literary a matter as the other gospels' relative prolixity.

Who then really killed Jesus and why? And why did Jesus submit to this? The only consistent thread in these narratives is that Christ was constantly handed over, or abandoned to another party. Judas betrayed his presence; the disciples deserted him; the Sanhedrin gave him up to Pilate; Pilate in turn to Herod; Herod back to Pilate; Pilate again to the mob who finally gave him over to a Roman execution, which somehow, improperly, they co-opted. Even in his death, Jesus was still being handed back and forth, as if no one actually killed him, but he died from neglect and lack of his own living space.

Given this strange account, the overwhelming response of modern New Testament scholars is to doubt its veracity, to such a degree that little of the Passion narrative is now seen as plausibly historical. In this chapter, however, I want to suggest a perspective from which the very strangeness of the features I have mentioned may in fact present some warrant of verisimilitude (at the very least). But at the same time this new ground for historical plausibility casts light upon the universal significance of Christ's death, as claimed by the first Christians.

Why are the gospel accounts today viewed with so much scepticism? There are two main reasons, one critically respectable, the other less so. The first reason is that the events presented appear utterly *exceptional* and even implausible in the light of what we know from sources other than the gospels. Most striking is the fact that nowhere else do we read of the purported Passover custom whereby the governor of Judea offered to release a prisoner every year. There is no mention of this in Rabbinic sources, nor in Josephus, who was favourable to the Romans, and likely to have mentioned any instances of their mercy. Furthermore, all we know of Pilate independently of the gospels suggests that he was a tyrannical ruler, not given to making concessions. Scholars also wonder exactly how early Christians could have been privy to private proceedings that took place between Pilate and Jesus in the Praetorium.[1] A few of them have in addition questioned the plausibility of the proceeding before the Sanhedrin: would Jesus really be thought to have transgressed Jewish law? Did he qualify as a blasphemer, since blasphemy for the Jews at this time was pronunciation of the secret name of God? If the Sanhedrin condemned Jesus, then would not they have stoned him to death, since there is evidence that they still had the power, even under Roman jurisdiction, to carry out this sentence, and in some cases did in fact do so? Scholars (such as A.N. Sherwin-White) who defend the plausibility of the Sanhedrin's condemnations and handing-over to the Roman authorities, nonetheless almost universally reject the idea that the final executioner was the mob stirred up by the chief priests and elders.[2] The ground for this rejection is twofold: first of all the lack of evidence for the Passover amnesty as already mentioned; secondly, the fact that Jesus died a Roman judicial death, which renders Pilate's real and metaphorical handwashing either implausible or else more insincere than the gospels seem to allow.

So the first reason for scepticism finds the events of the Passion to be so unusual as to render them most probably, in the main, ahistorical. However, if writers have embellished what is clearly intended (as scholars still allow) to be a historical account, then one must ask why? This is also a historical question. The main answer today given is that the four evangelists, writing at a time when the Christian community had become clearly separate from the Jewish one and wished to find an undisturbed place for itself within the Roman empire, desired to downplay the Roman involvement in the death of Jesus, and exaggerate the involvement of the Jewish authorities. The implication of this view is that Jesus was indeed seen as a dangerous political agitator by the Romans, and was executed as such; not, indeed, as the leader of a zealot party – else why should the disciples not have been arrested also? – but certainly as a potential focus of popular dissent either from Rome, or else from the established Jewish authorities, which for Rome could be almost equally inconvenient.[3] Or, of course, from both authorities. It is notable that in St John's gospel the high priest Caiaphas is presented as fearing that Jesus could become just such a focus, and eventually incite a terrible Roman reaction (John 18: 14).

The second reason for scepticism concerning the Passion narratives also concerns the issue of false attribution of blame to the Jews, but is much more driven by a presumption that the early Christians were anti-Semitic, and that any continued attribution of responsibility for Jesus's death to any Jews in Jerusalem at this time is a perpetuation of such an attitude. In particular, any taking-seriously of the role of the mob is seen as politically reprehensible.[4] However, even if one profoundly sympathizes with the underlying motivations for this attitude, there is no logic in any automatic presumption of anti-Semitism as constitutive of Christianity as such, and still less logic in the view that segments of a people too often victims cannot in certain instances have been themselves the persecutors. Therefore we are returned to the first reason for scepticism: the sheer atypicality of the events which the gospels narrate.

It is possible, I think, to whittle away the plausibility of this first reason, before stating my positive reason for believing what the gospels tell us. There is, first of all, a general methodological point to be made, and secondly, a series of considerations about details. The general point is that arguing against exceptions primarily as exceptions is a highly dubious historiographical procedure. It is only resorted to when there is a significant lack of confirmation that an event did in fact occur. For in point of fact, well-attested and yet extraordinary and unpredictable events do occur: as I first wrote this chapter I was just receiving news that the World Trade Centre in New York and a part of the Pentagon in Washington had been destroyed by hijacked aircraft. The immediate aftermath of this event illustrates the truth that we are often far more certain that something has happened, than *why* it has happened. The surprisingness and often inexplicability of precisely the most *outstanding* events renders them the most typical events – since an event, to be recordable, and so to be an event, must to some degree be an exception to 'the normal course of events', for which in reality only 'the course' (the instance of a particular culture, etc.) is really an 'event' in human history. This constitutive exceptionality of the event means that the most event-like events are necessarily surprising and very often inexplicable, since they exceed the normal expectations of causality. Indeed one can go further: given the complexity of human reasoning, human lack of reason and the contagion of mass behaviour, it may be true to say that the biggest events – those that most shape our experience and understanding – occur literally *without* sufficient causation. Causal explanation of, for example, the First World War, runs the danger of seeing it as, with hindsight, an inevitable event. In reality it is much more plausibly seen in Tolstoyan terms as arriving according to the gathering pace of its own mad momentum. There were preceding occasions, for this as for other greatest and most event-like events, but no causes in the strict sense.[5]

Of course, where events are insufficiently well-attested, then the problem is not simply one about cause and occasion, but a fuller reconstruction both of what took place, and of what led up to this taking-place. In the absence of much evidence, one has to resort to what is known in general about the circumstances in which the events are alleged to have taken place, in order to establish analogies and plausibilities and so forth. Nevertheless, one should only do so in a tentative spirit, and should try to discriminate between more-or-less possible exceptions on the one hand, and more-or-less-impossible exceptions on the other, while remembering that this exercise is itself more impossible than possible, given the foregoing methodological caution regarding the exceptional character of all events as such.

This caution is especially pertinent in the case of the gospels; one could argue that here it is most of all pertinent. For the gospels themselves assume that the events they are describing are unique and remarkable, even that they are the most exceptional and singular events that have ever occurred. In addition, they are also held to be the most important and the most meaningful; so much so that they are now to be regarded as the frame of reference within which everything else is to be understood. So here we have a purported hyperbolic instance of an event which is so exceptional and singular that it vastly exceeds as effect its own occasioning causes: just as Mary's fiat allowed but did not cause the Incarnation – not even in any degree (given that she could do nothing *in addition* to God) and John the Baptist's baptizing of Jesus allowed but did not cause the first hypostatic descent of the Holy Spirit at 'the down-rusher's ford' (the expression is David Jones's in his *Anathemata*). There can be no question that hyperbolic, uncaused events do occur, nor can one rule out *a priori* the possibility of a supreme instance of such an event, which renders all other events only instances within its own down-rushing course.

The claim that such a supreme instance has arrived in actuality and therefore belongs to real (not merely logical) possibility is an aspect of the claim that God has become incarnate. It follows, in consequence, that liberal criticism of the Bible is in double methodological peril; not only does it tend to rule out as historical what is different and unprecedented, it also can only contest orthodoxy by begging the very question that is at issue between itself and orthodoxy: namely, did Christ constitute an absolutely unique exception? The very 'evidence' which orthodoxy can cite for this claim, although it is indeed without genuine evidential warrant in a strict scientific sense, is seen by liberalism as evidence against the claim, but equally without genuine evidential warrant. (Of course liberal criticism veers also into the opposite error, when it dismisses any gospel event described in terms of typological repetition as *deficient* in the exceptionality that guarantees real historicity – here one makes the opposite methodological rejoinder: no *entirely* unique event can register with human beings.)

Even if one were to set aside the claims of orthodoxy to recognize in the life of Christ a hyperbolic and final event (announcing already the end of history), one would still be left with undeniable evidential warrant for the instance of an event in the strong sense of something unique and unprecedented. Without question, the gospels constitute, if not the record, then at least some sort of trace of the arrival of, an in many respects entirely new sort of religious institution, practice and belief. The danger, then, for liberal criticism, if it loses its sense of discriminatory balance, is that it will so disallow all that is exceptional in the gospel narratives that it will merely have postponed the problem of manifest exception for the consideration of the historical fact of the Church, and in such a way that the Christocentric aspect of this phenomenon will have to be implausibly played down or evaded – a mistake which is as great as trying to conceive of a Christ-event which prescinds from the always-already given presence of the reception of Christ by the Church, beginning with Mary and the disciples. (Here also the issue arises of why one should treat Josephus and rabbinic texts as independent background sources, and not accord the gospels the same status; is this to privilege official and established literature over insurrectionary and emergent voices?)

So much, then, for the first, general methodological point. As for the details, the objections cited are perhaps less convincing than is usually imagined. Regarding Pilate's known character, bread and circuses were proverbially never adverse to Roman tyranny, and the idea that a cruel and non-concessionary ruler would never have been obliged to let the populace have their way in certain circumstances is simply naive. As to conversations that could not have been overheard, there is simply no way of knowing what may or may not have leaked out of the Praetorium, but the main point is that one must allow for ancient historiographical conventions of reconstructed dialogue which by no means betray a cavalier disrespect for historicity. With respect to Jesus's infringements of Jewish law, certainly some but not others of the pharisees at the time would have objected to things like Sabbath-breaking; from Philo we know that blasphemy could be extended to any impious invocation of God; it is *not* the case that calling oneself 'Son of God' or 'Messiah', or invoking the coming of the 'Son of Man' were never seen as blasphemous – it depended on context and fortune. Certainly Jesus's metaphorical threats to the temple might have been taken non-figuratively and regarded gravely.[6] One can also imagine that if Jesus claimed to be *the* Son of God identifying himself with a pre-existent emanation of divinity like wisdom or the eternal law or the *Logos* (and we have no real grounds to doubt this, outside the bias against exception) this extraordinary claim would have met with ordinary judicial hostility.

When it comes to the executive powers of the Sanhedrin, then the scholarly consensus now is that they did not enjoy undisputed and autonomous powers to put to death; instances where they did fell during vacancies in the procuratorship and otherwise (as Simon Légasse notes) Josephus records two cases where, indeed, the Sanhedrin tried to get self-appointed prophets executed by Rome for essentially Jewish offences – one of them another man named Jesus. Sherwin-White explained how, as wielder of *imperium*, Pilate would have been able to try the crimes of non-Roman citizens by a process of personal *cognitio* that was *exceptional* to the regular *ordo iudiciorum publicorum*, without jury-courts or specific criminal laws and with absolute personal licence as to the punishments that could be meted out. (This process was significantly only allowed at the margins of empire; it was not permitted at the centre even for the Emperor himself – revealing the paradox that the optimum arbitrary power of the centre only appears at the boundary.) Nevertheless, both the presence of accusers and the answering of a charge were normally demanded: Pilate's demurral and then deferral to the Sanhedrin in the face of Jesus's silence is highly plausible. Yet if *cognitio extra ordinem* could easily extend by fiat to the recognition of alien religious and other charges in the interests of good order and appeasement, it does not seem to have been the case that it allowed powers of sovereign (rather than mandated) sentencing and capital execution themselves to be alienated. 'Pliny', says Sherwin-White, 'did not understand the charges against the Christians in Pontius, but he condemned them to a Roman execution without hesitation.'[7] It is then broadly agreed that there is little reason to doubt at least *this* 'handing-over' procedure.

This still leaves us with the problem of the Passover amnesty. Before discussing this, however, let us consider briefly the historical explanation given for the evangelists purported falsification of history. Is it really plausible? Certainly it is highly speculative, because we do not really know whether the synoptic gospels were written by Christians with a clear and distinct sense of their separation from Jewry. In addition, even John's gospel, let alone the synoptics, still attributes a great deal of blame to Pilate, and indeed presents him as cynical, sceptical, vacillating and submissive to the mob, rather than as tolerant and concessionary. (The gospel writers fall well short of the later occasional elevation of Pilate to a *figura* of the Church, and in the Coptic case, to sainthood.) If Rome was to be exonerated, could not the job have done better? One can protest here that the gospel writers could not evade the undeniable fact of a Roman execution, but there remains their superfluous presentation of Pilate as uncertain (especially in Luke), as cruelly playful (especially in John) and as a witness to the truth merely despite himself. (By contrast, the apocryphal *Report of Pilate the Procurator Concerning our Lord Jesus Christ*, and other similar fragments, presents Pilate as writing to Tiberius Caesar concerning the positive evidence of Jesus's astonishing powers.) Most of all it is striking that no attempt was made to present Pilate as indeed simply acceding to the Sanhedrin's wishes, even though the idea that Christ died under the Jewish law is expressed within Pauline theology and is semi-implied by the gospels themselves. Notably, the gospel writers do *not* present the Romans as executors of a Jewish sovereign will, and in this respect they accord with what we know of circumstances in the technically 'unfree' city of Jerusalem under the Roman jurisdiction.

If the evidence of a desire to exonerate Rome is after all not so clear, then what of the evidence for anti-Semitism? Again it is far weaker than usually claimed. Certainly John's gospel speaks of 'the Jews' in general as an actor, but this may reflect only the distance from Jewry of a Hellenistic or Hellenized Christian community. But even if the anti-Semitism of John's gospel is allowed, no general case is thereby established, since the synoptics report basically the same structural feature of the Passion proceedings – that is to say, a handing-over by accusing Jewish authorities to the Romans, and a later semi-handing-over by Pilate to the mob. A recent study by Jon A. Wetherby of the attitude of Luke-Acts towards the Jews concludes that there is no evidence of anti-Semitism, and that these books specifically make the leaders and people *in Jerusalem* in part responsible for Jesus's death and certainly not the Jews as a whole.[8] Indeed Luke (if it is he) in Acts is careful to record the defence of Paul by some Pharisaic scribes (Acts 23: 9). Wetherby also notes that Luke is, amongst the gospel writers, especially concerned to portion out the guilt also to Pilate, Herod (a non-Jew) and the Roman soldiers. What Luke stresses is the division of Israel with regard to Jesus, just as in Acts he stressed the division of the whole of the known world. Of course the idea that all nations are complicit in the death of Jesus, just as this very event brings all nations together (Acts 2) is in Luke a theological theme, but this does not prove that it is not also a meditation upon the actual course of events. As to his recording in Acts of repeated Roman defences of Paul against some Jewish elements, since Paul was a Roman citizen and the case in question would have been seen by the Romans as a Jewish sectarian dispute, there is little reason to ascribe this repetition to theological motives *rather* than the protractedness of the proceedings which Paul really underwent.

One can conclude that if Luke evinces no especial drive to blame the Jews, nor any in exonerating the Romans (which is unlikely, given his evident concern for the distressed and marginalized), then the shared structural features of the Passion procedure cannot really be accounted for by ideological motivations. In that case, at the very least, we cannot be so sure that the Passover amnesty is a typological construct based, for example, on the freeing of Jehoiachin in II Kings and Jeremiah, or written as a fictional fulfilment of Isaiah 53's prophecy concerning the suffering servant taking the punishment of the criminal upon himself. Even sceptical critics allow that 'Barabbas' is not an invented name, and that his release, if not under a regular amnesty, and not as a result of a plebiscitory choice, may well have occurred.[9]

These positions are adopted by Simon Légasse in the most recent and extensive book-length treatment of the trial of Jesus, portions of which have been translated by John Bowden for SCM Press. Much of what I have contended up till now is not so far removed from what Légasse is prepared to accept. However, along with the general consensus, he denies the historical plausibility of the Passover amnesty, the large role of the mob, and the dispensing with responsibility by Pilate. In doing so he considers the 1985 work of the Belgian classicist Jean Colin, entitled *Les Villes Libres de L'Orient Greco-Romain et L'Envoi du Supplice par Acclamations Populaires*.[10] Unusually, Colin defended the crucial role of the mob in the Passion narrative. He showed that in the 'free cities' of the Oriental empire, the Romans dealt with the fierce Greek sense of legal autonomy by a practice known as *epiboesis*, whereby people could be condemned and executed by popular vote and acclamation (including instances of preference between two people accused). He cites the later example of the Christian Attale of Pergamon, who, although a Roman citizen, was thrown to the beasts in the arena by the Roman governor to be 'agreeable to the multitude'.[11] Colin suggested that precisely *epiboesis* was resorted to the case of Jesus. Légasse, however, summing up the general consensus of the New Testament academic guild's reaction to this book, declares Colin's appeal to the Greco-Oriental rather than to the Jewish or Roman world to be irrelevant. He points out the obvious: Jerusalem was not a free city, and there is absolutely no evidence of this legal usage being deployed by Palestine. Naturally though, Colin knew this, and Légasse does not discuss the case he made out in its despite.

This was as follows: Pilate is known to have been in Caesarea, a free city, where he could have become acquainted with the practice; Herod must certainly have known of the practice from the Decapolis, the ring of free cities surrounding Galilee, where Herod held sway. Colin suggests that we take seriously Luke's gospel's presentation of Pilate as being at his wit's end when faced with Jesus; in such a state he might have resorted to an alien practice that was nonetheless countenanced within the *imperium*. Perhaps he thought of the idea himself; more plausibly, suggests Colin, it was suggested to him by the Greek Herod during the episode, recorded only by Luke, when Jesus is shuttled to and fro between the two Roman jurisdictions. Here it is notable that Pilate first hands Jesus over to Herod because he realizes that Jesus is a Galilean. Alternatively, one might claim that Luke – from the free city Antioch – fabricated the whole episode from his experience. This conclusion, however, conflicts with the structural consonance of the four gospel accounts, and the generally accepted historical secondariness of the Lukan version.

Once again, therefore, the issue concerns the question of an *exception*. In the face of the problems raised by Jesus's exceptionality, did Pilate resort to a locally exceptional legal procedure? It seems that one can only conclude that Colin's solution is not impossible, and perhaps more plausible than the now orthodox ones. As to the question of the supposed Passover custom of amnesty, it is perhaps significant that Luke *does* not mention a custom, which would be consistent with the notion that this release of Barabbas was *also* an exception; taken along with the Herod episode, this may imply that Luke's account is the most accurate one. (Nonetheless, given the paucity of available evidence, the silence of Josephus, Philo and rabbinic sources concerning the amnesty custom is not really conclusive, and one has no real warrant to doubt the witness of the other gospels.)

Another peculiarity of the Lukan account is the absence of the crowd welcoming Jesus into Jerusalem on Palm Sunday: at Luke 19: 36 it is *the disciples* who spread their garments. This might appear to betoken a Lukan *bias* against the mob, which would compromise his witness. However, Luke equally and inversely is unique in his recording of support for Jesus by 'a great multitude of the people' *after* he had been condemned by the mob, and they had led him away (Luke 23: 27). So here again Luke is the most notably even-handed of the gospel writers, perhaps out of historical fairness as well as symbolic appropriateness. According to him, a large number of people condemned Jesus *and* a large number of people wept for him.

This may seem to be all that one can really say on this topic. However, there is a way of going further, of increasing the plausibility of Colin's solution by showing that precisely *exceptionality* was paradoxically typical of Roman rule in general.

III

Although *epiboesis* was confined to the Eastern empire, a somewhat parallel phenomenon was recorded in the case of Rome itself and Roman law in general by Pompeius Festus, the late antique grammarian. In his treatise *On the Significance of Words*,[12] he tells us that, after the secession of the plebs in Rome, it was granted to the plebeians to have the right to pursue to the death (singly or collectively it is implied) someone whom they have as a body condemned. Such an individual was declared *homo sacer*, and his irregular death was not exactly homicide, nor punishment, nor sacrifice, since unlike regular capital punishment, it had to be carried out without purification rites. Such a person was *sacer*, simply in the sense of cast out, utterly abandoned, a sense of the word which may be more ancient than the connotation 'sacred', deriving from the specific sending forth which is sacrifice. This is the conclusion of the Italian philosopher and scholar of late antique philology Giorgio Agamben, in his recently translated book, itself entitled *Homo Sacer*.[13]

Agamben argues that there are isomorphic parallels between the recorded *homo sacer* procedure and other Roman practices: first of all, the *patria potestas*, or absolute right of the Roman father over the life and death of his son. One should note here that the law described by Deuteronomy 21: 18–21 presents a certain analogy to the *patria potestas*: here a drunken and gluttonous son who habitually disobeys his father and mother is to be handed over by both parents to the elders at the gate of the city, who in turn hand him over to all the men of the city to be stoned outside the gate. This exceptional action is deemed to be purgative in its effect; though whether it was ever actually effected is debatable. Nevertheless, such a concept may have provided a kind of residual background for a fusion of cultural horizons in terms of the kind of enacted exception which (I shall further argue below) was the death of Jesus.

The second parallel claimed by Agamben is the 'devotion' of oneself and one's enemies to a sacrificial death offered to the gods of the underworld in battle. If these enemies were not killed, then simulacra of them had to be offered instead, while the dedicated enemies from thenceforwards occupied a kind of ontological no-man's land, having no place amongst either the living or the dead. A similar thing was true, Agamben argues, of a dying Roman emperor, whose real life was also transferred to a simulacrum, ensuring the fiction of uninterrupted sovereignty. Here again, there are certain Israelite parallels, which could have formed the basis for a hermeneutic fusion. Robertson Smith noted (and in this case Agamben notes also) that the Old Testament speaks of a dedication (*herem*) unto utter destruction, and avoidance on pain of death (that is, contagion of such dedication) of a person, place or thing so dedicated or 'anathematized' (Micah 4: 13: 'You shall beat in pieces many people, and devote their gain to the Lord').[14]

Of all these parallels, the closest and most crucial is the *patria potestas*. For this power was absolute: to kill a son was to kill what naturally belonged to you – it was not murder, nor execution, nor sacrifice. And upon this mythical and real foundation, Roman notions of political sovereignty, unlike those of ancient Greece, were themselves founded.

Agamben characterizes all these legal instances, and especially *homo sacer* itself, in terms of the notion of exception. Here, normal legality is suspended: someone is reduced to bare life, to sub-humanity, and can be killed indifferently, yet not murdered, sacrificed nor executed, since the Roman power is *indifferent* to merely plebeian judicial decision. From certain parallels with *patria potestas* however, Agamben argues that the exception is the secret foundation of Roman authority. What establishes legality is the power of authority to break its own law, and sometimes to abandon those whom it is normally self-bound to protect. At bottom, as Augustine realized, in Roman logic legality is the self-bestowal of normativity by the *de facto* possessor of power. This means that at the limit, naked power will keep reasserting itself, and even the citizen must be (never mind the sub-citizen) by definition as a citizen, reducible to sub-human, natural, quasi-animal status, in such a way that he can be hunted down like a werewolf. For Agamben therefore (here invoking both Carl Schmitt and Alain Badiou), *homo sacer* is to be correlated with the aporetic structure of sovereignty as such: it works by including only what is simultaneously excluded, namely illegal exceptionality. And one can add to Agamben here a second *aporia*, which applies not only to sovereign will, but to will as such: for a will to be effective, something other than will must carry out the will's order – if my hand will not move, I cannot throw. So for political will to be effective, someone else must always perform the sovereign's will – every sovereign needs an executive. Yet this executive is unavoidably other, and therefore always a potential rival sovereign power in itself; in addition its difference from sovereignty must be one of interpretation and delegation, as well as execution, so it is also necessarily a partially actual lesser sovereignty. In this way the 'handing over' to the plebs involved in *homo sacer* belongs to any logic of a single sovereign centre. Such a centre, by its very claim to singleness, is doomed to duality.

One detail of Agamben's analysis can, however, be called into question from his own evidence. Is it so clear that *homo sacer* is not offered as a sacrifice? All that is certain is that he was to be killed without ritual purification – but this is still consistent with a total offering, as indeed the Israelite examples attest: totally unclean towns were to be offered to Yahweh. Agamben himself at one point says that the *homo sacer* was delivered over to chthonic gods.[15] Perhaps the difference from more ritualized expulsions concerned precisely a degree of impurity, or else, to the contrary, official indifference one way or the other. In either case, total absence of ritual still belongs to ritual, especially as the event was to take place within certain circumstances and therefore was brought within regularity, yet not within a punitive response to officially criminal irregularity. It would also follow that to 'sacralize' in the mode of expulsion might always have had sacrificial connotations. Certainly one should not confuse all banishing, including scapegoating, with vertical sacrifice (after the tendency of René Girard); nonetheless, a horizontal banishing could often be construed as a sending downwards and occasionally as a sending upwards.

IV

So now the inevitable question: was Jesus a *homo sacer*? Not most probably, in any consciously identified way, but possibly in a way conforming to the deep structure of Roman law which Agamben diagnoses. For this structure, the exception proves the rule; the exception is the ultimate paradoxical basis of order, always liable to erupt. When it does so, it re-enacts the foundational banishment – and Agamben notes that in Greece, as in other ancient legalities, the ban was the oldest form of punishment and of community self-definition and regulation.[16] Thus it would follow that liberal Biblical criticism is doubly guilty of *petitio principii*: once, because it assumes the non-verisimilitude of exception with respect to Christ, when this is the very thing at issue; and twice because it does the same thing with Roman law, when again the role of exception is what needs to be debated. And in the second case it is up against a certain amount of hard evidence and not simply faith.

Jesus is certainly presented by the gospels in a way that conforms with *homo sacer*. In fact he is presented as *homo sacer* three times over. Once, because he is abandoned by Jewish sovereignty to the Roman executive. Twice, because he is abandoned by Roman sovereignty to the sovereign-executive mob; three times (at least according to Luke and John), because he is in some obscure fashion handed over by the mob to the Roman soldiers and executed after all in a Roman fashion. But did he really and exactly undergo Roman execution? It is much more as if the mob were allowed to lynch him after the fashion of a Roman execution, and to place him among those truly executed according to the sovereign but exceptional power of *cognitio*. In like fashion, Jesus was only addressed and arraigned in mock fashion as King of the Jews by Pilate, but on the cross named really King of the Jews, as if (without a simulacrum) Jewish rule were thereby really destroyed. Again, was Jesus really condemned by Jewish law, or did the Sanhedrin altogether substitute for this condemnation the accusation that he had offended Caesar? But then the Romans sarcastically rejected this, and, apparently accorded plebiscitory authority to the mob. Yet by a final twist, it seems as if the mob enjoyed no real delegated executive power, as in the instance of *homo sacer*. Instead, Jesus was crucified only virtually, even though this really killed him; for neither Jewish nor Roman law had succeeded in condemning him. (The reader will recall from Chapter 2 that real violence always *is* ritual violence, a gaze upon abandonment.) Only the mob did this – *they* became in effect the sovereign power (under instigation from the priests and elders) and the Romans in a certain sense their irregular executive. But in this way sovereign power and plebiscitory delegation were uniquely collapsed into each other. The necessary exception of mob lynching coincided precisely with regular execution. Accordingly, one could argue that the Cross exposed the structure of arbitrary sovereign power in its ultimate exceptional yet typical instance (Matthew 26–27; Mark 14–15; Luke 22–23; John 18–19). This is its act of discernment of the worst human violence.

Did the gospel writers really fabricate these features (as most New Testament critics now think)? If so, then how did they alight upon a narrative which makes such sense in terms of the structures of Roman law and the interactions between incompatible, yet forcibly supplementary, Roman and Jewish jurisdictions? There seem to be good reasons at least to suspend one's doubts.

6

ATONEMENT

Christ the exception

I

Even were one unable to accept my arguments for the historicity of the Passion narratives in the previous chapter, one would still have to take seriously the surface structure of the texts, and their implications for the inter- actions of *ecclesia* with *imperium*. Does that mean that these arguments are only an interesting curiosity as far as theology is concerned? No, for two reasons.

First of all, even in the case of mythical and fictional thought, meanings and events are normally inseparable. There are no events outside the assign- ment of meanings, and there are no construable meanings not ultimately including some reference to an active rearrangement of things in time. The salt passes after I have asked for the salt to be passed: it is a mineral, but also a condiment, subject to meaningful convention. The situations where one deliberately drains events of meaning in order to confront their strangeness, as in physical or even historical science, or inversely one abstracts events from the normal course of events through mimicry in order to heighten meaning, as in drama, are clearly secondary and parasitic. Thus in the case of new legends, ideologies and fictions, one legitimately asks after the real occasions that have helped to give rise to such novel configurations of sense.

Secondly, there is the question of genre. Despite the normativity of a coincidence of meaning and action, there is always also a perceived interval which allows both science and drama to emerge: I know the salt lay for countless ages in fathoms indifferent to humanity; I know that it is the subject also of superstition and metaphor. So do the gospels ally their narrations more to the side of science or of drama? – given that all human language must ultimately partake of both, event and meaning being originally insep- arable. The simple answer 'drama' entirely misses the point of the specific drama which the gospels restage. For the entire content of *this unique* drama is the presentation of a situation in which, for the first time, there is no interval whatsoever between meaning and action. What they seek to present is the *Logos* become flesh: a situation in which the surplus of fictional and metaphoric meaning is here *none other* than the surplus of unknown

94

consistency and causation. None of Jesus's imaginings are ineffectual, unlike ours; none of his actions lack an infinite depth of meaning. There is no possibility that the consistency and causes of his actions might be meaning-less for humanity, since the depth of Jesus is God, the eminent locus of meaning and exemplar for our humanity. Even though Jesus in his humanity necessarily followed human examples, in his divine personhood, which means his ultimate singularity of character, he was without example, and imbued his human mimesis with an absolutely original creative power able to hold together without any interval between sense and occurrence.[1]

It follows that every claim that the gospels are 'merely legendary' must ironically rebound. For it entirely begs the claim of the gospels to present an absolutely exceptional phenomenon. Normally, a suggestion of fictive drama must count against scientific and historical accuracy, but if (although only if) the gospels' presentation of 'Incarnation' is successful, then here alone, where fictionality abounds, historicity must all the more abound. Of course the reverse equally applies.[2]

The implication of this unique state of affairs is that the gospel is immune to an idealist reading. Its meaning *is* that meaning has sloughed off its fallen impotence and is now fully actual and effective. If Christ be not raised, then our faith is in vain, because the new meanings offered in Christ only have significance (unlike all other meanings) if they are entirely effective. They must have arisen originally as events, indeed as hyper-events that more truly occurred than any other occurrences, else they would have no power now to be effective and to generate the event of reconciliation.

So theologically speaking, given the second reason, the broad accuracy of the gospels with respect to the Passion narratives is not dispensable. But given the first reason, even a secular outlook, besides a theological one, has to be concerned with the active occasioning of new significance. *Something* must have occurred to create a new exposure of the violence and terror latent in given social and political structures, and to give rise to a new social alternative. I have already tried to show that the alternative 'somethings' of New Testament critics are not adequate to the scale of the new irruption, unlike the gospels' own understandings of what this something was.

So let us ask again about the implications of the surface structure of the texts for the interaction of *ecclesia* with *imperium*, given that, theologically speaking, these surfaces must be understood as immediately conveying (without the usual interval of suspension of assent) the full depth of actual occurrence.

II

What are these implications? First of all, that Christ, the God-Man, died precisely a purely divine and a purely human, or even sub-human, death. He did not die the death of a martyr, as a witness for a universal cause, although later martyrs have died in cause of *him*. For his 'infringements' of the law were not such for many Jews; his apocalyptic prophecies were misunderstood; all that was comprehended and denied was his claim to be God. Herein lies nothing typical, nor inevitable. Two of the synoptic gospels declare that the high priests (Mark 15: 10) and the people (Matthew 27: 18) resented Jesus – they envied him his unique status, his absolute unreachability, his absolute height beyond height. No creature is in principle unreachable; hence God alone inspires ontological envy. All real envy is of God, and Jesus was envied because he was God in the flesh. The people screamed out their resentment to Pilate. It is true that it is only Matthew who appears to suggest that the crowd caught the contagion of envy from the high priests and elders. And perhaps to the contrary they warned the crowd that Jesus would destroy the temple, and it was this fear, and not resentment, which moved them. However, Jesus's subversiveness with regard to the law and the temple economy had been visibly demonstrated and Jesus had at first been welcomed by the people to Jerusalem. If the people now viewed themselves as protectors of the temple, then they shared a posture with the high priests and elders which both Mark and Matthew diagnose as in the latter case being but a cover for envy (since Jesus clearly was protecting the temple's integrity and was not out to destroy it). If supposed defence of the temple was a self-deceit for the high priests and elders, then it would logically be a self-deceit for the people also. Jesus was truly hated for his awesome elevation.

Nevertheless, Jesus did not die only a divine death. He also died the most sheerly human death – or a kenotic death of utterly emptied-out humanity. For he was not Socrates, dying for the truth: jesting Pilate denied him this dignity. Even if the gospels ironically know that Jesus did die for the truth since he was the truth, there is no clear question of truth being publicly displayed here; neither can the disciples see why Jesus has to die. Nor was he seen as leader of a party, since his disciples were ignored. Indeed the first handing-over by Judas seems to have been required because Jesus was seen as belonging only to this private group, within which alone he had influence, and to which alone one had to resort, in order to know about him. No, in the end, he died at what was possibly the whim of a drunken mob. To try to give Jesus a dignified death, like that of St Thomas More, is to miss the point: in his death, Jesus entered into absolute solidarity with each and every one of us. He died the death which any of us, under sovereign authority, in exceptional circumstances which always prove the rule, may possibly die. He died as three times excluded: by the Jewish law of its tribal nation; by the Roman universal law of empire; by the democratic will of the mob. In the whole summed-up history of human polity – the tribe, the universal absolute state, the democratic consensus – God found no place. He was shuttled back and forwards, with an undercurrent of indifference, as though not really dangerous, between their respective rules. He became *homo sacer*, cast outside the camp, abandoned on all sides, so that in the end he died almost accidentally. He died the death of all of us – since he died the death that proves and exemplifies sovereignty in its arbitrariness.

In this respect, it is ironically only by disallowing an anti-Semitic bias to the gospels (which is supposed to account for the story about the mob) that one can directly relate the death of Jesus to the death of those who died in the Holocaust. For Agamben points out that the Holocaust victims became in a sense *homo sacer* – killed in a way that was characterized neither as murder nor execution nor indeed – now for certain – sacrifice (despite the misnomer 'Holocaust'). Jesus imbued with his divine height precisely the death of absolute innocence, the death of the outcast, of people reduced beneath humanity into half-animality. Moreover, Agamben rightly warns us not to be sanguine about the end of totalitarianism, because the line between totalitarianism and liberal democracy is not after all so distinct. The liberal notion of natural rights guaranteed by a sovereign state itself plays directly into a first constitutive *aporia* of sovereignty. If these rights are 'natural' (and follow from certain given facts regarded as prior to valuation) as if they belonged to an animal, yet are only operative and recognized – and therefore existent – within the State, then the State assumes to itself a power over nature, a right even to define nature, and indeed defines itself by this power, and therefore secretly reserves to itself alone a supreme *de facto* right of pure nature prior to contract, by which in exceptional circumstances it may withdraw any right whatsoever. If you accord people 'human rights' by nature, it means (as Alain Badiou argues in his *Ethics*), that you already envisage people *primarily* as passive if freely wandering animals, who *might* be victimized: the ban actually creates the space for its own violation, just as St Paul saw was the case with all law outside the counter-law of charity. Agamben cites instances of reduction to half-life by liberal democracies and especially the United States: dangerous experiments upon prisoners condemned to death; drug testing in the third world; the dubious treatment of brain-dead organ donors – and one could of course add experiments upon foetuses and late abortion which is but disguised infanticide. Recently we have had instances of American politicians declaring that Taliban prisoners or suspected terrorists enjoy *neither* the rights of criminals *nor* the rights of prisoners of war. They have therefore become *homo sacer*, denied contradictorily *as* humans (since we would not really treat animals like this) any humanity whatsoever, and any mark of the *imago dei*.

Christ then, in Agamben's terms, was reduced to this bare life. Agamben struggles nobly but perhaps futilely to imagine an escape from the *aporias* of sovereignty. He suggests that we exit this structure which seems to encompass humanity as such, and instead identify with the outcast position of abandonment. Yet Agamben also seems to believe that the aporetic constitution of sovereignty is echoed at the ontological level: Being, like sovereignty, is itself nothing save through its inclusion of beings, whose contingency it must of course also exclude from itself as Being as such – as the reality that there is Being at all, whose secret every particular being assumes but can never disclose. Therefore beings, for Agamben following Heidegger, are abandoned by the Being that discloses them, and in this sense are in a condition like that of *homo sacer*.[3]

But in that case, one may well ask, just what is the point of identifying oneself with bare life in order to escape earthly sovereignty, only to fall into the hands of cosmic tyranny? Is not the latter bound always to reincarnate itself politically? And why do we still accept the metaphysical projections of semi-Nazi ideologues like Heidegger and Schmitt, however brilliant? And however much we can learn from their philosophies concerning the ways in which Nazism and Fascism were unfortunately rooted in aspects of the Western legacy?

Here it is notable that Agamben does seem to elide the Christian Middle Ages from his purview. Even the presentation of Roman law seems somewhat exaggerated, since however much the *patria potestas* operated as a reserved foundation, Roman rulers were also bound by customary and co-operative limitations upon their powers. True, unlimited sovereignty is rather a modern doctrine, developed by Bodin and Hobbes, which assumes a metaphysical background unknown to Rome of an infinite God, defined mainly by an unlimited will. Yet this new political theology – of which Carl Schmitt was the ultimate (one might vainly hope) legatee, was itself erected within the ruins of a Christocentric understanding of politics and sociality.

This understanding maintained consistency with the New Testament itself. What are the main features of the New Testament's understanding of our solidarity with Christ, the God abandoned as *homo sacer* upon the Cross?

III

First of all, the main stress is that, upon the basis of the rejected one, a new sort of community is to be built. But this is only possible because the rejected one is, bizarrely, also the most envied, unrepeatable one. If abandonment is the last word, then, as with Agamben, there is no real hope. Mere identification with a victim as victim confirms victimhood and diminishes us all. But Christ was never merely abandoned, even for a single instance. Even though all his friends deserted him in the garden of Gethsemane and he suffered thereby the worst extremity of human agony, he still did not endure ontological desertion. The cry of dereliction upon the cross recorded by Matthew and Mark (Matthew 27: 46; Mark 15: 34) involves no abandonment by the Father, but rather Jesus's deepest entering into the self-separation of sinful humanity from God: hence it is to God, not the Father ('My God, my God . . .') that Jesus as Son in his humanity cries out. When, by contrast, Jesus in his divine nature speaks as the Son to the Father, it is a question of serene deliverance in contrast to the cruel human handings over: 'Father, into thy hands I commit my Spirit!' (Luke 23: 46).

(I owe this point to David Hart. Yet one must also mention here that Luke does admittedly present a uniquely stoical dispassionate Jesus, and that Christ's 'bloody sweat' in Gethsemane, recorded only by Luke (22: 44), is not found in some early manuscripts and therefore is very likely an interpolation. Perhaps Luke had a semi-docetic worry about ascribing suffering to Jesus, and perhaps this was later detected by the redactor – though one can scarcely be sure. But this does not effect Hart's point about the exactly 'Chalcedonian' use of terminology by the gospel writers: Luke's serene commending to the Father is scarcely inimical to the spirit of the other writers, while it remains notable that they locate the anguished alienation as lying between manhood and Godhead, not between Son and Father.)

Christ failed to resist human power and went freely to his death because he knew that a merely human counter-power is always futile and temporary. But he also went to his death, and therefore was innocent of suicide (and perhaps only innocent for this reason) in trust of his return, his resurrection. Hence the New Testament does not speak of Jesus's death as a sacrifice in the rabbinic sense of a death atoning for sins, nor as something lost to earth to compensate for what we have taken from God. Nothing can be taken from the impassable God, and nothing can be added to his sum. This is why John's gospel is always ironically instilling the point that Jesus is the real initiator who gives himself, even when he appears to be constantly handed over. This does not at all denote an indifference to the historical causality of the latter proceedings (into which, to the contrary, John offers us a certain unique insight), but rather the coincidence of Christ's personhood with that of the *Logos*, so that Christ, moving genuinely in the realm of secondary causes, is also himself the first cause behind the very being of these causes. Jesus only submits to being handed over because he is in himself the very heart of all transition as really loving gift, and thereby able to subvert every betrayal and abandonment.

St Paul therefore speaks not of the offering of Christ to the Father, with whom he is really identical, but, instead, of our dying to sin and purely finite obsessions, including negative legality, *with Christ*, in order that we might immediately pass with him into a new sort of life. Christ and we ourselves are both killed by evil which is nothing, and so in dying to evil, we die to nothing whatsoever. Fully to die, for St Paul, means already and automatically to be resurrected (II Corinthians 5: 14: 'we are convinced that one has died for all, yet therefore all have died'; Romans 6: 5–6; Ephesians 2, Galatians 2, Philippians 2; Colossians 1–2; 3: 1–3 and 9; see also I Peter 4: 1–2). If any 'ransom' is offered by Christ, then it seems indeed that for St Paul, as the Fathers divulged, it is granted to the chthonic gods who are really demons, and to the demonic intermediate powers of the air (Galatians 4: 3–5: '. . . we were slaves to the elemental spirits of the universe.

But ... God sent forth his son ... to redeem those who were born under the law'; and see Colossians 2: 14 plus Ephesians 4: 9). As *homo sacer*, Christ is delivered over to the corrupt (or semi-corrupt?) angelic forces who are the guardians of laws and nations; yet Paul's point is that these powers are nothing, are impotent, outside the divine power which they refuse: hence such a sacrifice becomes, in Christian terms, absurd. Only in a comical sense was Christ, strictly speaking, a sacrifice. In a serious sense he was an effective sacrifice because he overcame sacrifice once and for all – because, in the absolute kenotic impotence of refusing to fight finite potency with finite potency, the ultimate of infinite irresistible power was disclosed. In refusing violence, Christ also exercised a militant opposition to violence. However, this counter-violent violence was disclosed as consisting in utter self-giving which is immediately return, as resurrection, and therefore also gift-exchange. Already, in dying, because he is God, Christ is not truly abandoned, but through apparent abandonment is finally and inexorably returned to us. In dying, as God, he already receives back from us, through the Holy Spirit which elevates us into the life of the Trinity, our counter-gift of recognition. Though to God we can really give nothing, by the humanization of the *Logos* we are given that hypostatic indwelling of the Spirit which is the ground of our deification, in such a way that we can, after all, in the Spirit, return the divine gift. Hence the divine answer to the original human refusal of his gift is not to demand sacrifice – of which he has no need – but to go on giving in and through our refusals of the gift, to the point where these refusals are overcome. Christ's abandonment offers no compensation to God, but when we most abandon the divine donation it surpasses itself, and appears more than ever, raising us up into the eternal gift-exchange of the Trinity.

It is the same for the *Epistle to the Hebrews*: sacrifice implies multiplicity, repetition, appeasement, whereas Christ the true Priest puts an end to sacrifice. He does this not really by offering a one all-sufficient sacrifice (this is to read over-literally and naively) but by passing into the heavenly sanctuary as both priest and victim, and making an 'atoning offering' there – in the one place where it is absurdly unnecessary, since offerings are only sent up to this altar from earthly ones. The point is that Christ's earthly self-giving death is but a shadow of the true eternal peaceful process in the heavenly tabernacle, and redemption consists in Christ's transition from shadow to reality – which is also, mysteriously, his 'return' to cosmic omnipresence and irradiating of the shadows (Hebrews 9: the Middle Platonic element here is essential). If nevertheless the heavenly altar must be cleansed, then once again this must be from the impurity of the cosmic powers, which infect even the very portals of Godhead (all that is not absolutely God). Yet though Christ's offering is even here unto death, the death that the *Logos* dies is a showing, within a death-dreaming cosmos, of that utter ecstatic self-giving which is eternal life itself. The heavenly altar that is purifed is, for the author of the *Epistle to the*

Hebrews, the psychic realm: 'your conscience'; and purification of this realm consists not in one more sacrificial 'work' – even a final such work – but rather in the final removal of the illusion of the need for such works. The 'blood of Christ will purify your conscience from dead works to serve the living God'. This offering of his blood is made by Christ, not as incurring a subtraction from his own resources, but instead 'through the eternal Spirit', which is to say out of and within the eternal mutually sustaining *donum* that holds together the Father and the Son (Hebrews 9: 14 and see Philo, *De Sacrificiis Abelis et Cain*, XXV, XXX, iii). Therefore in pouring himself as an apparent oblation upon the heavenly altar – which is the upper terminus for the escalating smoke of oblation, not its basement origin in bloodletting – Christ in truth passes as peaceful gift-that-returns beyond this altar to the right hand of the Father.

Both St Paul and the author of the *Epistle to the Hebrews* speak of Christ rather than the law as fulfilling the 'will' of Abraham. Both argue that a 'will' only becomes effective when someone dies (Hebrews 9: 17; Galatians 3–4, esp. 3: 15–18). It seems to me that something more than a banal legal reference is intended here. What is surely being invoked is something akin to my second *aporia* of sovereignty, which regards the relation of will to execution. For this *aporia*, a will is only effective in its own absence, when its wishes are carried out by another, just as a political sovereign requires, but is weakened by, a relatively distant executive, and an economic monopoly must bifurcate into two relatively independent parts in order to remain efficient – as symbolized for Jean Baudrillard by the erstwhile World Trade Center, whose sinister monopolistic character and Babelistic height made it an easier target, while its bifurcation weakened its solidity.

Hence the final guarantee of will, and for our *respect* for human wills, is death. This is exactly why we have legal wills, whose reality is poised somewhere between human worth and human terror (human freedom and human bondage, the honour due to father and mother, and enslavement to the past). Yet this reproduces constantly the entire sovereignty/executive problematic. By contrast, for the *Epistle to the Hebrews* Christ's will is indeed ratified by death and by blood, but not in a way that leaves it at the mercy of an executive. Instead, Christ's will is a new sort of self-emptying will that consists *entirely* in its passing out of itself to be non-identically repeated in another. It is only, in appearance and for a finite gaze, the blood of a deadly sealed contract, because it is secretly the infinite blood of life that flows in the firmament (Hebrews 9: 9–12). Likewise, for St Paul, the will of Abraham cannot really be fulfilled in the carrying out of injunctions which only keep us from worse wrongs, suggest to us temptations, and tend to impose on us over-precise categories, but only in the single living heir who fulfils the spirit of Abraham's legacy from the eternal Father. So whereas, as we saw in Chapter 1, Kant projects the separation of powers into the Godhead, the New Testament incarnates a new divine polity which uniquely abolishes all such separation, yet equally without any 'confusion' of the distinct powers, precisely because it reconceives 'unity' beyond 'singularity'.

In both St Paul and the *Epistle to the Hebrews*, one finds the tendency, as throughout the New Testament, and supremely in its Pneumatology, to promote the category of 'life'. It is almost as if it is suspicious of categories of human cultural institution and of the culture/nature divide.[4] The carrying through of 'will' involves a continuity and yet rupture between 'living' voice and 'cultural' inscription. The very order of sovereign arbitrary control depends upon this. Yet for the New Testament, there is neither 'natural' will nor regular conventional performance of will. Instead there is created will which participates in God, wherein life and *Logos* (Spirit and Son) communicate as one. Such a will is never the presupposed 'pure nature' of sovereignty and liberal rights theory. Instead it is already a will to reciprocity and to harmony with others according to an ineffable order and measure, which is yet not the measure of law. Such a will does not consist sovereignly in itself, and so cannot be betrayed by any executive – instead it only *is* in its always-already othering as execution: always for furtherance and not termination of life. Therefore by offering ourselves in and with Christ, we do not really lose ourselves, but live the genuine and eternal absolute life that returns as it proceeds outward.

This same promotion of life informs also the New Testament's over-coming of the first *aporia* of sovereignty. This concerns the rule of exception and the logic of inclusion which is also exclusion. For the Church is founded on Christ who was *entirely* excluded: by imperial Rome, by tribal-cum-city-state Israel, by modern democracy. But were Christ only the abandoned one, this would constitute a politics of naturalistic nihilism, a kind of cynicism in the antique sense, to which the New Testament stress upon uncontaminated natural life is curiously akin. Yet to the contrary, Christ as purely excluded is risen: therefore the life he is risen to is the possibility of life after exclusion from life, of a life beyond inclusion versus exclusion. If Christ is supremely exceptional, this is because he is the exception even to the law of exception: after Christ there is no more of that oscillation between norm and exception which paradoxically establishes the sphere of the norm. There is now only – so to speak – a series of exceptions, of pure outstanding and emanating (not caused) 'events' which are nonetheless consistent with each other. This is equally the new 'usual' beyond the usual: in truth an endless process of *variation*, since without the usual usual, there can be no *real* exception any longer. As for David Jones at the end of the *Anathemata*, Christ works in the mode of what has 'always been done', yet performs through this something 'other'. And as for W. H. Auden in *For the Time Being*, redemption is like the extraordinary event of stepping into the room behind the mirror: it entirely is, and entirely is not, the same room.

The New Testament is here very direct: Christ's blood makes peace, Christ's blood makes possible harmony between people; in Christ, there is no longer the inclusion/exclusion logic of race, nor of economics, nor of gender. There is in Christ no more black and white, master and slave, male and female. But this inclusion of differences does not mean their exclusion! No, they remain, as pure relations, pure passages of harmonious will. To the disappointment of liberal democrats, but the delight of Socratic (and socialist) critics of liberal democracy, hierarchical relations also remain: the subordinate are to obey freely, but masters to rule generously and with care. This is not to endorse the specific hierarchies of gender and slavery which Paul within his limited historical perspective was likely to endorse, and duly did, but it is to insist that Paul rightly recognizes the necessary 'educative' and architectonic hierarchies of the transmission of harmonious life which no culture can ever truly dispense with. (See Chapters 7 and 9 below.)

At the centre of this new social and even 'political' institution lies an absolute mystery: the insistence on Christ's specificity. For if there can be more to social life and hierarchy than arbitrariness, if there can indeed by 'harmony' or a passing of events in the 'right' way like music, then this suggests that there is a real 'affinity' to be constantly produced, discovered and enacted. Were this unnecessary, then Christ would be unnecessary; a mere command to 'be reconciled' would do, or a set of legal recipes, or books of wisdom. Of course we are to imitate Christ and to live ecstatically through exchange, losing our lives in order to gain them. But if *only* Christ reconciles us to each other – nation to nation, race to race, sex to sex, ruler to subordinate, person to person (and this is not because he has achieved something forensic outside our sharing in Christ – a reading of Paul that E.P. Sanders has forever destroyed),[5] then this can only mean that the specific shape of Christ's body in his reconciled life and its continued renewal in the Church (where it is authentic, which must also be ceaselessly discerned) provides for us the true aesthetic example for our reshaping of our social existence.

We live in Christ because Christ as *homo sacer* was archetypally a human being as a *creature* and not simply the *bios theoretikos* who is both inside and outside the *polis* – half animal of passions, half man [*sic*] of political reason. We also live in Christ because this typical abandoned man was nonetheless God, in whom we participate and from whom we all have our life. Our new political life in Christ is once more a merely natural life in the sense of created life, and of specifically human life which is orientation to super- natural deification. The Middle Ages started to think through the possibility of this life, but cut itself short by a dual development which invented a forensic reading of the atonement and a voluntaristic doctrine of sover- eignty in a single gesture (this is well attested by the theology of Grotius, but has earlier roots in Ockham and further back still). In the earlier mediaeval model, we are not ruled from above by a sovereign source which includes yet excludes us, but by blood flowing from the past which we imbibe, so that the outside is also the inside. For this vision we submit to the will of the past and its living hierarchical representatives, yet in such a way that we are to fulfil this will in the spirit not the letter, and carry it beyond and above the shoulders of the giants on whom we stand – as depicted in the overwhelming blue of the windows of Chartres Cathedral. (See further, Chapter 7 below.)

Today we must take up this project again and insist that the body of Christ is the true universality – against both the taboos of tribes (even though the law of Christ extends as well as abolishes taboos: see Chapter 10 below) and the universality of enlightenment, whose dark gothic secret is *homo sacer*. We must espouse and oppose the abandonment of potentially all of us to half-animality. We must oppose also the sacrifice without return of individuals to the state, to globalization, to the future, to ethical duty, to pagan fatality. Unlike Dante's Ulysses we must not once more abandon Penelope, sailing heroically beyond the pillars of Hercules, without hope of return, to the foot of Mount Purgatory, without hope of ascent. Instead, beyond the mediaeval venture, we must give ourselves to voyaging, unto death if necessary, like the English sailors John and Sebastian Cabot of Bristol (whose statue still stands there by the quayside) and before them the Portuguese sailors Magellan, Vasco de Gama and Columbus. Supremely we must follow the example of the Portuguese King Sebastian, lost at sea in one of Fernando Pessoa's poems (whom the Portuguese have believed will return to save them, as the British have believed of the Romano-British King Arthur) yet in sure knowledge that the created world is round – the world not only of sacrifice, but also of returning. So Pessoa invokes him: 'I spy through fog your dim shape turning back' (*Vejo entre a cerracao tue vulto baco que torna*).[6]

7

ECCLESIOLOGY

The last of the last

I

The Incarnation and the hypostatic descent of the Spirit inaugurated on earth a counter-polity exercising a counter-sovereignty, nourished by sovereign victimhood.

This counter-polity refused all the usual conditions of human rule, both psychic and political: the division of powers between sovereign and executive, the exclusionist logic of inside/outside, and government by emergency and exception. In heaven it is perfect, but on earth its sway is not utopian; for now we glimpse dimly its perfection within a process of reconciliation that is but fragmentarily realized – like a fleeting passage of an aerial creature amongst the trees, which we are scarcely sure we have glimpsed at all. Reality is still saturated by evil invented in the angelic and human event of the Fall; this ensures that even the apparently noble is always fissured by a deep and subtle corruption. As time advances, this corruption worsens – nor does the descent of the Son and the Spirit halt this worsening. It is rather that this descent inaugurates an altogether different possibility: it opens a narrow chink of light, allowing, albeit inchoately, a certain counter-movement of advance and of progress for the few (intensely) and the many (dispersedly) towards the source of this light.

The chink of light: the Philosopher's Stone, the curative herb *Moly*, the Holy Grail; this has been found. But it is incessantly lost again, and must ceaselessly be the object of a quest. Redemption remains a vague rumour, and only those possessed of a true light-hearted folly will dare to abandon everything else in order to pursue it.

The Church is the brotherhood and sisterhood of the Grail: of those ceaselessly questing for the Eucharist which is the source of the Church, and so perpetually questing for the Church itself.[1] The latter is not a given, but arrives endlessly, in passing. When it settles and becomes objectified as mere human sovereignty, its nature is lost. Only in the passage of time, as we saw in Chapter 3, is forgiveness exercised, and so only in passing is the Church the community of reconciliation. Reconciliation occurs in the truth, in the fusion of affinity, when all move together in their mutually right position-ings through time. As a result, the passage of the Church is also the passing of signs, of shadows that are foreshadowings. Each sign is inadequate and must make way for further inadequacies: yet in their passing, the signs com-pose a figure of broken beauty and of spasmodically peaceful co-existence. The way of reconciliation through appropriate exchange is also the *via crucis* which suffers the brutality and distortions of fallen time as the only fashion in which, for the time being, peace can be manifest amongst us.

Once again, there are two entirely co-incident aspects. We began with evil and violence; then we dealt with their remedies which are forgiveness and the *via crucis*. Now it is a question of how the new kingdom of forgive-ness and *imitatio Christi* is constituted. In fact its constitution is likewise double, and intra-convertible: the Church is established both as the truth of the *Logos*, which is revealed by the good of the Holy Spirit, and as the gift of the Spirit which is peace, the intermingling and co-ordination of all the Spirit's specific gifts, which are human talents.

Truth and peace: the former is shown to inward sight and requires an aristocratic ascent; the latter appears collectively and is democratically distributed. Yet they are not really external to each other; it is not at all that truth is one thing, and peaceful consensus another, nor that aristocracy and democracy are opposites in tension. The mixed constitution here is not a balance, but a necessity for the integrity of the respective ingredients. Without truth there is no peace of true consensus, because otherwise agree-ment would be based upon delusion, and therefore upon hidden coercion. But equally, without peace there would be no truth, because truth is not an epistemological mirror. For mere knowledge alone it is possible that there might be no truth, only endless shifting perspectives. If there is truth, then it is ontological – the fact that there are essences (however complex); the fact that there is a true way for things to be and a way things eternally are. Only in that case does it follow that things may be ultimately compatible with each other, as mere shifting perspectives need not be. If there is truth, then it must apply universally, and the truth of one thing must be compatible with the truth of all other things. But this is peace.

In consequence, there is only an echo of truth amongst human beings when their partial consensus mirrors eternal peace. While, indeed, the peace-ful community can only be established in truth and justice, it is *equally* true that there is only truth and justice for a visible gaze when there is already some practically embodied intimation of peace, since knowledge lies collec-tively in language and shared figuration, not just in private insight. This is the element of validity in American pragmatism, but its thesis that 'the true is the made' (to put it anachronistically in Vico's phrase) can only be accepted if also read backwards (as Vico intended) as 'the made is the true', in the sense that 'the truly made imitates the true'. However, one can accept that *only* the made can imitate the true, and that the true itself, as the generated

106

Logos, is 'infinitely made'. In other words, if truth is peace and peace truth, then *theoremata* and *pragmata* are also convertible and co-incident aspects.

I have already suggested that somehow all this involves a similar relation between 'aristocracy' (the theoretical aspect) and 'democracy' (the pragmatic aspect). Or, one could say, between hierarchy and levelling. Again, as we shall see in much more detail later, these two are not really opposites. This is first of all revealed in the circumstance that hierarchy is not simply private and esoteric, but also public and visible; while democracy is not simply exoteric and distributed, but also an internally established fiction, which only individuals can sustain in being though an attitude of ontological humility which accepts that all gifts, however hierarchically diverse, *equally* come from God. This contrasts with the post-Baroque false pseudo-humility, unknown to the Middle Ages, of pretending you are not talented when you know you are – such an attitude implies a *possession* of humility as virtue, and so a contradictory pride in humility, whereas authentic humility simply is dispossession: all my talents and achievements are the passing of gifts, nothing to do with me, nothing I could be proud of rather than be grateful for.[2]

There are not then two parallel hierarchies, the one internal and mystical, and the other public and political. Instead, for the authentic Dionysian tradition, there is but one hierarchy of the Eucharistic and ecclesial *corpus mysticum* which is at once mystical and political. The inner hierarchy is not a parallel hierarchy: rather, inwardness alone allows there to be hierarchy at all. Since hierarchy is always a convention, and since it involves 'stages', else it would be indeterminate – a mere perpetual sliding in which everything was simultaneously at the top and at the bottom – it is composed by esoteric 'leaps' which are entirely psychic in character (as neoplatonism taught).

This immediately suggests to the modern thinker that hierarchy is an ideology: external hierarchy poses as 'natural' by disguising its conventionality and ruptured non-continuity. But the neoplatonic and Dionysian traditions fully admit the interiority and reasoned conventionality of the stages and the links. Much more radically than modernity (though in a way compatible with postmodernity and with modern physics), they view material nature itself as manifestly discontinuous, as an hierarchical emanation and not as a 'caused' sequence. The latter conception cannot really acknowledge the instance of new events, because within the causal perspective the preceding always 'accounts' for the later. Emanation by contrast is not causality (efficient causality), and permits the event, because it views an effect as the development of the cause, which itself unfolds and defines its very nature – even if, at the top of the ladder there is *Unum* or *Esse* which holds in 'complicated' fashion the entire 'explicated' sequence (to use Nicholas of Cusa's terminology). If nature also is a discontinuous hierarchy, then it too must be sutured by *psyche* – unless it is a nihilistic randomness.

Social hierarchy (of an educative kind, not a fixed kind, based on birth not talent) need not necessarily then be ideological. Another way of showing this is by pointing out that visible democracy equally depends upon interior convention. A 'level' is a comparative notion, which is why even Locke's radical political theory is based upon the great chain of being: the equality of men follows upon their elevated dignity within the cosmos, and (we can add to Locke) at the same time upon their sub-angelic common genus which is differentiated by matter, whereas each angel is its own genus, and no angel is on a level with any other. As comparative, the 'level' is in fact the very invisible interruptive convention which sutures (both breaks and constitutes) the hierarchy. And just as hierarchy accords, by a judicial decision, value to specific difference – for example of intelligence – so, likewise, democracy accords value to a factor of equality only by *ignoring* all differences of degree. It is very hard to justify this ignoring, and to defend democracy from the charge of ideology: indeed as Nietzsche saw, it is far more obviously ideological than aristocracy. Really, there is only one stance that rescues democracy: this, as already intimated, is our truly humble recognition that we are all equally recipients of divine gifts, without which we would not exist at all. But further theological dimensions to democracy will be considered later.

From the foregoing one can see how both hierarchy and democracy are equally mystical and political, equally internal and external, even if hierarchy more naturally lines up with the esoteric, theoretical and truth-observing, and democracy with the exoteric, pragmatic and peace-realizing.

In what follows, I shall build up to a vision of the simultaneous hierarchy and democracy of the Church; showing that, contrary to all the assumptions of secular sovereignty, it is all the more democratic the more it is genuinely hierarchical. Moreover, that this is the only possible real democracy, and the most extremely democratic.

It will be already clear that this means that the Church has both an 'esoteric' and an 'exoteric' aspect. The esoteric aspect is mystical theology, which is theology pure and simple; theology as experience and discourse that is possible through reception of the Eucharist. The exoteric aspect is the actual dispersed life of the ecclesial community.

These two aspects converge inchoately around the notion of 'the rule' of the Church, its constitutional authority as established in canon law. The latter exhibits the parameters within which the Christian life must be lived, and within which theology can reflect and speculate. However, at the same time, canon law adverts to theology; it is mostly a digest of theology, from the basic conciliar decrees onwards, as Gratian's *Decretals* reveal, since theology itself is entirely concerned with the laws of ecclesiastical polity and already considers just wherein authority lies, the comparative authority of scripture, custom and reason and so forth.[3] And yet, the foundation of the Church cannot really lie in theology taken as theory. Theology presupposes and reflects upon the practice of the Church, and therefore, it would appear, it is a secondary aspect of the Church's life. Nevertheless, *ecclesia* can only exist at all through its essential constitution, since it is always more than its own endless failings. Thus by an irreducible paradox, theology presupposes from the outset not only the Church but also its own digest: canon law which is yet nothing but abridged theology.

This chapter then, occupies the uneasy pivot of canon law. It is finally concerned to expound, theologically, an ecclesiology. However, in obedience to the above paradox, one has to realize that theology *cannot* really frame ecclesiology, any more than vice versa. Both Karl Barth and Richard Hooker realized something like this: theology *only* expounds ecclesial law; dogmatics *is* 'Church Dogmatics', or 'The Laws of Ecclesiatical Polity'.

It follows that theology expounding an ecclesiology must also be theology that enters the abyss of self-reflexivity, and asks simultaneously about its own relation to the Church, which means its own sources of authority. An ecclesiology will have to be at the same time a treatise on 'theological method' – or rather a self-reflexive consideration of both the content and process of theology, since the two are inseparable (to avoid a foundationalist methodologism).

So to approach the question of the Church, the question of collective peace, we must from the outset ask, what authorizes theology?

II

The paradox which I have just enunciated seems more like a fully fledged *aporia*: if canon law is equally theological and ecclesial, then does theology – always *mystical* theology – found the Church, or the Church theology? Does aristocratic inwardly experienced truth hold primacy, or else external democratic peace and inherited consensus?

A contemporary way of putting this question would be to ask, should theology owe its prime allegiance to academic standards or to the Church community? Should it be (the 'aristocratic' view) primarily a 'public discourse' answerable to the critical norms and liberal values of free society in the West, or should it be the faith of the Church seeking understanding, according to a logic indissociable from this faith (the 'democratic' view)? The reader should notice that 'aristocratic' here more equates with 'liberal' and 'democratic' with 'conservative'.

Faced with such a stark alternative, many people are likely to propose instead a compromise. Given that the notion of a contextless reason, without presuppositions and affective practical commitments, is a fiction (as recent philosophy, both analytic and continental, has tended to conclude), then it is with and not contrary to reason to suggest that a well-established community and tradition may undertake to articulate its own implicit reasonings. However, if this reflection is not to be merely self-regarding, then it must also be subject to critical reflections coming from external sources: for example, the diagnosis of 'ideologies'.

Yet the problem with any mere compromise is that it piles up a double problem and compounds it with contradiction. One is still left with the question of an uncritical solipsism on the one hand and of the fictional perspective from nowhere on the other. If the two are combined, then one is trying to believe at once that reason founds itself and that this is impossible.

At this point some theologians have had recourse to semi-Hegelian solutions, often inspired by Jurgen Habermas. Critique is imminent: one must begin with a tradition and assumptions, but a negative process of unravelling contradictions in the first deposit gradually drives towards a universal logos.

This solution leaves us in no better plight. Traditions unfold by acts of hermeneutic discrimination as well as by the overcoming of contradictions. Something ineliminably subjective and feeling-imbued is just as involved in development as in inheritance, in continuation as in origin. And however long the process of formally objective logical negation, this cannot alter the positive status of the beginnings. One remains entirely inside a tradition. Conversely, if a logical process is still the only criterion for socially acceptable truth, then one is persisting with placeless, formal and self-founded criteria for reason. The idea that a tradition will edge towards the universal through the outworking of contradiction, or conversely that a foundation will finally emerge at the conclusion, is itself contradictory.

So one still has a compromise between two perhaps unsatisfactory positions which sustains the unsatisfactoriness of both and adds to this the unacceptability of downright incoherence.

Is it possible to do better? I want to approach this question by adverting already to ecclesiology as well as to theological method. One can note that a penchant for compromise invades also the sphere of ecumenism. Very often, documents issued in the name of joint doctrinal statements between different churches produce their results by toning down given differences or glossing over their ineluctable historical reality. So, to give a short example, it will be discovered that Aquinas and Luther have 'essentially the same' doctrine of justification. There can be much truth in this sort of conclusion, given that by Luther's day the nature of Aquinas's account of salvation had been obscured, and that since his day the views of both in this area have been yet further contaminated. Yet in the end, an irremovable difference which is significantly linked with their exceedingly different ontologies (realist/analogical versus nominalist/univocalist) tends to be passed over. Luther's nominalism will not really admit the Thomist paradox of righteousness that is entirely supernatural, yet also entirely ours since it is our deification. Instead, the younger more 'participatory' Luther is in fact developing the consequences of an almost monophysite Ockhamist and nominalist Christology which cannot really think two universal 'natures' in a single personal reality, nor think this reality other than on the model of a single finite thing 'within which' God has somehow entered.[4] (Actually Luther was *more* monophysite than the formal monophysitism of the 'monophysites' – although John Philoponus, at least, seems already to have espoused a form of nominalism.) Within such a perspective, the participation in Christ by which we are justified edges too closely towards mere identity and subsumption. Aquinas's apparently similar Cyrilline tendencies actually follow a totally different realist logic, which strictly preserves the integral finitude of Christ's human nature, and the apathetic integrity of his divine nature, while insisting that his unity of personality and Being is only divine, since there can be no other unity 'alongside' and conjoined with, the divine unity. Luther's nominalist univocalism finds another solution in his later extrinicist, imputational account of grace, which is more obviously alien to that of Aquinas.

This kind of upshot in ecumenical documents seems to me to do a disservice to the cause of truth and run the risk of making theology look, indeed, to be biased from an academic perspective. What seems crucial here is that while ecumenical reflection makes some use of historical research to upset prejudices about what different communities have believed from their outsets, it does not take this process far enough. At bottom it is a matter of developing mutual respect between different ecclesial bodies, not of questioning the very character of these bodies. In this respect, ecumenics is very much conducted on a basis that is internal to received variants of the faith. Yet here a more external, objective approach might be more inclined to ask questions about the common intellectual assumptions of both the post-Reformation and the post-Tridentine faiths, and the possible deviation of these from earlier Christian views.

There does in fact seem to be an increasing consensus amongst historians both of events and of ideas, that neither the Reformation, nor the somewhat elusive 'Renaissance', nor even the later 'Enlightenment' were anything like such crucial shifts in Western theory and practice as the multiple changes which took place before and after the year 1300.[5] Around that year, there started to be a far greater gap between specialists and non-specialists in all fields; administration became more technical and distant; clerical control over the laity further increased; sharper differentiations were made between academic disciplines; theology assumed a far more technical and difficult character; the traditional centrality in theology of participation, deification, apophaticism, allegory and the vision of the Church as something engendered by the Eucharist all were abruptly challenged, in a fashion that prove epochally successful. Meanwhile, much that had been taken for granted in the Aristotelian/neoplatonic synthesis and had been shared with Byzantine, Jewish and Islamic culture, was declared from henceforth unacceptable by the ecclesial authorities. Many historians consider that the later break-up of

111

Christendom was itself in large measure the upshot of these changes, and equally that the same changes already ushered in a drift towards 'secularity'. This has implications both for ecumenism, and for the debate about the relationship of theology to secular culture.

For sometimes great faith is invested in the possible upshot of Christian reunion, particularly within the 'Yale School' of American theologians: secularization is seen as a negative reaction to Christian disunity; re-unification as the key to renewed mission. Yet if the new historical consensus is correct, then it is rather the case that secularization, not ecumenism, is the prior problem. It might be that Christian division was itself an outcome of a severe weakening of the Christian vision, and that the key to ecumenical discussion would be a far more drastic critique of the character of existing ecclesial bodies.

What I have just said seems, however, to impose too much duality between theology and history. It cannot in fact be an accident that much of the new picture of the history of ideas and of the Church is itself inspired by theologians – but by theologians prepared to be critical concerning the contemporary norms of the ecclesial body to which they belong (over-whelmingly, this body is the Roman Catholic Church).

So far I have tried to interweave between debates about theology amongst the different Church denominations, and debates about its respective relations to the Church and to the academic community. We are talking, then, about the sources of intellection in theology, which very often are taken to be Scripture, Tradition and Reason. All too often, the Anglican commu-nity has presented itself as having a uniquely balanced orientation to all three *loci*. This way of understanding the grounds for theologizing is, however, wholly unsatisfactory; in fact it is ultimately an upshot of the 'crisis of 1300'. It tends to result in arguments for the predominance of one of these ele-ments or another, or else for compromise between their respective sways. But the problem with 'tradition' as we saw, seems to be solipsism; the problem with 'reason' seems to be its unreal and impotent abstraction; the prob-lem with 'scripture', one can add, is its magical positivity. Compromise between these three again compounds problems, and adds to these contra-dictions since (one can now go on to say) replete positivity does not need the supplement of community in time, nor of neutral reason; while tradition cannot admit a positive foundation that would render it redundant.

To overcome this hydra of an *impasse*, we need to understand from the work of many historians and theologians that Scripture, Tradition and Reason were simply *not* seen as separate sources roughly prior to 1300. Throughout these considerations, two questions will arise. First of all, should we want simply to *return* to this earlier perspective, or must we return with difference, given a certain validity to some of the newer post-1300 considerations? Secondly, how do we handle a situation in which there is a real secular sphere, as there was not in the Middle Ages? Can a certain earlier pre-1300 fluidity between faith and reason still help us out in our modern predicament?

The transformation of theology from the pre-1300 situation to the modern one will now be considered under three headings: the supernatural, the *corpus mysticum* and allegory. Through all these headings runs a fourth, which will not be explicitly considered on its own: this is participation. The first three categories derive mostly from the work of Henri de Lubac, especially as reinterpreted by Michel de Certeau, Jean-Yves Lacoste and Olivier Boulnois. The fourth category derives in part from Erich Przywara, Sergei Bulgakov, Hans Urs von Balthasar, Rowan Williams and again Olivier Boulnois.

What is at issue under the first heading is theology between faith and reason; under the second, theology under ecclesial authority; under the third, theology between scripture and tradition.

III

It is a correct Catholic view, proclaimed since the time of the Church under persecution, that truth should be freely pursued, since all knowledge points towards God. Coercion into understanding defeats its own object, since the divine truth freely shines out everywhere. There is no question, then, but that the Church should be on the side of free scientific enquiry.

Since at least the Counter-Reformation however, the Catholic Church has tended to construe its support of science in terms of a duality of the realms of reason and faith. In the thought of Cardinal Cajetan, the Thomistic paradox of a natural desire for the supernatural, a desire which must be already the lure of grace, since humanity cannot raise itself to God of its own accord, is lost sight of.[6] Instead, Cajetan underwrites the late mediaeval and unThomistic espousal of a purely 'natural beatitude' accessible by philosophy, according to which the latter is supposed to be able to attain by natural powers of intellect and will to some sort of positive knowledge and contemplation of the divine. By comparison, Aquinas had spoken of a philosophic reach to a negatively defined first cause, and in other statements indicated that even this reach is inseparable from a divine drawing forth by grace which defines humanity as such.[7] Cajetan instead espoused in effect a 'closed humanism' with its own transcendental reach that was essentially unrelated to the arrival of revelation. Since there was no longer any natural anticipation of grace, faith was now construed in very 'extrinsicist' terms as assent to a series of revealed propositions; gradually, in a process culminating in Suarez, revelation also lost its integration of inner experience with interpretation of outward sign, and was bifurcated between one or the other.[8] The realm of grace now concerned external positive data superadded to the conclusions of reason, or else an ineffable realm of inner 'mystical' experience, equally positive and equally subject to experimental testing for reality of 'presence'.[9]

113

As both Lacoste and Boulnois argue, modern 'philosophy' does not simply emancipate itself from theology; rather it arises in a space that theology itself has carved out for it: the space of pure nature.[10] To be sure, 'natural beatitude' was supposed to correspond roughly to the pagan *theoria* achieved by Plato and Aristotle. But this was a delusion: pagan *physis* was not Christian *natura*, since the latter exists only in paired contrast with the supernatural. It would be truer to say that the Platonic and Peripatetic philosophies contain some rough anticipation of the Christian supernatural, as much as they do of the Christian natural. For they both understand wisdom to be primarily the prerogative of the divine, and human wisdom as some degree of sharing in this replete wisdom.

Olivier Boulnois correctly radicalizes de Lubac's reading of Aquinas to show that the paradox of natural orientation to the supernatural in Aquinas is in fact in continuity with an entire cosmology and ontology which takes up themes from the Graeco-Arabic legacy, even though it transforms them in terms of a much stronger grasp of the idea of divine Creation.[11] Thus it is not simply that, as natural, we desire the supernatural, it is also that *intellect* as such, on the model of the angelic intellect that moves the celestial spheres, drawn in ceaseless perfect motion by the immoveable, only exists in the space of this paradox. Indeed, while all finite motions are proper to specific natures, nature as a whole is only in motion because drawn beyond herself by higher powers towards a stilling of motion. The motion of human intellect is like a more intense and reflexive influx and concentration of natural motion as such, while the celestial spheres combine the inwardness of the intellect of the separate substances that move them with the totality of circulating finite motion. In this way, the natural human destiny that looks towards the supernatural vision of God is only the outworking in a conscious, knowing and willing created nature of the paradox of creation as such: it is of itself nothing, and only exists by participation.

(Creation for this reason requires a *purer* sense of *methexis*, as grasped by the Biblical teaching of the presence of wisdom and glory in the cosmos; thus St Paul with self-conscious irony proclaimed *methexis* to the Athenians: 'God in whom we live and move and have our being.' Likewise, theurgic neoplatonists like Proclus and Iamblichus – the former more than the latter – who stressed that philosophy should culminate in worship, and taught a kind of kenotic descent of the divine powers into the cosmos, deployed the word *methexis* in relation to emanation, far more than did the non-theurgic Plotinus. For the latter, even though emanation is both caused and imaging, and therefore participatory – since *methexis* inconceivably blends the receiving of substance with the copying of an exemplar – the stress lies upon the tension between the pure source and the imperfect copying of that source which generates the next lower level, and this tends to a dialectical dissolution of participation. Finally, one must add, following Rowan Williams (see note 30) that, for all neoplatonism, the essence of the One cannot really be participated, since the One dissolves all distinctions and even all reasonings: to approach the One is aporetic, since such an approach tends to dissolve the thinker who approaches and yet, since neoplatonism is not pure monism, this cannot happen, and defeats the goal of thinking. By contrast, for Christian theology the hyper-diverse and eminently intellectual essence of God can, by the contradictory hyberbole of glory (para-doxa), be imparticably participated. Plato himself already intimated this notion; yet for him there remains a chaotic material residue that does not participate. It follows that *methexis* is logically more Biblical than Hellenic.)

Therefore everything, for Aquinas, not just humanity, is already as itself more than itself, and this more is in some sense a portion of divinity. (Everything is therefore 'engraced'.) It is not that something 'more' is added to the natural human soul – it is rather that the psychic is the conscious concentration of the paradoxical nature of every *ens* as such. Here, even though Aquinas rejects the Arabic doctrines of a single superhuman active intellect, he still nevertheless echoes their concern to attend to the phenomenology of thinking, which notes that we are never entirely in charge of thought: thought occurs to us, and so thinking is certainly something thinking in us, as well as something that we think (*De Spir. Creat.* x).

The collapse of the paradox of the natural orientation to the supernatural was an aspect of the collapse of this entire cosmology and ontology. Aquinas had sought a cause for finite being, *ens commune*, as such. But in the later Middle Ages – beginning, ironically, with Siger of Bribant – this was deemed a question that made little sense, since *esse* was no longer thought of as something superadded to essence; the latter conception renders an arriving accident paradoxically more fundamental than the essential itself in the constitution of the creature.[12] Instead, one could now only ask for the final cause of finite being in its given finite circumstances. Something finite as existing – the dog in its possession of being – rather than the why of it's being a dog, for example, was now regarded as making full sense in its own finite terms. Hence to know that an existence was from God was no longer held, as it was for Aquinas, to change the very character of the truth concerning that existence that could be known, since causal origin no longer marked the existentiality of finite things. This new space of univocal existence, of simple 'thereness' in abstraction from derivation, quickly became as much thereness for mere entertained thought as for ontic reality. Indeed, the emergence of this space was itself inversely encouraged by a parallel drift, ever since Roger Bacon, away from the Aristotelian view that knowledge is the realization of migrating species as pure forms in our minds, towards knowledge as representational mirroring of a reality having in itself no essential orientation toward understanding. Ideas and mental fictions now started to acquire ontological equality with real beings as all equally 'things' constituted through their self-standing, rather than instantiation of an essence, or real inter-relation.[13]

The new univocalist/representational space was the space that could be explored as the realm of pure nature. It extended beyond the finite: indeed as Boulnois points out, Duns Scotus found it contradictory that Aquinas had combined the view that the primary object of the human intellect is sensory, with the view that every act of understanding is orientated towards the supernatural.[14] Instead of Thomas's *aporias* and conundra, he substituted the view that the human intellect in its pure pre-lapsarian essence is naturally capable of the grasp of non-material essences: this (already, one wants to say 'transcendentalist' à la Rahner) reach of our intellect, is then the natural base for the reception of positive supernatural information.

The combination of a univocalist and representational conception of understanding (our intellect represents 'things' which are simply there in their differential exemplifying of a bare 'presence' outside participation) with the idea of a natural beatitude, permitted theology to encourage the emergence of independent philosophy faculties in the early modern period (the diverse presence of philosophy in mediaeval arts and theology facilities had represented a totally different intellectual economy). There were now professional 'philosophers', where previously philosophy had survived as a kind of pagan 'moment' within Christian theology, which was linked with the necessary discursiveness of our finitude. Ironically, the new division of powers had itself in part emerged to counter the threat of Latin Averroism, which was thought (probably erroneously) to pursue a philosophy altogether independent of theology. The only drastic way to achieve institutional control over such tendencies was to purge theology itself of an essential metaphysical detour through a vision of the participatory reflection of the divine essence in the cosmos, and to insist that it is rather a purely positive discourse founded upon the divine *potentia absoluta*, now regarded as a real unknown reserve of limitless options. In this way there can be a final court of appeal against wayward reason, a court whose procedures are not so much guaranteed by partial illuminatory intuition and dialectical discursiveness, but rather by recourse to positive sources and to methods for discriminating amongst and ordering those sources. This new positive approach was only really perfected in the sixteenth century with the new insistence on theological *loci*, especially in the work of Melchior Cano.

What is important to grasp here is the to us counter-intuitive link between a new autonomy for philosophy, and yet at the same time an increased censoring (at least in aspiration) of philosophy by theology. As Jean-Yves Lacoste has well described, this had well-nigh ludicrous consequences: granted autonomy to explore pure nature, philosophers quickly did not find what they were supposed to find – soon they were announcing materialisms, scepticisms, determinisms, rationalisms, pantheisms, idealisms and so forth. A little later they were disconnecting natural beatitude from any contemplation of the divine whatsoever. This meant that the only 'true' philosophy was mostly done with their left hand by theologians. Philosophy was supposed to be able to reach natural truth solely by reason; however, as faith knew that the higher truth of revelation overrides apparently sound reasonings, every philosophy conflicting with faith had to be denied twice over: once on positive grounds of faith, second in terms of a better reasoning which then had to be sought out.

Such convolutions surely have helped to bring Christianity into disrepute; yet they are entirely remote from the real outlook of the high Middle Ages. What is more, the 'bad' philosophers of modernity have always been more truly theological than the 'sound' ones. For they have refused to conclude to God from uninflected objective reason, and thereby have inadvertently, and in some measure, avoided idolatry: all this has been set out in superb detail, though from very different if complementary perspectives, by Michael Buckley and Jean-Luc Marion.[15]

But what we must now ask ourselves is whether or nor the same mistakes are still being perpetuated today. For some time now I have contended that Roman Catholic intellectual culture finds it very difficult, for institutional reasons, altogether to negate a false Tridentine legacy, and to pursue all the consequences of de Lubac's theological revolution (a subversion as real as it was stealthy). An enterprise of 'natural theology', which historians have now shown to go back at the very furthest only to Scotus, is perpetuated, along with a parallel discourse of 'natural law' considered in an unThomistic way, apart from the law of charity. This perpetuation is common to both 'conservatives' and 'liberals' – indeed it is that secret common ground upon which they are distributed *as* conservatives and liberals, stressing respectively either faith or reason, but both assuming a two-tier economy. Even someone as influenced by de Lubac as Hans Urs von Balthasar, and himself crucial for the *nouvelle théologie*, still at times pursued, unlike de Lubac, a 'metaphysical' prolegomenon to *sacra doctrina*. When discussing Heidegger, he falls into exactly the same trap as Gilson: Heidegger has recovered the ontological difference already known to Thomas, yet does not 'pursue questioning far enough' by leaving both the non-necessity of the ontic, and the excess of the ontological shown through this contingency, as a pure mystery. Further questioning is supposed to give rise ineluctably to the thought of being as a personal donor.[16] But of course it does not: such a recourse remains also a 'mystery'; while Heidegger has after all his own resolution of the initial mystery – Being is also nothing, or else is the continual presencing of absence in time.

In purely rational terms, Heidegger appears the more rigorous of the two, if by 'rational' one is speaking of the exploration of pure given nature as representable by our finite intellect and subject to the manoeuverings of our finite will. As Jean-Yves Lacoste contends, the space of pure nature must confine the human essence to what the human being is itself on its own capable of, and must equally confine true human understanding to this capacity in its cognitive aspect.[17] Within such a confinement, we may add, our world will be defined by technological capacity, by an empty reach towards a sublime unknown and by systematic indeterminacy – since limits turn out to be themselves the perpetual anarchic transgression of limits (the inevitable postmodern turn of modernity), as well as by the horizon of death. As Lacoste points out, even the later Heidegger's exceeding of these options in terms of a symbolic dwelling within the cosmos remains a resignation to the impersonal, without hope beyond death, and so in subordination of the desires and aspirations of the body.

It would seem then, that the history of modern ideas negatively bears out the view that no natural beatitude will be concluded to, save under the promptings of an explicit orientation to the supernatural. This situation is half-recognized in the papal encyclical, *Fides et Ratio*.[18] There philosophy is exhorted to be 'wisdom' rather than merely 'reason', and this means to take account of right desiring, of the link between thought and life and to be open to receive something beyond the grasp of reason. This is all well and good, but needs further defining. The 'autonomy' of rational enquiry is still advocated, and not merely in terms of legal freedom (which one should of course endorse, in keeping with the early Christian view that truth can only be freely consented to) but also in terms of some essential good proceeding from such autonomy. However, if right desiring and openness to revelation have entered the picture, then, according to the post de Lubac logic, this is already a work of grace, and already exists in some sort of typological, which is to say real historical, relation to scripture and tradition. What I mean by this is that all the traces of 'wisdom' on which philosophy might build in our modern world do not stand simply 'outside' Christian tradition, as far as this tradition is concerned. All ethical topics, for example, are marked by the passage of the gospel through the world, and even when philosophy appeals to the Greeks, it appeals to a legacy which is taken up, in part and in places, within the New Testament itself, and thereby is now a constituent element of Christianity.

However, the exaggerated and somewhat naive opposition of the encyclical to 'relativism', which militates against attention to historicity, means that the pursuit of wisdom cannot really be taken in this fashion. Instead, *Fides et Ratio* seems at some points to insist upon a reason that is the same in all times and places, and is an autonomous natural faculty without presuppositions. In that case we are back with all the old post-Tridentine absurdities: the world is granted leave to think autonomously, yet left to itself it turns out that it cannot do this. So the Church ends up teaching the contradiction that autonomy need assistance.

In the face of this situation, one natural reaction is a fideistic one. This reaction tells a story: once upon a time, it seemed as if the Church could rely upon metaphysical cosmology; then it seemed as if it could rely upon a metaphysical ethics, but now it must learn to cling to the Cross alone – perhaps construing even this as the tragic presence of God in his secular absence. It is the story told by Bonhoeffer (in his weaker, more Lutheran dialectical moments) and also the story told in large measure by von Balthasar, especially in *Love Alone: The Way of Revelation*, although Balthasar still adds to revelation the (essentially Kantian, in the end) props of a phenomenological aesthetic and personalistic ethics taken as prolegomena, if admittedly only in part.[19] My noting this must make it sound as if I favour a Barthian critique of Bonhoeffer and von Balthasar, and therefore a yet more purely fideistic recourse. But such is not in any way the case.

For the claimed maturity of the fideistic grand narrative of all three thinkers turns out to be only adolescent in character. What has been feverishly outgrown is not a natural childhood, but a non-innocent childhood of error which need never have happened – which is not *at all* to say that we should have remained forever in the culture of the twelfth and thirteenth centuries. No, it is an *unknown* future that we have missed and must seek to rejoin. Historical researches done since the 1960s make it abundantly clear that the metaphysical cosmology of the high Middle Ages was thoroughly informed by, and transformed through, the Biblical legacy. When this metaphysics was lost, with the nominalists, it was not on the basis of a rediscovery of a Biblical God of will, law and covenant, etc., but rather as the consequence of a catastrophic invasion of the West by ultimately Islamic norms (norms which we now turn back upon Islam, imagining it to be the 'other'). The very condemnations of 1277 by the Archbishops of Paris and Canterbury, which swept away a cultural legacy shared with Islam (as with Judaism and Byzantium), also repeated within the West a gesture of Islamic *kalam* orthodoxy: banish and regulate philosophy; impose instead a positivistic order based upon literal punctilinear revelation underwritten by absolute sovereignty, which is now the only trace on earth of an inscrutable deity. Caliphization of the West; the Bible now read as if it were the Koran.

In the light of these developments, it proved in fact extremely difficult to continue to think through the central Christian doctrines which depend upon realism of universals, reality of relation, and the truth of *methexis*: all denied by the terminists. In consequence, Ockham's Trinity becomes three ontic persons within one unity of an individual; his Christology appears monophysite, because he cannot think the divine hypostasis relationally as unifying two real essences; transubstantiation is trivialized into bilocation and extrinsicist miracle, and the Creation starts to acquire such autonomy that for Ockham there is no longer any 'reason' to ascribe its origins to God rather than to the Intelligences. In consequence, all these doctrines become lifeless things no longer informing reason, and are rather matters merely to be believed on pain of death in this world or the next. They are now left to the Church as a huge pile of nakedly ideological resources.

So the cosmos of participation was never 'argued against' in some unanswerable fashion. There was simply an epistemic switch (complexly linked with social transformations), to representation and univocity. Certain tenets of natural philosophy may have been disproved, but even here one can exaggerate: Thomas Torrance has rightly pointed out how much nearer Robert Grosseteste's Christian/neoplatonic cosmology of light, with its 'Cantorian' sets of nested differentiated infinites (and actually no celestial/ terrestrial duality) was to modern physics, than that of the later Middle Ages or of Newton.[20]

The point then is not at all that we must now cling to faith in ascetic nakedness. Instead we must pass beyond the still all-too-modern fideism of neo-orthodoxy, towards a 'radical orthodoxy' that refuses the duality of reason over against faith. The issue is rather that, what has recently passed for reason, is not, as far as the Catholic faith is concerned, the work of the *Logos* at all, or only jaggedly and intermittently so. Recent reasoning itself shows this, negatively, to be the case, since the rigorous upshot of its objective, representing regard, is to discover the role of unreason beyond reason, and the founding of sense in nonsense. Reason's domain is nihilism; whereas the discovery of a meaningful world governed by a *logos* can only be made by faith. This is perhaps the nearest one can get to an apologetic gesture (and I am echoing the thought of Jacobi), but it still does not decide the issue, ineluctably.[21] Reason can indeed *allow* the possibility that the infinite is an order that exceeds the finite contrast of order with chaos – and postmodernism tends to disregard this point – but it cannot truly rule out the possibility that the infinite is simply hypostasized chaos, or the chance control of endless meaningless formal 'orders' in set after sub-set. Moreover, reason alone, without *eros*, can more easily 'envisage' absolute chaos, than it can an inaccessible infinite order.

What has passed for reason is, as Lacoste suggests, a mere decision to see that which is Prometheanly within our capacity as the key to our nature and the key to unlock the secrets of the world, or else as the key to a knowable world limited to the truth that arises for our purposes. This of course has often been seen as a pious gesture: confine reason and nature within their limits, thereby let the gratuity of grace in its glory all the more shine out upon us. Even in the case of Kant, a true reading shows that he is trying to protect a rarified and anti-liturgical pietist faith from contamination by limited images, much more than he is trying to protect reason from contamination by religion (Kant, the last Scotist, Ockhamist, or Suarezian, as he had been variously described).

The Kantian attempt to acknowledge limits self-deconstructs, since limits will only appear if one claims absolutely to surmount them, and thus one gets Kant's dogmatic hierarchy of practically perceived noumena above theoretically perceived phenomena. Yet even a postmodern, deconstructed Kant, wherein the sublime overflows every temporary restraint, still erects a shrine to pure nature and the confines of reason: its mark is now the hypostasization of the unknown as only an empty void, and refusal of any possibility of 'beautiful' mediation between the invisible and the visible.

But this worship of limits which constructs pure reason is only a *decision*, without reasons. As Lacoste has best explained, such a decision adopts a hermeneutic of the human essence and of nature which makes that which lies within perceived capacity fundamental. But supposing the human aspiration to, or even openness to, that which lies beyond its capacity, were taken as the hermeneutic key instead? Lacoste here puts in a sharper light the insistence of many twentieth-century Christians – Charles Péguy supremely – upon the virtue of hope. Reason orientated only to a beatitude supposedly within our grasp dispenses with hope, only to land up as without hope, and at best resigned to this condition. Likewise, if such a reason is taken as hermeneutically decisive, it must downgrade the promptings, urgings and longings of the *body*. The supernatural in us may be intelligence as such, intelligence thinking through us, but it is also always conjoined with sensation, as Aquinas taught. Therefore intelligence begins as a bodily exercise, accompanied by desire that reaches into the unknown. Only by the exercise of an artificial abstraction can we prise reason apart from desire, which reaches beyond our capacity. This prised-apart 'pure reason' is also a totally individualistic reason, whether on the level of the single person or of collective humanity. For such a *logos*, I cannot be completed by the other, and so others cannot mediate to me the lure of a wholly other who is also 'not other' as *intimo interior meo*, according to the creationist logic of paradoxical priority of supplementation.

What *faith* proposes as reason, then, is taking as hermeneutic keys to reality first *hope*, and then *charity* which is the erotic lure of the other and our giving ourselves over to the other, as well as our free agapeic letting of the other be, independently of our immediate egoity.

How does such a perspective impact upon the task of theology today? Primarily, it absolutely forbids us to baptize the secular desert as the realm of pure reason, pure nature, natural law or natural rights and so forth. For this is not at all to acknowledge this sphere in its integrity, but rather it is to define it in terms of an impoverished Baroque theology – even though it still defines itself in this way, as if everyone were really a headless theologian. Rather what truly characterizes the 'secular' sphere is a postmodern simultaneity of remote times, places and cultures. It cannot be dealt with in terms of a single Western liberal narrative of pure nature, because this will only issue in bombs and destruction of the other. And none of this complex confusion is exactly 'outside' the Church. The Church should read it all in terms of multiple but converging narratives of typological anticipation, unrecognized scattering of the seeds sown by the incarnate *Logos*, and various fallings-away and partial survivals of Christian norms.

So the answer cannot be that of responsibility before a uniform liberal court. This court itself is a fiction, and one moreover whose dark inner secret is constitution by a voluntarist theology securing order through the formal regulation of chaos from a single sovereign centre. Such a liberal option in theology in fact remains confined within a logic constructed by extrinsicism. Its essentially authoritarian character is revealed when it stamps philosophical conclusions already arrived at with a theological seal of approval derived from doctrines which extrinsically symbolize supposedly universal truths.

But nor can the answer be a fideistic one. Revelation is not in any sense a layer added to reason. It arrives as the augmentation of illumination, and faith is found only in the highly complex and tortuous course of a reason that is hopeful and charitable. It is lodged in all the complex networks of human practices, and its boundaries are as messy as those of the Church itself. De Lubac's paradox forbids us to privilege either a human above or a human below. Rather, what has real priority in his scheme is the divine supernatural, which so exceeds our human hierarchies that it includes every degree of them in equality and is as near to the below as to the above. So although the lure of the supernatural takes precedence over nature that is drawn towards it (and this cannot be perverted into the transcendentalist terms of Rahner), this lure is only acknowledged by aspiring nature in all her lowly variety. Theological truth first of all abides in the body of the faithful.

Yet where are their plural bodies, especially today? Not neatly gathered in, that is for sure: rather, disseminated outwards into complex minglings and associations. A faith obedient to the Church is protected from solipsism precisely at the point where one recognizes that the Church has always been, as John Henry Newman recognized, itself the taking up and inter-mingling of many human traditions. It even consists from the outset in seeing how the diverse might cohere, and continues to enact this analogical mingling.

Therefore I do not find the plural space of the academy, as perhaps *best* symbolized by Religious Studies departments, wherein alone *alternative* traditions of reason are sometimes recognized, to be totally other to the space of the Church that is also pluralistic and also construes its truth, as does the Bible, to be in one of its aspects a certain narration of 'the history of religions'. The difference is that the Church has a project of integration, to which the theologian is bound. Within both the academy and the Church, the task of theology is to foreground the Christian difference and non-difference – to think through the Christian logic as something entirely exceptional which also continues and elevates what is most usual to humanity.

How exactly though, does theology relate to Church authority? This is the question we must turn to next, under the heading *corpus mysticum.*

IV

How are we to understand the nature of ecclesial authority and its bearing upon theology? Jean-Luc Marion has said in *God Without Being* that the key is to realize that the Bishop is the true theologian.[22] I think that he is precisely right, but that his point has usually been misunderstood (especially in the United States).

What he is invoking of course, is a vital link between theology and the Eucharist. The Bishop is the original President at the Eucharist; he is also the prime preacher of the Word, a function which he performs only in conjunction with his representing of the body and blood of Christ.

The idea that all theologians must sub-derive their authority as theologians from the Bishop is only authoritarian under an erroneous understanding of the relationship of the Bishop to the Eucharist, to the word of God and to his *cathedra*, which is at once his teaching office and also literally the place where he sits and presides, usually a city of long-standing.

However, such an erroneous understanding was already encouraged by shifts in the conception of the Church and its relation to the Eucharist in the late mediaeval and early modern period. As de Lubac described these transformations, the term *corpus verum* ceased, roughly after the mid twelfth century, to be applied to the Church, and was transferred to the body of Christ in the Eucharist. Inversely, the term *corpus mysticum* migrated from the Eucharist to the Church.[23] Gradually, the latter was drained of physical solidity, which was transferred to the transubstantiated elements. 'Mystical' slowly ceased to mean 'to do with the liturgical mysteries of initiatory passage, participation and ascent' and came to denote secrecy, absence and symbolism. Accompanying this transformation, was a change in the relation of both bodies to the historical body of Christ. Earlier, the sacramental and ecclesial bodies stood near each other, and both represented the historical body. But in the new scheme, the historical and sacramental bodies began to stand near each other as alien sources of authority over against the Church, which, as Michel de Certeau stresses in his brilliant commentary on de Lubac's *Corpus Mysticum* and *Exégèse Medievale*, increasingly came to be seen as an ideal space to be constructed in order to realize the dicta of authority, or else to make manifest a new inner 'mystical' experience which is the residue of liturgical ascent that finds no place in a more legal and less liturgical construal of the public sphere.[24]

As long as an essential relation between the three bodies remained however, strong traces of the older view persisted – for example in the thought of Bonaventure or of Thomas Aquinas. It remained the case that the historical body was mediated to the Church by the sacramental body. The Eucharist still 'gave' the Church, in such a fashion that, as Catherine Pickstock puts it, the Church was not a closed self-governing entity like most political bodies (whether hierarchic or democratic), but rather received its very social embodiment from outside itself.[25] At every Eucharist it had, as it were, to begin again, to receive itself anew from without, from the past and from the angelic Church above. Inversely, the transubstantiation of the bread and wine into the body and blood of Christ was seen as a dynamic action of divine self-giving inseparable from the bringing about and consolidating of the body of the faithful. (Incidentally, the term 'transubstantiation' is much older than the term 'real presence' which is only really current after 1550: *praesentia corporalis* was used in the Middle Ages but shied away from by Aquinas, and is dubiously linked with a static sense of exclusionary local presence that is also 'over against' the congregation.)[26]

The really drastic change came when, as de Certeau following de Lubac stresses, the sacramental body ceased to operate this mediating function. Then, instead of a triad, one had alternating dyads: a direct relation of either the absent historical body, as testified to by Scripture, to the Church, or else of the sacramental body to the Church, the Sacrament now being taken as a source of authority *independent* of scripture and rather deriving from a hierarchic transmission of ecclesial orders. As de Certeau concludes, this eventually brings about a total shift from a priority of the diachronic to a priority of the synchronic and functional. Previously, the past had really been made present again through the Eucharist, and the Church had re-emerged through its sustaining of a bond to the past and projection forwards to the future, by re-offering of the sacraments and reinterpretation of the *sacra scriptura*. Now instead, the past started to seem like a remote lost source of authority which historical detective work must flesh out (thus the rise of humanist concern with 'historicity'). As remote, it stood apart from and over against the Church, which no longer represented it. Its relationship to the other sacramental source of authority was bound now to be disputed, since the sacramental body was no longer seen as an essential way in which the lost historical body as traced out by the scriptures was 'performed' again in the present. Either sacraments as validated by tradition were seen as an essential supplement to the now remote scriptures, as in the late mediaeval and Tridentine views, or else the need for this supplement was rejected, and one was left with the Protestant *sola scriptura*. But de Certeau's drastic conclusion here is both rigorous and undeniable; the crucial shift was certainly not the Reformation: rather Protestantism and Tridentine Catholicism represented two alternative versions of 'reformation' which should be defined as the switch from the triadic to the dyadic account of the relation of the various bodies of Christ. It is this sort of realization which could be the ground for a more honest and self-critical ecumenism.

Under the new disposition, the power of clerical authority was necessarily increased. For when the historical body had been again made present in the Eucharist, and the Eucharistic body had been only fully realized in the congregation, primary authority had been both symbolic and collective, and initially bypassed vertical hierarchy. Only by a sort of reflex was episcopal authority constituted. The Bishop was first of all powerful as identified with a particular *cathedra*, which was a specific intersection of time and place that recorded a particular Christian fulfilment of a particular local legacy: thus nearly all churches were built on earlier sacred sites, and this was not at all

124

primarily a matter of propaganda, but of vital continuity in and through a surpassing. As president of the Eucharist and teacher from his chair, the Bishop enacted once again the essence of a certain place (usually the abode of sacred relics) and perpetuated the stream of glory refracted through it in a specific way. The Bishop held authority, from Ignatius of Antioch onwards, as symbolizing in his singleness the unity of the Church in a single *civitas*. Of course the Bishop was also the guardian and guarantor of correct trans- mission, and of course his exercise of these powers might often in reality over-step the mark of his representational and dramatic function. All the same, it remained the case up until the mid thirteenth century or so that clerical sacramental and preaching authority was much more 'mingled' with lay participation that it later became – although at first in the later Middle Ages the laity defended itself with the increased activity of semi-independent lay fraternities.[27]

It was nevertheless during this period that the techniques of remote, secret and invasive clerical control, as deployed through auricular confession, exorcism and staged miracles, first mooted in the twelfth century and promulgated through the Lateran Councils, were vastly extended. The 'gothic' realm of complex overlapping spaces and social participations started to give way to the 'gothick' realm of systematic terror through *surveillance*. It is no accident that one of the great 'gothick' novels of the romantic period, the Irish Protestant Charles Maturin's *Melmoth the Wanderer*, deploys a critique of the Spanish Inquisition also as a critique of Calvinist predestinationism and of modernity as such.[28]

This increased clerical control was inseparable from the new economy of the three bodies. For no longer was the transmission of authority carried through in a superhuman 'angelic' fashion by the liturgical action. No longer did the historical body pass via the Bishop into the mouths of communicants or (more often) the eyes of witnesses, who then 'performed' what the liturgical script suggested. Instead, the historical and sacramental bodies were now more like inert objects in need of human subjective assistance. For the magisterial Reformation, the ordained clergy were the privileged interpreters of the word, who quickly established 'orthodox' parameters within which it could be read, so neutralizing its supposedly self- interpreting authority, as Catholic critics swiftly pointed out. For Tridentine Catholicism, the ordained hierarchy was the guarantor of a Eucharistic miracle now seen as a spectacle quite apart from its dynamic action of 'giving' the body of the Church.

So we cannot possibly talk of an increased lay influence in Protestantism over against a Catholic clericalist reaction. Rather, in either case there is a substantial loss of mediaeval lay participation (as the British Catholic historians, John Bossy, John Scarisbrick and Eamon Duffy have all argued),[29] while in either case also, there is a significant rise in compensating lay pieties and mysticisms which try to colonize the no-man's land which had now

125

arisen in the gap between a closed humanism on the one hand, and an extrinsicist system of dogma on the other. As de Certeau argues, a 'mystic' discourse arises with a redoubling of the sense of the absence of a true ecclesial body, although it is very often recruited into the machinations of ecclesiastical discipline and the attempts to verify abstractions with experience, and build a new future on the basis of formal method.

It would seem then, that the earlier, high mediaeval model offers us a much better understanding of the relation of the Bishop to teaching and so to theological reflection. Theology is answerable to the Bishop as the occupant of the *cathedra* and as President at the Eucharist. But this means that the theologian is primarily answerable, not so much to a Church hierarchy in its synchronic spatiality – this is all too modern – but rather to a hierarchical, educative *manuductio* of the faith down the ages. Equally he is answerable to a specific locality, or even multiple specific localities, such that his sense of perpetuating a history must be combined with his sense of carrying out an archaeology and mapping a geography. Finally he is also answerable to the mode of the reception of sacrament and word by the congregation, even if this is now in the early twenty-first century frequently impossible and the theologian must exercise what is an excessively critical function by ideal standards.

But this sounds all rather abstract. Who really constrains the theologian and to what degree? The Bishop? The Congregation? And how are we to understand the workings of ecclesiastical hierarchy today in the realm of Christian knowledge and action, given the great approval that the Church appears to give to democracy in the secular sphere?

V

To try to answer these questions somewhat, I want to invoke the thought of Nicholas of Cusa in his early work, the *De Concordantia Catholica*.[30] Although this was a conciliarist treatise, Nicholas's later papalist position did not abandon its essential conclusions. It is very interesting from our point of view, because it almost uniquely preserves, at a very late date, a much earlier perspective upon the mediating role of sacramental signs between the historical and ecclesial bodies. At the same time, it shows traces also of more modern elements that are of a kind that are inescapable today: a new stress upon mass assembled participation in the present, and upon historical variation that is due to the cultural variety of human imaginings. In addition, Nicholas, following Augustine and other patristic sources, anticipates an apocalyptic time when the Church will be in terminal decline, which may be our current situation. So perhaps Nicholas provides some keys not merely to recovering the lost pre-1300 world, but also to going forward now to the future we might always have had, yet never yet have had.

126

Cusanus sustains the thesis that the Eucharist gives the Church. For him what stands topmost in the Church hierarchy is not a *de jure* legal power, but rather sacramental signs. In this way, in the tradition of Dionysius, the ecclesial and the experiential are still fused through the liturgical mysteries. The sacramental signs for Nicholas correspond at a lower level of the cosmic hierarchy to the Triune God at the very top of the hierarchy (given that a neoplatonic hierarchy involves a series of stages such that lower stages analogously repeat within their inner hierarchy, the pattern of inner hierarchy of higher stages: see Proclus, *Elements of Theology*, Prop. 108). God is said fully to know the members of the Church in love, and they are orientated to the Trinity through a desire that exceeds their intellection – a very 'Eastern' element here. The next rank below God within the heavenly *ecclesia*, the eternal Jerusalem (wherein God 'is' through all perpetuity, as in later Russian sophiology) is the angelic. The angels, in a rather Arabic fashion, see into all human intellects, and human thought especially puts us into contact with the separate intelligences. Within the ecclesial hierarchy, the priesthood is linked to the angelic in terms of its teaching function, and its occupancy of *cathedrae*, since the *Apocalypse* tells us that angels are guardians of ecclesial places. In the third rank comes the Blessed in Heaven who are linked to humanity on earth through the body, and who correspond to the body of the faithful within the Church militant here below.

There are certain complications within this scheme: the clergy in relation to their *orders* correspond to the first sacramental rank – but this seals the priority of their sacramental, transmissive function over their authoritative, teaching one. In fact the clergy span all three degrees, because in terms of their participation with the laity in intercessory offices, they belong to the lowest level which simply praises and does not mediate.

In addition, there seems to be a certain lack of consistency: the laity are the most bodily, and yet their function of praise is also a spiritual synthesis of sacramental sign and physically situated *cathedra*. The same unclarity pertains in the heavenly Church: the resurrected faithful are the most corporeal and yet their third psychic position (in keeping with the neoplatonic hierarchy of the One, *nous*, and *psyche*) also synthesizes through desire the Origin that is God and the intellection that belongs to the angels. The confusion perhaps has its source in the blending of Proclus with Trinitarian theology. For all these degrees also correspond for Nicholas to the respective persons of the Trinity, and though the Son is as *Logos* intellectual, as *imago* he is also somewhat 'corporeal' compared with the unity in desire shown by the Spirit.

It is in fact the presence of the Trinity at the top of the hierarchy that has a deconstructive effect at every level of the hierarchy; although Nicholas also inherits the deconstructions inherent in Proclean neoplatonism itself. He offers in this treatise perhaps one of the fullest exhibitions ever of the multiple paradoxes of hierarchy: indeed out of them he generates an early democratic theory. The idea that he simply 'mixed' mediaeval hierarchy with proto-modern democracy, as Paul Sigmund says, is simply not the case: instead he returns to earlier high mediaeval mystical and educative notions of hierarchy, and out of these notions themselves generates new democratic theses.[31] This gives a basis for conciliarism and consensus quite other to the contractualist one of William of Ockham, which blasphemously reduces Church government to a balance of power between formally considered individual forces.

Let us begin with the paradoxes already glimpsed by neoplatonism. Paradox one: a hierarchy, to be a hierarchy, requires stages, else it would be qualityless flux – a mere 'ramp' *without* distinctions or with infinite multiple distinctions, rather than a 'staircase' (see Proclus, Prop. 21) But then a stage can only be distinguished within a flux if it marks out a *level*, which will be a field of equality. And yet to sustain the ontological primacy of hierarchy – every emanation from on high is continuously diminishing – the level must itself be broken up as a hierarchy within a hierarchy, and of course this threatens a *mise en abîme*, indicated in Cusa's text by a slightly insane process of triadic sub-dividing on the part of an author who of course knew that finitude itself was subject to infinite division. A consequence of this logic of levels is that the subordinate within a certain stage is nonetheless equal – with its subordinateness entirely cancelled – to all members of that stage if one rises to a more fundamental hierarchical viewpoint (Proclus, Prop. 21).

It is this crux that provides Nicholas with his fundamental conciliarist principle. From the *highest* perspective, all that is created is equal; within the Church militant all its members are on a level, just as the sacramental and ecclesial bodies are on a level. Since the true ontological character of the Church, following Augustine, is peace and harmony, which for Cusa is extended into *discors concordia*, the first ruling principle within the Church is consensus. Not of course in the first place majority rule, but absolute consensus. For the Church is not first and foremost a vehicle of correct teaching: it is rather first and foremost the *event of concordantia*. (A concept almost identical to the Russian *sobornost*. For Sergei Bulgakov, as for Nicholas, truth is '*conciliarité*' and 'to live in union with the Church is to live in the truth, and to live in the truth is to live in union with the Church'.) Doctrine is about nothing but the giving of divine *concordantia* in the Creation and its restoration through the Incarnation and the Church, which is the arrival of reconciliation. Hence there cannot be true teaching without peaceful consensus – even if, one might add, this consensus and the key to harmony can dwindle to being present only in a few, as Augustine anticipates will eventually happen when there will be left only the 'last of the last'.[32]

It is for this reason that teaching is inseparable from the guarantee of the Holy Spirit's presence in the Church: in the long run and for the most part, the members of the Church will be reliable, because without this there could *be* no true doctrine. For doctrine is first of all a body and not simply words:

128

Christ was the supreme teacher as the event of the return of *concordantia* to the world. For truth there must be democratic consent, although this must also be a uniting in 'the right way', according to the true measure of harmony. If 'democracy' failed, the Church would cease to be; yet the keys to democratic consensus must much of the time be safeguarded by an ecclesiastical elite, gathered round the bishops, or a single protesting bishop, like Athanasius.

At this point the significance of the nested hierarchy within each level comes to the fore. It is not really a principle in opposition to 'democracy'. That is only the case where, within a closed immanent circle based upon a balance of interests between forces, a sovereign centre is granted *de facto* power. This is why liberalism always generates terrifying hierarchies not linked to the transmission of values: hierarchies of money and bureaucratic organization and policing. Here one has the necessary authoritarian counterpart to the mitigated anarchy of market society. By contrast, the power that Nicholas invested in the *cathedra* is a salve against the closure that the emerging sovereign state and later liberal democracy would soon place around a specific, often 'national' community. In fact, even a global community is closed against a wider democracy if it is only 'in the present'; this is the point of Edmund Burke or Alexis de Tocqueville's appeal to the votes of all the ages. The Bishop and those gathered round him must especially sustain the *concordantia* with the past and preserve the resources of the past for the future against the likely ravages of the present. Thus the Bishop is poised between the always arriving order of signs and the consensus of the people which can alone fulfil that order. His authority derives from both. But ultimately, of course, he must appeal to the widest democracy of all: namely the original *concordantia* of the whole cosmos, grounded in the consensus of the Trinity, which Cusa in this work already presents as the coincidence of the opposites of the one and the many.

Nicholas's ecclesiology results from the interplay between the democratic and aristocratic principles, combined with a monarchic one in terms of the papacy. But even in the latter case the stress is upon *cathedra*: the Pope's authority is that of an ancestral place.[33] A place which has been the focal intersection of so much for so long, evil as well as good, is likely to have a certain priority in terms of the persistence of the rhythms of the truth. The same applies to every episcopal seat in a lesser degree. So in fact a single principle legitimates *both* the democratic and the aristocratic aspects. This principle is 'for the most part'. Applied synchronically, one gets democracy: the consensus of the entire laity and clergy is the most reliable guide – a Newman-like principle. Applied diachronically one gets aristocracy: the longest-persisting locations and their representatives will be the least likely to err. Yet the entire diachrony merges with an eternal synchrony: the voices of all times and places are the final court of appeal, in so far as these voices sing with one true voice of praise.

Thus infallibility, speaking *ex cathedra*, works in the following way for Cusanus. True infallibility resides in the whole Church on account of the presence of the Holy Spirit, without which human salvation would be null and void. Then it resides in the conciliar assembly of the bishops, and finally in the supreme *cathedra* of Rome, the longest-abiding seat of sacred legitimacy. The Pope is the supreme guardian: he has the right to summons a general council. But the consensus of the council is a more reliable locus of infallibility than the Pope, as in turn it is weaker than the entire *ecclesia*. A council has the right to depose a false Pope – and Nicholas even sustained this view in his later papalist phase.[34]

But throughout these considerations, which owed much to Cyprian as well as to Augustine, Nicholas never lost sight of his sense of the primacy of the sacramental. This primacy, as Augustine recognized when dealing with the Donatists, ensures that even erring clergy can be true ministers. For the belief in the infallibility of the Church is not a peculiar superstition: instead it resides finally in our trust in certain signs. Since we cannot command the meaning of any sign, true signs will always outwit our worst intentions, and inhabit us promisingly despite ourselves. This is how the Holy Spirit is present in the Church.

A second paradox of hierarchy is that the higher element within a lower stage must always be more akin to the *lower* stages above itself than the higher stages above itself. This is aporetic, because stages involve not just a smooth descent but rather a regular folding back of the whole process upon itself to produce the instance of stages, such that the higher element within each stage re-invokes the summit *out of series*, while the lower element anticipates the nethermost base, also out of series.

Neoplatonism was fully aware that to produce a distinct new level which must in a measure 'hold back' the free fall of emanation, a new charge from the original source must somehow flow down the chain and to a degree interrupt the process of diminution: the principle of 'remission' (Proclus, Props, 56, 97, 100). Or to put this the other way around: a distinct new phase must somehow override the immediately higher intermediary and re-invoke the origin directly – as well as the entire series of higher causes above the most immediate one.

For example, if the hierarchy runs throughout from Spirit to Body, the higher elements in lower stages will be more spiritual than the lower elements within that stage, but more bodily than everything higher up, in such a fashion that these elements shift undecidably between 'more spiritual' and 'more bodily'. In consequence, there will be an increasing tendency as one descends the hierarchy to perceive even the topmost dimensions of stages as 'more bodily', and thus an asymptotic tendency *to reverse* the hierarchy in the lower stages altogether. Ethnographers have discovered that many local tribes with symbolic hierarchies actually carry through this reversal, so that, for example, 'male' will be on top in a higher realm, and 'female' in a lower.

This second paradox tends to produce explicit reversal in the lower realm, and parallel orders of hierarchy, albeit hierarchically arranged. In the case of Cusanus, this happens with the body of the faithful. In so far as they are more fleshly, then fleshly concerns here assume priority. The laity of the Church are governed by the Emperor within a separate hierarchy that owes direct responsibility to the Trinity.[35] The authenticity of the donation of Constantine is denied by Nicholas, and the crowning of the Emperor is seen as confirmation of an already proclaimed power, as applies also to the coronation of the Pope. Yet of course the realm of the Emperor still belongs to *ecclesia*: Cusa, unlike some thinkers soon to come (supremely, Jean Bodin), is not yet talking about 'the State'. Concerns of the flesh remain ultimately subordinate to those of the spirit, and the Emperor like the Pope is still answerable to the infallibility of the entire body of the Church. In so far as this is concentrated and focused in the Pope, he also remains in some sense answerable to Rome. Indeed he is of course the Holy Roman Emperor. (Nicholas's perspective is naturally Germanic.)

A third paradox of hierarchy is much accentuated by Trinitarian theology. The origin of a hierarchy cannot merely be the highest rung: as the source of every stage it must transcend hierarchy as such and even equalize within itself all stages of the hierarchy, negating their differentiation. This is the neoplatonic doctrine of the mystical One. However, the Trinity tends to turn this non-differentiation into preserval as much as obliteration of the many, as Nicholas stresses. This increases the sense that at the top, degree is crossed out, while inversely it allows lower degrees truly to participate in, and to reflect the One. Furthermore, as we have seen, hierarchy requires distinguished stages, and in fact a minimum of three stages, since if there were only two there would not be mediation and interval and therefore no stages at all. So Nicholas, like neoplatonism in general, posits three main stages, and subdivides his stages into three also. But the Trinity teaches that the One is also Three and therefore that it 'complicates' what hierarchy 'explicates', to use Cusan terminology. We have already seen that within every stage the totality of the stage ranks above the topmost rank within a stage, so that, for example, the Bishop is above the laity, but the whole Church is above the Bishop. The invocation of a Creator God makes this principle apply more emphatically to the totality of everything. Since all differences of rank are utterly subordinated to the qualitatively different difference of rank between Creator and Created, the totality of the cosmos emphatically comes next after God, rather than the created intelligences. (In Russian terms the whole cosmos is first the location of the created *Sophia*, akin to the traditional *anima mundi*, or Ralph Cudworth's 'plastic principle'.) Moreover, because in the Triune God the second and the third stage are equal and co-original, this means that the paradox of levelling as one ascends the hierarchical ladder is carried over into the Absolute itself, which thereby much more validates cosmic levelling. In this levelling, the Trinity is itself manifest. Therefore at the summit of the created hierarchy all the lower degrees are now fully equalized: body is restored to parity with spirit, as occurs in the resurrection of the dead.

The cosmos one is concerned with here, however, is really the totality of the restored cosmos concentrated in the heavenly Jerusalem: the angels and the resurrected faithful, plus God in his glorious presence. The latter is the heavenly glory that reflects the intra-divine *Sophia* that is the ontological ground of the emergence of the Son and the Spirit in the Trinity for modern Russian theology, or the primal active power of 'outgoing' that Gregory of Nyssa named *dynamis* and Dionysius in the plural *dynameis*. At this highest level one can infer therefore that the laity and the Emperor are equalized with the Bishop, while the latter's *cathedra* is equalized with sacramental signs now fully realized. Indeed via the resurrected body of the Lamb in the heart of the eternal city, the Bride Jerusalem is equalized with God and drawn through deification entirely into the life of the Trinity.

So the principle of hierarchical ascension guards truth against democracy, but the more ascension is enacted, the more also democracy is implemented in the truth. It is not that democracy is a compromise for here and now: it is rather that it can only finally arrive in the perfection of *concordantia* as deification. To eternalize democracy, and maintain its link with excellence rather than the mutual concessions of baseness, deification as the doctrine of the offer of equality with God is required. (Again this is close to the Russian theological embrace, and yet critique of, the egalitarian tendencies of modern times.)

Such divine democracy is approximated to here below in the processes of historical *traditio*. For Nicholas as a 'Renaissance' thinker, these now include a passage through the cultural relativity of different human fictionings: different sacraments and sacrifices in all human cultures, that nonetheless all really indicate the one sign of Christ and his sacrifice.[36] It is here that a 'modern' factor comes into the picture: a new sense that human institutions really do spring from collective 'makings'. Such a sense is also what pushes Cusa towards bringing out the latent democratic implications of an inherited and highly traditional – indeed in his day totally out-of-date – Trinitarian and liturgical hierarchical vision. Even hierarchical structures are erected by fashioned consensus, beginning with God himself. Truly Nicholas was 'radically orthodox'.

For Cusa, as for Augustine, the ontological diminution through emanation worked also downwards through time because of the Fall. For Augustine, the sixth age of the world inaugurated by Christ is human old age, marked by decline and a worsening of the Fall's effects. Yet here also, the paradoxes intrude, reinforced by Trinitarian theology: direct contact with the origin can be established even in senescence. At almost the end, there has been absolute rejuvenation: for Augustine 'progress' becomes possible for the first time in the era of ultimate degeneration. This is the Christianized temporal remission exercised by grace. It involves an absolute duality: as W.H. Auden understood in his libretto for the Christmas Oratorio *For the Time Being*, the Incarnation institutes a time of dread when we have to live in the partial meaninglessness of an aftermath to the appearance of the ultimate – to live in absolute waiting for the consummation of what was begun and yet is 'for the time being' suspended.[37] It is also the time of terrible demand for perfection and, in Augustinian terms, the time when evil in its nakedness as Antichrist will appear, as the response to Christ of always worsening evil. The world 'through the looking-glass' after Redemption, is the new world of wonder, and yet also of a new faerie dread. For Augustine, the faithful in the face of this uncanny peril are likely to be few and will get fewer, until we reach the 'last of the last'. Nicholas agreed, and thought he had reached that period. He gave the world 600 more years (writing in the *De Concordantia* in 1433) until Europe had been destroyed and yet Christ preached throughout the world. Therefore he anticipated in a sense both globalization and the end of Christendom. Yet this disastrous era is also for him precisely the time in which a conciliar and democratic ideal that will truly reflect the Trinity can at last be achieved on earth. Disaster will make us see more truly.

It is in a sense comforting to realize that our predicament was from the outset foreseen – for Augustine and Nicholas only build upon Christ's warnings and promises in the gospels. Neither triumphalism nor celebration of secular autonomy are here suggested. Rather there will be catastrophic refusal of charity. However, the hypostatic presence of the Holy Spirit on earth will not fail, and hence the 'time being' can be a time of meaningful realization of deified democracy: even especially in the further darkening period toward the end. There will be decline ... and yet there will be progress.

VI

Theology, therefore, is answerable to reason precisely in so far as it is answerable to the Church. And in the latter domain it is first of all answerable to the Triune God, since theology is a participation in the mind of God before it is obedience to any authority, whether scriptural or hierarchical. But as such it is equally a participation in the whole deified Church as *Sophia* or the heavenly Jerusalem. The latter is nonetheless only encountered through earthly mediation, and here theology is first answerable to the whole Church militant, although this involves a certain answerability to the Bishop in the way that we have seen.

But in what way is theology also answerable to Scripture? Here, once again, we can only see clearly when we refuse post-1300 dualities. As we saw, Protestantism privileged the historical body of Christ, Trent the sacramental body. Equally, this meant a preference either for Scripture or Tradition, respectively. But prior to Henry of Ghent, there had been no such juxta-position. He for the first time, reacting against Wycliffe and Huss's appeal to Scripture over against *traditiones humanae*, asked which had primacy: the *auctoritates* of the *dicta*, or those of the Church? Although Henry sees any discrepancy between the two as only an abstract possiblity, not as a reality, his question still reveals that something had already altered.[38] Now it seemed it was already the case that Scripture was a closed book in the past that needed supplementing by a separate oral command. Basil the Great had spoken of written and unwritten traditions, but the latter were seen by him and by later theologians as consisting in the 'performance' of the text itself. *Traditio* was the handing over of the text into practice. Gratian in his *Decretals*, following Augustine, identified reason and truth with the deposit of Scripture, whose authority is universal like that of the Church and so organically coincides with it (C.8): 'custom' is different, and regards the relatively unimportant; we praise custom however, when it is known not to impinge on Catholic faith (C.6 and 4). Thomas Aquinas likewise speaks of *sacra scriptura* as the sole authority for *sacra doctrina*, in a way that sounds 'Protestant' by later Tridentine standards (S.T. I. Q. 1. a 8). But he is not speaking of the Humanist Bible which the reformers and the counter-reformers equally inherited. There was, as yet, no single bound printed book, but many manuscripts of different books of the Bible – usually surrounded by patristic commentary. Gregory the Great had said that when he read and commented on the Bible, the text itself expanded.[39] It was up to the commentator to go on trying to achieve the Bible as the infinite Borgesian library spoken of at the end of St John's Gospel, as it was equally up to the painter and stager of miracle plays.

Such a Novalis-like or Mallarméan perspective was also presupposed by the entire practice of allegorical exegesis. This rendered theology possible by showing how Christological and ecclesial restoration of the world depended upon the assumption of a divine 'rhetoric of things'. Things referred to in the Old Testament were already redeemed, since they pointed forwards allegorically to Christ: in the 'time being' after Christ, we could be redeemed, because his deeds indicated and made possible our anagogical performances. As de Certeau says, all this depended upon a sense that there were 'essential' shared universal meanings between things; in consequence nominalism ensured the collapse of allegory as the real divine rhetoric and so of the true inner basis of Christian theology. Without intrinsic aesthetic connections, the ways of God in history became indecipherable, and one was left instead with a series of positive institutions, only linked as logically possible manifestations of the divine absolute power. Logical reflection upon this situation was now divorced from ontology, and the rhetorical dimension of Scripture and preaching was henceforth somewhat confined to mere human words. The 'treatise on sacred rhetoric' emerged within both a Reformation and a Counter-Reformation ambience.

It is nevertheless true that in various ways de Certeau exaggerates. Indeed his own somewhat 'nihilistic' (in a strictly technical sense) theology seems to require the later decadent situation of bodily absence to be normative. He exaggerates the negativity of the 'time being'. The Church is not just, as he says, a mystical substitute for the lost real Israel and the living body of Christ: it also truly is in all its physicality and placement in *cathedrae* still exactly both these things. It only lost this positivity through the processes traced by de Lubac and de Certeau himself. Moreover, are we to perceive the work of the univocalist/nominalist tendency within the Church only negatively? Without lapsing into Hegelian dialectic, one can acknowledge that catastrophe may help one to see more clearly, and that the nominalist critique exposes certain faults to view. There are three points to be made here.

First of all, in the face of nominalism and univocity, Nicholas of Cusa realized that both realism about universals, and analogical participation, require one to see the limited scope of the law of identity – for Ockham says with some truth that a common essence would be in the same respect both particular and universal (this would apply especially to Aquinas's view that the common *forma* is in things *as* this particular substance). Likewise he says that an analogous *essentia* would be in the same respect both shared and proper (and this would apply especially to Aquinas's view that the partici-pated *esse is* the particular existence of a finite being).[40] Nicholas saw that outside finite limits the law of identity no longer holds, although he also sustained a Platonic view that only the eternal *has* an unalterable identity and is fully *non aliud*. Finite things, though they exclude, and cannot be their opposite, are also involved in an infinite shifting 'approximation', and ceaselessly tend toward the opposite of what they are. For this reason, that which exceeds the law of identity also alone upholds it. In effect Nicholas's specifically post-nominalist perspective brings more fully to view a modifi-cation of Platonism and Christian ontology in terms of a far more emphatic affirmation of the infinitude of the absolute which is specifically a conse-quence of the idea of a simple and unified (but not individual) God with unlimited power (pure *possest* or *posse* for Cusa) to effect Being as such, in limited beings. And as with the Russian *Sophia*, infinity is for Cusa the inner reality of even the finite world; here he in part takes up again Grosseteste's innovations.

Secondly, Cusa's interest in human participation in divine creative power can also be related to Scotus and Ockham. Given their affirmation of univocity, they tend to say, unlike Aquinas, that creatures can fully bring about being. Hence Ockham declares that human beings in a sense create (QQ 2.9) Nicholas says this too, but he restores the creaturely bringing about of being in a finite thing to the context of participation and mediation that still sees being as really an effect of God alone. Nevertheless, in the wake of the nominalists, he talks explicitly of human acts of creation in a way that

Aquinas and Bonaventure did not, even if their thought does indicate a human participation in the process of *creatio continua*[41] and is in principle open to the Cusan development.

In the third place, Nicholas also realized, following the nominalists, that universals are indeed constructed through language, but that 'fictionalized' universals may still exhibit something that holds in reality, albeit in a more 'conjectural' fashion than acknowledged hitherto. Dietrich of Freibourg and Ulrich of Strasbourg, as Alain de Libera notes, sought to save the Dominican realist legacy by speaking of a purely internal mental construction of the universal, so at once returning to Plotinus and anticipating idealism. But by pursuing a more Proclean, theurgic path (that had always stressed the descent of the ideal in external liturgical and symbolic guises) in a new linguistic mode, Cusa instead opened out a new space for rhetoric, poetics and the human fabricatedness of history.[42] If Boulnois is right in saying that the Thomist paradox of the supernatural is in part inspired by the Aristotelian maxim 'art imitates nature', since for grace, as with art, a sustaining of nature also exceeds and completes it, then the new Cusan space suggests a more explicit coincidence of grace with the art that is intellect.

Such a coincidence, despite de Certeau, *is* found amongst certain exponents of sacred rhetoric. In, for example, the work of the Lutheran Matthias Flacius Illyricus, rhetoric is not reduced to ornament and propagandistic manipulation, nor is traditional fourfold exegesis totally abandoned. Instead one finds here a fusion of a human rhetoric which sustains a Longinian interest in the way words can both reveal and enact through performance the real (Longinus may have been close to theurgic neo-platonism), with a continued acknowledgement of the allegorical divine real rhetoric in created things.[43] The anagogic here continues to 'pro-duce' the past in the older sense of 'lead forth', but this production includes now also a moment of the creative 'production' of truth in words. Through a blending of Longinus with Augustine's rhetorical writings, that was oft repeated by both Protestant and Catholic writers in the sixteenth century, the indwelling of the Spirit is rethought in terms of a doctrine of poetic inspiration. The Biblical writings themselves are considered by Flacius Illyricus as human rhetorical construction as well as a divine allegory of the real. This was possible within a Longinian perspective that saw the style with the most sublimely persuasive 'coiled force' to be a 'brief', albeit figurative style, full of *res* and a minimum of *verba*. Such a fusion of human and divine rhetoric carries right through to the Anglicans John Dennis and Robert Lowth in the seventeenth and eighteenth centuries, and thence to the North German Hamann, and many in the nineteenth century, both Catholic and Protestant, influenced by him.[44]

All such people indicate how, in times of diminution, our task is not *only* to recover the pre-1300 vision, but also to acknowledge human consensus, co-operation and varied free poetic power in a way this vision did not fully envisage. High mediaevalism needs to be supplemented by a Christian socialism, conceived in the widest sense.

Theologians who may be the last of the last still have an ecclesial task before them.

8

GRACE

The midwinter sacrifice

I

The Church, as the body of Christ, follows the *via crucis*; in this way it restores peace. By so doing, it also mediates forgiveness to us, and so brings again the reign of goodness and truth. But how exactly does mediation occur? How is the regime of concordantia conveyed to the individual as the event of grace? In what way is reconciliation between specific individuals brought about?

Since I reject all Protestant accounts of grace as mere imputation (although there are many Protestant accounts not of this kind), an account of the arrival of grace must for me also mean an account of sanctification, and of ethics. At the same time, however, I shall argue that we are good *only* by grace, and that, in Kierkegaardian terms, the Good is only possible beyond the ethical, in the religious realm.

The schema of Chapters 1 to 6 has now been reversed. In those chapters, there was a sequence of two pairs (Chapters 1 with 2 and then Chapters 3 plus 4 with Chapters 5 plus 6). Each pair dealt first with the relatively private and then with the relatively public aspect of evil/violence and good/peace. But Chapter 7 dealt with the public peace inaugurated by Christ, since this is the primary effect of the Incarnation, and there is no grace not mediated by the Church (it being understood that the Church, like grace, is every-where). Now, however, we need to turn to the more personal complement of ecclesiology: the mediation of forgiveness by grace (Chapters 9 and 10 will sustain this reversal).

We saw nevertheless in Chapter 3 that forgiveness itself hovers between the personal and the political: between victimhood and sovereignty. In this chapter therefore, we shall at times appropriately reflect upon the arrival of forgiveness by grace in terms of the figure of the *king*, who combines in his *corpus* and *persona* both empirical individuality and symbolic generality.

II

Usually, Christianity is seen as suppressing 'moral luck', or the idea that, to a degree at least, we require good fortune if we are to be good. However, in this chapter, I want to argue to the contrary, that Christianity embraces moral luck to such an extreme degree that it transforms all received ideas of the ethical.

In the course of this argument I shall try to show that these received ideas of the ethical, which may or may not permit some play to 'moral luck', all subscribe to a 'sacrificial economy'. And that they do so in two different variants: either in terms of the giving up of the lesser for the greater, or else of a more radical notion of absolute sacrifice of self for the other, without any 'return' for, or of the self, in any guise whatsoever. The second variant, which would usually see itself as *escaping* the sacrificial economy of *do ut des*, but which I will argue is but this same economy taken to its logical extreme, has been recently espoused in different but profoundly analogous ways by Jan Patocka, Emmanuel Levinas and Jacques Derrida.[1] Against this view, which now enjoys a wide consensus, I shall argue that a self-sacrificial view of morality is first, immoral, second, impossible, and third, a deformation, not the fulfilment, as Patocka echoed by Derrida claims, of the Christian gospel.

The chapter has two phases: first, a consideration of 'moral luck' accompanied by an intermittent analysis of Shakespeare's late play, *The Winter's Tale*. Second, a more systematic spelling out of the implications of this analysis for a consideration of 'morality, gift and sacrifice'.

Let me first rehearse, briefly, the usual arguments concerning 'moral luck'.[2] Morality, for the Greeks, concerned the attainment of the truly happy life. True happiness was regarded as secure, abiding happiness, impregnable to assault. Hence it came to be associated with self-possession and 'autarchy' or *self-government*, whether of the city or of the self, and increasingly of the immaterial soul, deemed to be free of need. However, there was a tension implicit in this notion of a secure happiness. Happiness usually concerns reception of gifts from without, and a total immunity would lock a person within a tower where neither sorrow nor joy would be able to gain entrance. Hence Aristotle, for at least part of his output, articulates a compromise: the ethical life is to be found in the *relative* security of the well-born, good-looking man, owning sufficient store of goods to permit him to exercise a virtuous generosity, and *through this* to sustain his relative power and independence. This example indicates that while the Greeks fundamentally defined the ethical in opposition to fortune or luck, they were sometimes prepared to admit, to a degree, fortune or luck as a necessary precondition for the ethical: a circumstance which Martha Nussbaum terms 'the fragility of goodness', although she repeatedly loses sight of the fact that a security of self-possessed good *remains* Aristotle's fundamental determining notion. It is nonetheless true that, for Aristotle, just as we need good fortune to begin to be good, so we must continue to enjoy if it we are to remain good. If we fall for example, under the rule of a tyrant who commands us either to betray the city or else to allow a member of our own family to die, we have, by bad stroke of fortune, been tragically removed from the context in which we can continue to be unambiguously virtuous people.[3]

The Greeks therefore, *first of all* in defining the ethical goal as secure happiness deemed the Good and Fortune to be opposites, but in the *second* place did tend to admit an element of moral luck. And after all, their very deliberations involved a presupposition of the supreme moral luck of being born Greek and not barbarian. However, in later times of greater political anxiety, thinkers sought a more absolute total security of the inner citadel of the soul. Since such security precludes joy as well as sorrow, the goal of happiness tended to be redefined as a passionless *tranquility*: this, roughly speaking, is the Stoic position.[4]

Now how, in this late antique period and later, has it stood by contrast with Christianity? It will usually be noted that Christianity permitted no such Stoic security: the Christian was not offered any inner refuge against what time may bring, nor was an utterly passionless (in the sense of emotionless) life regarded as desirable. It may, however, also be noted that, for a Christian, 'to be good' was dependent on 'fortune' in the new guise of the grace of God. Such grace does involve external circumstance, since it is externally mediated by the Church (or by obscure pre-figuring encounters with the Church) and furthermore it renders *even the inner citadel of the soul* subject to an arrival from without. This observation already introduces a note of considerable uncertainty into construals of the Christian stance *vis-à-vis* moral luck.

However, it is also usually concluded that Christianity radically extirpates this thematic, since it holds that every person, whatever their birth and whatever their degree of learning (so one does not have to live the minority life of a philosopher) can always, in every situation, respond in a moral fashion – even in an unambiguously moral fashion. This is partly because virtue itself has now been redefined: the more apparently 'passive' modes of humility, patience, forgiveness, suffering unto death, even the non-despairing endurance of tragic dilemma, are modes universally available in every situation. These virtues can be perfectly performed by us 'alone'; they can be offered to the world as gifts all the more secure in their gratuity by the possibility of their derelict abandonment through the refusals of others.[5] One might, perhaps, qualify this in the direction of saying that one needs the initial fortune to belong to the *community* of such a novel form of practice: that to be able to give and forgive one must first have the sense that one is oneself given and forgiven; that one owes in gratitude a certain return and a certain repetition. In other words, it is true that for Christianity we never entirely originate our own virtuous acts – they are responses, even mere continuations in the face of the gift that we have always first received. However, this point is after all but a small qualification, since God, for the Bible, has never been without witnesses, and the Church through typology and prolepsis is a universal reality. No one anywhere, by virtue of mere human birth alone, would appear to be entirely outside the logic of donation, which seems to permit a certain immunity to moral luck.

Now I do not, without qualification, accept the above account as true. However, supposing, for the moment, that it is, there is one all-important point to take note of. This is that Christian ethics, so construed, retains the antique requirement of security and, indeed, maximizes it, yet wrenches it away from its original logical foundation in the pursuit of happiness which even the Stoics still followed – albeit to the point of logical collapse. Christianity apparently still thinks of the ethical life as the deepest identity, *as that of which we cannot be dispossessed*, and therefore as that which we have no excuse to lack, and yet this inner possession may not make us happy, at least in any recognizable worldly sense, and according to later mystical writers celebrating 'indifference', whose legacy passes to Kant, not necessarily happy in any sense at all.[6] Christian ethics, on this construal, has ceased to pursue 'happiness' and instead has become 'other-regarding'.[7] The orientation to the other by intentional gesture, is that which we alone can own. There is a latent paradox here, because the priority given to the other at the limit demands the laying down of our own life. Hence what we 'own', the ethical, is nothing other than radical self-dispossession. However – and this will become relevant for my wider argument – this paradox does not necessarily overthrow the logic of ownership: to the contrary, it dialectically preserves it at the limits of contradiction. The idea of a non-eudaemonistic other-regarding ethic implies finally that to be ethical is to offer your life as a gift without hope of return in time (since your offering outreaches your death). Such a stance remains always possible, for that of which we absolutely cannot be deprived is indeed (as Heidegger realized) our own death.[8] Hence also we cannot be deprived of the will to offer ourselves, if necessary, unto death.

This account of Christian ethics as 'other-regarding' appears then, at first glance, to be logically coherent. It regards the ethical attitude as essentially one of altruism, which is only *guaranteed* by the gesture of self-sacrifice, the willingness to give oneself even unto death. It is this gesture, or the latent will to this gesture, of which we cannot be deprived, which appears absolutely immune to 'moral luck'.

However, at this point, we need already to note something else. If this is the Christian stance *par excellence*, then it can be readily secularized, as Patocka argued, because omission of the hope for resurrection and eternal life will tend to purify the strictly other-regarding motive still further. Thus Patocka, and Derrida ambiguously in his wake, urge on us a 'heretical' Christianity that is nonetheless really a demythologized one, more Christian than Christianity so far. In this new, perfected Christianity, the injunctions of St Luke not to invite to feasts those who can invite you back (Luke 14: 12), thereby guaranteeing the austerity of your giving as 'unilateral' and self-sacrificial, is no longer to be contaminated at the eschatological level by the Lucan promise that such conduct will receive a reward from our heavenly father.[9]

Hence, if the construal of Christian ethics as most essentially 'other-regarding', and in consequence sacrificial, is valid, then it might well be the case that Christianity's true destiny is to be demythologized and secularized.

However, this construal may be called into question. *Should* one read Christian ethics as abandoning the antique concern with happiness, and yet sustaining its requirement for secure self-possession (even if this is now reduced to the willed gesture of absolute non self-possession)? Or can one construe things precisely the other way round? That is to say, that Christianity, unlike Stoicism, was able to stick with and even augment the goal of happiness or beatitude through a novel abandonment of the goal of self-possession, even in its mode of ethical reduction? And along with the notion of self-possession, to abandon also the cognate themes of self-achievement, self-control and above all self-government, which rule nearly all our inherited ideas of what is ethical? This is what I eventually wish to argue.

Let us, however, for the moment strategically remain with our two inherited notions of the ethical (as identified by Robert Spaemann) which are *both* linked to the supremacy of self-possession and self-government. On the one hand, classical eudaemonism; on the other hand, post-Enlightenment (perhaps post-Renaissance) other-regarding ethics, whether Kantian or utilitarian (the latter at least in its altruistic versions after Sidgewick). I now want to show (drawing freely on Spaemann, Derrida and Bernard Williams) how both notions are subject to inner dialectical collapse (or deconstruction), in a fashion that concerns precisely their attempts to manage and control 'fortune'.

First of all, eudaemonism. Can one secure happiness? No, it seems that it is never present as secure, and so never present as genuine happiness that need not turn its face away from reality to seek refuge in illusion. At most we have only 'virtual happiness'. Why? First, because to open ourselves to the most genuine happiness (for example, one including friendship, as Aristotle stipulated) risks also the greatest ultimate sorrow, and therefore for self-protection we must remain to a degree self-enclosed and will never be free from the anxious calculus of precisely to what degree this should be the case; exactly what balance of adventure and security we should espouse. Secondly, because happiness is not punctual: as Aristotle realized, it is rather the course of a whole life. Yet we never get to the end of our lives, nor their upshots; we are bound to 'die before our time', and only others will read our lives as a whole, rather than as still open to further development. It is for them to say 'happy' or 'unhappy', yet they *cannot* say this, since, as Spaemann argues, happiness retains something of a secret unpredictability and inviolability relating to one's specific physical body, whose movements are not entirely subject to cultural control.[10] Thirdly, happiness is comparative. To take Spaemann's example: for the Portuguese poet Fernando Pessoa in one of his poems, the shepherd in Arcadia is happy *over there*, for *me*, the non-Arcadian.[11] But no more than the shepherd will experience his own death, does he (even in Arcadia) know, reflectively and consciously, his own pastoral joy. Again, it seems that one's own happiness is known only by the other and yet it is still not *his* happiness. Happiness is nowhere replete and therefore never itself: nowhere in life and nowhere in space. Likewise in the fourth place, it is nowhere in time. For happiness must be present to us now, yet now is never, but always over or yet to come. Perhaps, indeed, happiness might be just this stretched-out tension, this 'joy over time'. But not, at least, in our time, since for now the past is always contaminated by loss and mourning, and the future by fear and anxiety. Happiness must be present without these negations, yet cannot be so. And in these four ways, not just ordinary joys remain elusive, but also our tranquil enjoyment and realization of a consistent ethical excellence (or even of an unperturbed entry into impersonal communion with abiding Platonic forms).

Antiquity, therefore, early and late, still underrated the contamination of morality by luck or fortune. How stands it, by contrast, with modern, 'other-regarding morality' from Kant and Bentham to Levinas and Parfitt? Its plight is equally dire. First of all, there is Hegel's critique of Kant, in its broad thrust: as soon as we act, with patience, humility, forgiveness, suffering unto death and so forth, we run the risk that this act will be mistaken, misinterpreted and abused (perhaps because we have badly *expressed* it, since aesthetics can always contaminate and ruin the ethical imperative) in a fashion that is both not our fault, and yet somewhat our fault, because of our tactlessness, and often both in a disentanglable fashion. What use then, are these derelict, abandoned acts: are they, as Jean-Luc Marion would have it,[12] still perfect gifts, since he takes the content of a gift to be a mere 'sign' of the real ethereal gift of intention, or more fundamentally as the unobjectifiable passage of the 'self-giving' gift itself? Surely one should argue, they are not, for intentions (or rather passages) are only ever instantiated in signs and gestures and are therefore always somewhat particular, somewhat content-specific. The abandoned, useless gift is to the contrary reduced to the most general and therefore impotent, unintending invitation to be patient, humble, suffer unto death and so on. Abandoned, inert, without upshot, it is reversely corroded even in its most original intention – it is, in short, objectified. A duty, therefore, which fails to make the other happy, surely ceases to be a moral act (and perhaps not just Hegel, but even Kant himself remained haunted by this thought). Other-regarding ethics *cannot* ignore happiness, yet happiness is often the child of whim and circumstance.

Therefore, 'other-regarding ethics' is also undermined, as we have seen, by the self-implosion of the notion of pure duty. But hard on the heels of this 'loss of duty' comes also, in the second place, 'loss of self'. Can we possess ourselves as ethical through a sacrificial self-offering in death? If this alone proves the good, then we *need* the misfortunes of others in order to demonstrate our worth – and therefore this seemingly ethical self is utterly lost in its secret longing for the sorrows of others as the occasions of its own heroism. Moreover, *till* we are martyrs, we can never be sure that we possess ourselves as ethical, since martyrdom is the paradigmatic test: passing it, at the end beyond ourselves, we also lose ourselves and *never* come to possess a good will. For always, in the next gasp before expiry we *may* despair, we may recant, we may come to curse the very one we think we propose to save. And if even the dying self is not immune to luck (the 'weakness of the flesh' in dying) then *a fortiori* we have lost the living self who enjoys his life but is subject to still greater uncertainties and contingencies.

These contingencies are, supremely, the *needs of others*. In the case of the moral subject of consequentialist ethics, this subject is liable to limitless persecution by the needs of others, who are regarded contradictorily as not subject to this persecution, but as somehow already in the endlessly postponed *telos* of 'enjoyment'.[13] And just the same bad infinite haunts the seemingly greater refinement of Kantian and Levinasian ethics. Both exhibit a similar obliteration of the living self in the form of the circular pointlessness of a subjectivity constituted through its respect for the (free or suffering) subjectivity of the other which is only subjective in returning that respect. Modern ethics, just because it enthrones altruism, is pathological in its degree of obliteration of the possibility of consummation, or of the beginning of beatitude in a time simply to be enjoyed, and a conviviality to be celebrated by the living self.

However, if, as we have seen, the living and dying self of self-sacrificial ethics is not after all secure – save in a bizarre kind of hope for a gesture of martyrdom which can never arrive, which is just how Derrida construes it[14] – nor, in the third place, is the self of the other whom we are supposed to 'regard' secure in its turn. In so far as the other is alive, I will tend to take her for granted, and her visibility (here I am strategically somewhat agreeing with Levinas) will tend to make her 'part' of me, like a kind of extension of my body. She cannot, by appearing, fully appear as other. Her otherness will rather emerge in her absence, especially her death, which partially defines her uniqueness and non-dispossessibility. When she is gone, I mourn, and first come to value her as irreplaceable, in a way that I could not have done while she lived. But now she can no longer speak to me, and so she has emerged as irreplaceable in that very moment in which she has lost that *other* crucial aspect of otherness, namely free spontaneity. Indeed, a mourning which neglects this second aspect of alterity can degenerate into the most ferocious mode of possessiveness. And moreover mourning, although it alone tends to reveal to us the subject as subject of our ethical concern (as irreplaceable), is also a domain in which we can sing an Orphic song but do no ethical deed towards the other, just as she can longer respond to us. For this reason there is no virtue in mourning, and yet if we cease to mourn, the other is lost and we forget the only occasion for the realization of the possibility of virtue and thereby become supremely evil. For what is more evil than to burn a human body like that of an unloved animal without a funeral? But if mourning is a vision, it is not a work, for the work of mourning or of coming to terms with loss is immoral and unchristian, since it would always mean that we *forget* the subject as irreplaceable. All the same, to act again towards the living we *must* recover, must betray the good, must become evil.

This situation is acutely dramatized when it is uncertain whether someone is dead or alive, for they have merely *disappeared*. In Michelangelo Antonioni's film *L'Avventura* (1959) a woman, Anna, disappears, and her fiancé immediately starts to court her best friend, Claudia. If she is dead, this relationship may retrieve something from her decease, yet if she is alive it is contaminated by guilt. But given her mere disappearance, a state of irresolvable uncertainty pertains: life simply cannot go forwards. Likewise, in the recent film *Le Colonel Chabert* (based on a short story by Balzac), a soldier returns 'from the dead' to find his wife remarried. Should she resume her previous life, or abandon a later life undertaken in good faith? Both the earlier and the later lives have now become unresumable as ethical imperatives. So, on one level, these stories show how we need *definite* death to sustain morality; to pass over to a new good, an earlier claim on our attention must be 'over'. And that in itself is enough to cast suspicion on 'morality' as such: why does it require absolute death for its repeated exercise? Yet at a deeper level still, these stories indicate how death itself functions only as disappearance. For we can only register the dead one as 'missing', not in a state of death, since death is not a state. Hence in any case, even if Anna is really dead, Claudia will be faced with the choice between guilt and a certain callous coldness, and the only answer to her dilemma, as to that posed by *Le Colonel Chabert*, is Christ's answer to the Pharisees that in heaven 'there will be neither giving nor taking in marriage'.

In the case of Shakespeare's late play, *The Winter's Tale*, we have the instance of a death and a presumed death which turns out to be only a double disappearance. But the one who mourns, Leontes King of Sicily, treats the death from the outset like a 'disappearance' which cripples the very possibility of moral action. Hence Leontes' courtiers beseech him to forget his dead wife and son and lost daughter and resume his rule again, for politics requires self-control, although morality seems after all to disallow it (Act V, Scene 1). Here mourning is complicated by guilt (but it usually is). Leontes' false accusation of his wife as adulteress has led to her death, the death of his heir, and the loss of his daughter, Perdita. His courtiers urge that he has now *atoned* through mourning, thereby claiming that mourning is a moral work that may be completed. But Leontes, echoing Lear's repeated 'Never' after the loss of Cordelia, absolutely denies this. *Nothing* could compensate for the monstrousness of his deed, since he has betrayed what for him are the unique, irreplaceable ones; only reconciliation with them could cancel out the deed, and that is impossible since they are dead and lost. Time, with its irreversibility, Leontes perceives, is stern: it permits justice and the punishment that sin automatically incurs. But it does not at first sight permit forgiveness and reconciliation, because that would be to trivialize a past that in the mode of the death of responding persons can be irretrievably lost.

Leontes, via his loss, has finally come to love. He loves because he is wounded, and so at last sees what is missing. He enjoys, one might say, this one advantage, that unlike those chronically wounded *by others*, he is not rendered incapable of love, and yet this advantage is cancelled in that his mainly self-inflicted wounds permit him only the futile *gesture* of love. Like the initially complacent in general, he sees what is lost with absolute clarity only too late, and therefore tragically. Hence in our world half the potential moral subjects – the *wounded* – see too late, and only through loss of the other, which is either their fault, or has been inflicted upon them from the first. By contrast, the other potentially moral subjects – the *apparently innocent* – who have abundantly received love from the living, and therefore are able to pass this gift on, are always infected by complacency, the non-realization of the fragility of the gift in its passage through time. They have always been too sheltered in their development from the knowledge of wounds inflicted elsewhere. Not having lost, they do not sufficiently attend to the voice of the present loved one. And since *all* are either wounded or complacent, or rather all are relative mixtures of both, since this is an exhaustive human typology, there exist *no* potential moral subjects at all. Rather we are all embroiled in the *aporia* of the present versus the absent other, where neither can adequately fulfil the role of the other; neither the living beloved, nor the dead.

'Other-regarding ethics', whose paradigm is self-sacrifice, has now therefore lost its duty, its self and its other to regard. It is ruinously subject to the vagaries of fortune in the first case, and in the second two cases to the universal bad fortune of temporal loss and death, combined with the subjection of even the best human wills to a kind of routinization in respect of the other, which sometimes, as in Leontes' case, spills over into suspicion.

However, things are worse than this. As Spaemann details, there are no criteria by which *to prioritize* either the pursuit of self-fulfilling happiness or attention to the other. To pursue *entirely* the latter path of self-sacrifice would pathologically erode the self which is alone able to offer itself. But then, when to live and when to give? A further anxiety enters the picture, and as Bernard Williams once suggested, a further dimension of moral luck.[15] Was the painter Gauguin right, asked Williams, to leave wife and children to go to Tahiti? (Against Williams one can conceive the pursuit of aesthetic self-fulfilment as *also* a moral choice, but this merely renders more acute the dilemma he invoked.) Williams suggested that only the success of Gauguin's wager on being a good painter can retrospectively justify this decision. He comes to enjoy the moral luck of finding he has talent (a 'gift'), or that his talent was able to come to fruition. But it might have been otherwise. Williams's analysis assumes that this instance is an anomaly, and that *normally* an intention to do something is not at all like Gauguin's intention to be a painter. Hence one can usually know that one can realize one's intention, and exactly what that intention is (whereas Gauguin does not really know what *kind* of painter he will turn out to be). However I think, to the contrary, that all of us are always in the situation of Gauguin. This is for two reasons: first of all, as Derrida suggests,[16] the giving of ourselves to one person or purpose frequently involves sacrificing other goods or people, and often without reason. Our sense of responsibility *must,* in order to fulfil itself, be always exceptional and particular, because attentive to a specific unique demand; yet to be responsible it must also by definition be answerable to a public forum. But how can these two demands ever be reconciled? And what explanation could ever be given to the neglected ones? There are *never,* it seems, any *adequate,* that is to say publicly stateable reasons for lavishing devotion on one person rather than another – to the public gaze this will always appear excessively aesthetic or erotic. Yet to the private impulse it may appear to fulfil the logic of the ethical itself.

Secondly, an intention is never precise until we begin to formulate it in words: which already amounts to a kind of actual performance. We never know in advance, strictly speaking, what we are going to do or say. Intentions 'come to us', as it were, from the Muses, and we are not in command of them. (Intention is therefore merely the way an intention turns out to be.) Heterogenesis of ends (beyond Hegel) has *always already begun.* Even to formulate a good intention it seems, we need moral luck.

But here, at last, at the most extreme point of ruination of even the ethical intention, everything can run into reverse. Christianity is perhaps (sporadically) the history of this running into reverse. Suppose it is the case that to be ethical is not to possess something, not even to possess one's own deed. Suppose it is, from the outset, to receive the gift of the other as something that diverts one's life, and to offer one's life in such a way that you do not know in advance what it is that you will give, but must reclaim it retrospectively. A total exposure to fortune, or rather to grace. Were it *simply* the former, then one would have run resignedly into nihilism; all the *aporias* of the ethical already sketched would still stand, but one would simply embrace the impossibility of the ethical and yet the necessity of temporal ethical conventions. Perhaps, in addition, one would qualify this, like Derrida (and Levinas?), with a mysticism of infinitely postponed hope for the arrival of the Good. Life would either be construed as utterly arbitrary after Lear or Schopenhauer, or else as a comedy beyond the ethical, in a 'postmodern' mode. However, the Christian construal of the total sway of moral luck is to understand fortune, as always, however disguisedly, the personal gift of grace: to believe therefore that only *utter exposure* constitutes the ethical.

It follows from this, that no secularization of Christian ethics along the lines proposed by Patocka is possible; we have already seen how the mere attitudes of patience, humility and so forth, regarded as things we can of ourselves perform, can turn out to be not ethical at all. To the contrary, they only assume an ethical complexion as a waiting on God – in other words, as a kind of meta-ethical trust that it *will* (beyond perpetual postponement) be given to us to be ethical, given to us again to receive and again to give in such a way that a certain 'asymmetrical reciprocity' or genuine community will ceaselessly arrive (for now in part and eschatologically without inter-ruption). It ceases, on this perspective, to be the case that the Christian is the person who knows that he can be good in any merely given situation. On the contrary, the Christian can rather be seen as the person who recognizes that there is no *apparent* good to be found or performed in any given situation. Original sin and death (the results of the Fall) are perceived as locked in a complicity which prevents the ethical from coming to pass. (For a supreme analysis of the morally corrupting effects of natural decay see the late W.J. Sebald's great German but also East Anglian novel, *The Rings of Saturn*.) By naturally and culturally inherited contamination of our wills, we are all either wounded or complacent or both, capable only of valuing what is lost; obliged therefore to take measures to prevent future loss; congratulating ourselves on these measures (law) and so secretly celebrating loss as the occasion for our greatness, and instead of festively enjoying present loved ones, subject to boredom with them tending always to suspicion. Death, the experience of loss, contaminates our wills: this leads in turn to more barriers, more wars, more loss. Loss is ineradicable, and so we tend to assume that ethics is a sort of maximum possible minimization of loss. Yet I have shown that so long as there is loss, there *cannot* be any ethical, not even in any degree. Hence hope, hope that it may be given to me in the next moment to act well, is inseparable from hope that there may be universal acting-well, and at last a non-futile mourning; to be ethical therefore is to believe in the Resurrection, and somehow to participate in it. And outside this belief and participation there is, quite simply, no 'ethical' whatsoever.

From these considerations I would argue that there are three aspects to ethics. First the mundane, everyday hope that community is possible, that people and objects can analogically blend beyond identity or difference, though we can never prove such a possibility *a priori* or *a posteriori*. We can only receive instances that we judge to constitute such blending and seek, in hope, to perpetuate them: here hope is conjoined to receptive Charity. Both the living out and the search for such a life in common is neither simply eudaemonistic nor 'other-regarding', but as Spaemann puts it 'ecstatic'. However, this is neither a self-sacrificial nor a sado-masochistically erotic ecstasy (and are not these two things secretly natural counterparts, as I argued in Chapters 1 and 2?) since both these recourses are unto death and thereby subject to the *aporia* I have already outlined (we cannot live to enjoy it). Rather, the true ecstasy passes *through* death, or in trusting it *will* be given to us to offer through death, and not just to death (which would be moral/masochistic) but through death, because in hope of our own return along with the return of others. Thus to look for our collective participation in divine fullness of being is to transcend in an 'objective' and self-less manner either egotistic or self-sacrificial concerns. For Spaemann this ecstasy is epitomized by the *feast*, in which mere bodily need is transfigured in collective celebration: here we eat only because and when others eat, and yet we do not renounce ourselves, for we eat also.[17]

Hence the everyday ethical hope naturally leads to hope for resurrection. By contrast, the second two aspects of ethics are not mundane, but mythical, miraculous, enchanted, indeed in a sense child-like (and therefore Christian). After Shakespeare had written *Lear*, there was no possibility of him remaining with the unsurpassibility of the tragic, because this would actually be to *underestimate* the end of *Lear*. Since this play discloses a universal tragic sway (we cannot redeem our losses and misdeeds, there is no forgiveness), one cannot either mitigate this circumstance nor come to terms with it; that is to say accept it, even though it is true. It is so bad, that it *should* be turned away from, and yet it cannot be. It *must* be turned away from because it leaves *no possibility for the ethical*. This is where 'a piety of the tragic', like that of Donald Mackinnon, simply will not do, partly because it *still*, after all, *evades* the tragic, by hypostasizing it in a speculative fashion. (Mackinnon failed to see that Speculative Idealism espoused exactly the romantic and not perhaps very Greek cult of the tragic, which he himself perpetuated – revealing thereby his own idealism despite all his explicit disavowals, rooted in his Kantianism.)

Hence the late Shakespeare has to imagine 'another place', or a mythical post-tragic sphere. Herein lie the second two aspects. First of all, Christianity refuses, having recognized a universal tragic condition, to ontologize this, but makes the extraordinary move of seeing the universal itself as but a contingent narrative upshot. Hence the story of the Fall, and to ontologize this story in the gnostic manner of Hegel and Schelling is to miss what here profoundly disturbs the entire project of 'ontology' itself. For without the Fall, or with the substitution of the notion of a necessary Fall, one starts with an irreducible scarcity and egotism, and the ethical becomes that which reacts to a bad situation which it is secretly in love with, and needs ceaselessly to reinstate, despite the fact that this compromises the very character of the ethical. Therefore one needs the myth of the Fall in order to think a genuine Good, which to be non-reactive can only be an original plenitude.

However, the danger here is to imagine that the Fall originated in the *doing* of something bad. How can this be, if originally and by divine intention, to give or receive the gift in ignorance is always to give or receive an unknown good action? If, that is to say, the *entire* field of action is by definition 'good' in a manner that cannot be qualified by the character of an intention. In this case, original sin must instead mean *refusal* of the field of action itself, defined as giving with joyful uncertainty in faith, a refusal which commences in the suspicion that one does not, after all, receive a good gift from the other. This is articulated better by Shakespeare than by Genesis: in *The Winter's Tale*, Leontes and Polixenes, Kings of Sicily and Bohemia respectively, passed their boyhoods in seeming innocence, as if outside of time. Early in the play, Polixenes interprets their meeting with women, their future wives, or the arrival of 'the other' in the course of time, as the moment of fall. But Hermione (Leontes' wife) to the contrary ascribes marriage still to the reign of innocence, and indeed views the arrival of the women as the event of grace itself (an association that is maintained throughout the play: see here Act I, Scene 2). This is an ironic passage, for in the context of the play the Fall is still to come, and involves not a first misdeed by Leontes, but rather a first suspicion that Hermione has committed the sin of adultery. Here the Fall is not an act, but rather a first mistrusting of the joyfully confident 'risk' and uncertainty constitutive of the field of action (or, one might say, it is a first diminishing of act). Leontes misreads the *signs* of Hermione's affection for Polixenes, and thereby offends against necessary trust in the secrecy of the other. Hence 'original sin', on this rendering, is the imagination of sin, the reading of the unknown as source of threat or poison rather than potential or gift. (In Locke's *Essay Concerning Human Understanding* the philosopher notes that the Hebrew words for adultery (*niouph*) and jealousy (*kinneah*) could have been invented by Adam[18] before the *actuality* of adultery on the grounds of suspicion alone.)

This reading of original sin therefore understands original blessedness by implication, not as deliberately 'doing good', but as a state of good moral luck or reception of grace. And original sin is here seen as nothing but the imagination that there could be a perversion of the field of action, malice from the other, such that the bad dream gives birth to a bad reality: evil is only virtual, but then we step through Ballard's malign and merely dramatic – and not Auden's or Bonnefoy's enchanted and really transforming – looking-glass. (See Chapter 6, note 2 above.)

The third aspect of ethics we have already indicated as hope for resurrection. Again *The Winter's Tale* is instructive. Were this play more 'realist' in the mode of Shakespeare's earlier plays, it could not be post-tragic. Were Leontes to relent from mourning, resume control over his kingdom and ask pardon from Polixenes whom he has accused of adultery with Hermione, it would not, after all, for reasons we have seen, reinstate the ethical, although equivalents to such actions are our only usual recourse. The ethical, to the contrary, only returns fabulously with the return of Perdita and the seeming 'resurrection' of Hermione (Act V, Scene 3). The reappearance of the latter as at first apparently a statue, who only gradually moves, is of crucial significance. For it dramatizes our fracture between a world of life which is real, in which the other person can speak to us for a time and yet is doomed to be lost in a manner which renders life irredeemable, unforgivable and therefore meaningless, with a world of meaning or 'art' (one could say language and culture) which is permanent, deathless and yet sterile, like human drama itself: the statue cannot speak (and indeed only speaks again once, to acknowledge Perdita, the lost daughter). This fracture between meaningless life and lifeless meaning is another way of expressing our fallenness and incapacity to be good. Hence when Hermione returns, she is not just resuscitated, but returns as *both* life and art (and therefore Christomorphically: see Chapter 6, above), returns indeed like a kind of *perfected human intention*, where it is known that the only good deed that could be given to us would be the capacity to raise another from the dead (after the fashion of the one good man who walked on earth). And, in addition, Hermione's continuing to be a statue means that her loss as living person is not simply cancelled – the spectators continue, we are told in the play, to sorrow, and are not sure whether their surprised ecstasy is one of mourning or of joy. In the resurrection of the dead, the dead one is given back to the living as in a sense still dead, still wounded, and yet uniquely innocent, so that he or she appears in the space of living exchange as surprising gift, beyond our life now in time, which is always the mere pursuit of security. In other words, Shakespeare ceases here to articulate mere stage-magic on this earth, but instead intimates real enchantment within another, transfigured earth which is the world given back as manifest gift, rather like the walking crippled boy and the once again blooming garden of the forever mourned dead wife of the Lord of the Manor, in Frances Hodgson Burnett's *The Secret Garden*.[19]

The eucatastrophic transfiguration at the end of *The Winter's Tale* culminates in a double marriage: first of all of Perdita to Florizel, and so of Sicily to Bohemia (Act V, Scene 3). Thereby, in a final mutual giving of all future time, fallen anxiety is mended: for this had begun with the separation of bounded political kingdoms that were traditionally close allies. Again this separation had commenced with suspicion, not deed. Leontes considered that Polixenes had become too friendly with Sicily (in the person of Hermione); conversely, Polixenes wondered whether he had already stayed too long as a guest – in other words, received too much from Leontes, thereby incurring an unreturnable debt (since he comes from poorer, less exotic, northern Bohemia). The lack of permanent bonding, the lack of marriage and the ceaseless need for guarantees, with the consequent problematic of interpretation of signs, means that there is an anxiety about duty and extent of duty between the two kingdoms, an anxiety about *when* to live, enjoy and consummate, and when to sacrifice and give to the other. This, as we have seen, renders ethics undecidable and impossible. Anxiety is only surmounted when enjoying and giving coincide in a communal ecstatic feast which is perpetual and so secure, no longer in need of any contractual re-establishment (which is not to preclude the need for constant mutual readjustments within the security of faith). Marriage is clearly a figure for this, as is confirmed by the second marriage in the play, of Camillo (Polixenes' servant) to Paulina (Hermione's maidservant) as its final deed. Camillo had been in service to Leontes, but deserted to Polixenes, because he refused to go along with Leontes' suspicions. He nonetheless longed to return to Sicily, but Polixenes says to him that as he has come to rely on Camillo's sacrificial gifts of service, if Camillo ceases to give them, he will in effect take back all that he has so far given. (George Herbert was soon to confront God with the same *aporia* in his poem *Gratefulnesse*.) Here an *aporia* of gift follows from a situation of forced obligation and alienated exile. But once again, marriage restores free but mutual giving in asymmetrical reciprocity, since in marriage there is no interval of *debt* between gift and return (which would reduce gift to a contractual economy) but rather absolute eternal coincidence of gift and exchange in the same moment which is ceaselessly perpetuated. Once Camillo is returned to his home, once political order is restored in the light of resurrection, the *aporias* of gift and the ethical are both suspended and resolved.

Nonetheless, we must at this point bear the examples of *L'Avventura* and *Le Colonel Chabert* in mind; Leontes might have remarried and yet still resurrection could betoken a healing of the inevitable guilt involved. If the angelic state (as Christ says) does not inaugurate new marriages, then this implies a compatibility in the resurrected order of all erotic unions entered into on earth, since somehow they will all be taken up into the more general eschatological marriage of the Church as Bride with the crucified Lamb of God.

The opposite to the condition of married reconciliation in *The Winter's Tale* is the condition of utter abandonment. When Perdita was lost, she was left in the capitalist north (Bohemia) with a cache of money (Act IV). As *only* alive, estranged from the inheritance of honour down the generations (which is all her mother Hermione declares she lives for: Act III, Scene 2, 92–115), she is reduced to a thing, a commodity. For that which is abandoned, outside donation, reception and mutuality, is after all such a mere *object*, and *not* as Marion would have it, a gift. Hence Derrida, Marion, Levinas and Blanchot have all failed to see that the private, supposedly 'free' gift of market society is identical, precisely *as* abandoned, with the commodity of the capitalist mode of exchange.[20] So in Bohemia the abandoned Perdita has fallen into the world of calculating exchanges for money presided over by Autolycus, son of the mediating god Mercury.

This is already the world in which we live, a modern world in which nothing shields *everyone* from tragedy or the doom of endless choice, which results in the sacrifice of some for others and unresolvable dilemmas and unhealed regret: a poisoning of the heterogenesis of ends which issues in ceaseless perversion of our intentions. Am I saying that our mercantile reality then reveals the raw truth of life in fallen time? Yes, but I am not, like Derrida, ontologizing this truth. For I insist instead on the possibility of imagining the counter-reality of resurrection, and the possibility that this world already mysteriously participates in that reality. Embracing this possibility leads us to hope, even now, after the Fall and before the End, for the gracious arrival of something better and to act within this hope. Such hope will note that the resolution of *The Winter's Tale* is political as well as religious – that Camillo, at home in the restored *polis* and *oikos*, can at last give freely. Hence should our polity be restored by grace, would not anxiety about our necessary preference for some but not others, and our apparent sacrifice of some for others, be eased in the knowledge that we are to love our *neighbours*, because we know that others are loving theirs?

In other words, we would rediscover that even the condition of *agape* can only be fulfilled within a *polis* where each of us exercises a specific – or rather unique and non-identically repeated – role. In point of fact, the cruciality of role within the *polis* is yet more emphasized by Christianity than by antiquity. Its transmutation of an ethic of virtue into an ethic of gift (especially in Paul) means that there is a break with the Aristotelian notion that to be virtuous means to possess individually a balanced instance of all the virtues in harmony; a corollary of this view was that only those in *elite* roles, with a leisure that freed them from specialization, could be virtuous. For Christianity, this harmonization is only possible on a collective level as the *ecclesia*, and the most humble specialization can still partake of replete virtue. To belong to the virtuous life in common now means to exercise well the specific gifts (*charismata*) that one has received, which dictate a particular role within the Church community. One is thereby liberated from a pagan anxiety about the ways in which one does not enjoy the capacity, time or space to perform certain good acts. There is indeed, as we saw with Augustine (in Chapter 1) already a romanticism here: to be good is now to exercise one's peculiar preferences beneficially; to be good, as Kierkegaard saw, is now to seek out one's own exceptionality, even though this can only be truly located through the blending with others. It is no longer to follow a general abstract law, but to enact one's own unique charisma.

Equally, the lesson of the wintry wind is that should hopeful ventures be encouraged and not thwarted, we would tend to rejoice at the course taken and laugh at the courses thereby not taken, in the confident knowledge that everything is in any case excess, and there is an infinity on which all roads may be taken in the end. And third, if we lived in an economy of gift we would not be indifferent to the consequences of our acts, now treated like sellable products, but we would 'go' with our gifts, and others in receiving them creatively would continue to care for us in this employment. Joyfully estranged from ourselves, we should sometimes find in this loss our gain, and always know that it would finally be so.

III

Through the above reflections, incorporating a partial rereading of one of Shakespeare's late plays, I have sought to suggest, first of all, that the ethical is only genuinely imaginable as a mutual and unending gift-exchange, construed as an absolute surrender to moral luck or absolute faith in the arrival of the divine gift, which is grace. Secondly, that the sustaining of such an exchange requires a notion of resurrection and faith in the reality of participation in resurrection. The first element, gift-exchange, is paradigmatically figured either as feast or as marriage, and therefore is appropriately combined with the second element, resurrection, in terms of images of the heavenly banquet, or the eschatological marriage of God and humanity, heaven and earth. Outside an overcoming of the present economy of death *as well as* sin, I have argued, and a practice which seeks to anticipate the resurrection Sabbath, there can be no notion of the Good that does not fall prey to irresolvable *aporias*. Hence, in theological terms, I am arguing that resurrection is an inseparable moment of atonement, or that sacrifice is only ethical when it is also resurrection.

This complex of ideas, or characterization of the ethical as gift exchange, feast, marriage and resurrection, I am seeking to set in deliberate opposition to a recent consensus which would try to understand the ethical as *primarily* self-sacrifice for the other, without any necessary 'return' issuing from the other back to oneself. This consensus itself involves an alternative complex of ideas: first of all, one has the notion that only an entirely sacrificial giving without any expectation of a counter-gift distinguishes the gift from a form of self-interested contract. Secondly, one has the notion that *death*, far from being complicit with evil (as theology would understand it to be), is the *necessary condition for the event of the ethical as such*.[21] This is supposedly for two reasons: first of all, only our *vulnerability*, the possibility that we might die, allows us to make an appeal as needy people to our neighbour; only this circumstance provides the condition for an ethical demand. Secondly, only the capacity of the ethical subject to respond to the needy person, if necessary with his own death, guarantees his deed as truly ethical, as a truly disinterested gift. Thirdly, one has the notion that 'God' must be reduced to a shadowy hypostasized Other lurking just behind the human other, because any God who interfered to 'reward' the disinterested giver would undo the purity of this disinterest and the purity of the ethical realm. And so, in the fourth place, one arrives at the paradoxical affirmation that the true nobility and purity of religious self-sacrifice is only realized in a *secular* sphere, that here alone a dying for the other achieves genuine sacred value. These positions are common to Patocka, Derrida and probably Levinas, while the first point is espoused by Marion (although logically it should lead to the other three).

I shall now summarize and make more explicit the grounds for my rejection of ethics as unilateral and sacrificial in favour of ethics as gift-exchange and openness to divine grace, dealing with each of these four notions in turn. First, the idea of a fundamentally sacrificial, or unilateral gift, makes absolute one's inalienable self-possession of a will to sacrifice and so *preserves* the Hellenic notion of the ethical as the overcoming of moral luck or the arrival of that which unperturbably belongs to one, even if, or *especially* if, as for Derrida, this belonging or identity is only secured when one *is* no longer, when one is dead, and even if, or *especially* if, this identity is construed, as with Marion, as the debt to a giver which inaugurates subjectivity as such (for this subjectivity supposedly outside all agency and judgement is thereby all the more inviolable).

There is no true respect for the other involved here, since the gesture which allows the other to persist outside of his communication with you is seen as more definitive of the Good than the living communication which you enjoy with the other: consequently Levinas sees the other as only genuinely present in its 'trace', not in present image. But if we truly value the other, we must value meeting him in his specificity and therefore my presence before the other is ineradicable from a situation which is paradigmatic for the ethical. Of course, one's celebration of such an encounter may require one in certain circumstances to sacrifice oneself, even unto death, and one can go further to say that in a fallen world the only path to the recovery of mutual giving will *always* pass through an element of apparently 'unredeemed' sacrifice and apparently sheerly unilateral gift. But the point is that this gesture is not *in itself* the Good, and indeed I have argued, is *not* good at all outside the hope for a redemptive return of the self: albeit that this is an eschatological hope which never permits us to expect a return at any particular place or specific moment of time, or to elicit any specific *mode* of return. To speak of such a return is not at all, however, to surrender to the lure of contract, because it is not the case that actual, self-present life is a mode of self-possession which we then surrender in the sacrificial gesture unto death. Quite to the contrary, it is when we are giving, letting ourselves go, at certain times or always in fallen time with unavoidable sacrificial pain, that we are always receiving back as ever different a true, abundant life (this is the Gospel). Therefore the resurrection hope preserves this logic at the limit: we do not hope (as Patocka and Derrida allege) for an extrinsic super-added reward for our giving up of an illusory self-possessed life; rather we take it that a final surrender of an isolated life, a life indifferent to the pain of others, issues of itself – dare one say *automatically* – in a better more abundant life (and this 'automatic' self-realizing dimension of

Jesus's resurrection, clearly articulated in the New Testament, is shamefully glossed over by the pseudo-piety and mythologizing bent of exegetes who wish to speak only of a 'mighty act of the Father': John 11: 25; 12: 24).

The fuller more abundant life is a return of life always afresh, always differently. Hence what distinguishes gift from contract is not the absolute freedom and non-binding character of the gift (this is our Western counterpart to the *reduction* of exchange to contract, which remains entirely uncriticized by Derrida and Marion, who are unable to assimilate the more truly critical lesson of Mauss), but rather the surprisingness and unpredictability of gift and counter-gift, or their character in space as *asymmetrical reciprocity*, and their character in time as *non-identical repetition*.[22] It should also be noted here that Derrida regards the event of a gift construed as a free, unilateral gift as an *impossibility*, since short of death one always does cancel one's giving in receiving something back, be it only the consciousness that one is a giver.[23] Only the dead person, on this account, only the subject who has passed beyond subjectivity, can be a true giver, just as the only disinterested gift is to an absolutely anonymous other – paradigmatically the enemy, says Marion – and cannot possess any identifiable content beyond the gesture of giving, because there is nothing about an object on *this* construal that makes it in itself a gift. But to the contrary I would argue that the content of a gift alone determines whether it is an *appropriate* gift, and therefore a gift at all.[24]

For Derrida, therefore, a gift is only ever a promise of a gift, perpetual postponement. And Marion's attempt to show that this impossible gift is really a phenomenologically reduced gift, having its special mode of being present outside the 'presence' of Being and the mutual coincidence of giver and receiver, will not work. For this reduced gift which is no identifiable object, derives from no known source, and passes to no known willing recipient, can only be 'recognized' in a fashion that can make no conceivable difference to actual ethical life. Such recognition acknowledges only the idol of an abstract God, whose gift is as effectively abyssal and absent as that of Marion's atheistic interlocutors. Moreover where there is no intimation *whatsoever* of the donating source, a gift is simply an impersonal intrusion, whose lack of objectifiable content further renders it arbitrary on our part to interpret it as gift, rather than as violent rupture. Equally, where there is no knowledge of a recipient, and one assumes even that he is hostile, there cannot truly be a gift, because a true gift must be a considered gift appropriate to its donee; hence one must *already* have entered into an exchange with her. Before a gift can be given, it must already have started to be received. For gift-giving is a mode (*the* mode in fact) of social being, and in ignoring this, both Derrida and Marion remain trapped within Cartesian myths of prior subjectivity after all. However, Derrida is right, against Marion, to deconstruct his unnecessary Cartesian starting point, and one can agree with him that a unilateral, purely sacrificial gift can never occur. If there is a gift that can truly be, then this must be the event of reciprocal but asymmetrical and non-identically repeated exchange.

The second element in the complex of notions which construes the ethical as sacrificial is the idea of death as the ground of morality. I have already indicated how this manifestly celebrates something negative as the precondition of something positive in a way that is self-contradictory, and I have also already shown how a self-surrender without hope of self-return gives up on the hope for ecstatic communication, for 'feasting' and for 'marriage', which is the only viable paradigm for the Good itself.

Although I take this paradigm to be fully articulated only by Christianity, it is notably anticipated by Plato in the *Phaedo* when he insists that warriors who die for the city out of fear of loss of honour are trading lesser fear for greater, and lesser pain for greater pleasure of anticipation of undying fame (*Phaedo* 68d–69e). Socrates, in this dialogue, refuses this idea that virtue is a kind of coinage, and therefore refuses an ethical market economy which is also a *sacrificial* economy – something is given up, abandoned, in order to gain more. By contrast, *the philosopher* is in his essence a person who begins with absolute confidence, with the vision of the Forms as that which cannot possibly be endangered. He therefore acts with genuine positivity, without fear and not with a merely apparent fearlessness that is in thrall to an even greater fear. For this reason the philosopher is good as first merely knowing, or *receiving* the vision of the Forms, and not as acting or as sacrificing in the sense of giving up something. (And indeed the Pythagorean tradition which precedes Plato already refrained from bloody, sacrificial rituals.)[25] Only in a secondary moment, out of the plenitude of vision, does he offer himself entirely, giving his whole body over to death if the occasion arises (as it has, for Socrates). This is not, as modern philosophy tends to claim, *itself* an aspect of a sacrificial economy, in the sense of a 'giving up' of the body and the passions for the gain of knowledge, since formed materiality and the passions are, for Plato, simply weak participations in a fuller ontological and erotic reality. Imitation of this reality is only possible by derivation from this reality (by its *charis*, grace) and so there is in some sense a sharing, and not simply *mimesis* alone. Nothing real is lost here: in *this* exercise of virtue, there only occurs a passage from lesser to greater. In the Christian era, the stories of the deaths of martyrs record a similar acceptance of suffering out of an already commenced plenitude of paradisal vision.[26] (One should also note that the above implies a qualification of Nussbaum's verdicts on Plato and Aristotle: it is the latter, seeking a relatively secure inner citadel in time who limits 'moral luck', whereas for Plato one entirely abandons oneself to the Forms which arrive through the erotic lure of the other.)

This leads me to a discussion of the fourth notion in the complex of ideas which define the ethical as sacrificial: the idea that the sacred is fully realized in an atheistic or demythologized mode. What this notion occludes from our view is the ever-present role of the city or the State intervening in order to maintain civic order[27] within our relationship to the other person or to God. Such mediation is fundamentally inscribed in the very historical 'transport' of sacrifice from practice to metaphor. One can mention two moments here in particular. First, the way in which, as Marcel Detienne has recounted, in Greek sacrifice the same scents and spices were involved in erotic play as in religious sacrifice, and it was in consequence thought important to divert an excess of sensation from the horizontal to the vertical plane. Unlike the Platonic instance, the bodily erotic is here not regarded as participatory, but as a fully real thing to be limited, kept in its place and to a degree 'given up'. The burning spices should most appropriately spiral upwards to the divine realm. Here then is a kind of 'giving up' or offering of material passion in favour of its sublimation, and so a limitation and confinement of its scope of operation.

In this context one should note that the specific language of 'sacrifice of passions' does not, as far as I can see, occur in Greek philosophy. This is because, after Pythagoras, the more immaterialist philosophy tended to advocate a non-bloody, non-civic, sacrifice in which the passage upwards of smoke indicated not so much the *offering* of passion, as the transmutation of passion within the philosopher into a higher passion.[28] So amongst the Neoplatonists sacrifice is specifically construed as *initiatory passage*, rather than as gift or offering.[29] It is only, perhaps, with Paul in *Romans* that one gets the language of 'sacrifice of passions' and so an 'internalization' of sacrifice – but the import here is entirely different from the vertical deviation of horizontal scents and spices. Rather, Paul is talking about an offering of self (soul and body) to a personal God which implicitly involves a trust in a return of self as a more abundant living soul and body.

The second moment concerns, as Martin Hengel has described, the way in which the death of the hero for the city was construed by the Greeks (and later still more by the Romans) as equivalent to sacrifice, and as indeed as rendering the hero himself a fit recipient of sacrifice in turn.[30] In both these instances – that of the pagan religious sacrifice of passion and of the sacrifice of the hero – one has the idea of the subsumption of something ontologically real and irreducible into a greater whole: in the one case the cosmic order, in the other the city. There is a notion in the latter case of loss without return, save for the posthumous praise of celebration of one's austerity or bravery. A return of the *living self* is not involved, save in rather shadowy intimations of an after-life. But the point to grasp here is that modern secularity gets rid of even such intimations, and so *perfects* pagan logic, a logic of sacrificial obliteration of self either for an ideal, or for the city, or for both. Such a logic promotes *an abstract space*,[31] the notion of the perpetually abiding notion or community which outlasts the lives of its citizens and is elevated in value above the lives of individual humans, even where this is disguised in the form of the notion of 'sacrifice for future generations'. For since *every* generation should logically be subject to the same imperative, consummation is forever postponed, and indeed morality itself is defined as perpetual postponement or else as self-sacrifice (this *aporia* applies both to consequentialism focused upon the capital of pleasure, and to Kantianism focused upon the capital of 'freedom'). Hence, already (as I have recounted elsewhere),[32] nineteenth-century positivism proclaimed that the secular, science-based community understands the true sacrality of sacrifice as 'altruism' or surrender of the self for the sake of the future, for science, and for the State. And when our contemporary 'post-modern' or else Levinasian thinkers discover the Good, or the moral act of self-giving sacrifice, to be perpetual postponement, they are simply perfecting this cruel and annihilating logic under whose tyranny we all now live.

The opposite to this tyranny was remarkably articulated by the great Scottish novelist John Buchan in his strange novel *Midwinter*, in which (in a highly Kierkegaardian fashion) the Jacobite hero of the story puts the salvation of a young girl in whom he is erotically interested before the well-being of his political cause, and indeed, according to the plot of the novel, destroys that cause altogether. The extremity of his situation is not down-played: 'He saw his clan, which might have become great again, reduced to famished vagrants', and yet, encouraged by a fictionalized 'Dr Johnson', and the mysterious 'Midwinter', who represents in the story the mysteries of Diana, he is reconciled to his option as a truly Christian one:

> Love had come to him, and he had passed it by, but not without making sacrifice, for to the goddess [Diana] he had offered his most cherished loyalties. Now it was all behind him – but by God, he did not, he would not regret it. . . . He had sacrificed one loyalty to a more urgent, and with the thought bitterness went out of his soul. Would Lochiel, would the Prince, blame him? Assuredly no.[33]

Reduced to a Lear-like 'nakedness', he is yet consoled by the thought that instead of sacrificing the singular to the all, he has sacrificed an (after all idolatrous and finally merely nominal) 'all' to the singular, and so affirmed the Resurrection hope for the return of each and every one, beyond the *aporia* of sacrificial options.

My claim therefore, is that the idea of self-sacrifice unto death without return for the sake of 'the whole', even if that be the rule of moral duty to an unspecified other, is *not at all* the true moral kernel of the Jewish and Christian legacy, but much more a transcription of secular modernity, which reads time not as a gift-of-self in the hope of an eternal return, but rather as a giving-up-of-self in time for a future absolutized space which will never truly be set in place. One may note, for example, that parents who entirely sacrifice themselves for their children thereby betray them, since they fail to present them with any *telos* and example of a lived, enjoyed (and sexual) adult life. This claim can be substantiated from the evidence of the Bible.

Ancient Near-Eastern Studies and Biblical criticism show that a typically near-Eastern idea that 'doing good' is a one-way operation proceeding downwards from the King towards those in need – 'the widows and orphans' – was heavily qualified in the inter-testamental period by the influence of Greek notions that good can be done by anyone – even a slave – and is more reciprocal or exchangist in character.[34] (And it would also be premature to conclude that the earlier Jewish perspective is wholly 'unilateral'; this would ignore in particular the notion of 'covenant'.)[35] A tension between the two perspectives appears to be registered in the New Testament itself, where in Luke's gospel 'benefactors', or those who wield power by giving are regarded with suspicion; where one is adjoined to love one's enemies and also, as already noted, *not* to invite to feasts those who can invite you back (Luke 6: 32–35).[36] (Though one may contrast this with the way Jesus' death is preceded in this gospel by a *symposium* amongst friends.)

This is Derrida's favoured focus for the Christian essence, and yet it is surely to be contrasted with St John's gospel, where there is no mention of loving enemies, where love seems to ceaselessly circulate amongst friends – I in you, and you in me – where there are erotic gestures (between Jesus and Mary of Bethany) and where the disciples are described as the Father's 'gift' to the Son, just as the Son is his gift to the disciples. Also one finds here an integration of Hellenistic notions (deriving from the Socratic paradigm) of a dying for friends rather than the city, which is also a dying for the truly *ethical.*

Now it may very well be argued that Christianity has combined both perspectives on giving, but if it has done so it is surely more fundamentally under the *aegis* of reciprocity, even though the eschatological character of this goal requires 'an absolutely unilateral' moment for the gift in our fallen present time. The sovereign gift from the divine height (to 'widows and orphans') is received only as a gift also returned from below, in the incarnation of the *Logos*, as the return of humanity to the Father. Likewise, God ceases to be a gesture of lonely superabundant giving, but instead his gift which is the Holy Spirit only *results* from, and is the manifestation of, the perfect mutuality of Father and Son. And finally, the Son offers himself *not at all* for the earthly city, and not at all as the giving up of something for the sake of an even greater something else, not even himself for the sake of the cosmos or the other. For the manner in which 'he dies for his friends' is indeed not that they should live their self-possessed lives while he has lost his – as if he had saved them from drowning, or defended them in war – but rather in defence of the truth he has secretly proclaimed to them through mysterious deeds and enigmatic words; the truth of which is the absolute creative power of the Father, a truth only maintained and indeed fully taught in Christ's resurrected return. It is this return that is commemorated when, in the eucharistic gesture, there is offered up to God *without division* bread and wine, and yet the people immediately consume this all themselves in its return to them as God's very flesh and blood.

In the eucharistic liturgy, humanity enters in advance into the divine Sabbath, the eschatological banquet and the cosmic nuptial, into the realm where once again we can entirely trust our every act as good precisely because we know that it will not merely follow our intention but be transformed and given back to us in a different and surprising mode.

Here, therefore, in the Eucharist, we see the only possible paradigm for gift and forgiveness, and therefore for ethics, not as one-way sacrifice, but as total surrender for renewed reception. Within this paradigm we can realize that to the degree that we are involved in some sense at certain times in both 'feast' and 'marriage' we are transported by the divine *Logos*, which gives by forgiving only to those reclined at the *symposium*, already above the time of death, such that we participate already in the time of resurrection. At this *symposium* and within this *connubium*, we give up everything, but not for the terrestrial city, and not even primarily for others: here we give up everything 'absurdly' to God in order to confess our inherent nothingness and to receive life in the only possible genuine mode of life, as created anew. Here we hold on to nothing, here we possess nothing securely, in contrast with exclusively ethical models which are also sacrificial. Here instead we render ourselves entirely a prey to the mere good fortune that it might turn out that we have been ethical. But the name of this fortune is secretly grace, the *Donum* or the Good; those names which convey all our Western longing.

9

POLITICS

Socialism by grace

I

How is the peace of the Church mediated to and established in the entire human community? I still believe that the answer is 'socialism', an originally mainly Christian concept, arising first in France and Britain and then Germany, later appropriated by German atheists, with the unfortunate consequence that the Church then pursued in reaction to this development unfortunate hybrids of the Christian socialist legacy with market liberalism and traditionalist reaction.

Yet despite resurgent (but deeply confused) unease about the economic and social consequences of the untrammelled free market and of globalization, socialism like religion now assumes a merely spectral reality in the modern secularized world. It has ceased to appear either plausible or rational, and has instead been consigned to the realm of dreams. All the same, as with Christianity in the West, we remain haunted by its ideal excellence, because nothing has emerged to replace it; we sense that just as the story of a compassionate God who became human was the 'final religion', so also the hope and to a degree the practice of a universal fraternity based on sharing was 'the final politics'. With its demise, we are delivered over to something somehow more secular than politics – to a future of infinite utilitarian calculations by individuals, States and trans-national companies of the possible gains and losses, the greater and the lesser risks.[1]

There will, however, be those on the left who will protest here that such a perspective upon socialism's demise is a false one, in thrall to postmodernist propaganda. The problem rather, they would argue, is that we have lost confidence in the rationalist legacy of the Enlightenment, to which socialism belongs. But it is clear that, to the contrary, socialism first emerged in a climate heavily imbued with *counter*-Enlightenment elements following the collapse of the hopes of the French Revolution: it was concerned with re-establishing, albeit in a more egalitarian mode, bonds of fraternity and solidarity which transcended a mere formalistic respect for the freedom and happiness of the other person, and was grounded in a shared vision of

162

the substantive Good which the first socialists often assumed would be a religious one, expressed in some mode of ritual practice.[2]

By contrast, the untrammelled free market, along with a bureaucracy governed by purely procedural norms, is clearly an expression of an Enlightenment commitment to the fully universal, the clearly comprehensible and the exhaustively justifiable, since only an empty consistency of method is able to meet these criteria. Compared with this reality, debates about the onset of the 'postmodern' are trivial: for while the emptiness of the modern, enlightened legacy tends to nihilism, the attempts to fill the gulf with modes of purely human self-assertion disclosing a human essence are not likely ever entirely to abate.

For the above reasons, we are now bound to ask whether capitalism is not the *definitive* shape of secularity, and whether by contrast community is not an intrinsically religious, mythical matter, so that with the demise of common belief, only a competitive market system in all spheres can organize and manage the resultant pursuit of remorseless self-interest by individuals and groups. Such a conclusion is perhaps now espoused by many on the left, but the reality it discloses is either positively endorsed or negatively refused. Endorsed, by 'libertarians' who fully embrace the secular, and refused by 'communitarians' who in some way or other tend to invoke the religious. I want now briefly to characterize these two intellectual parties, and indicate the problems with their respective positions, before suggesting why both groups may *share* an inadequate understanding of what 'community' means.

First of all, in the case of libertarians, one is confronted with the phenomenon of a Whiggism undismayed by any evidence. The most astonishing thing about this tendency (as represented by Anthony Giddens and others)[3] is that it remains more attached to the most metaphysical element of the Marxist legacy, namely its fatalist and logicist belief in capitalism as 'a necessary stage' in human history, than to its more rigorous and scientific aspect, namely its deconstruction of the logic of capitalist organization. Hence it implies that global neo-liberalization since the 1970s must be understood as a necessary and continuing sweeping away of paternalist, almost quasi-feudal relics: the new world-wide 'revolt against deference' shows that socialists were wrong to assume that the road of the liberal *via negativa* had been travelled to the end.

A little later I am going to indicate what I think is the major fallacy here, but for now I want to highlight the post-Marxist pathos of this tendency, whereby having largely abandoned the thought of a socialism still to come beyond capitalism, it still nevertheless seeks little dialectical twists of hope, crumbs of false historicist comfort. For while libertarianism insists that the future lies with the isolated 'reflective' individual, managing and manipulating a plethora of life-choices, chances and risks, it nonetheless seeks also to claim that civil society is in good heart, and that new forms of community are emerging: one cites sporting associations, women's support networks, single-issue groups, groupings around sexual orientation. But of course, all these things, however worthy, are rather evidence of lack of community: they are the resorts of people without community, who perhaps do not want community, but instead, having abandoned their singularity *in favour of an essence*, or in other words a hobby, or a badge – being-a-woman, being-a-black-man, being-gay, liking a kind of rock music, being obsessed with a particular kind of threatened animal, and so forth – they wish to foregather with other foreclosed singularities in order to offer mutual support, aid and encouragement. There is no community here, first of all because there is no *difference* and therefore no encounter; secondly, because there is no degree of self-sufficiency, of *societas perfecta*, or of potential to survive without outside aid, as there is with say a family or a parish, which can emigrate, and still survive and propagate, like the Pilgrim Fathers. The relationship to both space and time of such emergent 'identities' is too deficient to allow the term 'community'. These are essentially *reactive* groupings – often sustaining a semi-mythical sense of victimage, without positive innovative programmes with implications for the whole of humanity. There is, I think, rarely much genuine friendship to be found here, because association *for its own sake* – association with the other and the surprising with whom one nonetheless finds one can blend to increase mutual strength – is not the goal. Instead, it is a matter of input and output, and of a *trade* in mutual support.

The appeal to the rise of 'networking' therefore confirms and does not qualify a historical slide towards individualism. It does seem to me curious when socialists celebrate this; when, for example, they argue that it is pointless to protect the family – that 'last bastion of primitive communism' in Michel Houellebecq's phrase – because it is historically doomed. Proponents of such a position appear not to realize or else fatalistically to accept that the same capitalist forces which are undermining traditional heterosexual monogamy will *also* tend to undermine *any* stable relationships, however defined.

We should therefore cease to reach for spurious dialectical comfort, and instead recognize that capitalism of its most innate tendency precludes community. This is because it makes the prime purpose of society as a whole, and also of individuals in particular, to be one of accumulation of abstract wealth, or of power-to-do-things in general, and rigorously subordinates any desire to do anything concrete in particular, including the formation of social relationships.[4] Where individuals are commanded 'accumulate!' it will not be possible to restrict their accumulation except through the rules of a regulated struggle of all with all. And where society recognizes only the general imperative 'accumulate!' it will not be possible to arrive at any notion of an intrinsically just distribution of roles, resources and rewards. Instead, a set of rules for exchanges between *things* which reduces them all to a fictional abstract measure, will both disguise and organize (as Marx realized) relationships of arbitrarily unequal power.

The purely libertarian option on the left, must, therefore, part company with socialism. However, there are problems also with the left-of-centre communitarian position. It seems to bask in nostalgia for a state of nature that never was, and never can be. This state of nature somehow combines capitalist market *exchanges* with a compensatory social *organicism*, to which it hopes the economy can be finally subordinate. It is not malicious to point out that it shares this goal in common with Fascism. Here, community is thought of in an organicist way precisely because it is taken to exist apart from exchange – which always exposes a unit, whether the individual or the group, to an outside, to an exchanging partner. Because community *rather than* exchange is seen to be the final context, the sites of community here privileged are quasi-totalizing monads: the family, the locality, the nation. Thus if the libertarians tend to underestimate the importance of *relative* self-sufficiency to real community, the communitarians overestimate it, precisely because *absolute* self-sufficiency can never be arrived at. For every community exchanges outside itself, with the infinite unknown.

There are, I think, two further errors also at work here. First of all, exchange cannot be outplayed; it cannot be allowed its rein like the horses of force and desire in Plato's chariot of the soul, only to be pulled in at the last by the communal *logos*. Indeed this position does involve a kind of dubious pseudo-Platonism, which thinks of the *self-governing unit*, whether the individual or the city, as the final context. By contrast the truth, throughout all nature, is that every totality is continuously breached, and is always already breached – or, one might say, is always involved in an exchange beyond itself, not within an ultimate circle, but within an unending chain of exchanges throughout space and time. For this reason, the organization of exchange is fundamental, and will tend (along with production) to govern everything else, including every attempt to circumscribe a totality. This then, is the degree of truth in economic determinism; the priority of what breaches, flows into a thing and out again, and thus the priority of both production and exchange (production being in some respects an exchange – with nature, with the outcome, between producers in a hierarchy of production – and inversely every exchange producing a new outcome).[5] It is of course true that exchanges are not necessarily *economic*, and not necessarily of a legally formalized kind, acknowledging only *contractual* encounters. Nevertheless, exchange *has* been reduced to the economic and legally formalized in our capitalist society.

It follows that since exchange has, along with production, an ontological primacy, in our society capitalist market relations and contractual formalism, if untransformed, will remain determinative. Or, in other words, if community is not enshrined in exchange itself – and capitalism is precisely the exclusion of community from exchange – there is no other social site, no family site, no local site, no national site, in which community can take refuge. For in reality, families, localities and nations are *in* themselves only exchanges outside themselves, and therefore in a capitalist economy are doomed to be undermined, to be subject to the general process of invention of the 'individual' as a supposedly indivisible unit which negotiates directly (ignoring family, place and nation) with the invisible market centre – that macrocosmic individual who exists to accumulate and perpetuate the illusion of self-government at a cosmic level.[6]

This leads me to the second error of communitarianism. However, this is an error essentially *shared* by its libertarian opponents. It concerns a certain historical picture which they both have in the back of their minds, according to which community is essentially something which once was, and resided in an organic society of the past; in a *Gemeinschaft* which went along with the pervasive ordering of society by religion. By contrast, the movement of secularization is seen as a movement to *Gesellschaft*, to individualism and to individual expressivism.

II

Of course, there is no gainsaying this picture altogether, and let me to begin with partially confirm it in three significant respects (postponing to the next section my elaboration of the second error). First of all, community and religion in a broad sense do indeed go together (as Durkheim and so many others have suggested); so much so that the claim may in fact be tautologous, because community where it exists is an end in itself, is not *for* anything else, and is therefore, as Maurice Blanchot once contended, *ineffable.*[7] It cannot adequately be represented or told about, because it is a singular event or a series of singular events. One has to know about it from a vantage-point within it in order to experience it, not because it is not externally expressed, but because it is always *that* particular series of expressions grasped from *these* particular points of view. Communitarians, in the wake of Alasdair Macintyre and others, are fond of recommending 'thick' virtues like justice and truth in contrast to 'thin' virtues like 'respecting liberty' or 'promoting happiness', which seem grounded simply in mutual self-preservation, or else the preservation of the whole society, such that nothing in the community experience is here seen as objectively right and just. However, this perspective does not go far enough, and needs supplementing by Blanchot's considerations: for if one starts to *justify* or to argue for thick virtues, one is soon reduced to referring to something like social cohesion, or the cohesion of the individual – Aristotle does this just as much as Locke and Mill.[8] A genuinely thick virtue, a genuine model of social bonding valued for its intrinsic quality, would have to be difficult (yet not entirely impossible) to name, and semi-ineffable (to qualify Blanchot).

166

Here one may note that Plato, with his notion of the Good as a transcendent plenitude which we partially recollect only through *ever new* occasions for recollection encountered in a forward movement through time, is much closer to grasping 'ineffable community' than Aristotle.[9] Augustine gave this intrinsic quality its perhaps only possible general name – which is 'Peace'; but like St Paul, he did not take this as something one could contrive, or formally plan for. Instead it is what arises 'by grace' as a thousand different specific models of social harmony, a thousand different gifts of specific social bonding, a thousand kinds of community.[10]

Presently I shall show how this reflection can help remove the thought of community from a somewhat reactionary tinge. For now I must mention a second respect in which community is both organic and religious. This is the fact that it has nothing to do with *need*. 'Consider the lilies of the field': the sun pours upon the earth its abundance, and there was never any need to work or produce.[11] Community must have arisen of an impulse beyond mere necessity: either out of the dark desire of some to possess and therefore to make things scarce for others and thereby control them (as the Church Fathers thought); or else in order to celebrate, in order to *raise supernatural edifices*, and accumulate in order to expend in offerings and sacrifices to the gods[12] (it has been known for a long time that the raising of symbolic tombs preceded the discovery of agriculture). Or most probably, community arose for both reasons at once. But this renders community either rational and sinister, or else irrational and most probably sinister. The irrational latter aspect, which never seems lacking in societies deemed primitive, renders community always coterminious with a specific *mythos*, a specific narrative without rational grounds.[13]

In a third respect also, religion, organicism and community seem to belong together. This concerns the *economy* of primitive societies. As anthropologists have for a long time told us, so-called primitive societies do not make our divisions between public contract and private gift, nor between the free active subject and the inert object. Hence for these societies, a thing exchanged is not a commodity, but a gift; and it is not *alienated* from the giver but expresses his personality, so that the giver is *in* the gift, he *goes with* the gift. Precisely for this reason, a return on the gift is always due to the giver, unlike our modern 'free gift'. Yet this gift is still a gift and not a commodity subject to contract, because it returns in a slightly different form at a not quite predictable time, bearing with it also the subjectivity of the counter-giver.[14]

However, this economic mode was possible only within tight communities possessing strong familiarity of blood and tight expectations of what would be appropriate gifts. Despite the definition of gift with reference to the non-identical counter-gift which alone permits a gift to be transferred, the archaic gift sustained the same fetish, the same story of the same cycle of giving through all its exchanges. It moved in an organic circle, and outside that circle, for the purpose of trade with strangers, barter or early forms of contract were already resorted to.[15] Moreover, however much we may celebrate the archaic gift, its reverse aspect, or the reverse aspect of organic collective identity, was always *war* with the other, not to mention the many ways in which gift-giving was used (as hierarchy tended to increase) to secure arbitrary power within the clan itself. The gift-community possessed automatically its own form of violence. But our historical tragedy is that replacement of the gift with contract – which means the treating of all and everyone as a stranger – entails another and equally terrible, though more subtle from of violence. We should therefore realize the following: to say 'gift is violence, but contract is also violence', is the same as to say, 'myth is violence, but reason is also violence', or else again, 'community is violence but lack of community is equally violence'.[16]

<h1 style="text-align:center">III</h1>

So far I have been going along with the idea that community and organicism belong together. And this is the common inherited view. Now, however, as promised, I want to show how it can be, at least to a degree, disturbed. Let us revert to the issue of the relation of community to exchange.

The entire organic community is a *self-governing* community; therefore it is a community that has ceased to relate to bodies outside of itself. It follows that if it treasures community within itself, it can only do so by falling into self-contradiction. For community is not a *fusion*, as J.-L. Nancy points out, or at least it is not a *complete* fusion (a totality without asymmetrical reciprocity), because that just produces another isolated individual totality.[17] So to value community is to value encounter, and the meeting with the other and different, albeit that it is *equally* to value a harmonious sharing and blending (this goes along with the element of 'relative self-sufficiency'). If one gives ultimate value to community within a community, it becomes in consequence entirely contradictory to set absolute bounds to that community, or to its new encounters outside itself, within time and space.

It appears then that the self-governing organic community is already the individual subject writ large, and that it is not accidental that such communities often celebrate founding heroes, who are precisely individuals who *break with* preceding communities.[18] Of course heroic individuals only express *collective* values, unlike the modern expressive individual. Nevertheless heroism makes its own heroism ultimate, and the same metaphysical logic of *self-government* orders both the predefined individual of antiquity and the more unpredictable individual of modernity. Equally, it is true that the self-government of the modern rational society repeats in a formal-instrumental mode the self-identity of *mythos* – this is shown by the way in which individual differences get reduced in our society to quantitative variations, and are often more apparent than real in their acknowledged instance. Just as pagan myth-governed collectivities were at bottom individualist, so equally, modern capitalism is at bottom collectivist. It follows that the *Gesellschaft/Gemeinschaft* contrast of the sociologists is a simplification. By contrast, Otto von Gierke, Theodor Adorno and today J.-L. Nancy were right: ancient society and modern society, pagan myth and secular reason, are profoundly in agreement.[19]

However, between these two, in the middle of history, Gierke identified something else; the *free-association*, or relational unity with the other, whose near-oxymoronic character allows it to be brought into conjunction with the gift, which is somehow at once *free in relation to* and yet also *bound to* the other.[20] For we can now point out that, for all its confinement within an organic enclosure, it is also the case that the gift, like a kind of universal portent of the gospel of love and grace, necessarily had to breach this organicism. As Marcel Mauss declared, a gift already broke with status, and was already a negotiation with an unknown other.[21] It had to be, because any human family (given the incest taboo) arises out of exchange with the other, such that organicism is a specifically *patriarchal* illusion, an attempt to expurgate the strangeness of wives. Always working counter to this, as Annette Weiner has shown, was the active subjectivity of the gift itself, which meant that women as gifts, far from being reduced to mere objects, since the gift is not an object, exerted in many places an active power of breaching, opening and arrival of exteriority.[22]

Hence, *even to some extent from the outset in archaic society*, community has been *with* exchange, and gift has been possible, not simply because of organicism, but because there are strangers. Likewise, community *needs* strangers, *these are* the only available neighbours. It is not that they need to be received *into* the community, it is rather that the arrivees are always the only people to have community with, though most arrive through time by birth (the circumstance of 'natality', whose fundamental import was explored by Hannah Arendt).[23] But the human problem is this: how to escape Scylla and Charybdis? That is to say, both organic community and alienated contract, remembering that both are modes of 'individualism', and both exclude community. What would the way through be, what is the character of the oxymoronic third way spoken of by Gierke?

We would have to name it *universal* gift. Instead of the treating of even neighbours as aliens (though this was transcended even in primitive societies in the case of guest rituals) one would substitute the treating of even aliens – when encountered – as neighbours: a universal practice of offering, a universal offering in the expectation or at least hope of receiving back not a price due to us, but others themselves in their counter-gifts, because we aim for reciprocity, for community, and not for a barren and sterile self-sacrifice (which as we saw in the previous chapter is the alternative of *both* nihilists *and* Levinasian moralizers who take capitalist exchange to be the definitive form of exchange).[24]

This universal gift of asymmetrical reciprocity would perforce be also universal *mythos*, universal non-identical repetition of the same yet always different story. (The recipient of the gift who gives back is also the Piercean/Roycean 'third' as the interpreter of the proffered sign of the first giver: hence gift is metaphor – and the interpreting Holy Spirit is eminently *donum*.) Here would be found an all the more genuine community, because all the more ineffable and not strictly repeatable. By contrast, both the traditional organic community and the modern capitalist community equally try to hold onto identity in spatial form, in order to define it and store it, thereby *de-sacralizing* it, subordinating it to a self-preservation which is ultimately self-cancelling, since the self is in flux: the 'preserved' self logically turns into the postmodern 'voided' self. And this is why every god has always died.

IV

The universal *mythos* would be an alternative *logos* to the *logos* of reason, which always seeks to produce a final human essence and thereby exercise tyranny, whether as state socialism or technocratic capitalism. However, the point of this invocation is not at all to appeal back to myth and ritual in despair at the failures of reason. To the contrary, one of the merits of Catherine Pickstock's work is to indicate the irrationality of a reason that rationally acknowledges no surplus to itself, but seeks to be self-sufficient and 'pure'. Such a reason is doomed to regulate and preserve inviolate its own void 'heart of darkness'. Since it is confined by its purity to the entirely formal, methodical and procedural, the content it does promote, and which no formalism can entirely avoid, will assume the form of a crushing demonic ritual, sustaining no point or meaning save its own identical repetition. Hence, as Franz Kafka implied, bureaucracy operates not so much as naked coercion, but as a habit of procedure and protocol which we internalize, such that we are held captive by the numbing and sterile mystery of its strange futility.[25] Likewise, the market induces us to idolize novelty as merely pointless variation, to bow down before the mesmerizing sublimity of endless quantifiable increase and to follow the deceitful lure of abstraction.

Meanwhile, as Pickstock describes, our social life is entirely governed by the empty rituals of manners and fashion, which enshrine no abiding sense of the collectively valued, and therefore are never to be trusted, since they may always be the masks of insincerity and manipulation.[26] As she also shows, the peculiar characteristic of these three aspects of 'secular ritual' (the bizarre 'religion' that is essential for the reproduction of the irreligious) is that they all pursue a process of 'spatialization'. For since, like all rituals, the modern ritual aims at security and stability, and yet, unlike other rituals (for the example the eucharistic liturgy which 'gives' the Church) it cannot appeal to norms outside its own recurrence – and is indeed intended to block all invocation of such norms – it must perforce seek to erect an absolutely secure space, immune to temporal ravages. Yet this is obviously a superstitious and impossible project, more insanely 'idolatrous' than anything known to 'primitive' peoples. Since the absolutely secure space never finally arrives, and since in addition, it commands only form not content – or rather commands content only formally as a command to be there and to increase – the modern ritual also demands a ceaseless and unremitting sacrifice of the past and present to the future, without any traditional 'return' of benefit to the already dead or to those still living, in the shape of an eternal life.

Opposed to spatialization stands an appeal to transcendence. The latter alone can mythically and rationally sustain the 'universal gift'. This is because such a gift must be semi-ineffable, somewhat sacral as to its content, for otherwise it would have no value, would confer no benefit, and therefore be de-natured as gift. But at the same time, if it is a gift that can be passed on into the unknown realm of strangers, or be received in return from that realm, then this content cannot be circumscribed after the fashion of primitive, local societies. As we have seen, this proviso in no sense dilutes the sacrality of the gift, but rather the reverse, since the more the value of the gift is fetishized and confined to a narrow range of permissible forms, the more it becomes self-referring in a mode that is like a kind of concrete pre-figuration of the abstract self-reference of pure reason. Hence the sacred ineffability of the gift is more sustained where a horizon of unknown variation is allowed, but this horizon can only be envisaged under the Sun of transcendence. Only if reality itself is regarded as 'given' from some beyond does it become possible to trust that that which is communicated and circulated may assume new meanings which can blend seamlessly with the old. Or inversely, a reality limitlessly receptive to the renewal and perpetuation of gift, understood as that which both surprises and unites (surprising to unite, uniting to surprise), must be a reality that derives from a source that is always and eternally the plenitude of such blending.

Yet is it not outrageous for a political discourse to appeal directly to the theological (which for many people simply represents the fantastic and unbelievable) in this manner? No, because it has already been seen how the secular sustains a certain equally 'irrational' and yet nihilistic variant of the theological. And this variant is but one possible mode, one possible idiom of universalizing. To be human, to be linguistic, is to universalize to some degree, but the regime of spatialization is also the attempt at secure, ideal abstraction, immune from the vagaries of the sensible, and the transports of time. As Pickstock further argues, and as the great modern French poet Yves Bonnefoy long ago claimed in a slightly different fashion, this drive to the pure concept (or pure *mathesis* for Pickstock) is itself an attempt to evade death.[27] But since all actual, real, specific things in time must die, this evasion refuses also everything finite, which means everything alive with which we are acquainted. For this perspective, the remembered gleanings of things are but tokens of absence, or else the false consolations of accumulated ciphers.

By contrast (for both Pickstock and Bonnefoy), there exists another possible model of universalizing. In this mode, it is recognized that a ceaseless passing and a ceaseless dying is the very condition of life itself, which allows its dynamic and its development. But this further suggests that only an impossible, embalmed, absolute finite life (as aimed at by spatialization) would be perfectly dead. By contrast, what really lives is never for a single instance of time or an iota of space perfectly alive, but rather always already passed away and transported beyond our horizon. But if life is only the passing of life, the ecstatic memory of life, then, as Augustine suggested, it only occurs as a sign of an absolute eternal life, as a desire for more of itself that would be more like itself. Since life passes and is only mediated to us through memory and desire, every specific concrete instance of life is always also something other than itself, part of a larger, dimly imagined reality, disclosing only partially something that draws us to its hyper-presence.[28] Within this perspective also one must universalize in order to construe (to speak, to live humanly), but here the universal is disclosed in particulars regarded as retrieved as well as lost through death. Here as for Bonnefoy, the fundamental language of human life is paradoxically that of monumental *tombeaux*. Here also, by the same token, the *élan* to the eternal beyond is the same *élan* which causes us to attend to the next instance of time, the next step in space, which alone sustains and reveals for us the preceding step, in expectation of new disclosures from an eternity also reaching down towards us.

A mere myth absolutely irrelevant to practical politics? A *mythos* certainly, as well as a *logos*, but by no means irrelevant. For the problem about pure reason is that it brutally abstracts from all specificity and ineffable attachment, and although its global regime may be sustainable unto delirium, it also destroys the common run of human well-being and motivation. In general it induces a schizoid cynicism, whereby, as with some modern evangelical Christians, a very thin and kitsch-laden content is regarded by its adherents almost exclusively from the perspective of promotion, marketing and re-packaging in order to make it blend forever more seamlessly with the abstractions of virtual life.

On the other hand, there are problems, equally, about fanatical and closed attachments, as all history so readily attests. Today indeed the incipient self-referentiality of such attachments fuses all too smoothly with the self-referentiality of abstraction, in such a way that all the machinery of market and bureaucracy may be used to press for the rights to expression of certain identities that are at times little better than reconstructed 'heritage' fetishes. And where one wishes to go somewhat further than this, and to insist, like John Gray, on the living diversity of local cultures, resulting in distinctly different forms of capitalism (Chinese, Japanese, Indian,

German, Italian and so forth), then there still arises the question of what idiom – economic, cultural, political – mediates these different practices.[29] If one is resigned to mere postmodern Isaiah Berlin-style pluralism, then it is inevitably true that at the meta-level what rules is the purest, most spatialized abstraction. And it is exactly this abstraction which, as Gray himself describes, is responsible for the most ruthless and globalizing drive for profits: resulting now not just in the destruction of cultures, natural environments, welfare states and trades unions, but also in the inevitably consequent decline of economic demand and the rise of regional over-production. Hence to celebrate even an extra-liberal pluralism, that is to say in a Berlin-Gray postmodern mode to promote the toleration of non-liberal societies, does not really contradict globalization, for it still only allows us to mediate between diverse cultural visions in an abstract fashion. This is essentially to substitute free-choosing cultures for free-choosing individuals; and given the sheer cultural diversity of so many parts of the world, it would mean that in practice the free-choosing individual was still very much to the forefront.[30] Therefore any attempt to restrain the global market would require some sort of appeal to rival universality. Yet all universalities supposedly deducible from the universally human have all, hitherto, issued in the formally empty and thereby destructive, whether one is speaking of capitalism or state socialism. Detached from all attachments, such human-isms inevitably land up destroying every attachment as too tinged with the arbitrary, in the name of the black sun of nihilism itself: that absolute transcendental arbitrariness, which, within an arbitrary economy, is alone 'non-arbitrary'.

So one is returned, once more, to the need for at least some modicum of universal attachment, universal *mythos*. But here, as I have suggested, transcendence offers a thought of the universal not as something clearly grasped, spatially fixed and operable, but rather as something eternally present yet not fully accessible. This universal is instead only available as diversely mediated by local pathways, as Augustine already divined (see Chapter 1, above). But inversely, it is only by virtue of a local ecstatic opening to this universal that one has giving, or community, or sacred locality at all. It is not that one is suggesting that there is an absolutely unknown transcendence, accessible by one's own cultural pathway, each as good as every other. For this transcendent would be an uncharacterizable black hole, and therefore the most perfect of abstractions, while concomitantly all the indifferently good pathways would lack any concrete, actualizable idiom for mediation. Such religious 'liberalism' would be thoroughly apolitical. Instead, if one is to say that an open pathway, or many open pathways, are disclosive of transcendence in some degree, this implies that, constantly and dynamically, one is on pilgrimage from sacred site to sacred site, weaving them together along a coherent line or spiral, and thereby out of smaller sites constantly tracing the margins of greater sites, and then returning to locate within the greater realm each specific place once again. In this fashion a recognition of the transcendent requires not just the legitimizing – beyond modern abstraction – of infinitely many regional perspectives, but also the constantly renewed attempt to characterize the one human 'region' in the cosmos, and to erect, as it were, the universal totem.

But all this, one might claim, is precisely the endeavour of the so-called 'axial' religions – Judaism (later Christianity and Islam), Socratic Philosophy and Buddhism – which all emerged around the same period before Christ. These movements (less emphatically Buddhism, though this was its tendency *vis-à-vis* Hinduism) all inculcated notions of transcendence. Now for the political left to understand the political significance of this inculcation, it is crucial that it lay aside Whig and Marxist biases towards linear historiography. As Marcel Gauchet argues in his book *The Disenchantment of the World*, instead of speaking of 'progress' towards the State and global culture, it is better to think of 'primitive' societies without the State as *electing* (in some fashion) for an absolute stasis provided by a fixity of ritual and mythic repetition which helps prevent internal rupture, economic inequality and economic scarcity.[31] Conversely, it is better to think of the modern abstract release of political power and abstract wealth as an option for absolute novelty and full realization of all possible human powers. Between these two options, Gauchet locates the axial religions' appeal to transcendence.

However, still in thrall to Whiggery, he is only able (from his *own* option for the modern perspective) to conceive of this appeal as a transitional hybrid, destined eventually to disappear from the cultural horizon.[32] Yet a continued option for transcendence suggests another, at least equally plausible historical perspective. As has been seen, the 'primitive' ensures a perfectly rational and proto-formal self-enclosure which foretells pure reason, while the modern erects a yet more perfect spatial stasis based upon the most extreme 'tabooing' ever known – namely of all semi-ineffable attachments as dangerous. Given such a converging of apparent opposites, the invocation of transcendence can appear, by contrast, as the real alternative: arising not at the end of history but in the middle (as why not? asks the non-Whig).

But this timing is after all not so accidental, because the axial religions emerged in a period after the emergence of gigantic empires, focused on a sovereign centre. It is tempting here to see a simple alliance between monotheism and the centralized State, for indeed the sacral bureaucracy and eminent imperial ownership of Babylon were accompanied by a severe pruning of the pantheon. And yet it is clear that, to the contrary, the axial religions all invented modes of community intended to qualify the untrammelled sway of the State and its abstractions. More vividly than anyone else hitherto, Pickstock has shown how Socrates and Plato sought to

174

re-invoke and yet re-invent the mythical, the ritual, the recollective and the oral in the face of an already secular and 'modern' programme for sheerly manipulative politics, purely market economics, preferential individualism and cognitive scepticism acknowledging only the drift of temporary power.[33] (And it should be remembered here that the *polis* was *already* in some measure a reaction against empire and was 'more archaic' in the role it allowed to oral participation as against written decree.) Likewise Israel, while deploying State thematics, also renewed attention to the ancestral, the oral and the pastoral within her expanded city-state.[34]

In either case, instead of the start of a transit to modernity, what one has is already a critique of the modern in advance, which re-invokes the primitive (so that the Bible always was 'out of date') and yet not in a spirit of pure nostalgia, since it seeks to be more universal than the primitive. For if anything represented such a transit, it was rather the object of this critique, namely the Asiatic empires like that of Babylon. Here one finds already a secularization of law (contrast Plato's *Laws* and the *Torah*) and already extreme penalties for the violation of private property rights (contrast the *Torah's* focus on the sundering of intra-human bonds).[35] Yet these things were strangely correlated with a theocratic absolutism and a simplified pantheon tending to the monotheistic. This was because the sacred had been increasingly understood as a source of power which could be channelled and manipulated by a codified divination. Outside this imperial monopoly of the sacral, a drained and thereby 'secular' sphere started to emerge. And indeed, without such secularization, theocracy is inconceivable, since a theory which limits rule only to a sacral class with a monopoly on divine mediation, *requires* there to be a distinct secular sphere over which to exercise this authority. By contrast, where access to the divine is mediated throughout by an elusive participation (as in Athens and Israel) the secular is less distinct, and theocracy finds no scope for its peculiar logic. Hence, as Pickstock emphasizes, the emergence of theocratic 'divine right' theories based upon a *de facto* channelling of divine will and power through a sovereign centre (rather than upon an elective participation in divine practice), which occurred at the end of the Middle Ages, went paradoxically hand in hand with secularization. At this time a 'Babylonian' pattern of monotheism reasserted itself, in a fashion manifestly subversive of prior Christian and Jewish construals of God and community.

In the light of these considerations, we can reappropriate our Western legacy, not as the history of an evolutionary progress away from religion and towards human freedom and control, but rather as the history of a tremendous revolt against *either* particularism *or* the cult of universalizable power, in the name of the transcendent Good. Capitalism represents the gradual collapse of this revolt; socialism (in its more syndicalist forms) the attempt to renew and intensify it. But if the creeds of transcendence in the West (Judaism, Christianity, Islam) are expressions of this revolt, then it is clearly absurd to regard them as local cultic preferences in contrast to universalizing reason. On the contrary, their entire point is that they represent a mode of universalizing other than that of enlightenment, and one that, since it is more respectful of the particular and ineffable, holds more promise of a distributive justice enacted through consent, rather than through terror and forced purchase. Yet the precondition for such agreed distribution remains, as I have argued, some mode of universal religious attachment, some kind of collective totem. Thus the religions of the West have focused upon symbols, practices and authorities utterly specific, yet also moveable and transferable from culture to culture, and variable from place to place.

The problem, of course, is that they present us with rival versions of a 'universal totem' and this is a problem not readily resolvable, though it should also be remembered that the degree of overlap in symbolic as well as conceptual consensus is also considerable. Catherine Pickstock has, however, provided us with an exemplary account of how one 'universal totem', namely the Catholic eucharist, supremely operates in a fashion that is at once entirely tangible, and yet equally non-fetishistic and non-socially divisive. She has also shown how, when such a totem becomes *merely* portable (as with the Protestant bound and unvarying Bible, or the Counter-Reformation regulated and unvarying Mass) and loses local variation along its journeying, it tends to become once more a fetishized object which is increasingly a mere cover and a pretext for the rule of reified abstractions. (This is the fate of all 'fundamentalisms'.)

Pickstock's analysis of the social import of the Catholic Mass cannot be bypassed, just for the reason that, as I have argued, the pre-condition for collective solidarity and just redistribution beyond the liberal formalities of respect for person and property must be some kind of collective and supra-rational devotion. Indeed, all societies retain some such devotion, but where it is marginalized, it tends to become debased and fanaticized, so that should it ever erupt once more into the centre (at once protesting against and yet reinforcing the lack of true liturgy), the consequences are likely to be (and were in the last century) diabolical. For this reason alone the matter of collective devotion must be one of general political concern. Moreover, such devotion can never be simply conjured up *de novo*; we have to reckon with a given inheritance. Here Pickstock reminds us that the first source of European collective identity was the sense of being literally part of the body of Christ, an extension of divine humanity.[36] Such a sense has left a unique legacy, a conviction of the possibility of limitless human exaltation, abso-lutely qualified by an equal conviction that such exaltation is an attentive reception of an invisible *Imago* that utterly exceeds the human, even though it can be perfectly blended with it according to an ineffable affinity. We should surely pause and ask ourselves whether this legacy is not uniquely valuable, and whether any other imagery or ritual could have ensured it? For, as Pickstock argues, what is so striking about European collectivity is

176

that it is imagined as ceaselessly reconstituted entirely from without: the body of Christ, which we are, is nonetheless what we must first of all receive and then receive again. And this has the consequence that ultimate authority resides not in a person, nor in an institution, nor in a legal norm over against the community and judging it.[37] As we saw in Chapter 7, this symbolic power is not, primarily, mediated by a human hierarchy: on the contrary, it is in the first place mediated by the general ingestion of these symbols throughout time. Thus community, on this model, is not self-governing, and yet the government of the transcendent other is mediated by the gradual emergence of a complex consensus attained not just in contemporary space, but across all the successive generations.

V

Does this not suggest that the notion of the 'body of Christ' involves something much more politically complex than the usual notions of 'democracy', 'civil society', 'human rights' and so forth? In particular it suggests a *politics of time* surplus to our normal questions of who should possess authority and freedom within a circumscribed *space*. This politics has several aspects.

First of all, we have seen how the politics of endless acquisition and of deferred enjoyment in expectation of an absolute future rest upon an illusory ontology which seeks to erect a secure spatial edifice in defiance of death. A politics of time would, instead, treat life and the moments of life as only passing, and focus on how they might pass gloriously. Thus instead of the sacrificial cult of instrumentalization which encourages us to think of most processes – education, journeys to work, technology, administration, communications – as things to be endured if we are to reach the really valued (but increasingly elusive) ends, we would rather focus on the cyclical 'pointlessness' of life (eating to work, working to eat, etc.) and then see in this cycle itself the point, a kind of dance to be performed well, as if for the delectation of the gods. This, as Pickstock has reminded us, is how Plato finally conceived the life of the city.

Secondly, a politics of time would insist on the priority of the other-worldly as the pre-condition of justice. This is the hardest crux of all for the secular left. But it is easily explained. I am not speaking of the other-worldly as something opposed to the world-in-time; as Pickstock points out, it was only after this world had been reconceived as a sacrally leached, unyielding space, that the Church's concern became more exclusively to do with the fate of the individual soul in another dimension.[38] But a reality seen as passing tends to be seen as permanently invaded by an elsewhere which it mediates, although it is equally true that what passes can be seen as ultimately valuable only for what it portends. Of course such a perspective can lead to an oriental neglect of the political and social, or can be used ideologically to placate the dispossessed, but this need not be the case where what passes is allowed to pass well, and where one rejoices in its passing, since only such passing allows us to construe the world as a continuous theme or tune, as Augustine insisted.[39] Here the ephemeral is celebrated, but not as something that might be possessed or accumulated. The latter realization, if not deployed selectively and ideologically, in fact uniquely removes the entire *raison d'être* from the desire to possess and accumulate more than anyone else, since it reveals this aim to be illusory and impossible.

Thus whereas a secular socialism appears to withdraw from egotism with reluctance and rancour, as if it desired to prevent some people from holding too much of the *genuinely good*, religious socialism, with far less austerity, insists like Augustine that only that which is in common is truly good at all, or can be truly possessed, though only in the mode of reception of a gift, which must be relinquished and passed on. Moreover, this common good – the wealth of being which passes like a flash of light – is always enjoyed (Augustine again) from different perspectives as something absolutely individual and unique, whereas a limited spatial good shared out equally is supposed to grant a portion of the same kind of thing to all.[40] In other words, where what is 'in common' is seen as metaphysically and truly in common, collectivity is seen to arise through the uttermost individualism, just as the transcendent universal is only available through local and specific refraction.

In the third place, a politics of time refuses the inevitable secular oscillation between humanism and nihilism. In the former case, the criterion of autonomy may place restrictions on the coercion of one by another, as well as upon the idolization of false, supposedly external absolutes, and also upon many inequitable inconsistencies. And yet the same autonomy, with an implacable logic, tends eventually to be manifest as the terror of collective and majority force, the idealization of human freedom whatever its elections, and the absolute rightness of whatever legislates without and yet through exceptions. Here as we saw in Chapter 1, it is not enough, like Hannah Arendt, to accuse Adolf Eichmann of perverting the 'without exception' of the Kantian categorical imperative into the 'without exception' of consistently administered state law, whatever its content – which in this case was genocidal.[41] For Eichmann was more right than he knew: Kant's *Metaphysics of Morals* makes it clear that the 'without exception' of submission to sovereign state power which sovereignty demands is endorsed by the 'without exception' of the categorical imperative, as we cannot *universally* will that outraged individual consciences should remove the very source of political legal order.[42] Since this order is seen by Kant as merely positive, and as legitimated by its proceeding from free autonomy, no 'natural' norms or restraints can be appealed to (as for the Middle Ages) over against the *de facto* exercise of sovereignty. This of course reveals that the 'without exception' is really the rule of the arbitrary exception in a state of permanent emergency, as we saw in Chapters 5 and 6. Thus Kantian

178

liberal humanist logic and Nazi logic are seamlessly linked, and Nazism was nothing but an unhindered attempt to raise man as a God, to unleash and perfect the power of human freedom.[43]

Yet such pure humanism also slides into nihilism. With too great an immodesty free will may be seen as surmounting fate, and yet with too great a modesty the same free will may often be seen as but the manifestation of fate, the temporary instance of a blind power as much denied as manifest in its instantiations, which are therefore destined always to disappear (this is the gist of all the various Nietzschean and Heideggerean semi-Nazisms still current). But both these faces of the secular equally eradicate time, since humanism seeks an impossible permanent defeat of time and death, while nihilism celebrates time as pure destruction, and therefore as the spatial void which overrides time and reduces its instances and differences to unmeaning. The first face – humanism – denies the inherent nothingness of things which are temporal, while the other face – nihilism – hypostasizes this nullility, such that, for its perverse theology, apparent presences are seen as inevitable primitive denials of the *nihil*, through which the *nihil* nonetheless is alone manifest. By contrast, only the orientation to transcendence, to the eternal, interprets the intrinsic nothingness of things in time as their existing by participation, as their subsisting always and primordially as gifts which declare to us ever-renewed and freely granted human possibilities.

In proceeding from this vision, which regards all temporalities as nothing and yet as the way to everything, a politics of time is able to outwit both the immodesty of autonomy and the false modesty of abandonment to fate which places limits on the chances of human reconciliation, and encourages only a free-market play of transhuman forces. Thus a politics of time, construed as grounded in liturgical devotion, is able, as Pickstock suggests, to inscribe heteronomy in the heart of autonomy itself. For where the ruling principle is a deferral to a plenitudinous unknown Good which is always still awaited, rule itself is (at least in principle) understood as the possibility of a self-critique through attention to what lies beyond the self (individual or collective). Pure autonomy must arbitrarily elect some facet of self as essential and inviolable, in order to refer to this as a measure; in this way, of course, it collapses into heteronomy after all. But liturgical rule is able to await on further capacities of the self as yet undisclosed or ungranted. At the same time it does not appeal to any finite, hypostasized heteronomous principle: on the contrary it is precisely as a new disclosure of the self that the rule of the transcendentally heteronomous can be registered.

All this may sound abstract and removed from practice. But it is not, because social justice and political democracy require absolute self-critique, and yet at the same time an avoidance of any absolutization of the self making this critique, since this leads to the fascistic worship of will or fate – and then to attempts to enact a final divine judgement in the here and now in order to produce a utopian 'heaven on earth', whose corollary will necessarily be a 'hell on earth' to which all those tinged with imperfection will be condemned. (On these grounds Jacob Rogozinski has demonstrated that the Holocaust was the supreme consummation of secularity.)[44] Only a culturally imbued sense of transcendence is able to sustain this balance between self-critique and non self-adulation. From this sense, and from this balance, flows a valuing of time, since future contingencies are no longer subordinated to the eternal spatial measure of human arbitration or else ultimate vacuity. Within the scope of the latter measures, these contingencies are reduced to random instances, but for a politics of time what is still to come may disclose or remind us of more of that which is eternal, beyond both time and space. Hence for this practice alone, contingency partakes of ultimate and not subordinated significance.

But here a caveat must be entered: were the future contingency to arrive through time alone, then it would merely be seen as another manifestation of the same one thing, already given, like a flower issuing forth from a shoot. Since, by contrast it arises also from another space, or from a space forever constituted by externalities (unlike the utterly finished, surveyable space of a *mathesis*) then it is guaranteed that the future contingency is super-added to the present, and not emergent from it by mere instrumental causality – whose absolute sway would demand that everything was given from the very first instance of time. In this way a non-foreclosed space is also required for the temporal arrival of significant contingencies, like the endless variations of tidal waves upon a sea-shore (just as equally, the genuine externalities of this space only appear through the open-endedness of time). Pickstock is therefore right to insist upon a liturgical *chronotope*, not upon a triumph of time over space, which, as she says, would be but another mode of spatialization.[45] Another way of conveying this point is to say once more that exchange is as fundamental as production.

A politics of time, therefore, seeks first of all to ritualize life as passage, in order to capture in the lineaments of passage certain traces of the eternal. In this fashion it is fundamentally liturgical. Secondly, it insists that this eternal is alone what we individually possess and possess in common, like light, which we all see together and yet from singular perspectives. Thirdly, it recognizes that government by the eternal is at once heteronomous and autonomous: 'middle voiced' as Pickstock puts it. More concretely, we can now recognize these three components as festival, education and profession. These are the 'three modes of liturgical order'.

VI

Festival, first of all. Where life is realized and enjoyed as passage, there wealth lies in glorious expenditure, and personal freedom in acts of generosity which bond us to others. This passage is, as we have seen, a passage of gift,

180

which as Pickstock says, cannot begin or cease to be gift, if it is ever to be given at all, since a thing given is regarded as always having had this fundamental destiny, if we are not to devalue the recipient; while a gift must go on giving itself, if it is not to lapse into mere possession, in forgetfulness of the donor. In consequence life celebrated as passing gift is life thankfully received from the outset, and also life shared without restraint. Doxology and charity are here inseparable, but also consummated in the shared festival, for to obliterate oneself as recipient is to blaspheme the transcendent giver; while to refuse the return gift of gratitude from the one to whom one gives is to celebrate's one will to give (in Kantian, Levinasian or Derridean mode) instead of the miraculous and unpredictable arrival of achieved affinity and surprising reciprocity. Hence Pickstock restores to our gaze the full dimensions of charity as also celebration, kinship, fraternity, *eros* and ritual.[46] From this perspective charity ceases to be an anxious duty, just as bereavement ceases to be an unmediated private loss; instead to give has its seasons, and loss its place in a general economy, although neither in an exhaustively prescribed fashion.

Giving, therefore, is primarily a matter of shared expenditure and celebration. 'Primitive' societies know this, and group themselves around such ecstatic transition, not around accumulated illusions. In modernity, by contrast, without a collective understanding of why things pass (from whence they come and to where they are going – out of apparent night through a single day and back to night, like Bede's sparrow flying through the mead-hall), and a public celebration of this passing, there increasingly are no public, central spaces – which are always as Bonnefoy stresses, marked by tombs ornamenting death, and towers narrowing upwards.[47]

Without collective mourning and collective offering, there arise no sufficiently extravagant public works erected out of limitless and exorbitant demand – like the massive stone circles of the Atlantic seaboard erected, perhaps, through the cyclical co-operation of tiny adjacent chiefdoms, or even through more egalitarian exchanges.[48] Only such works, as Georges Bataille asserted, ensure any sufficient brake on the private appropriation of capital, since merely pragmatic public purposes are too finite in scope to absorb the insanely infinite stockpiling of credit. Bataille was, however, wrong, as Pickstock rightly avers, to assert the secularity of all production.[49] To the contrary, where the smoke of offering does not vanish into an abyss, but ascends to a plenitude which has already received it, and therefore ascends with unquenchable hope of future benefit, there it will be seen that every production, just to the degree that it is produced only to be lost, expended and offered, nonetheless exhibits in its specific lineaments the benefit of participation, of further received gift. For here there is no real contrast, as for Bataille's (conventional and conservative) nihilism between holding and losing: on the contrary, if what is held must be lost, it is also the case that this losing is an increased self-expression, allowed to us by the

181

transcendent as the most we can ever hold. Thus the Pickstockian notion of 'liturgy' adds to the current academic thought of 'gift' an equiprimordiality of productive work with exchange, yet without any descent into a reductive materialism. Liturgy is an offering, a kind of spontaneous non-regulated taxation. But it is also 'the work of people'. Therefore it is both the occasional riot of festival and the steadiness of everyday tranquil craft. But festival *as* craft, and craft *as* festival.

VII

Next comes *education*. Within a spatialized politics (common to both right and left), it is assumed that education is only a temporal instrument which subserves a spatial outcome that is political, social, economic and technological. Broadly speaking, this renders education but one field within the space of the political. However, from the perspective of a politics of time, it is rather that the political (and the social, economic and technological) is but a moment of the pedagogic or of *Paideia*. This is because the point of human life is taken to be ultimately *theoria*, or the contemplation of the eternal. Therefore the whole of life is regarded as a reception and a learning. Education, it can be seen, lies for this perspective very much within a liturgical economy. And concomitantly, if life is a pedagogic reception, then it is also a pedagogic transmission: freedom here must be first of all the generous imparting of what one has learnt in order that it might be learnt better. But in that case we have a primary pedagogic mode of sociality which (like the body of Christ) is very hard to specify under the usual spatialized 'political' categories. For clearly, education can never be democratic: this was Socrates's subversive realization, beyond any subversive thoughts normally available to the 'left'. The sheer singular uniqueness and contingency of wisdom is unable to subordinate itself to any majority, and if one is to learn, one must first submit. Likewise if the past (as Edmund Burke demanded) is to be given a 'democratic' voice, one must first of all yield blindly to tradition, before one gains insight into its logic or a capacity to modify it. Thus certain modern pseudo-radical *soixante-huitarde* (for all its otherwise glory) phenomena like 'student rights' and 'children's rights' are evidence of an understandable perplexity that spatialization never perfectly completes a sway supposed to be exhaustive; but at the same time they are testimonies to an inherent limit of this project which exposes its final absurdity.

Nevertheless, if education is not 'democratic', nor is it 'hierarchical' in the usual (but debased) sense of something fixed. For the initial hierarchy involved is self-cancelling in the sense that the aim of a downwards transmission is to raise up the one beneath, and ideally beyond one's own height (as with the mystical hierarchies of Dionysius and Cusanus), since the pupil responds with the surplus of wise innocence over the teacher's mere experience. This pedagogic rhythm of self-cancelling hierarchy is far truer to our fundamental human ontology than merely political arguments about how space is to be shared out and administered, as though it were a given surveyable fixity which we all occupied with equal intensity. It is not just in school that first of all we must learn, and then, perhaps, overtake our teachers. On the contrary, throughout life also we must learn to recognize when we must now receive in turn from those who were initially indebted to us. Therefore a 'democracy of time' involves not levelling, but complex cycles of exaltation and abasement: abasement of the student for her exaltation; kenotic abasement of the exalted teacher in order to transmit and herself develop.

Given this circumstance, it is absolutely impossible that education could ever (in the most fundamental sense) be 'politically' organized. No 'majority' can decide on the form pedagogy should take, since this majority itself is only the outcome of a certain pedagogic process it can never control. Therefore democracy, in the usual spatial sense, should never govern education; if anything education *must* govern democracy and determine its quality. Every time the government or corporate inspectors arrive (as they increasingly do) at our schools, colleges and universities with their spatialized checklists, academics should send them back, and instead return their own emissaries to assess the government according to the (inexhaustible) canons of eternal wisdom. Indeed, it is arguably only the truly educated who can determine to what degree, at any one given time, a spatial democracy should operate: for as St Augustine argued, democracy is only a just arrangement where a majority of people have been educated into wisdom and virtue.[50] But of course we should remember that under a Christianized understanding of wisdom as love, and of truth as something infused throughout the social body by the Holy Spirit (in such a way that it is always likely on the whole to prevail, as we saw in Chapter 7), the biases against elitist rule and in favour of majoritarianism become much stronger than for the ancient Greeks. Christianity accords a far higher place to the responsive wisdom of 'childish innocence'. So the point is not to question all formal mechanisms of democracy, but rather to insist on the priority of an educative culture which will sustain and extend them. Otherwise, a corrupt majority will yield, not to the sway of good teaching, but to the lure of manipulative propaganda. For 'propaganda' is the debased evidence of pedagogic primacy when this primacy is denied. Likewise, inescapable hierarchy does not vanish when its instance or value is refused, either by the left or the right. Instead, in the absence of any sense of hierarchy as initiating into truth, and so as self-cancelling, one gets all the more rigid and spatialized hierarchies in which those who lead do so by chance, by opportunism, by possession of capital, by ability to seduce and, most often, by sheer force of acceptable stupidity and mediocrity.

But education, if it is not governed by a majority, is subject . . . to what? To reason? Clearly not this alone, since before we can reason we must receive a tradition and can never quite comprehend this foundation. And clearly not reason alone, if education seeks above all to know and inculcate the good life, or the basis of community, which, as we have seen, is semi-ineffable. Education in fact seeks, almost impossibly, to discover and transmit this semi-ineffability. Therefore if it seeks to frame universal concepts, it also seeks to shape the universal totem. Education obeys a liturgical rhythm which can only be denied in the mode of distortion.

VIII

Finally, there is the notion of *profession*. Where the transcendent governs, it does so, as we have seen, neither autonomously nor heteronomously, but rather through an instilled sense of right patterings, shown in examples and repeated by skill. Education should be about nothing but this instilling, such that it can only occur within a liturgical *polis* in miniature, just as the *polis* at large is a macrocosmic academy. As Plato argued, where a populace is instilled with the right modes and rhythms, there is little need for written laws: his was the true, ordered anarchy. And here Augustine added that coercion only becomes necessary when people turn away from common, 'educative' goods to the false goods of possession; for this perspective, as he points out, state punishment is benign, since all it need threaten is the removal of such illusory goods and a re-education into the truth.[51] Thus where devotion to transcendent value is instilled, one has the possibility of self-regulation that necessarily includes an internalized sense of the role of practice – technical, medicinal, pedagogic, economic, artisanal, etc. – within the wider society. One can call such devotion, such virtue 'professionalism', provided one prescinds from some of the usual connotations of this word, possessing a bureaucratic flavour. If one is a member of a profession, then one's education ensures that one does not, for the most part, understand self-interest in a sheerly base or even purely egotistical fashion. To take the example of medicine: medical doctors do not normally and as a rule (at least in Europe) pursue money alone, because they would despise themselves, and others would despise them, if they did so. Here (at least since Hippocrates and until very recently), there is no pure egotism, for it is not that the doctor ironically withdraws from what he does in order to cash in his performance as abstract wealth or prestige. No, he *goes* with what he does, becomes the gifts he bestows; this generosity *is* himself, not an ego, but something expended if it is to be renewed. In return, society provides him with what he needs in terms of instruments, prestige, material well-being and leisure in order to be a giver in this specific mode. Therfore as Marcel Mauss rightly argued, the idea of the profession continues to be bound up with the notion of the gift.[52]

In this light, we can grasp the profound significance of capitalist *de-professionalization* being carried forwards in our day. In every realm – first of all manufacturing and retail, but then successively management, medicine, education (at all levels), science, technology and finally politics itself – the same pattern pertains (as the insurgents of May 1968 already intimated). Innovation is to be made the prerogative of a very few, and even their brief is (mainly) functional manipulation and reproduction (most of their 'innovations' being but variants on the same). Beneath this level no one is any longer to be *trusted*, but instead must be endlessly spied upon, and measured against a spatial checklist of routinized procedure that is alien to all genuine inculcation of excellence. Trust is now impossible, because, as Pickstock has shown, public trust depends upon publicly accepted signs charged with a liturgical depth. Substituted protocol, by contrast, requires endless additional confirming protocols: the bad infinite of inspection tending inevitably to the terminus of a new terror. (Government inspectors at British universities – always second-rate, semi-failed academics – now turn on their victims deliberate 'dead eyes' and threaten to phone them in the middle of the night.) Thus today, all temporal pedagogic procedures that can never quite be regulated through economic supply and demand are subject instead to voracious bullying and policing: the application of rules and nominal requirements which must be endlessly renewed. And yet the irony beyond terror is that a spatialized check can only ever deliver an *appearance* of conformity, since the real proof of performed excellence is already past, or else will only be shown up in the future. Ironically, only the self-judgement of the professional under transcendent norms ever *could* be reliable.

But if one mark of contemporary market and state extremism is de-professionalization, then may not this suggest that an extension (rather than retreat) of the instance of 'the profession' is a crucial and at least potentially practicable possibility for left-wing politics? Central state planning, regarded as the main vehicle for socialism (although certain essential enterprises should surely still be run by state or pan-state-instituted corporations) has clearly failed, and in any case the project is an archetypal spatializing *mathesis* doomed always to misrepresent and distort temporal and unmappable processes (Hayek was right about this). The alternative vehicle is some mode of syndicalism or co-operativism, yet the problem here is to mediate relations between independent co-operative institutions, since, given merely market mediations, a non-subordination of workers' shares to profits will not be matched by the non-subordination of fair prices to profits. Moreover, given the necessity of hierarchy for production, it remains always likely that a managerial and then capitalist elite will re-emerge. Therefore what is essential for syndicalism is some kind of professional ethos, as recommended by John Ruskin and the guild socialist tradition; some sense that that which is produced is primarily a gift to the community which will relate to community values in crucially important ways. Thus every member of a group of producers or retailers or traders should first be initiated into a certain *mystique* of his calling – a certain professional pride in a mode of operation and an upshot which harmonizes with the semi-ineffable meaning of his whole society. Here once again, the dimension of time would be restored, since every initiate would cease to value (in herself and others) the mere amassing of abstract wealth, and instead would conceive of herself as inheriting, developing and passing on a particular strange skill requiring certain 'gifts' for its best exercise; gifts themselves offered for the wider manifestation of human *charisma*. No one not in some way initiated and trained after this fashion would be allowed to operate in business or production. (We need to invent a programme for seizing and subverting business and management schools in this direction.)

Where the product was also regarded as a gift, then, of necessity, internal syndicalist co-operation would be linked with a wider economic collaboration. There would remain, of course, a market, and one that is essentially free. The point for socialism is not (at least primarily) to 'limit' the market, but rather to reconstrue exchange according to the protocols of a universal gift-exchange: that is to say, in every negotiated transaction, something other than profit and loss must be at issue. At every turn, at every specific point of economic interaction, the exchange entered into must also represent what here, and in relation to everything else, is held to be justice, a truly shared benefit and a bonding as well as a division of exchange. Without doubt these no longer purely 'economic' exchanges, though encouraged by every inner syndicalist ethos, require also to be overseen not only by professional guilds, but also by co-operative banks and financial courts (consisting of both business and local or central government representatives) who would ceaselessly advise, and also legislate and execute on the acceptable range of fair prices, fair profits and fair capital returns – thought of in terms of reasonable compensation for the gift of ownership temporarily foregone in order to promote some public work. Business syndicates or even whole guild organizations perverting guild monopoly into power-advantage, or accumulating progressive abstract profit beyond equity, or exploiting their customers and damaging the environment, would be disciplined by the guilds, banks and courts, and *in extremis* shut down.

Naturally, this is idealistic, but not utopian, since it is grounded on the notion of education into virtue extended into guild regulation, which we know, historically, can be a partial success (and partiality is all we can hope for in fallen time). Moreover, many more mitigated capitalisms all over the world already sustain certain small degrees of the features I have enunciated. Pure, naked capitalism is still not yet quite the rule, or is even forever impossible. Hence the ideal politics of time which I propose – a renewed socialism, on a liturgical basis – is also a matter of small incremental gains worth pursuing, and small resistances to a total eclipse.

Such resistances can, indeed, be considered as local resistances to globalization. But at the same time, they will only be finally effective and liturgical if they blend, universally, to encompass the globe as a sacral locality.

10

CULTURE

The gospel of affinity

I

How can we bring about peaceful reconciliation in the contemporary world? Or how can we perpetuate the *ecclesia* and socialism in the twenty-first century? To perpetuate is to re-enact, and this involves once more the directly personal and existential dimension as well as that of collective organization. If we are to perform peace, then how are we to be forgiven and how are we to mediate forgiveness? Can we still be reconciled?

Our contemporary situation has most widely been described as 'post-modernity'. But what is postmodernity? Not postmodernism as a set of theories, but postmodernity, as a set of cultural circumstances.

Above all it means the obliteration of boundaries, the confusion of categories. In the postmodern times in which we live, there is no longer any easy distinction to be made between nature and culture, private interior and public exterior, hierarchical summit and material depth; nor between idea and thing, message and means, production and exchange, product and delivery, the State and the market, humans and animals, humans and machines, image and reality – nor beginning, middle and end. Everything is made to run into everything else; everything gets blended, undone and then re-blended. There are no longer any clear centres of control, and this means that new weight is given to plurality and the proliferation of differ-ence. However, none of these differences ever assume the status of a distinct essence: rather they are temporary events, destined to vanish and be displaced.

Let us consider some of the main instances of boundary confusion. First of all, the blurring of the distinction between nature and culture. One important aspect of modernity was the sense that human beings could make and remake their own cultural universe. On the other hand, this was usually seen as being done against the backdrop of fixed laws of nature. To some extent, because humans were also recognized as natural, such laws were seen as impinging on the human sphere also – limiting the range of freedom for human self-making. Thus humans were sometimes seen as by nature more fundamentally self-preserving, fear-avoiding, happiness-seeking, sympathetic or else productive creatures. But just recently, all this has appeared to change. First of all, people no longer seem to find any need to identify a human essence; no longer is human auto-creation regarded as operating within given parameters. Humans, it seems, might make anything of themselves; we are our own anarchic laboratory and can manipulate ourselves into a million shapes. Perhaps the only figure of essence which remains here is the idea that humans are productive, but as much the *result* of productive processes as agents *in command* of production. In consequence, the asymmetrical teleological and hierarchical aspects of human existence tend to get flattened out into degrees of intensity along a quantitative scale: no longer are there firm characteristics of childhood, middle or old age; no longer are there clearly any men and women, less and less is there much acutely bounded heterosexuality as opposed to the single, univocal (and therefore transcendentally 'homosexual') proliferation of multiple desires.

At the same time, the frontier of culture has so invaded nature that inversely culture appears to be amidst nature, and is no longer like a mind or fortress surmounting it. We can now intervene, technologically, in the organic realm. The prospects of hybridization of pre-given natural kinds have increased exponentially. Here, also, boundaries are being transgressed. But already, in the case of the AIDS epidemic, and the phenomenon of global warming, the unintended consequences of human intervention involve natural forces becoming much more palpable actors within the cultural sphere. And no doubt genetic manipulation will lead to many more instances of this uncomfortable rebound.[1]

But at a more profound level, our perceptions of nature and culture seem to be merging. Accounts of supposedly 'material' realities become more and more ethereal: increasingly, with the decay of any sense that we as humans are governed by natural law, we come to wonder whether 'laws' are not a projection by humans upon nature in general. Modern physics, for a long time now, has tended to think in terms of irreversible temporal processes, engendering not so much laws, as relatively fixed habits. And such habits are not really the habits of material items; it is much more that the material items are the deposits of highly abstract depositions. Likewise, in the sphere of biology, the talk of 'codes' and 'codings' is not intended in any merely metaphorical sense: if there is metaphor involved here, then it is in the very operation of biological metamorphoses themselves.

Conversely, however, human mental life is increasingly thought of as an embodied life: manipulable in terms of all sorts of narcotic stimuli, health regimes and gymnastic exercises. While nature is viewed in terms of the communication of signs, human thought is seen in terms of the processing of electronic inputs in the endlessly complex patternings of plus and minus signs, which point our way, without elective mediation or judgement through the garden of forking paths, whose only sure fatality is the arrival of the next proximate intersection and the next reductive binary alternative. From the outset, the computer developed in analogy to the steam engine, and information to thermodynamics: both energy and information are the temporary harnessing of chaotic dispersal; both, likewise, are doomed to entropy. The engine runs on irretrievably lost and un-Newtonian energy; information (unlike truth) is only for now; it informs *because* it is doomed to obsolescence and this is why we need more and more of it.[2] Like steam also, it is effective only where it is gathered in concentration: to be worth acquiring it is essential that it is not everywhere, and hence the freedom of information, as was argued in Chapter 2, is only apparent. To be 'informed' is to have accumulated more signs as fast as possible, while their value holds, than most other people, who are thereby deprived of cognitive capital. These signs only appear to convey to convey definite knowledge or to sustain the mystery of the unknowable: in reality their false mediation refers to closed formal systems that include only pre-circumscribed indeterminacies.

In these circumstances of merger between the phyisical and signifying, it is not surprising that, once again, Spinoza enjoys a huge vogue, for he was the philosopher who proclaimed that there is a dual aspect to all phenomena: that the 'order and connection of things' is also 'the order and connection of ideas'. Ideas already inhabit things; but conversely, for us to think is to rearrange reality; not to mirror it, but actively to alter its characteristics.

II

After the blurring of the boundary between nature and culture comes the new confusion of interior and exterior. And there is a deep connection. For in modern times, the private self guarded the boundary between culture and nature: he (*sic*) daily returned from public work to the sanctum of his home, with its supposed 'natural' family, and looked out upon his cultivated back garden with its intimation of wilderness. Today, however, there is no such sanctum. The home, most of all, is invaded by the public voices of the media, with their scarcely veiled instructions and commands. Now also the computer terminal gives domestic access to the global public space – not a real space, but a new, virtual spatiality.

Meanwhile, what has happened to the old, real public space: the space for promenading, for civility and overlooked courtship? In the United States, it has already largely vanished. Instead of the public piazza we have the interlocking of semi-private spaces, so that one walks from shopping mall into hotel foyer into set of office spaces and so forth. Increasingly, houses are situated within enclaves guarded by bad dogs and their unsavoury minders. In this situation, most of our modern 'liberal' political discourses start to appear completely meaningless. For they are all predicated on a mutual agreement to protect the right to do what one likes with one's own, so long as this does not interfere with the rights of the other. How can this criterion any long apply to the real interlocking 'rhizome' of material spaces, or to the fluid highway of virtual space? The shared covered walkway is pragmatically negotiated, not constructed according to general formal requirements of universal association, while the telephone and electronic mail give licence to endless mutual intrusion and surveillance. 'My' website, my informational contribution has already decided certain things for others, in a space that is theirs as well as mine, like a common grazing ground.

No wonder that, for some people, the information highway seems like a simulated communist utopia. This perspective, nevertheless, is deluded, for what is 'shared' here is only the immediate proximity of everywhere to everywhere else, which lacks in affinity, 'nearness' (as Heidegger already pointed out) or inherited communality. It is therefore only a place without place of total estrangement. The difference from a liberal organization of discrete spaces is really but the implosion of a hyper-liberalism: I can choose anything anywhere, but these choices will always be for the choices of others, selecting me. Since anything can now be mine, nothing will really be mine. Since I am offered absolute Kantian liberty without the guidance of education of my judgement, I will be perfectly manipulated: absolutely controlled in my important choices (for the exploitative outlet for sub-standard coffee for example, or the exploitative lifestyle website, that some poor individual imagines they have freely invented), and within this allowed a measure of predetermined indifferent laxity (a shot of this or that sickly flavour to disguise the third-rate coffee-blend, the sub-choice of lifestyle that gives me the illusion of interacting with the Internet . . .). Liberalism always depended upon the principle that the inalienable private possession is in principle alienable: it is yours just because you can sell it or give it away. But now, everything is entirely possessed as inalienable and already enacted in its constitutive possible alienability all at once. I release immediately to all who care to look my website choice: I advertise to others and market-brand my own image, clutching my polystyrene coffee-holder.

III

The new interfolding of inside and outside is exhibited also in a third set of confusions, between all the traditional modern economic categories. It is this confusion which produces the age of *information*. We still find it hard to believe that the production of abstract and ephemeral signs pointing to other signs can have become the driving force of the economy. In the United Kingdom, many still refuse to recognize that the almost total collapse of its automobile industry may actually now be giving Britain a certain advantage over Germany, where a relatively up-to-date automobile industry still thrives. Backwardness in one phase is an advantage for the next

– as Germany, who missed out on the phase of steam, once discovered. In that early industrial era, most people insisted that the production of food must always be the driving economic motor. Instead, as we know, agriculture became subordinated and was itself mechanized. Today, manufacturing is being subordinated and itself informationized. But areas like Los Angeles or London that work on the most abstract sector of the economy are the most booming areas and also the new foci of global command.

Nevertheless, this development is not without contradictions. The assumption of information priority can glibly overreach itself, just as earlier and still today one neglects a measure of agricultural self-sufficiency at one's peril. In the United States, the free market and the free information web has invited a huge invasion of its sovereignty by alien powers and this has led to the possibility of enemies of the market using the market against itself. One aspect of the so-called 'war against terrorism' is a realization that the market requires a new mode of totalitarian policing if state sovereignty and capitalist hegemony are to be saved.

In the age of information, production often consists almost immediately (and sometimes entirely so) in the exchange of the product. Likewise, the consumption of the product can already be a type of labouring, while promotion and marketing become themselves the prime generators of profit, rather than its secondary accomplices. Likewise, expenditure of informational capital can be equally an investment of such capital in future production. Furthermore, there is no longer any clear disciplinary structure between worker and management operating within a real distinct site, like a factory or an office, nor within a clearly demarcated firm or company. Instead one has networks of intellectual workers dispersed through real-space working somewhat for themselves, and somewhat for varying others. These workers are auto-controlled through the pressures of the need to compete, or desire for knowledge and influence. No one is telling them how many hours they must labour, but internalized mastery increasingly forces them to work without ceasing. (Again, see J.G. Ballard's *Super-Cannes.*) On the other hand, the boundary between this work and their leisure time is becoming hazy, since the seeking out of affective 'contacts' is increasingly vital to work performance.

Alongside this sphere of the production of signs however, it is important to mention also the increased importance of 'service' industries – medicine, education, catering, transport, beauticians, etc. etc. – which cater more directly for the needs of minds and bodies. However, these services are increasingly operated through levels of higher abstraction which allow them to benefit from global expertise and fashion.

In these areas also, deregulation ensures that hours worked tend to multiply. Meanwhile, in the older manufacturing industries, longer hours are directly enforced, because globalization and informatization has destroyed the bargaining power of manufacturing workers. Thus we can glimpse a gigantic paradox: the increased freedom, deregulation and differentiation of work in the postmodern era nonetheless permits concentrated capital, and in particular the multi-national corporations, to reap vastly increased profits from the vastly increased amount of surplus labour that is now expended in every sphere of production. The times of postmodernity are in no sense post-capitalist times, but rather times of capital writ still larger. Indeed, capital has always been a force of abstraction; today it reaps even larger material benefits from increased abstraction. Even from its inception, capital produced and marketed signs and fashions, and would not have engendered a new abstract equivalence between commodities if it had not done so. It is in a way simply that something always latent in modernity is now much more clearly foregrounded.

IV

Perhaps more drastically novel than informatization is a fourth mark of postmodernity, namely globalization. For this has to do not with a blurring of divisions within the economic realm, but rather with a merging of this realm with the political sphere. For a long time, the sovereign nation-state assisted the extension and regulation of the free market, but it nonetheless tended to subordinate the making of profit to military strength, and ethnic or national unity. Capitalism always tended to overflow state boundaries and today it can operate far more effectively by its capacity to shift human, material and financial resources swiftly, right across the globe. However, this does not mean that the state and politics have come to an end: to the contrary, the market requires more than ever the international state-ordering of virtual reality, international legal checks on financial speculations, and international policing of popular or ethnic or religious dissent.

Alongside the global market is emerging a kind of global empire, a new sort of postmodern empire, which, as Michael Hardt and Antonio Negri argue, continues a specifically American project of neo-Roman Republican empire.[3] This is not, like the old British and French empires, an empire of centre and subordinated colonies, but instead an empire of endlessly expanding frontiers, an empire of inclusion, not remote control, and an empire able to distribute power to its peripheries. Its expansion is enabled, in part, by the constitutional division of powers. This seeks, like ancient and Augustinian politics, a mixed constitution of the Monarchic One, the Aristocratic Few and the Democratic Many. Yet from the outset, federalists like Madison (but in contrast to conservatives like John Adams, as well as radicals like Thomas Jefferson), inserted a Machiavellian and Hobbesian dimension into the genuine Christian Republican tradition that descended from the Venetians and (in part) from James Harrington, and had much older early mediaeval Italian roots. For the federalists, 'the Few' are not truly the virtuous sustaining the common good, but rather they are potential sources of elite faction, which must be dealt with through the 'counter-acting' of 'ambition by ambition'. The Few then compose an agonistic balance of interests amongst power-groups. 'The One' is then merely a heterogeneous upshot of their interplay, while this *agon* prevents any direct Jeffersonian participation by the Many. (Jefferson was a kind of early distributist, who wanted each adult male to be given fifty acres of land, and desired legislation against primogeniture and entail. Unsurprisingly he greatly influenced French and Russian anarcho-socialists.) The 'division of powers' now emerges as an attempt permanently to defuse the greed of the Few on the part of the Many, and equally or more to defuse the insolence of the Many on the part of the Few. Totally abandoned here is the antique and Christian notion of the Republic as *paideia* as well as politics, whereby the One, the Few, and the Many aspire always to congruence and mutually supply contributing factors to a harmonious entity, rather than warding each other off through en endless equilibrium of litigation. In this modern mode of 'republicanism' and of states' confederation, a prime aim seems to be to prevent a 'faction of the Many' which would disturb not merely the higher rights of self-ownership of will and conscience of the Few, but also their lower private property rights.(Madison failed in contrast to Jefferson to see that the actual exercise of higher rights depended upon the equitable distribution of lower rights.) This meant for Madison especially agricultural private property rights, although he favoured a limited growth of a pan-federal commercial society in keeping with the need for an agonistic balancing of interests.

This system, of course, still sadly 'works' after two hundred years. From the outset, it refused both a more flexible British-style conservatism and equally the more dynamic French radical tradition of continuous revo-lution. It has consequently trapped the United States in a sad deistic stasis which has subordinated its true Christian and Jewish, agrarian and civic republican genius – which is still extraordinarily alive amongst many of its citizens.

To sustain this stasis indefinitely, the bureaucratic *agon* must be laid out also as an economic one within endlessly expanding frontiers. As Hardt and Negri show, this project was suspended once territory had been filled up during the more European and civilized era of the New Deal. But ever since the 1960s, Wild West expansionism had been renewed, given scope by the new frontiers of the market, information and outer space. This new scope constitutes the American 'empire', an extended sovereignty ever threatened by the anarchic forces of globalization, and which therefore requires 'anti-terrorist' policing. Thus its new, more invisible, distributed power is becoming all the more a controlling power. Within this empire, the United States, the United Nations, various non-governmental agencies and the multi-national corporations, all tend to share and blend functions of dominion. The political and the economic are by this means fusing.

193

Nor should one be sanguine, like Hardt and Negri, about this fusion. It is crazy to imagine as they do, that political and economic refugees are secretly 'political actors', or that capitalist development is driven *mainly* by manoeuvers in relation to work-resistance (though this plays a part) rather than by a self-sustaining search for expanded profit. (This is an aspect of Negri's tendency, shared by Alain Badiou, to downplay the supremacy of the economic under capitalism.) Certainly, it is true, as Rosa Luxembourg realized, that capitalism has hitherto relied upon a non-capitalist third-world imperial sphere for both primary accumulation and a supply of demand less eroded by the drive to extract surplus value from workers. Yet the erosion of this sphere by globalization by no means betokens necessarily yet another illusory 'final' crisis of capitalism, such that socialists need only passively await this outcome, or else work negatively in its favour, without a constructive imagination and proto-formation of a counter-globalization. There is instead, little doubt that capitalism already is able to solve temporarily its eternal *aporias* in new ways: by creating relatively under-capitalized enclaves everywhere, and by a global play between different speeds and intensities of capitalization.

V

So far then, we have seen that postmodernity can be characterized in four ways, which all have to do with the dissolving of fixed limits. These ways are: (1) the blurring of the nature/culture divide; (2) the merging of public and private; (3) the mode of the information economy; and (4) economic and political globalization. But before one asks, how is the Church to conduct its mission and articulate its intellectual vision on this postmodern terrain, should we not first ask, does postmodernity, of itself, possess anything like a religious dimension?

Here we should note that the blurring of boundaries has a cultural presupposition. That presupposition is one of *immanence*. An ordering of the world in terms of essences and relative values is linked in some way to teleology and hierarchy, or else, alternatively, to spatialization. In premodernity it was a matter of the former – everything had its appointed goal and relative value in relation to a distant, transcendent source which was equally foundation and finality. Both thought and social nature mirrored this assumption. In modernity, by contrast, from about 1300 onwards, the world was gradually accorded full reality, meaning and value in itself, without reference to transcendence: what Gilles Deleuze called 'the plane of immanence' was born. But in modern times this plane was seen was consisting in a kind of fixed spatial grid. Although height had been lost, depth displaced height and there still persisted fixed natures, especially human nature. In postmodernity, however, neither height nor depth remains, but only a shifting surface flux, because immanence is now conceived in terms of the primacy of time, not space. Possibility, productivity and change have been set free, both for nature and culture, which, as a result, are increasingly indistinguishable. It follows that both modernity and postmodernity are relentlessly secular, meaning by that (1) that they explain and evaluate without reference to transcendence, (2) that they see finite reality as self-explanatory and self-governing, and (3) that they see this finite reality which is the *saeculum* – the time before the *eschaton* for Christian theology – as being all that there is.

In these senses, postmodernity is not more open to religion than modernity – indeed, as more emphatically immanentist, it is really less so. Nevertheless, just as there were strange modern modes of religiosity, so there are strange postmodern modes of religiosity. Two of these are worth mentioning. First of all, academic exponents of relatively Marxist versions of postmodernism (Deleuze, Negri, Hardt, etc.) are fond of giving a Spinozistic twist to their atheism. The plane of immanence is seen as the sphere of active, productive forces, which manifest themselves in human terms as desire and love: the still beckoning communist future is seen as an apocalyptic refusal of negative, resentful, tragic and death-obsessed emotion as being unnecessary, and as hitherto imposed upon us by alien oppressors. Something of Spinoza's 'intellectual love' or his *Deus Sive Natura* persists in all this – there is to be a joyful reception and active contemplation of the immanent totality. For indeed, once oppression is surpassed, liberated nature-going-beyond-nature fully appears.

The second example is at a far more popular and widely dispersed level, and at first sight it seems quite different and not postmodern at all. This is the phenomenon of 'new age religions'. These religions all stress that salvation is to be located in a higher self, above the social, temporal, remembered self. This higher self can put one in harmony with everything, with the whole cosmos. This seems unpostmodern, to the extent that it takes to an extreme modern individualism, and seems to advocate retreat within an absolutely private, interior space. But this position shares with the Spinozistic one an assumption of immanence, of a self-regulating cosmos. Moreover, its higher-self-merging-with-the-cosmos is really rather like the ironic remove of the Spinozistic subject from its own process in flux – it is akin also to the Wittgenstein of the *Tractatus*, able to speak of what belongs to the subject as somehow standing impossibly outside the 'all' of things that can be spoken of. There are also parallels to Emmanuel Levinas's tendency to demote the graspably visible world as the regime of totality, and to Michel Henry's proclamation of a world counter to this totality, which consists in the pure, never visible interior of matter manifest as 'life' or 'auto-affection'.[4] Thus in postmodernity, alongside the stress of fluid and permeable boundaries, we have a new affirmation of the sanctity of an empty mystical self able to transcend, identify with, and promote or else refuse the totality of process in the name of a truer 'life' which is invisible. It will be apparent that even organized religion gets infected today with this kind of spirituality.

We need then to add the linked notions of 'immanence', 'self' and 'life' to nature merging with culture, inside merging with outside, information era and global regime if we are to envisage the full dimensions of postmodernity.

VI

Having sketched out these five dimensions, we now have to ask, how is the Church to evaluate these circumstances? In answering both these questions, I want in general to suggest that we regard postmodernity, like modernity, as a kind of distorted outcome of energies first unleashed by the Church itself. If that is the case, then our attitude is bound to be a complex one. Not outright refusal, nor outright acceptance. More like an attempt at radical redirection of what we find. In recommending such a redirection, I suggest that neither a reiteration of Christian orthodoxy in identically repeated handed-down formulas, nor a liberal adaptation to postmodern assumptions will serve as well. The latter response would clearly be a betrayal, but the former might well be betrayal of a more subtle kind – allowing us the illusion of a continuation of the faith in merely formal, empty terms, which discovered no real habitation for faith in our times, either with or against them. Instead, we must allow the very critical engagements with postmodernity to force us to re-express our faith in a radically strange way, which will carry with it a sense of real new discovery of the gospel and the legacy of Christian orthodoxy.

My assertion here is not intended as a general, methodological remark about Christianity in relation to culture, which might easily be taken as but another mode of liberalism. Instead, it is based upon the inevitable, if wary, affinity, which must exist between Christianity and postmodernism. Postmodernism, I have said, is the obliteration of boundaries. And Christianity is the religion of the obliteration of boundaries. Secular commentators like Deleuze, Hardt and Negri assume, in all too modern and essential a fashion, that there is some sort of 'natural' human desire which demands deterritorialization without end. I suggest, more cautiously (and partially following Alain Badiou) that Christianity itself invented a discourse and tradition of living beyond the Law, and that the West is still thinking and living through this idea. This idea is a not 'natural' given, but had to arrive 'by grace' as an event. For Christianity did, indeed, explode all limits: between nations, between races, between the sexes, between the household and the city, between ritual purity and impurity, between work and leisure, between days of the week, between sign and reality (in the Sacraments), between the end of time and living in time, and even between culture and nature, since Jesus advised us to follow the mute example of the lilies of the field. Indeed the category 'creature' enfolds and transcends both the natural and the cultural; culture for the gospels (and to this degree Henry is right) is only a higher and more intense 'life'; while, inversely, all of nature is the divine artifact. But above all, with the doctrine of the Incarnation, Christianity violates the boundary between created and creator, immanence and transcendence, humanity and God. In this way, the arch taboo grounding all the others is broken.

However, there is an apparent problem here. Judaism (and the religion of the Old Testament also) is not the religion of the obliteration of boundaries. Indeed it is perhaps the very opposite: the religion of the reassertion of boundaries. Primitive cultures are marked by rigid marking out of limits, often described as 'taboos'.[5] Later, when these societies are captured by state formations, taboos are removed, or else subordinated to more abstract laws which are imposed from outside, not inscribed in ritual practice. Ancient Israel, however, appears to have reacted against state formations like Egypt and Babylon by making a kind of half-return to the primitive, and inventing a new system of more universalized ritual boundaries. All the primitive tribal boundaries had to do with restricting complexity, confusion and so conflict. But while they are thus comprehensible in functional terms, the actual instances of taboo can often seem utterly arbitrary. The provisions of the *Torah*, by contrast, although often strange-seeming, exhibit a more cosmic scope and a more unrestricted interest in limiting the shedding of blood and the confusion of categories, which could lead to instability and struggle. It is as if the Jewish people took up, in a more universal mode, the instinctive sense of all primitive peoples that barriers must be erected against future danger and the augmentation of human and natural power.

Are we to take it, then, that Christianity really reverses this mission of Israel to the world? But such an interpretation is forbidden to us by all patristic teaching. To take this view, would be at once to side wholeheartedly with postmodernity, and to refuse, as the work of a demiurge, the revelation of the old covenant. Postmodernity, not Christianity, is the final refusal of all taboo, and it is worth mentioning here the Jewish anthropologist Franz Steiner's suggestion that the Jews were destroyed by the Nazis not – as for Emmanuel Levinas – in the name of totality, but rather as the people of the limit, in the name of the transgression of every limit, by immanent crowned power.[6]

Steiner also pointed out, in 'On the Civilising Process' (one of the greatest six pages ever written), that this process has not really increased human control over nature, as usually assumed, so much as massively increased human terroristic power over other humans: we can now certainly destroy ourselves forever, but are still able only to damage or control nature in very restricted ways. This increase of internal threat is Steiner's famous 'march of danger into the heart of creation'. The demons of thunderstorms, floods or crop failures are mild compared with the demons of the

Stock Market crash or the effects of modern weoponry upon whole popu-laces. The Holocaust exceeds slavery in horror; Hiroshima exceeds the nightmare of the 'wars of religion'.

And Steiner, perhaps uniquely, prophesied the new 'anti-terrorist' phase of 'the civilising process'. This would be, he thought, the miltiary police operation that would ensure 'the exclusion of the demons from inter-personal relations'. The demonic that once lay in nature without is now within society itself, but will one day (the day that may now be already upon us) 'be within individuals', once all external terror has been pacified.

This is a vision of pure psychic horror, of protesting desires denied any outlet. A vision, therefore, of mass mental breakdown. But it is also a vision of a situation in which anti-terrorist policing finally turns us all into potential terrorists. In the totally policed society, every individual will be a latent psychopath, and one moreover increasingly able to resort to the miniatur-ization of weapons of mass destruction.

Steiner concludes his essay:

> Whoever recognises this, lives in the black night of despair, illumined by but a single star, the star of a dual discipline:
>
> regarding man, who was created in his image;
>
> regarding society, whose boundaries are immutably set forth in the covenant.

So in considering the equally dual discipline of Law and Gospel, are we here presented with some sort of clue to the riddle of our times? Some thread through the postmodern labyrinth? Is postmodernity the misreading of the Gospel's surpassing of Law? Does it overstress the passing beyond boundaries at the expense of the virtue of boundaries? And does the cure for our postmodern condition lie in a healing of the rift between the seemingly opposed Christian and Jewish principles? Or rather does it lie in rediscovering that the Christian going beyond-the-law nonetheless preserves and elevates the Law? This would mean nothing less than discovering a hidden mean between process and limit, between movement and stasis: in theological terms, the co-belonging of grace with Law, and not a dialectical duality of Law and Gospel.

VII

It is this clue which I now want to follow up in terms of the Church's response to the five aspects of postmodernity. First of all, the question of the merging of nature with culture.

Religious people tend, instinctively, to feel uneasy in the face of a general collapse of all that was one regarded as natural. They are tempted to fall back on an insistence that God has made the human species and all others to be as they should be, and that either nature, or God's positive law, has given clear and firm guidance for the conduct of human sexual relations and reproduction. The trouble though, with this approach, is that an open-ended transformation of the natural world has always been regarded by Christian theology as proper to our *humanum*, and even as intrinsic to the redemption of humanity and the cosmos, looking towards the *eschaton*. Already, throughout history, we have drastically altered both nature and our bodies, and questions of right and wrong here have never been decidable *merely* in terms of what has been pre-given by (as it were) initial divine design. Certainly, that must be ceaselessly attended to, but questions of right and wrong in these instances more ultimately require a discernment of teleology, and a ceaseless discrimination of what is good in itself. In this way, the Baconian tradition rightly saw technological transformation as a work of Charity (the 'elevation of man's estate') and was at first actually very ecological in character, concerned, under the aegis of eschatological hope, with the beautification of nature. (Thomas Jefferson's explicitly Baconian outlook and practice still retained a strongly ecological aspect, even though he had lost most of its theological foundation.) Moreover, the influence of Comenius after his visit to England amongst the interregnum Hartlib group tended to recover against Bacon himself the symbolic, emblematic dimension of nature.[7]

Comenius was one heir of the Renaissance unleashing of a sense of human creativity along with a sense of the undeveloped potential of natural forces. This did not automatically go along with a loss of a sense of teleology and of participation in God. The new awareness of creativity and power was not at all simply the counterpart, as Gilles Deleuze and Antonio Negri tend to claim, of Scotist univocity, which encouraged thinkers to speak, for the first time, of finite being *qua* being without reference to God.[8] Instead, one can see that alternative interpretations were offered of human creativity, in terms *either* of univocity *or* analogy. In terms of univocity, human creativity is taken to mean that, in a certain domain – for example, politics, or mathematics, or even physics (as with Galileo) – human beings have, univocally, the same kind and extension of power as God has. It is *this* interpretation that engenders what Hans von Balthasar called 'Titanism'. In terms of analogy, however, as especially worked out by Nicholas of Cusa, who thought (as we saw in Chapter 7) within a Dionysian perspective, human creative power and natural power is never equal to God, and yet in its very creative exercise participates in the divine *Logos* or *Ars*, and registers 'conjecturally' a sense of how things should develop towards their proper goals. Even in its originating moment, creativity remains discerning. And such discerning *poesis* is essential, because human beings cannot be content with mere nature, and rightly prefer the stars of fable to the mere stars of

199

astronomy – as Tolkien declares in his essay 'On Fairy Stories' (see Chapter 6, note 2 above), this is the crucial sign of our supernatural destiny.

When it comes to contemporary practical examples, we need to continue to exercise this power of creative discrimination. For example, surrogate father or motherhood is not wrong because it violates the pre-given process of reproduction. Rather, we have to ask very complex questions about what such procedures will do to human identity – and whether the different identities which may thereby emerge are richer or weaker identities, more viable or else more unstable and threatened. (The answer is likely to be the latter.) Ultimately, we have to ask whether the general co-belonging of sex and procreation (which does not imply that every instance of sexual intercourse must be oriented to specific physical procreation) alone sustains human beings as more than commodities, because they are thereby the outcome of personal encounters at once both accidental and yet chosen, in a fashion that is irreplaceable, and essential to an ontological grammar which we should continue to elect. But such reflections involve not a refusal of choice, nor a mere postmodern resignation to choice, but a kind of higher level 'choice about choice'. At present, of course, we woefully lack cultural practices which might mediate our intersubjective metachoices.

Another example here is cosmetic plastic surgery. All theologians could compose knee-jerk pietistic assaults upon this increasingly widespread practice, speaking of sacred iconicity and so forth, but this could be to ignore the misery of ugliness, and the clear theological truth that the Fall has distorted human beauty. Creative restoration of beauty throughout the cosmos is part of the work of *charis* and *caritas*, and again the real issue here concerns judgement and discrimination. In this sphere also, it is not 'alteration' *per se* that is wrong, but only certain alterations discerned as distortions. So the problem with much of the practice of cosmetic surgery is not that it violates a given – as if we all really felt *entirely* psychically in tune with our aspects – but that it subserves false, standardized, sublimated standards of beauty, and is over-inclined to dismiss the resources of what is sheerly given. The more that ancient inherited cosmetic practices drift away from art and *maquillage* towards technology and the scalpel, the more also they drift away from genuine creative transformation.

From this example we may develop a general observation. *Ars* appears lightly to alter the surface of the given (as with the practice of painting in every sense), whereas *techne* appears capable of drastic transformations. But this apparent contrast is totally deceptive. In actuality, the light alterations of art really do, by small adjustments, reveal something totally new (the touch of lipstick), just as written fictions can invoke a truly other reality. And conversely, the heavy alterations of technology are secretly bound to a shallow *mimesis* (the surgically inflated and re-sculpted lips that copy a standard blueprint). Thus art (through costume, trappings, roads, hostelries, story and song) can render travel delightful beyond the mere motion of nature; technology, however, can only imitate motion and render it faster. So in the first case one has small yet qualitative shifts and adornments which make all the difference; in the second case large yet purely quantitative shifts which makes less difference than one imagines. If increased speed, for example, does effect a large difference, this tends to be one that actually damages and inhibits the scope of both nature and art.

In the case of new computer technologies, this truth is yet more marked: art can invoke truly other worlds, but virtual reality offers only a mimetic simulacrum of the world we in any case have. It can make features of this world apparently more readily available at will, but always the illusion disappoints, because it has not the three-dimensional solidity of that which simply has happened to arrive before us, or else, more importantly, *has freely chosen us*. A simple comparison makes this crystal clear: the feigned satisfaction of a simulated other disappoints, whereas the memory of a lost real other, or even the imagination of, or intimated encounter with a real other 'elsewhere', obscurely consoles.

At present, the postmodern fusion of nature with culture is more like the collapse of nature into a routinized culture, as *techne* increasingly makes the large difference of spoliation. The Christian question here might be as to whether this emphasis should be reversed. For while we must accept and embrace the revisability of the given world, this dynamism need not and should not refuse notions of nature and essence, not as what is exhaustively given, but as what may eventually be disclosed as valuable abiding gift with and through time, rather than despite it. Certain transformations and graftings may develop and unfold more of a partially pre-given and desirable identity, certain others the reverse. Certain hybrids should find their place, certain others not. One may note here that dangerous, commercially driven genetic transpositions from one species to another rest paradoxically on the assumptions of an already exploded, naively *essentialistic* biology, according to which biological identity is 'pre-given' in a single genetic code stored in DNA. This is not a true essentialism of course, but rather a reductive biological atomism. More recent evidence, which undercuts the work of Crick and Watson, is more compatible with a genuine essentialism. This suggests that biological identity is ultimately sustained by complex patterns of inherited habitual interaction between DNA, RNA, proteins and cells. In nature also, it would seem, an essence is something constantly constructed and arriving, and is non-identically repeated, as proteins 'read' genetic blueprints in unpredictable and yet not simply random ways. Nature also, one might argue, works the subtly new by *ars* as well as *techne*, such that to impose upon it too crude a *techne* in proud ignorance of the possible upshots (tampering with DNA structures as if this were all-determinative), is to attempt a mere quantitative mimesis that will actually lead to monstrous degeneration (as may already have occurred – see note 1).

Likewise in the field of surface engineering, certain interventions within the rhythms of nature still permit and uphold them, as for Heidegger the true ornamental bridge primordially discloses to us the banks of the river. But certain other interventions run a clear risk of upsetting these rhythms, like the flyover whose ugliness declares that it wishes the river were not there, and therefore declares also that it regards itself as an unfortunate necessity. All mere *techne* tends to view itself only as overcoming restrictions, and therefore detests its own exigency and is thoroughly reactive. This is the hidden source of the tendency of technology without art (a tendency that is as unnecessary for 'high' as for 'low' technology, even if it is more likely that the former will succumb) to depressing coldness and squalor.

So to judge concerning a transformation, to decide as to whether, in this particular instance of *techne*, there is also an instance of art which elevates and further reveals *natura*, is entirely a matter of discernment, according to no pre-written rules, precisely because we have faith that we do live in a Creation where discernment is possible. In this sense, the transgression of boundaries is not antinomic, because it is rather the ceaseless extension of the Book of the Law in real positive enactments. It is the constant retracing of the real eternal boundaries which we but partially intuit.

The contesting of the postmodern lies precisely in this trust in discernment and the discrimination amongst resting places. Postmodernity inscribes, tyrannically, only one law: produce, alter or make different, such that yesterday's transgressive innovation is today's crime of stasis. In this sense its antinomianism enacts a new law and is not, like the Gospel, really beyond the Law at all: the untruth of information is entropy without appeal. Thus pure anarchy is after all the law of identical repetition and ultimate destruction, in the same fashion as *techne* without *ars*. If there are truly no essences or natures, no 'proper ways' for anything to be, then nothing should be attended to beyond that minimal instance which is already a waste of time; nothing should be regarded in its hidden possibilities for its *own* development – rather, every possibility must imply that its realization requires an act of arbitrary (and not at all creative) destruction.

Certain Spinozistically inclined postmodernists are fond of speaking of the extension of the bonds of love and solidarity on the basis of compatible emotions and understandings: this is an aspect of the Stoic *oikeosis* or Spinozistic *conatus*.[9] But this is to invoke the primacy of *affinity*, and there can only be affinity between things that can be in some fashion *characterized*, even if such characterization is provisional. Otherwise there are only affinities of accident, whose instances convey no freight of enacted truth, and which instantiate no proleptic hope of a final chain of affinities with no exterior of exclusion. Indeed, given the Spinozistic rooting of passive resentment in the limited perspectives of the finite modes, there must always be exclusion, save for the privileged attainment of the active perspective of the one substance by a fated few. Furthermore, without the *convenientia* of analogy, the binding of differences under affinity can be no more than merging and coalescence into a single super-difference.

The Gospel concerns, above all for us today, this issue of affinity. For Christians, God became human and denied the division between Creator and Creation. However, in doing so, he also preserved it. God, in becoming human, in no way changed in himself, in no way entered within time – to claim that he did so would be, as it were, theologically anti-Semitic and antinomian (in a bad sense). Nor was anything that Christ did in any way 'mixed' with his divinity, except at one point: namely that of personality or of character. Jesus was God because his *affinity* with God was so extreme as to constitute identity; but an identity between humanity and divinity, not of substantial nature, but of character, *hypostasis* or *persona*. And Jesus communicated to his disciples, not simply teaching, but precisely this *character*, which they were to repeat differently, so constituting a community of affinity with Jesus. Not a community of nature (not a family) nor a coerced association (a State) nor yet a postmodern market proliferation of differences. Rather a community of differences in identity, but an identity diffused through the non-identical repetition of character, or of affinity.

Affinity is the absolutely non-theorizable, it is the almost ineffable. Affinity is the *mysterium*. And it is the beyond-the-ethical which alone gives us the ethical, for without affinity, love can only be the merely moral and immanent command to put the other first, a self-abasement before the rival egotism of the other, which she would in turn have to renounce. Instead of modern selfishness, one would then have a kind of postmodern endless postponement of egotism (Levinas and Derrida). By contrast, there can only be more than egotism, there can only be *love*, if there is ecstatic reciprocity and interplay of characters who naturally 'belong together'. In this way, the chain of affinity, beyond nature, discovers a higher nature (the super-natural, the gift of grace). It is for this reason that loving God, in the Bible, involves not just our being well-disposed towards God, but being 'like' God, akin to God, made in his image. This image does not fundamentally consist in any single human property – our reason alone, for example, abstracted from all other aspects – but rather in the whole person (even if this be specifically a whole rational person), and indeed according to Gregory of Nyssa, only in the totality of all human persons linked together (*On the Making of Man*, 12:17). Thus we cannot say *in what respect* we are like God; the image simply is an ineffable likeness, a dynamic *oikeosis* (becoming 'at home with' – as Nyssa also taught), both mimesis and sharing, an affinity.

I think that lack of trust in affinity, lack of the mediation of affinity through the Church, might to a degree explain the *sexual* crises and confusions of our time. However, Christians can only say this with fear and trembling, because throughout much of their history and yet much more especially in the period since the Reformation, they have failed to realize that affinity puts the erotic at the heart of *agape*, which cannot be merely the empty and nihilistic gaze of well-wishing on its own (many a vicar's smile at the Church door) although it is most certainly creative gift as well as discovered affinity, most certainly the diffuse effort of philanthropy as well as the concentrated depth of myriad intimacies.

It is in fact the blending of creative self-offering with discovered likeness which ensures that affinity is not simply that chemical metaphor deployed as an alibi for adultery which Goethe appears to condemn in his novel *Elective Affinities*. ('Elective' here means mearly the quasi-inclination of one chemical element for another, in Romantic theory.)[9] Affinity is not merely a *given* impersonal bond of attraction; it is rather the arriving *gift* of something that we must partially discover in patient quest, active shaping and faithful pursuing.

Because having a liking for someone, falling in love, etc. seems uncontrollable we have tended to think that they are non-moral or unmoralizable spheres. But to the contrary, these phenomena are both controllable and uncontrollable, and as such are the very pre-conditions for the exercise of morality. Affinity or ontological kinship is a kind of aesthetic of co-belonging of some with some, and so ultimately of all with all, not formally and indifferently (as if every person were equally near every other, as on the internet, which not accidentally is awash with prostitution in multiple guises) but via the mediation of degrees of preference. Without the recovery and restoration of this ontological kinship, there can be no possibility of real peace and reconciliation, only a kind of suspension of hostilities.

We have to *wager* upon this possibility, like the Pascalian gambling gangster Sky Masterson in Wolf Mankowitz's great filmed musical, *Guys and Dolls*. Masterson bets with another gangster that he can take the Salvation Army 'Mission Doll' to dine with him in (non-capitalist) Havana. If he wins, then the gangsters, who are arch-capitalists, reducing all – horses, women, the consumption of cheesecake or strudel in the deli – to abstract value, will turn up to be converted at the mission meeting. This is therefore a wager *against* the capitalist rule of wagering. Masterson acknowledges this, for when he wins the bet, he says that he has not really won, without the real unforced consent of Sarah Hemmings, the Mission Doll (she complies at first only to save the mission). At the same time, the bet also wagers against the rule of the mission's limited puritanical construal of love. What the mission has omitted from its commitment to charity as duty is the unexpected arrival of unformulatable affinity. Thus both the anarchic calculus of the gamblers and the steady calculus of the mission is outplayed by Sarah's falling for an utterly surprising future spouse.

It should nevertheless be said that 'the wager' is not really a simply individual matter. The musical ends with an ecclesial marriage, and so the location of a specific affinity within the wider Church. It is the Church which already foreshadows the Kingdom of realized peace through the infinite web of affinity, and it is within this collective foreshadowing that the local gamble of faith becomes possible.

And yet the universal is also the sum of specificities: as Pavel Florensky pointed out, marriage, though it mainly concerns only two people, is as equally sacramental as the Mass, which concerns equally all. Certainly the dyad of affinity (or strings of affinity beyond a literal 'two') must appear before the 'third' of community (which may be of any number from one to infinity), in order to avoid a collapse into the monism of mutual reflection, where two people (or more) drown in each other's depths. Nevertheless the community is exclusively composed of sequences of 'dyads' of spiritual affines. In the end the third 'judging' and generally philanthropic moment of one-way gift is also infused with the spirit of gift-exchange and loving fusion, while inversely all true erotic and filial love must already discern somewhat detachedly its own instance, and the various proportions and placings in which it is expressed. It is clear that the ecclesial logic at work here is also a Trinitarian one.

In the light of these sorts of considerations, I think that we are totally wrong to approach contemporary sexual issues as primarily a moral matter, or of what should and should not be done. On the whole, disagreements about sexual morality are a farcical unreality, masking grotesque depths of hypocrisy. 'Liberals' always seek more fidelity and security than they own up to; 'conservatives', in practice, will usually put life before principle. In this realm, the sham of argument is forever overshadowed and defeated by anxiety. So the Church should forthwith cease its participation in these unedifying disputes. Marriage is not a matter of morality, but of the basis of morality in occurrence. As with the earlier mediaeval tradition, it is either there or not there – entirely willed by the partners and by them alone, only because God himself has joined them together. This is Christ's teaching, and like him we should keep ironic and blushing silence about everything else, and leave it to the discernment of individuals and pastoral guidance.

Equally horrendous is the conservative attack on 'sex outside marriage' (with no real warrant in Christian tradition – especially lay tradition, which from Marie de France onwards has reflected in narrative upon the unresolved tensions between nature, love and generally necessary law) and the 'liberal' slandering of romantic fidelity, which is a slandering of sexuality itself and its deeply ethical jealousies. This same slandering fails to observe the increasing displacement of erotic affinity by a general system of market competition for sexual conquest that is entirely complicit with the pursuit of economic power and advantage (as the French novelist Michel Houellebecq has demonstrated in his brilliant novel, *The Elementary Particles* [*Atomised* in the UK]). The contradiction that obtains between formal freedom and real deprivation in the economic sphere now pervades the sexual sphere also. Modernity cannot accept that our strongest physical desire is hostage to the gift of another, and that in a fallen world a true trysting with *eros* may require at times, or even in cases all of the time, a sacrificial foregoing if we are not to betray others and ourselves. Like a siren it lures us into imagining that there is a 'right' to sexual fulfilment, but in practice this fantasized sphere means the exercise of a right to pursue sex as a commodity which depends upon the general failure of most and the supposed 'success' of a few.

Both liberals and conservatives also tend to perpetuate the ludicrous untruth that erotic excitement and fulfilment increases with the new and the altogether strange, and lapses with time and familiarity – whereas, to the contrary, common experience proves that real sex is impossible save in the relaxed presence of the ever-different-familiar, even if familiarity can descend from the outset, like a miracle. Freedom, innovation and passion grows here most surely with custom alone, as much as in the exchange of words, musical notes or witticisms. It is not that sex outside marriage is wrong; simply that it is impossible, and never what anyone ultimately desires.

It should in addition be said here that modernity, specifically (ever since the Renaissance) has always oscillated in sexual matters between a disciplinary puritanism unknown to the Middle Ages on the one hand, and promotion of a dark, death-obsessed and narcissistic eroticism on the other. (This is the coincidence of the moral and psychopathic which was discussed in Chapter 2, and which is particularly well diagnosed in the tradition of the Scottish novel from James Hogg through Walter Scott [*Rob Roy*] and R.L. Stevenson to Neil Munro, Eric Linklater and John Buchan – the latter alone suggesting a Catholic way to overcome the Scottish schizophrenia of Demonic-Tory-Jacobite versus Capitalist-Whig-Rational.)[10]

Often postmodernity accentuates the path of a dark eroticism, but here once again, it privileges entirely the flow of difference over the fertile pools of relatively constant essence. In particular, it tends to despise the mystery of the general difference of masculine and feminine, in favour of a supposedly more exciting dispersed and unpolar differentiation. Yet this ungeneric, ungendered and so, of course, unsexual differentiation cannot then truly allow any arrival of the event of affinity in its most intense sexual mode, since it thereby lacks any vehicle of mediation. Sexual difference is more ontologically resistant than people suppose; thinking otherwise is entirely patriarchalist. This is the reason: Aristotle noted (*Metaphysics* 1058a29–1058b24) that 'male' and 'female' are only possible features of the same human species, like white or black. However, he then noted a problem: not just all humans, but all of the *genus* animal are male or female (whereas they may be any number of colours). Is then sexual difference substantive and generic he asks? He only answers 'no' because his sexist biology declares femininity to be a material accident of deficiency. Without this sexism (which the Thomist *esse* level at least implicity surmounts) sexual difference is a disjunctive transcendental quality (exhaustively male or female or a hybrid) of 'animality' as such, perhaps life as such, and even perhaps, analogically, material Being as such, or even Being as such.

Moreover, male/female sexual difference, while it is indeed mysterious and sublimely ineffable, nevertheless does not entirely escape articulation, else it would be a vacuous difference that made no difference. In general, certain (but not by any means all) inherited generalizations truly do hold, although they must be further nuanced forever: men are more nomadic, direct, abstractive and forceful, women are more settled, subtle, particularizing and beautiful – though both sexes are equally innovative, legislative, commanding and conservative within these different modes. These differences are grounded, as Luce Irigaray argues, in different phenomenological inhabitations of the world that derive from different bodily structures, different bodily histories, different bodily cycles and a different relation to the rhythms of the cosmos. (It is simply obvious that gender difference is *somewhat* biological, whereas racial difference is an ideological fabrication.)[11]

A preponderance of counter-instances could of course be held to disprove this assertion, yet equally they could be held to witness to the abolition of gender by a ruthless postmodern capitalism which wishes to engender only 'individuals', turned narcissistically to themselves and to the abstract centre, never to the embodied other who displays a radical generic otherness that truly unsettles our egoity. The same abolition requires the ideal synthesis in a new individual of 'masculine' autonomy and self-control, with 'feminine' compliance and sociability (these traditional qualities being more culturally and ideologically induced, one might argue). It desires neither men nor women. None of this can be 'proved', but it is often important to state boldly what one sees and cannot in the nature of the case demonstrate: this is after all the real crux of responsibility. And the issue in the end concerns not bald fact, but rather the question of what is really desirable: an equality of the sexes without sexual difference (and as I have said, an *entirely* inexpressible difference is no difference, even if one must struggle forever to articulate it), or a new equality of the sexes which seeks to enhance a sexual difference that it also affirms, teleologically and eschatologically.

Equality of difference: without the feminine settled, male abstraction is not an abstraction but only another, arbitrary, settled view. Inversely, without abstraction the settled is not settled, but another abstraction in its very embrace of place, immune to the specific shifts of life and time. (Here also Christian abstraction is necessarily betrothed to Jewish specificity.) Instead, without this marriage, we are speaking of multiple narcissisms and purely active and so self-expressive desires without need and lack (for lack can persist non-negatively within fulfilment). This kind of sexuality is 'transcendentally homosexual', and this must be the outcome, where male–female relations are not seen as paradigmatic of the sexual as such. There need be no problem whatsoever with the idea that homosexual practice is part of the richness of God's Creation (nor with co-habiting gay clergy) and indeed its often parodic and ironic character (which springs at once from its need at times to mimic sexual difference, and its non-heterosexual logic, for which two enamoured partners may share a desire for a third) can hint toward the life of angels. The genderless angels can unite non-narcissistically with each other, because each angel constitutes its own genus and species; yet humans also, participating in their full existence in the divine *esse*, possessing significant accidents that equal their natural substance in defining significance, including the accident of homosexual orientation, can, as individuals, partially transcend their collective essence.

But where homosexuality is seen as equal in specifically *human* sacramental significance to the unity in difference of man and woman (where it is supposed that people of the same sex can 'marry', although their unions should certainly be brought in some fashion within sacramentality) then as a matter of logic, one has chosen the superiority of homosexuality over heterosexuality, and denied the place of the non-angelic within the cosmic and erotic order. If both are 'the same', then, indeed, 'the same' triumphs: transcendentally speaking there are simply many 'persons', all in theory potential sexual partners. It seems that there can be no 'neutral' characterization of sexuality as such: one has to choose, even if what seems subordinate *qua* human, gestures more specifically toward the higher angelic order. Here is double hierarchy, rather than flattened formal equality. Within this perspective one can go on to say that, just as marriage is equal in human sacramental significance to the Mass, so the adelphic rites uniting same-sex partners can be seen (beyond the received tradition) as equal in cosmic sacramental significance to those of marriage.

It is, however, in a way heterosexuality and sexual difference which the Church finds *really* difficult to accept, even though it lies at the very heart of its mystery. There is first of all the mystery detailed in the Wisdom Literature of God as *Sophia*, the 'female' birth of the Creation as not-God that is also the act of God, and therefore in some sense within God (enfolded in the generation of the *Verbum* and the procession of the *Donum*). There is also, in the second place, the mystery of Christ and his Bride the Church: gender equality within difference requires us, beyond the limitations of Catholic tradition, now to see the Bride as enhypostasized by the descent of the Spirit (in her full eschatological plenitude of commencement and ending) and so as *equal* with the Bridegroom. Until we can accept this, then (as Luce Irigaray has been near to suggesting) sexual equality will not be symbolically validated, nor will sexual difference be validated as grounded in God (the relative 'masculinity' of the *Verbum*; the relative 'femininity' of the *Donum*).

Despite this centrality, romantic heterosexuality was persecuted by old puritanism, and now is denied by the new pious indifference towards gender, for which all that matters is 'friendship'. The male homoerotic has after all partially dominated the life of the Churches for centuries: it is all too easy for past patriarchy and misogyny to be today writ larger in an apparently liberative guise, that is but the ruling *gnosis* of campdom. In

208

addition, the production of a normative 'homosexual' subjectivity (which actually threatens homosexuals also, including the difference between male gays and lesbians) serves the deepest purposes of capitalism: thereby the production of children can be increasingly commodified, and handed over to state and market regulation, so that human beings may be the better subordinated to the increase of profit and the stockpiling of abstract power.

No, the test of its real embracing of incarnate mystery will come when the Church is able to accept and no longer to trivialize human sexuality in its most humanly paradigmatic heterosexual guise.

VIII

In the face of the fusing of nature and culture therefore, the Church should proclaim the 'gospel of affinity'. It is the Church of all the marriages and quasi-marriages (including homosexual unions), the Church of all natural and spiritual offspring. Appropriate responses to other aspects of post-modernity then follow from this central insight. In the face of the blending of private and public, the Church needs in a sense to accentuate the private existential pole as the underplayed one, as earlier it identified that of nature. Since the Church fuses *oikos* and *polis*, values of nurture and reconciliation need to constitute our interweavings, not locked doors, barren highways and dangerous animals. We must learn to take literally the idea that we are 'grafted' into Israel, that we now belong with Israel in one spiritual bloodgroup, and we must think of all of our human relations in terms of extended family. The computer screen makes us equally near the whole world – but we need to resist the illusion that this is possible. We are finite and we cannot love all equally, except in loving God and trusting that they are loved by others. We need rather to love properly those that we are destined to love: including the endless strangers who constantly turn up. (Charles Dickens's novel *Bleak House* is very instructive here concerning the delusions both of loving at a distance, and of loving only near at hand.)

And such extensions of family must invade also the entire realm of law and punishment. The Church should promote the sense that such processes must be processes of penance and reconciliation as well as of justice. It must have done forever with Luther's two kingdoms, and the notion that a State that does not implicitly concern itself with the soul's salvation can be in any way legitimate.

Therefore reconciliation needs to be added to affinity. In the face, thirdly, of the information age, the Church needs to be wary of the secular tendency to promote the abstract, and should come to realize that only Christianity fully celebrates the concrete and bodily. For if the immanent world is all there is, then it tends to reduce to our abstract grasp of it, and we come to believe that it consists in these re-arrangeable abstractions. For this outlook, there is neither being, nor knowledge, and the affinity between them, but rather a shifting flux of the semi-concrete and the semi-abstract (the realm first located by Avicenna in terms of multiple formalities co-existing within a single individual substance and by Duns Scotus in terms of the formal distinction).[12] By contrast, we are only able to acknowledge a depth in things when we see them as surpassing our finite grasp, and as grounded in God the Creator. In this way, only recognition of participation in God gives bodies their solidity, because to grant them this we need to see how in God bodies persist as eternal. Likewise, we only have true knowledge of them when we share something of God's insight into how he wished them to be. So if an over-abstracting secular world has lost bodies and truth in favour of information, we need to reclaim both those realities. With Spinoza this time, we need to develop a less world-denying spirituality, which insists that to participate more in God we need always to enter further into true, temperate, corporeal pleasures (ascesis nevertheless remains crucial, for without refinement and abstention there is no delight). The insinuation of both puritans and Sadean atheists (Cathars, *tous les deux*) that one must choose either sensual pleasure *or* God, always sacrificing either one or the other, must be exposed as a reduction of God to the ontic: considering him as if he were a finite recompense for the loss of something finite.

So we now have affinity, reconciliation and embodiment. In the face of globalization and the new American empire, we need to counterpose Augustine's counter-empire, the City of God. We may do this alongside many secular co-workers: socialists, communists and anarchists. We should not refuse their co-operation, yet we should insist that they have little grasp of the counter-empire, since for them it is still a matter of simply unleashing more undifferentiated liberty, going yet further beyond the Law. For us, rather, it should seem that the impossibility of pure flux and unmediated difference will inevitably bring with it an arbitrary and oppressive deter-ritorialization. The only way, by contrast, to escape restricting terrain, is to refuse even the opposition of territory and escape. If there *is* any human nature, perhaps it resides in the desire to be at once at home and abroad. But this is only possible where one admits the lure of supernatural tran-scendence. For then immanent dynamism and immanent stasis are both outplayed, then the flux is not itself an immanent God, the pure space of pure movement, but consists rather in the relay stations themselves, the open but identifiable essences along its course. Then (as Jean-Yves Lacoste has declared) we are not postmodern nomads, but ecclesial pilgrims.

So to affinity, reconciliation and embodiment we can now add not only the City of God but also transcendence. Immanence appears to be demo-cratic and mobile, but it always re-erects a hierarchy of self-government that sunders the totality between the static and the mobile, or else the other way around. If the mobile is on top, as in postmodernity, then, of course, its truth can never arrive in the world, and the postmodern or new-age self perceiving this truth, is ironically removed from the world and its real selfhood of memory and hope. We can then never be liberated, nor redeemed. No gift will ever be given. Instead, since pure flux, pure deterritorialization, will never be manifest, the urge towards this illusion will always engender the surrogate of formal, arbitrary and oppressive control of the flux by a sovereign empire.

By contrast, transcendence appears hierarchic and fixed, but its onto-logical height resides beyond all immanent heights, and therefore is as close to ontic depths as to ontic elevations. For this reason, its truth *can* be mediated to us and we *can*, one day, be liberated.

For this reason, super-hierarchical transcendence offers us its gift of affinity through reconciliation in our bodies on pilgrimage within the City of God here below.

NOTES

PREFACE

1 I am indebted here to the very insightful discussion of my own and Catherine Pickstock's theology by Olivier-Thomas Venard in his article 'Radical Orthodoxy: Une Première Impression', in *Revue Thomiste*, July–September, 2001, 409–44.
2 Here I have clearly linked my own ideas with those of Catherine Pickstock in her *After Writing; On the Liturgical Consummation of Philosophy* (Oxford: Blackwell, 1998).

1 EVIL: DARKNESS AND SILENCE

1 See Joan Copjec, ed., *Radical Evil* (London: Verso, 1996); Jean-Luc Nancy, *The Experience of Freedom*, trans. Bridget McDonald (Stanford: Stanford UP, 1993); Slavoj Zizek, *For They Know Not What They Do: Enjoyment as a Political Factor* (London: Verso, 1991). See also, to some extent, Jacques Derrida, 'Faith and Knowledge: The Two Sources of "Religion" at the Limits of Reason Alone', in *Religion*, ed. J. Derrida and G. Vattimo (Cambridge: Polity, 1988), 1–79. On theology and evil, the crucial recent works are Kenneth Surin, *Theology and the Problem of Evil* (Oxford: Blackwell, 1986); Charles T. Mathewes, *Evil and the Augustinian Tradition* (Cambridge: CUP, 2001); Rowan Williams, 'Insubstantial Evil', in *Augustine and His Critics*, ed. R. Dodaro and G. Lawless (London: Routledge, 2000), 105–24.
2 Immanuel Kant, *Religion Within the Bounds of Mere Reason*, trans. George di Giovanni, in Immanuel Kant, *Religion and Rational Theology*, trans. and ed. Allen W. Wood and George di Giovanni (Cambridge: CUP, 1996), 57–213.
3 Hannah Arendt, *Eichmann in Jerusalem: A Report on the Banality of Evil* (London: Penguin, 1992).
4 Hannah Arendt, *Love and Saint Augustine* (Chicago: Chicago UP, 1996) and the introduction by J.V. Scott and J.C. Stark, 'Rediscovering Hannah Arendt'; Mathewes, *Evil and the Augustinian Tradition*. Mathewes in particular establishes beyond dispute the vein of Augustinianism in Arendt.
5 Arendt, *Eichmann*, 137.
6 See Michael Halberstramm, *Totalitarianism and the Modern Conception of Politics* (New Haven: Yale UP, 1999).
7 For a good account of this, see Roy F. Baumeister, *Evil: Inside Human Cruelty and Violence* (New York: W.H. Freeman, 1997), esp. 375–88.
8 See Jacob Rogozinski, 'Hell on Earth: Hannah Arendt in the Face of Hitler', in *Philosophy Today*, Fall 1993, vol. 37, no. 3/4, 257–74, esp. 267.

9 Kant, *Religion Within the Bounds of Mere Reason*, 6:20–6:53, pp. 69–97.
10 See Richard L. Rubenstein's classic text, *The Cunning of Reason: Mass Death and the American Future* (New York: Harper and Row, 1975).
11 Dionysius the Areopagite, *The Divine Names*, Book 4, 19–35, 716D–736B, esp. 31: 'it is not principles and powers which produce evil, but impotence and weakness.'
12 Dionysius, *The Divine Names*, Book 4, 20: 'Abolish the good and you will abolish being, life, desire, movement, everything'; Augustine, *City of God*, XIV, II: 'The choice of the will . . . is genuinely free, only when it is not subservient to faults and sins.'
13 See Slavoj Zizek, 'Selfhood as Such is Spirit' in Copjec, ed., *Radical Evil*, 1–30. In the same volume, see Jacob Rogozinski, 'It makes us wrong: Kant and Radical Evil', 30–45. See also Jean-Luc Nancy, *The Experience of Freedom*, Chapter 12 'Evil: Decision', 121–41. For a dissenting voice, see Alain Badiou's superb *Ethics: An Essay on the Understanding of Evil*, trans. Peter Hallward (London: Verso, 2001), 58–89.
14 Both Paul Ricoeur and Pierre Watté interpret Kant as offering the finest interpretation of a Pauline 'Self-Inhibition' in a fashion that 'frees' the theme of liberty from cosmology and discovers the seed of evil to be purely in the will taken as a positive assertion of self. The whole of this present chapter is designed in part to demonstrate that such a view is historically false, pseudo-profound and profoundly dangerous. Ricoeur also sees such positivity of evil as anticipated in primitive 'symbolization' of evil as visible taint or disorder. However, this aspect of aesthetic disharmony was rightly viewed by Dionysius as also privative: nothing that *appears* to us lacks beauty – rather what offends the eye is a deficiency of appropriate, requisite order that should pertain variously in any given instance. Thus evil for him, while negative, is also 'an inharmonious mingling of discordances': *Divine Names*, 4, 31. The invocation of an aesthetic aspect to privation does, nonetheless, serve to emphasize that evil as privation is not purely and simply nothing: as 'substance' it may be nothing, but in its effect of removal and deficiency it engenders a distorted positive act, even though, as positive, this act is not distorted. See Pierre Watté, *Structures Philosophiques du Péché Originel: S. Augustin, S. Thomas, Kant* (Gembloux: J. Duclot SA, 1974) and the preface by Paul Ricoeur, esp. p. 8, and Paul Ricoeur, *The Symbolism of Evil*, trans. Emerson Buchanan (Boston: Beacon, 1967), 70–100.
15 At this point these thinkers are incorporating a Levinasian thematic.
16 See Zizek, 'Selfhood as Such is Spirit'. And F.W.J. Schelling, 'Philosophical Investigations into the Essence of Human Freedom and Related Matters', in *Philosophy of German Idealism*, ed. Ernest Behler (New York: Continuum, 1987); *Of Human Freedom*, trans. J. Gutman (Chicago: Open Court, 1936).
17 See Watté, *Structures Philosophiques*, 128–215.
18 Augustine, *On Free Choice of the Will*, trans. Thomas Williams (Indianapolis: Hackett, 1993), Book 1: 1, 4, 12, 13; 25; Book 2: 14, 16, esp. 13, p. 57: 'this is our freedom: when we are subject to the [infinite] truth.'
19 Augustine, *City of God*, XIV, 13; *On Free Choice of the Will*, Book 1: 8.
20 Augustine, *On Free Choice of the Will*, Book 1: 11: once 'inordinate desire' has gripped the mind after Adam, it takes 'false things' for true, and becomes a prey to 'fear' and 'anxiety'. See further Book 3: 3, 4, 18, p. 106: '. . . as it is [since the Fall] they [humans] are not good, and it is not in their power to be good, either because they do not see how they ought to be, or because they lack the power to be what they see they ought to be'; 'because of our ignorance we lack the free choice or the will to choose to act rightly'; 'or . . . even when we do see what is right and will to do it, we cannot do it because of the resistance of carnal habit'

Here Augustine is commenting on Romans 7: 18: 'To will the good is present to me, but I find no way to do it', and Galatians 5: 17: 'You do not do what you will as flesh and spirit lust against each other.' Augustine continues, 'thus we who knew what was right but did not do it, lost the knowledge of what is right, and we who had the power but not the will to act rightly lost the power even when we have the will'. He then has to face the objection that if our free will is so inhibited by loss of vision and incapacity, then we are not to blame for failure to will the good. But he answers (p. 107), 'Perhaps their complaint would be justified if there were no victor over error and inordinate desire. But in fact there is one who is present everywhere and speaks in many ways through the creation that serves him as Lord. He calls out to those who have turned their backs on him, and instructs them who believe in him.' Desire of the Good remains possible through grace, and so our lack of vision and incapacity is exceeded and potentially overcome (since the Pauline impotence, recognized *after* grace, is not really seen by Paul as an absolute check). See also Book 2: 16 where it is made clear that the discernment of truth by will/desire is also the kenotic descent of divine wisdom towards us. At section 52 of *On the Spirit and the Letter* Augustine stresses that free will itself is the supreme gift of grace, while in *De Gratia et Libero Arbitrio* at 4:8, citing Matthew 19: 10–11, he notes that while marriage as sexual union is supremely what we *will*, marriage is also the sacramental *gift* of God. Here then again, what is given to us by God is to will.

21 See Martin Luther, 'The Bondage of the Will' in *Martin Luther's Basic Theological Writings*, ed. Timothy F. Lull (Minneapolis: Fortress, 1989), 178–82 and 206. For Luther, in a Scotist lineage, the will only 'inclines' to God under grace; the natural will has no natural orientation to God. But for Augustine, without the latter (always through grace) there is no will at all. Recent attempts theologically to assimilate the two thinkers ignore this metaphysical divide.

22 See note 20, above and the passage quoted from *On Free Choice of the Will*, Book 3: 18, p. 107.

23 *On Free Choice of the Will*, Book 3: 18, p. 107: 'You are not to blame for your unwilling ignorance [the legacy of Adam's sin], but because you fail to ask about what you do not know. You are not blamed because you do not bind up your own wounds [the post-Adamic incapacity], but because you spurn the one who wants to heal you, for no one is prevented from leaving behind the disadvantage of ignorance and seeking the advantage of knowledge, or from humbly confessing his weakness, so that God, whose help is effortless and unerring, will come to his assistance. When someone acts wrongly out of ignorance, or cannot do what he rightly wills to, his actions are called sins because they have their origin in that first sin, which was committed by free will. The later sins are the just result of that first sin.' This shows that Augustine's account of original sin is objective, collective, historical and realist, and involves no contorted doctrines about an inevitable willing of the bad for which we are to blame. These rather descend to us from Luther and Kant.

24 James Alison, *The Joy of Being Wrong* (New York: Crossroad, 1998).

25 *On Free Choice of the Will*, Book 2: 19.

26 *On Free Choice of the Will*, Book 2: 9, p. 49. Augustine associates the common true/good with light, enjoyed by all sight at once, unlike a touchable object, which we can only touch one at a time, in turn. However, it seems to me implicit in Augustine that in the Eucharist 'sight' and 'touch' are fused since here the most intimate touching that is tasting is a simultaneous and collective eating of a body not 'used up', and not enjoyed exclusively 'one at a time'. So here a body is like light, and in this fashion the Eucharist supremely combines the most

common and the most intimate. Therefore the Eucharist most exemplifies true willing or desiring and restored participation. Augustine in this dialogue also aligns the dialectic of common and particular with the co-belonging of 'wisdom' with 'number.' Here he is not always easy to follow, but roughly it seems that 'number' is at times associated with the eternal divine ideas, and at other times with the diversity of the creation – as in the case of God numbering sparrows and the hairs on our head. By contrast, wisdom is associated with the kenotic 'reach' of omnipotence to the ends of the earth, as with the figure of personified wisdom rushing to meet us, which Augustine alludes to. In this way the eternal numbers reach to the created numbers, and Augustine indicates that the diversity of instance and preference is not alien to the common, universal, eternal and measured.

27 Immanuel Kant, *The Metaphysics of Morals*, trans. Mary Gregor (Cambridge: CUP, 1991), 183 [378], 193 [389]; *Critique of Practical Reason*, trans. L.W. Beck (Upper Saddle River, NJ: Prentice Hall, 1993), Part I, Book I, Chap. I, II, 65–8; *Religion Within the Bounds of Mere Reason*, 6:22, p. 72 and asterisked footnote; 6:24–6:31, pp. 73–8.

28 This is why the 'revisionist' attempt to read Kant as a virtue ethicist cannot be rendered plausible.

29 *Religion Within the Bounds of Mere Reason*, 6:29, p. 77; *Groundwork of the Metaphysics of Morals*, trans. H.J. Paton (New York: Harper and Row, 1964), Preface vi–viii, p. 57 [389–90].

30 *Metaphysics of Morals*, 201–2 [400]; *Groundwork of the Metaphysics of Morals*, 128–9 [460], *Critique of Judgement*, trans. J.C. Meredith (Oxford: OUP, 1989), Book I, Part I, § 4, pp. 46–8 § 6, p. 51; § 26, p. 103; § 29, p. 120.

31 *Religion Within the Bounds of Mere Reason*, 6:30, p. 77.

32 *Groundwork*, 128–9 [460]; *Critique of Practical Reason*, Part I, Book I, Chapter I, 32–3, 43–52; Chapter II, pp. 70–4; *Critique of Judgement*, Book I, Part I, § 29, p. 121; § 30, p. 134; § 59, pp. 221–5.

33 *Groundwork*, 128 [460];

34 *Critique of Judgement*, Book II, Part I B, § 28, pp. 109–14.

35 *Critique of Practical Reason*, Part II, pp. 161–3.

36 *Religion Within the Bounds*, 6:33, p. 80.

37 *Religion Within the Bounds*, 6:36, p. 82; 6:22, p. 72.

38 Schelling, *Of Human Freedom*.

39 See J.-L. Nancy, *The Experience of Freedom*, 4, 'The Space Left Free by Heidegger', 33–43.

40 Nancy, op. cit. and 'Evil: Decision', 121–41. Nancy also gives analyses of freedom highly compatible with Augustinianism, which describe it as that which 'surprises us, rather than as something we control, and as primordially 'sharing', since every free expression must 'give' something of oneself to others. See 'Impossibility of the Question of Freedom: Fact and Right Indistinguishable', 21–32.

41 For example, Dionysius, *The Divine Names*, Book 4, 26: 'there is no evil nature – rather evil lies in the inability of things to reach their *acme* of perfection.'

42 Augustine, *City of God*, XII, 7: 'To try to discover the causes of such defection . . . is like trying to see darkness or to hear silence.'

43 Jean-Luc Marion, 'Le Mal en Personne' in *Prolégomènes à la Charité* (Paris: La Différence, 1986), 11–43.

44 For Scotus and after, see Catherine Pickstock, *After Writing* (Oxford: Blackwell, 1999), 121–67. Privation theory plays little role within Leibniz's *Theodicy*. See G.W. Leibniz, *Theodicy*, ed. Austin Farrer (La Salle, IL: Open Court, 1985).

45 See, for example, Augustine, *On the Free Choice of the Will*, Book 3: 15, 100–1.

46 *Critique of Judgement*, Book II, Part I B, § 28, pp. 112–13. Jacques Lacan, 'Kant with Sade', trans. James Swenson, *October 51* (Winter, 1989); Slavoj Zizek, 'Why is Sade the Truth of Kant?', in *For They Know Not What They Do*, 229–41; J.G. Ballard, *Super-Cannes* (London: HarperCollins, 2001).
47 *Religion Within the Bounds of Mere Reason*, Parts III and IV, pp. 129–215.
48 *Religion Within the Bounds of Mere Reason*, Part VI: 94–5, pp. 129–30.
49 *Religion Within the Bounds of Mere Reason*, Part IV, 6: 151–6:202, pp. 175–215 esp. 6:153, p. 176.
50 Luther, 'The Bondage of the Will'.
51 See Halberstramm's discussion of Arendt's use of the *Critique of Judgement* in *Totalitarianism* (see note 6 above)
52 See Kathleen M. Brown, *Good Wives, Nasty Wenches and Anxious Patriarchs: Gender, Race and Power in Colonial Virginia* (Chapel Hill: North Carolina UP, 1996).
53 Arendt, *Eichmann in Jerusalem*, op. cit.
54 *Religion Within the Bounds of Mere Reason*, Part VI: 139–43, pp. 165–8.
55 Immanuel Kant, *Metaphysics of Morals*, Part II, Section I, 44–48, pp. 123–8.
56 *Metaphysics of Morals*, Part II, Section I, ' 49, pp. 129–33, and Immanuel Kant, 'Perpetual Peace' in *Kant: Political Writings*, trans. A.B. Nisbet (Cambridge: CUP, 1991), 124.
57 See the magnificent book by David Depew and Bruce H. Weber, *Darwinism Evolving: Systems Dynamics and the Genealogy of Natural Selection* (Cambridge, MA: MIT Press, 1997).

2 VIOLENCE: DOUBLE PASSIVITY

1 See my discussion of Jean-Yves Lacoste on this point in Chapter 7, below.
2 Badiou, op. cit.
3 See John Milbank, *Theology and Social Theory: Beyond Secular Reason* (Oxford: Blackwell, 1991), 380–438.
4 See Michel Foucault, *Discipline and Punish: The Birth of the Prison*, trans. Alan Sheridan (London: Penguin, 1986) and Talal Asad, *Geneology of the Secular* (Baltimore: Johns Hopkins UP, 2002), Chapter 2, 'On Agency and Pain'.
5 See *The Sublime: A Reader in British Eighteenth-Century Aesthetic Theory* (Cambridge: CUP, 1996), ed. A. Ashfield and P. de Bolla, 30–40, 131–40, 180–95.
6 Plato, *Republic*, 439e–444a; Augustine, *Confessions* Book III, ii.
7 See John Milbank, *The Word Made Strange* (Oxford: Blackwell, 1997), Chapter 8, 'The Force of Identity'.
8 See Catherine Pickstock, *After Writing: On the Liturgical Consummation of Philosophy* (Oxford: Blackwell, 1998), 47–100.
9 Talal Asad, *Genealogies of Religion: Discipline and Reasons of Power in Christianity and Islam* (Baltimore: Johns Hopkins UP, 1993), 55–79.
10 I am indebted to discussions with Catherine Pickstock at this point.
11 See John Milbank, 'Stories of Sacrifice' in *Modern Theology* 12:1, January 1996, 27–55.
12 J.G. Ballard, op. cit.
13 See the discussions of the protagonists in Alan Wall's novel, *The School of Night* (London: Vintage, 2001), and Chapter 8 below. And see also John Milbank, 'Poetry is not Fiction', in *The Mercurial Wood* (Salzburg: Salzburg UP, 1997), xii–xiv.
14 This can be related to Kierkegaard's treatment of Socratic irony.
15 Plato, *Republic*, 376c–412a.
16 Franz Baermann Steiner, 'Orientpolitik, Value and Civilization', in *Selected Writings*, ed. Jeremy Adler and Richard Pardon (New York: Berghahn, 1999).

I am indebted to long-standing discussions with Michael Mack about all this. See also his *Anthropology as Memory* (Tübingen: Niemeyer, 2001).

17 See Bernard Williams, *Shame and Necessity* (Berkeley: University of California Press, 1993), *passim*. There is now a tendency in America to assume that all 'just war' theorists will be apologists for Bush, Cheney *et al*. But if one concludes that nearly all modern wars are 'disproportionate' in terms of both *ius ad bellum* and *ius in bello*, it is *only* just war theory that can conclude this.

18 S.T. II. II. Q. 22 a 1; Q. 24 aa 1–12; Q. 26 aa 6–11.

19 Charles Péguy, *The Mystery of the Charity of Joan of Arc*, trans. Jeffrey Wainwright (Manchester: Carcanet, 1986). See also Georges Bernanos, 'Joan, Heretic and Saint', in *The Heretic Face of Innocence* (Edinburgh: T. and T. Clark, 1999), 19: 'If one approaches her with distrust one sees only . . . a kind of spiritual police force.'

20 For all its evidently rabid bias, Charles Maturin's *Melmoth the Wanderer* (Oxford: OUP, 1995) still proffers a subtly penetrating critique of monasticism.

21 With regard to erotic love, see Guillaume de Loris and Jean de Meun, *The Romance of the Rose*, trans. Frances Hogan (Oxford: OUP, 1994), Chapter 11, 'The Sermon of Genius', 19409–20638, pp. 300–18. For example, 19461: 'But if a man strives with all his might to preserve Nature, keeps himself from base thoughts and toils and struggles faithfully to be a true lover, let him go to paradise crowned with flowers'; 19569: 'When they are first created, God has the same love for all, and gives rational souls to men as well as to women; therefore I believe that he wants every soul, not just one, to follow the best path and to come as quickly as possible to himself. So if he wants some people to live chaste, the better to follow him, why would he not want others to do so? What reason would deter him? In that case it would seem as though he did not care if generation ceased' [this essentially follows through the logic of an Augustinian as opposed to Greek patristic position on sex and procreation]; 19855: 'Concentrate on leading a good life; let every man embrace his sweetheart and every lady her lover with kissing, feasting and pleasure. If you love one another loyally, you ought never to be reproached for it. And when you have played enough in the way that I have recommended, remember to make a good confession so as to do good and renounce evil, and call upon the heavenly God, whom Nature acknowledges as her master. It is he who will come to your aid in the end, when Atropos buries you. He is the salvation of body and soul, the fair mirror of my lady, who would never know anything were it not for this fair mirror. He directs and governs her, and my lady knows no other law. He taught her all she knows when he took her for his chamberlain.'

Later in this chapter, the blighting of the Golden Age and the arrival of work and sterility is ascribed, after Virgil, to the jealousy of the Olympian gods. The Christian God, by contrast, elevates humanity to paradise, and knows no jealousy of human beatitude, nor of corporeal pleasures (since of course his infinite spiritual nature is not a lack of anything). The White Lamb (Christ) has conserved always the fold of the earthly paradise, and this still awaits us (20213) even with its flowers that 'are neither too closed nor too open' (19901).

With regard to chivalric warfare, see A.T. Hatto, 'An Introduction to a Second Reading', in Wolfram von Eschenbach, *Parziful* (London: Penguin, 1980), 412–39: 'Before, during and after Wolfram's time there is historical evidence of a deep desire in lay circles to be more closely associated with clerical institutions in piety somewhat short of the taking of monastic vows'; 'the function of the Great Society . . . is to inculcate an image of self-discipline in young men and women in joint service to God – coupled with and despite high living'; 417: This

Graal milieu was a 'second paradise' though it might involve tournaments and dancing. Hatto stresses that Parzival's almost exclusively outward activity, the activity which wins him the Graal when at last he pursues it in the right spirit, is that of knightly combat. He goes on to say that 'The chivalric orders had from the outset enshrined lofty Christian principles in their statutes, which, however, were often more neglected than observed. It was Wolfram's aim through a sympathetic discussion of knighthood as reflected in the early life of Parzival to raise this *latent potential* in the general chivalric order. In order to do so Wolfram had to shield the knighthood from the wounding arrogance of the ascetic clergy, who took the uncharitable view that as men of blood knights were damned. Apart from his positive teaching, mainly through the mouth of Parzival, Wolfram furthered his aim by the simple device of having no other clergy in his story than those required for the formalities of baptism, marriage and celebration of the mass, leaving confession and discussion of such burning issues as homicide, rebellion against God and religious despair to his laymen' (414).

22 I am entirely indebted here to Alison Milbank.

3 FORGIVENESS: THE DOUBLE WATERS

1 Dante Alighieri, *Purgatorio*, Canto 28. And see Jacques Madaule, 'Dante: Une Liturgie Poetique du Pardon', in *Le Pardon*, ed. Michel Perrin (Paris: Beauchesne, 1987). I am grateful to Alison Milbank for discussions about the *Purgatorio*.
2 In Michel Perrin, ed. *Le Pardon* (Paris: Beauchesne, 1987), see Danièle Aubriot, 'Quelques Réflexions sur le Pardon en Grèce Ancienne,' 25–7, and Alain Michel, 'Le Pardon dans l'Antiquité: de Platon à St. Augustine', 49–60, plus Chong-Hyoun Sung, *Vergebung der Sünden* (Tübingen: J.C.B. Mohr, 1993), especially 75–7. See also Oliver O'Donovan, *The Desire of the Nations: Rediscovering the Roots of Political Theology* (Cambridge: CUP, 1996) *passim* for immensely important historico-theological reflections on the relations of clemency to governance. For the Irish sources of some mediaeval penitential practice, see Thomas O'Loughlin, *Celtic Theology: Humanity, World and God in Early Irish Writings* (London: Continuum, 2001) 48–68, 109–28. In addition, see L. Gregory Jones, *Embodying Forgiveness: A Theological Analysis* (Grand Rapids: Eerdmans, 1995).
3 See Michel, 'Le Pardon dans l'Antiquité: de Platon à St. Augustine', and André Crepin, 'Pardon Chrétien et vengeance Germanique dans l'Angleterre du Haut Moyen Age', also in Perrin, *Le Pardon*.
4 See the *Oxford English Dictionary* entries for these words.
5 Søren Kierkegaard, *Works of Love*, trans. H.V. and E.H. Hong (Princeton, NJ: Princeton UP, 1995), 294–5.
6 *Purgatorio*, Cantos 28 and 33.
7 S.T. III. Q. 86 a 2.
8 Kierkegaard, *Works of Love*, Supplement, 314.
9 S.T. III. Q. 86 a 4 resp; a 6. See also John Bossy, *Christianity in the West 1400–1700* (Oxford: OUP, 1985).
10 S.T. III. Q. 86 a 2; a 4 resp; a 6. See Bossy, *Christianity in the West*, and Catherine Pickstock, *After Writing: On the Liturgical Consummation of Philosophy* (Oxford: Blackwell, 1998).
11 John Milbank, 'Can A Gift Be Given?: Prolegomena to a Future Trinitarian Metaphysics', *Modern Theology* 2, no. 1 (January 1995): 119–61.
12 See David Hart's brilliant article 'A Gift Exceeding Every Debt', in *Pro Ecclesia* VII, no. 3, 333–49.
13 *Purgatorio*, Canto 33.

14 See Aubriot, 'Quelques Réflexions sur le Pardon en Grèce Ancienne', and Michel, 'Le Pardon dans l'Antiquité de Platon à St. Augustine'.

15 See Aubriot, 'Quelques Réflexions sur le Pardon en Grèce Ancienne'.

16 See Sung, *Vergebung der Sünden*, 66; K. Koch, 'Sühne und Sündenvergebung um die Wende von der exilischen zur nachexilischen Zeit', *Evangelische Theologischezeitschrift 26* (1966): 217–39; John Milbank, 'History of the One God', *Heythrop Journal* XXXVIII (October 1997): 371–400.

17 See Sung, *Vergebung der Sünden*, and Koch, 'Sühne und Sündenvergebung um die Wende von der exilischem zur nachexilischen Zeit'.

18 See John Milbank, 'History of the One God'; and 'I Will Gasp and Pant: Deutero-Isaiah and the Birth of the Suffering Subject', *Semeia* (1992): 59–73.

19 See Jacques Ribard, 'De Don au Pardon: à l'écoute des oeuvres littéraires des XIIe et XIIIe siècles', in Perrin, *Le Pardon*, 117–30, esp. 129. See also Christiane Marchello-Nizid, 'Adultère et Pardon dans le Roman Courtois', in the same volume, 131–9.

20 Vladimir Jankélévitch, *Pardonner?* (Paris: Le Pavillon, 1971) and *Le Pardon* (Paris: Aubier, 1967); and Alain Gouhier, 'Le temps de l'impardonnable selon Jankélevich', in Perrin, *Le Pardon*, 269–82.

21 See John Milbank, 'Sacred Triads: Augustine and the Indo-European Soul', *Modern Theology* 13, no. 4 (October 1997): 451–74; and Catherine Pickstock, 'Music: Soul, City and Cosmos after Augustine', in *Radical Orthodoxy*, ed. J. Milbank, C. Pickstock and G. Ward (London and New York: Routledge, 1999).

22 Augustine, *Confessions*, XI, 26.

23 Jorge Luis Borges, 'The Rose of Paracelsus', in *Collected Fictions*, trans. Andrew Hurley (New York: Penguin, 1998), 504–8.

24 See Joan Copjec, ed., *Radical Evil* (London: Verso, 1996); Jean-Luc Nancy, *The Experience of Freedom*, trans. Bridget McDonald (Stanford: Stanford UP, 1993); Slavoj Zizek, *For They Know Not What They Do: Enjoyment as a Political Factor* (London: Verso, 1991).

25 Depew and Weber, *Darwinism Evolving, passim.*

26 See John Milbank, 'Problematizing the Secular: The Post-Postmodern Problematic', in *Shadow of Spirit*, ed. P. Berry and A. Wernick (London and New York: Routledge, 1993), 30–44; and 'La fin des Lumières: Postmoderne and postseculière,' *Concilium*, no. 2 (1992): 57–68.

27 See Robert Spaemann, *Glück und Wohlwollen: Versuch über Ethik* (Stuttgart: Klett-Cotta, 1990).

28 Kierkegaard, *Works of Love*, 380.

29 Geoffrey Chaucer, *The Pardoner's Prologue and Tale*, ed. A.C. Spearing (Cambridge and New York: CUP, 1994).

30 Cited in Gouhier, 'Le temps de l'impardonable selon Jankélévich'.

31 Julian of Norwich, *Revelations of Divine Love*, trans. Elizabeth Spearing (Harmondsworth: Penguin, 1998), *passim.*

4 INCARNATION: THE SOVEREIGN VICTIM

1 S.C.G. IV 55 (15).

2 See David Hart, 'A Gift Exceeding Every Debt'.

3 See Frederick Bauerschmidt, *Julian of Norwich and the Mystical Body of Christ* (Notre Dame, IN: Notre Dame UP, 1999), introduction and *passim.*

4 S.T. III. Q. 1 a 2.

5 S.T. III. Q. 1 aa 1–4.

6 S.T. III. Q. 1 a 2.

7 Gilbert Narcisse, OP, *Les Raisons de Dieu: Arguments de Convenance et Esthetique Théologique Selon St. Thomas d'Aquin de Hans Urs von Balthasar* (Fribourg: Editions Universitaires Fribourg Suisse, 1997), esp. 165–80.

8 See Bauerschmidt, *Julian of Norwich and the Mystical Body of Christ*.

9 S.T. III. Q. 1 a 2. resp: 'and there are many other advantages which accrue, above man's apprehension.'

10 S.T. III. Q. 1 a 3 ad 1; S.C.G. IV. 42 (4).

11 S.C.G. IV. 55 (3); S.T. III. Q. 1 a 1.

12 S.T. IV. Q. 95 a 1; 99 a 1 a d 3. See Richard Cross, *Duns Scotus* (Oxford: OUP, 1999), 113–26, for a clear exposition of the difference from Scotus at this point.

13 S.C.G. 55 (2): The Incarnation is 'not contrary to the order of things . . . because, although the divine nature exceeds the human nature to infinity, man in the order of his nature has God himself for end, and has been born to be united to God by his intellect.' Also 55 (4)–(17). In addition, see S.T. III. Q. 1 a 2 resp: the Incarnation is 'convenient . . . with regard to the full participation of the Divinity, which is the true bliss of man and end of human life; and this is bestowed upon us by Christ's life.'

14 S.T. III. Q. 3 a 5. Of course he is usually misunderstood and travestied at this point.

15 S.T. III. Q. 1 a 3. ad 5.

16 On this entire issue, see Michel Corbin, *L'Inoui de Dieu: Six Etudes Christologiques* (Paris: Desclée de Brouwer, 1979).

17 S.T. III. Q. 16 a b ad 2; Q. 17 a 2 resp; Q 2 a 7 ad 3. And see Richard Cross, *Duns Scotus*, and his article (unfavourable to Aquinas) 'Aquinas on Nature, Hypostasis and the Metaphysics of the Incarnation', *The Thomist* 60, no. 2 (April 1996): 171–202. See also now Richard Cross, *The Metaphysics of the Incarnation: Thomas Aquinas to Duns Scotus* (Oxford: OUP, 2000).

18 For example, S.T. III. Q. 17 a 2. resp.

19 Corbin, *L'Inoui de Dieu*.

20 See S.T. II II Q. 2 a 7; Q 5 a 1; III Q. 1a 3. And see also John Milbank and Catherine Pickstock, *Truth in Aquinas* (London and New York: Routledge, 2000), Chapter 2, 19–60. Some passages from this chapter written by me, and from Chapter 3, 60–88, written by both of us, have been recycled and adapted in the present chapter, as they are indispensable here. (The modern theologian, like the Baroque composer, is often and quite properly, a journeyman!)

21 See Milbank and Pickstock, *Truth in Aquinas*, Chapter 2.

22 Ibid.

23 See Richard Cross, *Duns Scotus*, and Rowan Williams's article on later medieval Christology, 'Jesus Christus III: Mittelalter', *TRE* 16 (1987): 748–53.

24 See Andrew Louth, *Maximus the Confessor* (London and New York: Routledge, 1996), 54–9.

25 S.T. III. Q. 2 a 1 ad 1 and ad 2; a 3 resp. and ad 2; a 5 ad 2; a 12 ad 2; 16 a 1 resp.

26 S.C.G. IV 41 (7) (11); S.T. III. a 3 ad 2. For a much fuller discussion of the significance of the hand analogy, see John Milbank and Catherine Pickstock, *Truth in Aquinas*, Chapter 3.

27 Aristotle, *On the Soul*, trans. W.S. Hett (Cambridge, MA: Harvard UP, Loeb Editions, 1996), Books II and III; Thomas Aquinas, *A Commentary on Aristotle's De Anima*, trans. Robert Pasnau (New Haven: Yale UP, 1999), 54–82. Again, for a much fuller development of this thematic, see Milbank and Pickstock, *Truth in Aquinas*.

28 S.C.G. IV 41 (12).
29 S.T. III. Q. 2 a 3 resp.
30 Duns Scotus, *Ordinatio*, 2.30–32; 1.4.n.19; Olivier Boulnois, 'Duns Scotus: Jean', in *Dictionnaire Critique de Théologie*, ed. J.-Y. Lacoste (Paris: PUF, 1998).
31 Duns Scotus, *Ordinatio* 1.3.1; 1.8.3.
32 See Duns Scotus, *Ordinatio* 3.7.3.n.3; Cross, *Duns Scotus* 127–9; Williams, 'Jesus Christus III: Mittelalter'; and Boulnois, 'Duns Scotus: Jean'.
33 S.T. III. Q. 2 a 1 ad 2; a 3 resp; Q. 17 a 2 resp. See also Williams, 'Jesus Christus III: Mittelalter'.
34 Duns Scotus, *Ordinatio* 3.13.4.n.8; Cross, *Duns Scotus* 124; Williams, 'Jesus Christus III: Mittelalter'; and Boulnois, 'Duns Scotus: Jean'.
35 Boulnois; 'Duns Scotus: Jean'.
36 Duns Scotus, *Ordinatio* 3.1.1.n.3.
37 Duns Scotus, *Ordinatio* 3.1.1.n.9; and Williams, 'Jesus Christus III: Mittelalter'.
38 For Scotus's view that we cannot love negations, see Duns Scotus, *Ordinatio* 1.3.1.2.
39 Duns Scotus, *Ordinatio* 4.15.1.n.6; Boulnois, 'Duns Scotus: Jean'.
40 Duns Scotus, *Ordinatio* 4.15.1.n.6; Boulnois, 'Duns Scotus: Jean'; and Cross, *Duns Scotus, passim*. For the formal distinction of attributes in general in Duns Scotus, see *Ordinatio* 1.8.1.4.
41 See Milbank and Pickstock, *Truth in Aquinas*, Chapter 2.
42 Duns Scotus, *Ordinatio* 1.8.1.4; *Quodlibet* 14. 14, 5 S.
43 Duns Scotus, *Ordinatio* 1.8.1.3.
44 Duns Scotus, *Ordinatio* 1.3.3.
45 See Milbank and Pickstock, *Truth in Aquinas*, Chapter 2. See also Catherine Pickstock's unpublished essay on Anselm's *Proslogion*.
46 Duns Scotus, *Ordinatio* 4.16.2.nn.6, 9–12; Boulnois, 'Duns Scotus: Jean'; and Cross, *Duns Scotus*, 107–13.

5 CRUCIFIXION: OBSCURE DELIVERANCE

1 See, for example, John Dominic Crossan, *Who Killed Jesus? Exposing the Roots of Anti-Semitism in the Gospel Story of the Death of Jesus* (San Francisco: HarperCollins, 1995), 111. I am indebted to discussions with Harry Gamble of the Department of Religious Studies, University of Virginia on the current state of scholarly thinking concerning these points.
2 The view that the Sanhedrin had strong autonomous powers of judgement and execution was put forward by Lietzmann and Juster and repeated by Paul Winter in his book *On the Trial of Jesus* (Berlin: De Gruyter, 1961). It is demolished by A.N. Sherwin-White in his *Roman Society and Roman Law in the New Testament* (Oxford: OUP, 1961) and Simon Légasse, *The Trial of Jesus*, trans. John Bowden (London: SCM, 1991), vi and 52ff. However, they both still reject the historicity of the role of the mob (Sherwin-White with Anglican discretion – or cynicism? See *Roman Society*, 26: 'One may here leave aside the worked-up sections concerning the release of Barabbas, and other material, such as the story of Pilate's wife in Matthew, and the sending of Christ to Herod in Luke, none of which is part of the *cognitio* proper.').
3 See Légasse, 65ff.
4 Again, this is Winter's view. And Légasse's at 69. See also Crossan, *Who Killed Jesus?* 82–133.
5 See Jean-Luc Marion, *Étant Donnée* (Paris: PUF, 1997), 169–251.
6 See A.C. Harvey, *Jesus on Trial* (London: SPCK, 1976), 77.

7 Sherwin-White, *Roman Society*, 35. And see Légasse, 138. I am indebted to Russell Hittenger for the point about *cognitio extra ordinem* being only exercised by Governors at the margins. On the dangers of leaving things to judges' solo authority, see Thomas Aquinas, S.T. II. II. Q.95 a 1 ad 2.
8 Jon A. Wetherby, *Jewish Responsibility for the Death of Jesus in Luke-Acts* (Sheffield: Sheffield Academic Press, 1994).
9 Légasse, 68 and 144.
10 Jean Colin, *Les Villes Libres de L'Orient Greco-Romain et L'Envoi au Supplice par Acclamations Populaires* (Brussels: Latonus, 1965).
11 Colin, 16.
12 Cited in Giorgio Agamben, *Homo Sacer: Sovereign Power and Bare Life*, trans. Daniel Heller-Roozen (Stanford, CA: Stanford UP, 1998), 71.
13 Agamben, *passim.*
14 Agamben, 76–7.
15 Agamben, 96.
16 Agamben, 104–12.

6 ATONEMENT: CHRIST THE EXCEPTION

1 I am indebted here to conversations with Regina Schwartz concerning Milton's *Paradise Regained*. The present chapter should be related always to Chapter 4 above and to my earlier piece, 'The Name of Jesus', which is Chapter 6 of my *The Word Made Strange: Theology, Language, Culture* (Oxford: Blackwell, 1997), 145–71.
2 See J.R.R. Tolkien, 'On Fairy-Stories' in *Poems and Stories* (London: George Allen and Unwin, 1980), 75–113. Tolkien here famously speaks of the gospels as uniquely true fairy-stories. However, since for him all genuine fairy-stories truly invoke what is in some sense a real other world of *faerie*, what he says more precisely is that in the gospel story Divine 'primary creation' and human 'secondary creation' uniquely coincide. This means that whereas normally a fairy-story dimly discloses an impinging yet absent world, where all is rearranged by enchantment, the gospels record a fully actualized entrance of enchanted transformation into our everyday reality. This renders the events they record a genuinely magical drama; whereas normally, for Tolkien, drama is suspiciously pseudo-magical, mere stage-magic. By contrast, third-person narrative evokes an absent true enchantment, which the imagination can reach beyond the range of vision, yet reach without reaching, in a fashion that sustains the mystery of distance. By appearing to render the enchantment present, drama tends to betray the imagination and the real power of literature.

Tolkien's suspicion of Shakespeare here is fascinating. Yet surely he might have remarked that Shakespeare's non-classicism deconstructs dramatic presence; that he tends to refuse the visual closure of *either* tragedy or comedy, and that he accords a great role to fetishized or magical objects. (Tolkien rightly complains that most drama is too personalist, and downplays the role of symbolic objects which outlast humans through time. Perhaps the Ring-Master envisages himself as in competition with Wagner as well as Shakespeare here.)

In future work on the Gift, I will include an analysis of this astonishing essay: its account of fairy-story as supreme 'sub-creation', of creative imagination as entry into a real world of *faerie*; and its subtle critique of drama as pseudo-magic which falsely entrances us in a frozen presence, compared with the liberating effects of diegesis, and its theory of the special status of 'things'.

3 Agamben, 59ff., 188.
4 See Michel Henry, *C'est Moi la Verité: Pour une Philosophie du Christianisme* (Paris: Editions du Seuil, 1996).
5 E.P. Sanders, *Paul and Palestinian Judaism* (Philadelphia: Fortress, 1977), 502–8. But Sanders fails to disprove Paul's antinomian bent (in a certain sense). Sanders rightly asserts: (1) that justification in Paul means participation in the body of Christ; (2) that death does not for Paul, as for the Rabbis, atone for transgressions, but that we are to die to the power of sin and live to another power; and (3) that Paul denies the salvific efficacy of the Jewish covenant. Sanders goes wrong in (1) arguing that participation in Christ, though it substitutes for the old covenant, does not involve belonging to a new group; he argues that *ecclesia* does not imply 'Church' in the later sense, whereas 'Church' meant later (at least up till the late Middle Ages) precisely participation in the Body of Christ; (2) exaggerating the non-legalism of the Rabbis regarding salvation: see Donald A. Hagner, 'Paul and Judaism', in Peter Stuhlmacher, *Revisiting Paul's Doctrine of Justification* (Downers Grove: IVP, 2001), 86ff.
6 Fernando Pessoa, 'The Last Ship', in *O Mar sem Fin/ The Boundless Sea* (Lisbon: Instituto Portugues de Patrimonio Arquitectonico/Mosteiro des Jeronimos, 2000) [unpaginated].

7 ECCLESIOLOGY: THE LAST OF THE LAST

1 This is Catherine Pickstock's idea. See John Milbank and Catherine Pickstock, *Truth in Aquinas* (London: Routledge, 2001), 109–111.
2 I am indebted to Lawrence Hemming for arguments concerning this point: he takes the opposite view.
3 Gratian, *The Treatise on Laws With the Ordinary Gloss* (Decretum DD 1–20), trans. Augustine Thompson OP trans. James Gordley (Washington, DC: CUA Press, 1993), *passim.*
4 See Graham White, *Luther as Nominalist* (Helsinki: Luther-Agricola-Society 1994), 231–99; Henry Chadwick, 'Philoponus the Christian Theologian', in Richard Sorabji, ed., *Philoponus and the Reflection of Aristotelian Science* (London: Duckworth, 1987); William of Ockham, *Quodlibetal Questions*, 5.10. See K. Lehmann and W. Pannenburg, eds, *The Condemnations of the Reformatiom Era: Do They Still Divide?* (Minneapolis: Fortress Press, 1990); 'Joint Declaration on the Doctrine of Justification', in Anthony S. Lane, *Justification by Faith* (Edinburgh: T. and T. Clark, 2002) esp. 87–96; 158–67. I agree (from a Catholic stance) with Lane's evangelical view that an Aquinas–Luther consensus has been exaggerated and that the 'Joint Declaration' is ambivalent regarding imputation: both playing down its Protestant role, and yet seeming (paras 23–4) to leave (unlike Newman or Kung) the possibility that the forensic declaration of righteousness rather that its consequent effectiveness is what renders us 'just'. But Chapter 3 above established that for Aquinas God's saving gift is *as* gift entirely effective and productive. See further for a critique of Otto Pesch's Luther/Aquinas approach, S. Pfürtner, 'The Paradigms of Thomas Aquinas and Martin Luther', in H. Kung and D. Tracy, eds, *Paradigm Change in Theology* (Edinburgh: T. and T. Clark, 1989) 130–60. I also dissent from the Finnish view that imputationism is read back from the Kantian rupture between knowledge and 'things in themselves'. No, univocity and nominalism themselves engender Kant. See C.E. Praaten and R.W. Jensen, eds, *Union with Christ* (Grand Rapids: Eerdmans, 1998) *passim.* Finally, *theosis* in Luther presupposes the incarnation, in Aquinas it is the other way round – see Chapter 4 above.

5 See Michel de Certeau, *The Mystic Fable*, trans. Michael B. Smith (Chicago: Chicago UP, 1992), 79–113 and Eric Alliez, *Capital Times*, trans. G. van dem Abbeele (Minneapolis: Minnesota UP, 1996).

6 Henri de Lubac, *Surnaturel* (Paris: Aubier, 1946); *The Mystery of the Supernatural,* trans. Rosemary Sheed (London: Geoffrey Chapman, 1967). See also Jean-Ives Lacoste, 'Le Desir et L'Inexigible: Préambules à une Lecture' in *Les Études Philosophiques,* no. 2 (1995), 223–46 and Olivier Boulnois, 'Les Deux Fins de L'Homme' in the same issue, 205–22.

   Recently, J.-P. Torrell OP has shown that, while Aquinas never uses the phrase *natura pura,* he does in a few places use the phrase *pura naturalia* (J.-P. Torrell, 'Nature et Grace chez Thmas d'Aquin', in *Revue Thomiste,* special issue *Surnaturel,* January–June 2001, 167–202). By this Aquinas means, following Augustine (significantly), our capacities to eat, build houses, cultivate fields, deploy *techne,* have friends, marry and so forth. These capacities survive the Fall and the loss of sanctifying grace. So it would appear that these capacities are independent of our supernatural orientation. However, Torrell points out that they are all impaired by the loss of grace, and that the state of true unfallen nature was an integral state where true nature was guaranteed by the supernatural orientation under grace. To Torrell I would want to add that it is all in the end a question of degrees of intensity: remarks of Aquinas elsewhere show that all reasoning powers, practical as well as theoretical, only exist in terms of an inchoate intuition of the supernatural end. The problem with de Lubac's position has always been that it appears to threaten a distinction between the divine action of Creation and the divine action of Supernatural Elevation. To me though this is a pseudo-problem; for reasons set out in the main text, there is, indeed, only a difference of degree, albeit qualitative degree, between these two receptions of the single divine action. This position far better observes the doctrine of divine simplicity and the *aporia* involved in the very fact of the existence of Creation.

7 See John Milbank and Catherine Pickstock, *Truth in Aquinas* (London: Routledge, 2001), Chapter 2: 'Truth and Vision', 19–59.

8 See John Montag SJ 'Revelation: The False Legacy of Suarez', in *Radical Orthodoxy: A New Theology,* ed. J. Milbank, C. Pickstock and G. Ward (London: Routledge, 1999), 38–64; Cajetan, *In Primam* Q.12.a1; *In Primum Secundae* Q.12.a8.

9 de Certeau, op. cit.

10 Lacoste and Boulnois, both op. cit.

11 Boulnois, op. cit.

12 See Olivier Boulnois, *Être et Représentation: Une Généalogie de la Metaphysique Moderne à L'Époque de Duns Scot (xiii–xiv siècle)* (Paris: PUF, 1999), 463ff.

13 Boulnois, *Être et Représentation,* passim.

14 Boulnois, 'Les Deux Fins de l'Homme'.

15 Michael Buckley, *At the Origins of Modern Atheism* (New Haven: Yale UP, 1987); Jean-Luc Marion, *I'Idole et la Distance* (Paris: Grasset et Fasquelle, 1977).

16 Hans Urs von Balthasar, *The Glory of the Lord: A Theological Aesthetics vol. V: The Realm of Metaphysics in the Modern Age,* trans. Brian McNeil et al. (San Francisco: Ignatius, 1989), 635–57.

17 Lacoste, op. cit.

18 John Paul II, *Faith and Reason* (London: Catholic Truth Society, 1998).

19 Hans Urs von Balthasar, *Love Alone: The Way of Revelation,* ed. Alexander Dru (London: Sheed and Ward, 1977).

20 Thomas Torrance, 'Creation and Science', in *The Ground and Grammar of Theology* (Charlottesville, VA: University of Virginia UP, 1980), 144–75; 'The Theology of

Light', in *Christian Theology and Scientific Culture* (New York: OUP, 1981). This is a decisive essay for the theology of the future. But one must of course, unlike Torrance, admit fully Grosseteste's Neoplatonism and escape the Scottish Presbyterian's straining at the limits of Calvinism.

21 See John Milbank, 'Knowledge: the Theological Critique of Philosophy in Jacobi and Hamann', in *Radical Orthodoxy*, 21–38.

22 Jean-Luc Marion, *God Without Being*, trans. Thomas A. Carlson (Chicago: Chicago UP, 1991), 139–61.

23 Henri de Lubac, *Corpus Mysticum: L'Eucharistie et L'Église au Moyen Age* (Paris: Aubier-Montaigne, 1949). See also, Catherine Pickstock, *After Writing: On the Liturgical Consummation of Philosophy* (Oxford: Blackwell, 1998), 121–67.

24 De Certeau, *The Mystic Fable*, 79–113.

25 Pickstock, 158–66.

26 I am indebted to conversations with Augustine Thompson OP of the University of Virginia on this matter. See also Jean-Yves Lacoste, *Être* [c] in *Dictionnaire Critique de Théologie*, ed. Jean-Yves Lacoste (Paris: PUF, 1998). Even the Council of Trent stresses that *praesentia realis* does not imply an exclusionary presence disallowing other *reales*, but a presence *per excellentiam* beyond mere locality. This is exactly *why* such presence is *substantialis*. Transubstantiation safeguards an apophaticism that 'real presence' tends to obscure (Denz. 1651).

27 This is how I am inclined to interpret some of Eamon Duffy's evidence. See Eamon Duffy, *The Stripping of the Altars: Traditional Religion in England 1400–1580* (New Haven: Yale UP, 1992); John Bossy, *Christianity in the West 1400–1700* (Oxford: OUP, 1985); J.J. Scarisbrick, *The Reformation and the English People* (Oxford: Blackwell, 1984).

28 I am indebted to discussions with Alison Milbank about this topic.

29 For a summary and synthesis of their views, see Catherine Pickstock, op. cit.

30 Nicholas of Cusa, *The Catholic Concordance*, trans. Paul E. Sigmund (Cambridge: CUP, 1995). Most of the following discussion is based upon Book I, paras 1–68. On participation in Neoplatonism in general, see the discussion by Rowan Williams in *Arius: Heresy and Tradition* (London: SCM, 2001) 215–30. On Proclus, see H.D. Saffrey, *Récherches sur Le Neoplatonisme après Plotin* (Paris: J. Vrin, 1990).

31 Paul E. Sigmund, 'Introduction' to Cusa, *The Catholic Concordance*, xxxvii–xxxix.

32 For *conciliarité*, see Sergei Bulgakov, *The Orthodox Church*, trans Elizabeth S. Cram (London: Century Press, 1935), 79. For the 'last of the last', see Augustine, *Ad Hesychium* (PL 33, p. 913), cited by Nicholas Book I, para. 14.

33 Cusa, *The Catholic Concordance*, Book I, paras 56–9.

34 Sigmund, 'Introduction', xxxiii.

35 Cusa, *The Catholic Concordance*, Book III, paras 294–312.

36 Cusa, *The Catholic Concordance*, Book I, para. 1 4.

37 W.H. Auden, *For the Time Being: A Christmas Oratario*, in *Collected Longer Poems* (London: Faber and Faber, 1968).

38 I am indebted here to the unpublished work of Peter Candler, of Duke University. See Henry of Ghent, *In Sent.* Prol 10.1; Yves Congar, *Tradition and Traditions* (London: Burns and Oates, 1963), 99; George Tavard, *Holy Writ and Holy Church* (New York: Harper and Row, 1959), 22ff.; Heiko Oberman, *The Harvest of Medieval Theology* (Cambridge, MA: Harvard UP, 1963), 369ff.

39 See de Certeau, *The Mystic Fable*, 222, citing the work of Pier Cesari Bori on Gregory the Great's reading of Ezekiel's vision.

40 William of Ockham, *Quodlibetal Questions* 4.12; 5.12; 6.9. resp. and 14, *Summa Logicae* 1.16. For Nicholas of Cusa, see Nicholas of Cusa, *Selected Spiritual Writings*, trans. H. Lawrence Bond (New York: Paulist Press, 1997), *passim*.

41 See John Milbank, *The Religious Dimension in the Thought of Giambattista Vico, 1668–1744, Part One: The Early Metaphysics*, 27–40.

42 Alain de Libera, *Introduction à la Mystique Rhenane* (Paris: PUF, 1984). For Cusa and Language, see Milbank, op. cit.

43 See Debora Shuger, *Sacred Rhetoric: The Christian Grand Style in the English Renaissance* (Princeton, NJ: Princeton UP, 1988), 73–6 and *passim*.

44 See John Milbank, 'Pleonasm, Speech and Writing', in *The Word Made Strange* (Oxford: Blackwell, 1997), 55–84.

8 GRACE: THE MIDWINTER SACRIFICE

1 Jan Patocka, *Essais Hérétiques sur la Philosophie de l'Histoire*, trans E. Abrams (Paris: Verdier, 1981); Jacques Derrida, 'Donner la Mort', in *L'Ethique du Don*, eds J.-M. Rabaté and Michael Wetzel (Paris: Metailié-Transition, 1992); Emmanuel Levinas, 'Time and the Other' (Extract) in *The Levinas Reader*, ed. Sean Hand (Oxford: Blackwell, 1989), *Autrement que l'être ou au-delà de l'essence* (Paris: Kluwer, 1990).

2 Bernard Williams, 'Moral Luck' in *Philosophical Papers 1973–80* (Cambridge: CUP, 1981), 20–39; Martha Nussbaum, *The Fragility of Goodness: Luck and Ethics in Greek Tragedy and Philosophy* (Cambridge: CUP, 1986). Similar considerations to those of this chapter might be opened up in relation to Williams's other great themes of shame and honour developed in that work of polite *lit. hum.* nihilism, *Shame and Necessity* (Berkeley: California UP, 1993). Again Williams is wrong about Christianity, and even Augustine: Charity, since it is a mode of glory (doxa) *is* also honour, not just interior will – it cannot be a light under a bushel indifferent to reputation, even if there can be a kind of hidden repute, appearing only to God. Likewise Christian guilt *is* also shame: our conscience is clarified for us only by others and by the Church. See my 'The Force of Identity', in *The Word Made Strange* (Oxford: Blackwell, 1997) 194–219.

See also John Bowlin's excellent and important book, *Contingency and Fortune in Aquinas's Ethics* (Cambridge: CUP, 1999) 167–213. This present article follows essentially the same line as Bowlin: Christian theology (represented by St Thomas) generalizes and extends moral luck as providential grace and so offers good fortune to all. The context of grace and universal providence means that it does not at all need to modify the Aristotelian position in a Stoic direction which sees achieved virtue as essentially interior, and luck or success as an extrinsic added element less essentially to do with the ethical. Beyond Aquinas though, I am trying to provide a historicized and 'poeticized' version of this position; a version which sees grace as mediated by the 'heterogenesis of ends'.

The ethical positions of this chapter are also clearly indebted to Kierkegaard, to Barth's reading of Kierkegaard, and to Bonhoeffer's theological appropriation and modification of Nietszche.

3 Aristotle, *Nichomachean Ethics* 1109630–111068.

4 See Robert Spaemann, *Glück und Wohlwollen: Versuch über Ethik* (Stuttgart: Klett-Cotta, 1989), 85–95: 'Die Antinomien des Glücks'.

5 As seems to be affirmed by Jean-Luc Marion. See Ésquisse d'un concept Phénoménologique de Don', in *Archivio di Filosofia* LXII (1994) N.1–3, 75–94.

6 See Hans Urs von Balthasar, *The Glory of the Lord, Vol. V, The Realm of Metaphysics in the Modern Age*, trans. Oliver Davies et al. (San Francisco: Ignatius, 1991), 451–597.

7 See Spaemann, *Glück und Wohlwollen*, for this characterization, esp. 'Vorwort' 9–11.

8 Martin Heidegger, *Being and Time*, trans. John Macquarrie and Edward Robinson (Oxford: Blackwell, 1978), 279–312.

9 Derrida, 'Donner la Mort', 64–5.

10 Spaemann, 85–95; 'Die Antinomien des Glücks', 110–22; 'Vernunft und Leben', 123–40; 'Wohlwollen'.

11 Spaemann, 89.

12 Marion, 'Ésquisse d'un concept Phénoménologique de Don'.

13 For the arid pursuit of such conundra to their bitter end without *Aufhebung*, see Derek Parfit, *Reasons and Persons* (Oxford: OUP, 1984).

14 Jacques Derrida, *Given Time: I Counterfeit Money*, trans. Petty Kamuf (Chicago: Chicago UP, 1991).

15 Bernard Williams, 'Moral Luck'.

16 Jacques Derrida, 'Donner la Mort', 54ff., 64ff.

17 Spaemann, 110–22: 'Vernunft und Leben', especially 114–15.

18 John Locke, *An Essay Concerning Human Understanding* (Oxford: OUP, 1975), III, VI, 44–7 and V, 1–8.

19 Frances Hodgson Burnett, *The Secret Garden* (Oxford: OUP, 1993). These magical aspects are very well brought out in Agnieska Holland's film of this novel (1994).

20 Marion, 'Ésquisse'.

21 See, especially, Derrida, 'Donner la Mort'. And for a critique of this, Catherine Pickstock, *After Writing: On the Liturgical Consummation of Philosophy* (Oxford: Blackwell, forthcoming), Chapter 3 'Signs of death', 101–19.

22 John Milbank, 'Can a Gift be Given?' in *Rethinking Metaphysics*, ed. L.G. Jones and S.E. Fowl (Oxford: Blackwell, 1995), 119–61 and 'The Soul of Reciprocity', in *Modern Theology*, Part 1, 335–93 July 2001, Part 2, October 2001, 485–509.

23 Jacques Derrida, *Given Time*.

24 See Milbank, 'Can a Gift be Given?'

25 Diogenes Laertius, *Lives* VII, 13, 22 and see Marcel Detienne, *The Gardens of Adonis* (New York: Hassocks, 1975).

26 I am indebted to Villiers Breytenbach for this point.

27 Detienne, *The Gardens of Adonis*.

28 I am grateful for discussions with Hildegard Caneik-Lindemaier on this point.

29 See Robert Alun Jones, 'Robertson Smith, Durkheim and Sacrifice', *Journal of the History of the Behavioural Sciences*, XVIII (April 1981), 184–205.

30 Martin Hengel, *The Atonement*, trans. John Bowden (London: SCM, 1981), 1–32. I am indebted to Wolfgang Stegemann for the point that Antique texts often use *sphagein* (whole-offering) rather than *phusia* in this context. Hildegard Caneik-Lindemaier thinks Hengel and Stegemann exaggerate lightly metaphorical usages, but in view of the cults attached to heroes, this objection seems implausible.

31 See Pickstock, *After Writing*, Chapter 2.

32 John Milbank, 'Stones of Sacrifice' in *Modern Theology*, vol. 12, no. 1, January 1996, 27–56.

33 John Buchan, *Midwinter: Certain Travellers in Old England* (Edinburgh: B & W Publishing, 1993), 229–30. The 'Sacrifice to Diana' which Buchan has of course derived from reading J.G. Frazer and Margaret Murray is here deployed typologically (a) as a figure for genuine Christian sacrifice – a trope used also in the equally remarkable *Witchwood* – and (b) to suggest that since the foretype is still included, there can be an integration of a Platonic erotic and romantic

moment in Christianity. Again *Witchwood* conveys the same message and suggests that a 'Catholic' and 'Platonic' Christianity holds the balance between a bleak uncharitable puritanism and a demonic neo-paganism; in the latter novel it is Calvinist 'justified sinners' who are also devil worshippers, implying that a fatalistic construal of grace, where our 'return' of love is irrelevant and the divine decree is impersonal and arbitrary is *dialetically identical* with an equally 'returnless' love for the powers of darkness and destruction.

34 See Henrik Bolkestein, *Wohltätigkeit und Armenpflege in Vorchristlichen Altertum* (Utrecht: A. Oosthoek, 1939) and Willem Cornelis van Unnick, 'Eine Merkwürdige Liturgische Aussage bei Josephus (Jos. Ant 111–113)', in *Josephus-Studien*, eds O. Betz et al. (Göttingen: Vandenhoeck & Ruprecht, 1974), 362–9.

35 See Milbank, 'Can a Gift be Given?'

36 See Willem Cornelis van Unnick, 'Die Motivierung der Feindesliebe in Lukas VI, 32–35' in *Novum Testamentum*, vol. VII, 1966, 284–300.

9 POLITICS: SOCIALISM BY GRACE

1 See Ulrich Beck, *Ecological Politics in an Age at Risk*, trans. Amos Weisz (Cambridge: Polity, 1995).

2 See John Milbank, 'On Complex Space', in *The Word Made Strange* (Oxford: Blackwell, 1998), 268–92 and 'Were the Christian Socialists Socialist?' in *Papers of the Nineteenth Century Work Group (American Academy of Religion)*, ed. Jack Forstmann and Joseph Pickle, vol. XIV, 1998, 86–95 (available from the Graduate Theological Union, Berkeley, California).

3 See Anthony Giddens, *Beyond Left and Right: The Future of Radical Politics* (Cambridge: Polity, 1994), and also, in some ways, Roy Bhaskhar, *Scientific Realism and Human Emancipation* (London: Verso, 1986). The mistakes of Bhaskhar and his followers are: 1. To imagine that there are identifiable 'laws' more ultimate than the contingency of flux and event. 2. To fail to see that these 'laws' are no more than the projections of human instrumental reason and its encountered limits on to an imagined 'reality'. 3. To fail to see also that the social is in no sense a 'reality' over against us, since it is *us*, and therefore entirely co-terminous with our endlessly revisable interpretations: the social world both *is* an act of interpretation, and also endlessly subject to reinterpretations which *really* alter how it 'is' or how it occurs in time. Thus 'Realism' spatializes the real, in such a way that the reality of occurrence (time, history) is obliterated. 4. Still to lust after a false marriage of socialism and scientific objectifying reason.

4 Still crucial are Chapters 1–3 of Karl Marx, *Capital*, vol. I (London: Lawrence and Wishart, 1983), 43–145.

5 See Michel Serres, *Angels: A Modern Myth* (Paris and New York: Flammarion, 1995).

6 See John Milbank, 'Sacred Triads: Augustine and the Indo-European Soul', in *Modern Theology*, vol. 13, no. 4, October 1997, 451–75.

7 Maurice Blanchot, *La Communauté Inavouable* (Paris: Editions du Minuit, 1983).

8 Albeit that the former has a richer account of the individual, and more assumes that what counts as true self-preservation is in accord with a generally accepted social norm.

9 See Jean-Louis Chrétien, *L'Inoubliable et L'Inéspéré* (Paris: Desclée de Brouwer, 1991) Chapter 1 and Catherine Pickstock, *After Writing: On the Liturgical Consummation of Philosophy* (Oxford: Blackwell, 1998), 3–46.

10 See John Milbank, *Theology and Social Theory* (Oxford: Blackwell, 1990), 380–438.

11 See George Bataille, *Theory of Religion*, trans. Robert Hurley (New York: Zone, 1992).
12 Op.cit.
13 See Milbank, *Theology and Social Theory*, 259–438.
14 Marcel Mauss, *The Gift*, trans. W.D. Halls (London: Routledge, 1990); Georges Davey, *La Foi Jurée* (Paris: Felix Alcan, 1922); Bronislaw Malinowski, *Argonauts of the Western Pacific* (New York: E.P. Dutton, 1961).
15 See John Milbank, 'Can a Gift be Given?', in *Rethinking Metaphysics*, ed. L.G. Jones and S.E. Fowl (Oxford: Blackwell, 1995), 119–61.
16 See Milbank, *Theology and Social Theory*, 278–326.
17 Jean-Luc Nancy, *The Inoperative Community*, trans. Peter Connor et al. (Minneapolis: University of Minnesota Press, 1991). See also Giorgio Agamben, *The Coming Community*, trans. M. Hardt (Minneapolis: University of Minnesota Press, 1993).
18 See T. Adorno and M. Horkheimer, *Dialectic of Enlightenment*, trans. John Cumming (London: Nelson, 1992), 3–81.
19 I am here indebted to discussion with Paul Heelas of the Department of Religious Studies, Lancaster, around this point.
20 Otto von Gierke, *Political Theories of the Middle Age*, trans. R.W. Maitland (Cambridge: CUP, 1987); *Natural Law and the Theory of Society, 1500–1800*, trans. Ernest Barker (Cambridge: CUP, 1958).
21 Mauss, *The Gift*.
22 Annette Wiener, 'Trobriand Kinship from Another View', in *Man*, 14 (1979), 328–48. And see John Bossy, *Christianity in the West 1400–1700* (Oxford: OUP, 1987), 19–21.
23 See Hannah Arendt, *The Human Condition* (Chicago: Chicago UP, 1958); *Between Past and Future* (New York: Columbia UP, 1961).
24 See John Milbank, 'Sublimity: the Modern Transcendent', in *Religion, Modernity and Postmodernity*, ed. Paul Heelas (Oxford: Blackwell, 1998), 258–85.
25 See, for example, Franz Kafka, *The Castle*, trans. Willa and Edwin Muir (London: Penguin, 1971), 60–1: 'Again he [K.] had this sense of extraordinary ease in intercourse with authorities. They seemed literally to bear every burden, one could lay everything on their shoulders and remain free and untouched oneself.' See also Slavoj Zizek, *For They Know Not What They Do: Enjoyment as a Political Factor* (London: Verso, 1991), 229–41.
26 Pickstock, *After Writing*, 146–9.
27 Op. cit. 101–18; Yves Bonnefoy, 'Les Tombeaux de Ravenne', in *L'Improbable* (Paris: Mercure de France, 1959), 9–34.
28 Augustine, *Confessions*, Books X–XI; *De Libero Arbitrio* Book II, 16.
29 See John Gray, *False Dawn* (London: Granta, 1998).
30 See Catherine Pickstock's essay 'Liturgy, Art and Politics', in *Telos*, 113, Fall 1998, 19–41.
31 Marcel Gauchet, *The Disenchantment of the World: A Political History of Religion*, trans. Oscar Burge (Princeton, NJ: Princeton UP 1997).
32 See my review of Gauchet's book, 'Rendering the Strange Off-Limits', in *The Times Literary Supplement* 4996, 5 June 1998, 7–8.
33 Pickstock, *After Writing*, 3–46.
34 See John Milbank, 'History of the One God', in *The Heythrop Journal*, vol. 38, no. 4, October 1997, 371–400.
35 Op.cit.
36 *After Writing*, 146–58, 158–66.
37 Op. Cit. and see Pickstock, 'Liturgy, Art and Politics'.

38 *After Writing*, 146–58, 158–66.
39 Augustine, *De Libero Arbitrio*, Book II, 16: '. . . do not doubt that there is an eternal and unchangeable form that sees to it that these changeable things do not perish, but pass through time in measured motions and a distinct variety of forms, like the verses of a song.'
40 See Augustine, *De Libero Arbitrio*, Book II and the discussion in Chapter 1 above.
41 See again Hannah Arendt, *Eichmann in Jerusalem: A Report on the Banality of Evil* (London: Penguin, 1992), 135–7.
42 See again Immanuel Kant, *The Metaphysics of Morals*, trans. Mary Gregor (Cambridge: CUP, 1991), 129–33.
43 See again Jacob Rogozinski, 'Hell on Earth: Hannah Arendt in the face of Hitler', in *Philosophy Today*, vol. 37, no. 314, Fall 1993, 257–74. Rogozinski cites Hitler to Rauschning (267): 'I am founding an Order, that of man as the measure and centre of the world, of the Man-God . . . a splendid figure of Being [who] will be like an image to be worshipped.' Rogozinski rightly comments: 'In other words: Nazism is a humanism.'
44 Rogozinski, 'Hell on Earth'.
45 *After Writing*, 233–8.
46 *After Writing*, 135–57. See also Rowan Williams, *Lost Icons* (Edinburgh: T. and T. Clark, 2000), on 'Charity' and *passim*.
47 See Bonnefoy, 'Les Tombeaux de Ravenne'.
48 See Colin Renfrew, *Before Civilization: The Radiocarbon Revolution and Prehistoric Europe* (London: Penguin, 1973), 161–82. But for a critique of this view which I am inclined to favour, see Julian Thomas, *Time, Culture and Identity: an Interpretative Archaeology* (London: Routledge, 1996).
49 Pickstock, 'Liturgy, Art and Politics'.
50 Augustine, *De Libero Arbitrio*, Book I, 6.
51 De Libero Arbitrio, Book I, 15.
52 See Mauss, *The Gift*.

10 CULTURE: THE GOSPEL OF AFFINITY

1 See Bruno Latour, *We Have Never Been Modern*, trans. Catherine Porter (Cambridge, MA: Harvard UP, 1993). Perhaps a general comment is in order here about the entire sphere of 'bio-ethics'. I tend to agree with Alain Badiou that the very notion of bio or medical ethics is sinister, since it inevitably implies an ethics that belongs to medicine taken as a science rather than traditionally as an art. I would add that this notion seems to suffer from a blind spot. This is that the sinister character of our bringing more and more of nature within the realm of our ethical and political decision lies less in the new capacities of humans to transform nature than in the character of our inherited ethical-political culture, which already poses as 'natural', and under this guise has for a long time reduced nature, including human nature, to a commodified abstraction. To give one example here: to be sure it is dreadful if insurance companies require personal genetic information. But given the inherited character of insurance companies, they are bound to do so. The demand is appalling because the *very notion of insurance as such* – making money out of the chances of life and death, and so already extorting from nature – is totally iniquitous.
   See also Barry Commoner, 'Unravelling the DNA Myth: The Spurious Foundation of Genetic Engineering', in *Harper's*, February 2002, 39–48, which reveals that the real moral questions do not concern 'what to do about new

scientific possibilities' but rather the questionable nature of certain supposed possibilities and the ethics involved in imagining there to be such possibilities and in obscuring their dangers.

2 See Mark C. Taylor, *The Moment of Complexity: Emerging Network Culture* (Chicago: Chicago UP, 2001), 78–84. This book gives fine analyses, even though I dissent from Taylor's conservative capitalist embrace of the information age, and from his argument that information systems truly mediate chaos and order.

3 See Michael Hardt and Antonio Negri, *Empire* (Cambridge, MA: Harvard UP, 2000). The present essay is heavily indebted to their analyses throughout. For the following reflections upon the United States, see A. Hamilton et al., *The Federalist* (New York: Random House, 2000), in particular no. 10 (Madison), 53–61 and esp. 57: 'the *causes* of faction cannot be removed . . . relief is only to be sought in the means of controlling its effects'; also no. 51 (Madison or Hamilton), 330–55. In addition see Richard K. Matthews's extremely good book, *The Radical Politics of Thomas Jefferson: A Revisionist View*, 97–119 and *passim*; James Harrington, *The Commonwealth of Oceania and A System of Politics*, ed. J.G.A. Pocock (Cambridge: CUP, 2001).
    I am indebted also to conversations with Augustine Thompson OP concerning his research into early mediaeval Catholic Republicanism in Italy, and the likelihood that J.G.A. Pocock has underplayed the importance of the more Catholic Venetian as opposed to the Machiavellian Florentine tradition, for Atlantic Republicanism.

4 See John Milbank, 'The Soul of Reciprocity: Parts One and Two', in *Modern Theology*, July and August 2001.

5 See Franz Baermann Steiner, 'On the Civilising Process', in *Orientpolitik, Value and Civilization* (New York: Berghahn, 1998), 122–8. I am again indebted to conversations on these matters with Michael Mack.

6 Steiner, see previous footnote.

7 See Charles Webster's supreme labour of love, *The Great Instantiation: Science, Medicine and Reform 1626–1660* (London: Duckworth, 1975), *passim*.

8 See Hardt, op. cit.

9 J.W. von Goethe, *Elective Affinities*, trans David Constantine in *Selected Works* (New York: A. Knopf 1999), 121–383 and Nicholas Boyle's extremely illuminating discussion of this work in his 'Introduction', xli–xliv. One may legitimately ask whether Goethe's refusal of Christianity already leads to a polarization between a merely impersonal affinity on the one hand, and the attitude of pure disinterested self-sacrifice on the other. Boyle rightly makes a comparison and a contrast between this novel and *Mansfield Park*. Does not the latter offer more of the truly ethical middle path?
    Apparently in contrast to me, Oliver O'Donovan, in his brilliant and unique book *The Desire of the Nations: Rediscovering the Roots of Political Theology* (Cambridge: CUP 1996) 266–8, sets affinity in small groups over against reciprocity in larger ones. By affinity he means primarily something biological, but also something more metaphorical and cultural; by reciprocity he means the more objective observations of justice and mutual respect between cultures. I would stress however that affinity already crucially involves structures of reciprocity, and that inter-cultural reciprocity if it is to be more than formal should involve elements of affiliation (though not imperial absorption). This seems reasonable if one observes that the idea of discrete cultures is a fiction. I imagine that O'Donovan might not be adverse to these remarks, although I see the Kingdom in its entirety as an *oikos* as much as a *forum*. I am also grateful to

Stuart Hall (the patristics scholar) for discussions regarding affinity in Gregory of Nyssa.

10 See Ian Duncan 'Introduction', in Sir Walter Scott, *Rob Roy* (Oxford: OUP, 1998), vii–xxix. Duncan shows that Rob Roy is not, like the Northumbrian recusants, the mere *opposite* of market Whiggery: rather in Fergusonian mode, his barbarism can be re-recruited by modernity as its dark face. This is then the tie of the Scottish North/South theme to the Jekyll and Hyde theme. For Buchan's *aufhebung* of schizophrenia, see Chapter 8 above. His near-Catholicism is shown also and more explicitly in *Sick Heart River*.

The Scottish tale of duality is often emplotted in terms of the 'Journey to the North' on the part of a rationalistic young man. As one advances in time, so the North recedes: for Scott and Stevenson it is the near Highlands; for Munro it is the far Highlands; for Buchan, the Shetlands (*The Island of Sheep*); for Linklater the Faroes (*The Dark of Summer*).

11 See Luce Irigaray, *An Ethics of Sexual Difference*, trans. C. Burke and G.C. Gill (Ithica: Cornell UP, 1993); *Sexes and Genealogies*, trans. G.C. Gill (Ithica: Cornell UP, 1993).

12 See Catherine Pickstock, *After Writing* (Oxford: Blackwell, 1998), 121–67; Oliver Boulnois, *Être et Représentation* (Paris: PUF, 1999), 17–107.

INDEX